BESTSELLING BOOK SERIES

Washington D.C. For Dummies,®
1st Edition

Cheat Sheet

D1415004

Metro Stops for Washington, D.C.'s Top Attractions

Attraction	Line	Station
Air and Space Museum	●●●●	L'Enfant Plaza
American Theatre Project	●	Anacostia
Arena Stage	●	Waterfront
Arlington Cemetery	●	Arlington Cemetery
Bureau of Engraving & Printing	●●	Smithsonian
Capitol Building	●●	Capitol South
Capitol Children's Museum	●	Union Station
Convention Center	●●●	Metro Center
Corcoran Gallery	●	Farragut West
Discovery Theatre	●●	Smithsonian
Downtown	●●●	Metro Center
Federal Bureau of Investigation	●●●	Metro Center
Folger Shakespeare Library	●	Capitol South
Folger Theatre	●	Capitol South
Ford's Theatre	●●●	Metro Center
Freer Gallery	●●	Smithsonian
Hirshhorn Museum	●●●●	L'Enfant Plaza
Holocaust Museum	●	Smithsonian
House Where Lincoln Died	●●●	Metro Center
Iwo Jima Memorial	●●	Rosslyn
Kennedy Center	●●	Foggy Bottom-GWU
L'Enfant Plaza	●●●●	L'Enfant Plaza
Library of Congress	●●	Capitol South
Lincoln Memorial	●●	Foggy Bottom-GWU
Lincoln Theatre	●	U-Street Cardozo
Mazza Gallerie/Chevy Chase Pavillion/Chevy Chase	●	Friendship Heights
MCI Center	●●●	Gallery Pl-Chinatown
Nat'l Airport	●●	Nat'l Airport
Nat'l Aquarium	●	Federal Triangle
Nat'l Archives	●●	Archives-Navy Mem'l
Nat'l Gallery of Art	●●	Archives-Navy Mem'l
Nat'l Geographic Society	●	Farragut North
Nat'l Museum of African Art	●	Smithsonian
Nat'l Museum of American Art	●●●	Gallery Pl-Chinatown
Nat'l Museum of Women in Arts	●●●	Metro Center
Nat'l Portrait Gallery	●●●	Gallery Pl-Chinatown
Nat'l Postal Museum	●	Union Station
Nat'l Theater	●●●	Metro Center
Nat'l Zoo	●	Woodley Park-Zoo
Pavillion at the Old Post Office	●●	Federal Triangle
Phillips Gallery	●	Dupont Circle
Renwick Gallery	●●	Farragut West
Sackler Gallery	●●	Smithsonian
Shakespeare Theater	●●	Archives Navy Mem'l
Shops at National Place	●●●	Metro Center
Shops at Union Station	●	Union Station
Smithsonian Castle	●●	Smithsonian
Supreme Court	●●	Capitol South
Textile Museum	●	Dupont Circle
Vietnam Veterans Memorial	●●	Foggy Bottom-GWU
Warner Theater	●●●	Metro Center
Washington Monument	●●	Smithsonian
White House and Visitor Center	●●	Federal Triangle
Woodrow Wilson House	●	Dupont Circle

- ● RED LINE
- ● ORANGE LINE
- ● BLUE LINE
- ● GREEN LINE
- ● YELLOW LINE

For Dummies™: Bestselling Book Series for Beginners

Washington D.C. For Dummies®, 1st Edition

Cheat Sheet

The Metrorail System

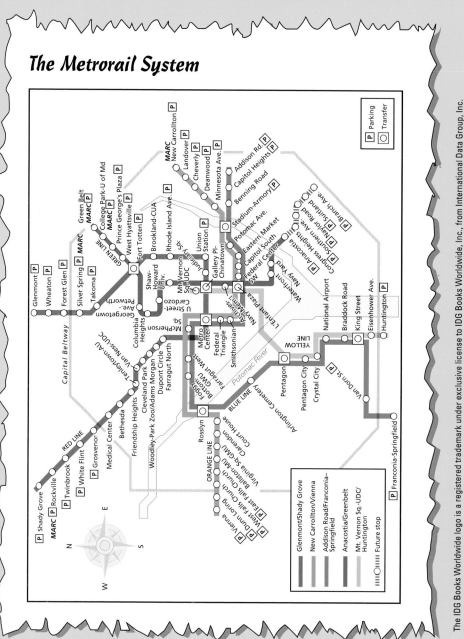

The IDG Books Worldwide logo is a registered trademark under exclusive license to IDG Books Worldwide, Inc., from International Data Group, Inc.
The ...For Dummies logo and For Dummies are trademarks of IDG Books Worldwide, Inc. All other trademarks are the property of their respective owners.

For Dummies™: Bestselling Book Series for Beginners

Washington, D.C.

FOR

DUMMIES

1ST EDITION

Washington, D.C.

FOR

DUMMIES®

1ST EDITION

by Beth Rubin

IDG Books Worldwide, Inc.
An International Data Group Company

New York, NY ✦ Cleveland, OH ✦ Indianapolis, IN

Washington, D.C. For Dummies,™ 1st Edition

Published by
IDG Books Worldwide, Inc.
An International Data Group Company
909 Third Avenue, 21st Floor
New York, NY 10022
www.idgbooks.com (IDG Books Worldwide Web Site)
www.dummies.com (Dummies Press Web Site)

Library of Congress Control Number: 00-110912

ISBN: 0-7645-6290-8

ISSN: 1531-7587

Printed in the United States of America

10 9 8 7 6 5 4 3 2 1

1B/RU/QS/QR/IN

Distributed in the United States by IDG Books Worldwide, Inc.

Distributed by CDG Books Canada Inc. for Canada; by Transworld Publishers Limited in the United Kingdom; by IDG Norge Books for Norway; by IDG Sweden Books for Sweden; by IDG Books Australia Publishing Corporation Pty. Ltd. for Australia and New Zealand; by TransQuest Publishers Pte Ltd. for Singapore, Malaysia, Thailand, Indonesia, and Hong Kong; by Gotop Information Inc. for Taiwan; by ICG Muse, Inc. for Japan; by Intersoft for South Africa; by Eyrolles for France; by International Thomson Publishing for Germany, Austria and Switzerland; by Distribuidora Cuspide for Argentina; by LR International for Brazil; by Galileo Libros for Chile; by Ediciones ZETA S.C.R. Ltda. for Peru; by WS Computer Publishing Corporation, Inc., for the Philippines; by Contemporanea de Ediciones for Venezuela; by Express Computer Distributors for the Caribbean and West Indies; by Micronesia Media Distributor, Inc. for Micronesia; by Chips Computadoras S.A. de C.V. for Mexico; by Editorial Norma de Panama S.A. for Panama; by American Bookshops for Finland.

For general information on IDG Books Worldwide's books in the U.S., please call our Consumer Customer Service department at 800-762-2974. For reseller information, including discounts and premium sales, please call our Reseller Customer Service department at 800-434-3422.

For information on where to purchase IDG Books Worldwide's books outside the U.S., please contact our International Sales department at 317-572-3993 or fax 317-572-4002.

For consumer information on foreign language translations, please contact our Customer Service department at 800-434-3422, fax 317-572-4002, or e-mail rights@idgbooks.com.

For information on licensing foreign or domestic rights, please phone 650-653-7098.

For sales inquiries and special prices for bulk quantities, please contact our Order Services department at 800-434-4322 or write to the address above.

For information on using IDG Books Worldwide's books in the classroom or for ordering examination copies, please contact our Educational Sales department at 800-434-2086 or fax 317-572-4005.

For press review copies, author interviews, or other publicity information, please contact our Public Relations department at 650-653-7000 or fax 650-653-7500.

For authorization to photocopy items for corporate, personal, or educational use, please contact Copyright Clearance Center, 222 Rosewood Drive, Danvers, MA 01923, or fax 978-750-4470.

About the Author

Beth Rubin moved to Washington, D.C., as a student — before there was a Kennedy Center, Watergate, or Metrorail. Since then she has survived 10 presidential administrations while escorting her two kids, numerous relatives and friends, and the occasional alien around Washington. While enduring Potomac Fever and D.C. traffic for close to 40 years, Beth has come to know the nation's capital intimately, warts and all.

In the early '90s she parlayed her knowledge of the city into *Frommer's Washington, D.C. With Kids,* now in its 5th edition. Beth's features, on a variety of subjects, have appeared in *Frommer's Dollarwise Traveler;* the *Washington Post; Roll Call, Ski Resort,* and *Washington Dance View* magazines; and numerous other Washington, D.C. area publications. She thinks her marriage to *Washington, D.C. For Dummies* is a match made in heaven. If the book is a hit, she's thinking about buying the Washington Monument and turning it into an all-night delicatessen.

When not chasing her mouse, Beth can be found roaming the District with paper and pen in hand. She lives in Annapolis, Maryland, 35 miles by motorcade from the White House.

ABOUT IDG BOOKS WORLDWIDE

Welcome to the world of IDG Books Worldwide.

IDG Books Worldwide, Inc., is a subsidiary of International Data Group, the world's largest publisher of computer-related information and the leading global provider of information services on information technology. IDG was founded more than 30 years ago by Patrick J. McGovern and now employs more than 9,000 people worldwide. IDG publishes more than 290 computer publications in over 75 countries. More than 90 million people read one or more IDG publications each month.

Launched in 1990, IDG Books Worldwide is today the #1 publisher of best-selling computer books in the United States. We are proud to have received eight awards from the Computer Press Association in recognition of editorial excellence and three from Computer Currents' First Annual Readers' Choice Awards. Our best-selling ...For Dummies® series has more than 50 million copies in print with translations in 31 languages. IDG Books Worldwide, through a joint venture with IDG's Hi-Tech Beijing, became the first U.S. publisher to publish a computer book in the People's Republic of China. In record time, IDG Books Worldwide has become the first choice for millions of readers around the world who want to learn how to better manage their businesses.

Our mission is simple: Every one of our books is designed to bring extra value and skill-building instructions to the reader. Our books are written by experts who understand and care about our readers. The knowledge base of our editorial staff comes from years of experience in publishing, education, and journalism — experience we use to produce books to carry us into the new millennium. In short, we care about books, so we attract the best people. We devote special attention to details such as audience, interior design, use of icons, and illustrations. And because we use an efficient process of authoring, editing, and desktop publishing our books electronically, we can spend more time ensuring superior content and less time on the technicalities of making books.

You can count on our commitment to deliver high-quality books at competitive prices on topics you want to read about. At IDG Books Worldwide, we continue in the IDG tradition of delivering quality for more than 30 years. You'll find no better book on a subject than one from IDG Books Worldwide.

John Kilcullen
Chairman and CEO
IDG Books Worldwide, Inc.

Eighth Annual Computer Press Awards ⮕1992

Ninth Annual Computer Press Awards ⮕1993

Tenth Annual Computer Press Awards ⮕1994

Eleventh Annual Computer Press Awards ⮕1995

IDG is the world's leading IT media, research and exposition company. Founded in 1964, IDG had 1997 revenues of $2.05 billion and has more than 9,000 employees worldwide. IDG offers the widest range of media options that reach IT buyers in 75 countries representing 95% of worldwide IT spending. IDG's diverse product and services portfolio spans six key areas including print publishing, online publishing, expositions and conferences, market research, education and training, and global marketing services. More than 90 million people read one or more of IDG's 290 magazines and newspapers, including IDG's leading global brands — Computerworld, PC World, Network World, Macworld and the Channel World family of publications. IDG Books Worldwide is one of the fastest-growing computer book publishers in the world, with more than 700 titles in 36 languages. The "...For Dummies®" series alone has more than 50 million copies in print. IDG offers online users the largest network of technology-specific Web sites around the world through IDG.net (http://www.idg.net), which comprises more than 225 targeted Web sites in 55 countries worldwide. International Data Corporation (IDC) is the world's largest provider of information technology data, analysis and consulting, with research centers in over 41 countries and more than 400 research analysts worldwide. IDG World Expo is a leading producer of more than 168 globally branded conferences and expositions in 35 countries including E3 (Electronic Entertainment Expo), Macworld Expo, ComNet, Windows World Expo, ICE (Internet Commerce Expo), Agenda, DEMO, and Spotlight. IDG's training subsidiary, ExecuTrain, is the world's largest computer training company, with more than 230 locations worldwide and 785 training courses. IDG Marketing Services helps industry-leading IT companies build international brand recognition by developing global integrated marketing programs via IDG's print, online and exposition products worldwide. Further information about the company can be found at www.idg.com.   1/26/00

Dedication

For Rachel, Tony, Joshua, and Jaymie Lightbourne, Eric and Lisa Kates Rubin.

Author's Acknowledgments

To Naomi Kraus, my editor at IDG Books, and the many individuals in the nation's capital who shared their expertise and time. Thank you one and all.

Publisher's Acknowledgments

We're proud of this book; please send us your comments through our IDG Books Worldwide Online Registration Form located at www.dummies.com.

Some of the people who helped bring this book to market include the following:

Editorial

Editors: Allyson Grove, Naomi P. Kraus

Copy Editor: Ellen Considine

Cartographer: Roberta Stockwell

Editorial Manager: Jennifer Ehrlich

Editorial Assistant: Jennifer Young

Senior Photo Editor: Richard Fox

Assistant Photo Editor: Michael Ross

Cover Photos: John Skowronski/Folio, Inc. (front); Ron Jautz/Folio, Inc. (back)

Production

Project Coordinator: Regina Snyder

Layout and Graphics: Sean Decker, LeAndra Johnson, Heather Pope, Julie Trippetti

Proofreaders: Susan Moritz, Angel Perez, York Production Services, Inc.

Indexer: York Production Services, Inc.

General and Administrative

IDG Books Worldwide, Inc.: John Kilcullen, CEO; Bill Barry, President and COO; John Ball, Executive VP, Operations & Administration; John Harris, CFO

IDG Books Consumer Reference Group

> **Business:** Kathleen A. Welton, Vice President and Publisher; Kevin Thornton, Acquisitions Manager
>
> **Cooking/Gardening:** Jennifer Feldman, Associate Vice President and Publisher
>
> **Education/Reference:** Diane Graves Steele, Vice President and Publisher; Greg Tubach, Publishing Director
>
> **Lifestyles:** Kathleen Nebenhaus, Vice President and Publisher; Tracy Boggier, Managing Editor
>
> **Pets:** Dominique De Vito, Associate Vice President and Publisher; Tracy Boggier, Managing Editor
>
> **Travel:** Michael Spring, Vice President and Publisher; Brice Gosnell, Publishing Director; Suzanne Jannetta, Editorial Director

IDG Books Consumer Editorial Services: Kathleen Nebenhaus, Vice President and Publisher; Kristin A. Cocks, Editorial Director; Cindy Kitchel, Editorial Director

IDG Books Consumer Production: Debbie Stailey, Production Director

IDG Books Packaging: Marc J. Mikulich, Vice President, Brand Strategy and Research

♦

The publisher would like to give special thanks to Patrick J. McGovern, without whom this book would not have been possible.

♦

Contents at a Glance

Cartoons at a Glance

By Rich Tennant

page 127

page 175

page 97

page 41

page 263

page 283

page 7

Cartoon Information:
Fax: 978-546-7747
E-Mail: richtennant@the5thwave.com
World Wide Web: www.the5thwave.com

Maps at a Glance

Table of Contents

Introduction

● ●

*W*hen John and Abigail Adams moved into a mostly unfinished White House in 1800, Washington, D.C. was a mosquito-infested swamp. Today it is hailed as a political powerhouse, and praised for its beautiful parks, superior architecture, and cultural and historic attractions. The city has also been labeled a political wasteland, a modern traffic nightmare, and a hotbed of sin and scandal.

Perhaps no city in the United States is as mundane and at the same time as inspiring as Washington, D.C. This is a town where legislators pass laws, then turn around and break them. Where the streets in the tourist areas are squeaky clean, but the behind-the-scenes political machinations are anything but. Where money is printed, but city officials plead poverty. The site of Watergate, Iran-Contragate and Monicagate, D.C. is also home to the Kennedy Center, the beautiful cherry blossoms, and the renowned Smithsonian Institution. Certainly one can find more here than just fabulous museums, magnificent monuments, and a textbook's worth of American history.

The city's diverse nature, as well as its ability to make everyone feel at home (after all, many "natives" come from someplace else), attracts travelers in the tens of millions each year. No matter what you want in a vacation — be it attractions that exercise the mind or body) you'll definitely find it in Washington. Even after 40 years of life in the capital city, I still find it a thrilling experience, and I'm willing to bet you will too.

About This Book

You picked this book because you may be too busy to wade through a sea of information or have zero interest in planning a trip. Perhaps you're a first-time visitor who doesn't know where to begin. Or maybe you're frustrated by all the detail in conventional guidebooks. (You know what I'm talking about, you want to find out when a museum opens and the author tells you how to *build* one.) Don't panic. Armed with *Washington, D.C. For Dummies, 1st Edition,* you'll feel like a Capitol Hill insider in no time flat.

I don't overwhelm you with choices, either. Or rhetoric. I cut through the prevailing political doublespeak and give you the bottom line — everything you need to know to plan and enjoy a visit in the nation's capital. This book even tells you how a VUP (very unimportant person) can get special White House passes or sit in on a session of Congress or the Supreme Court. I also let you know where you can enjoy a free concert or a panoramic view of the city, find a great hotel that won't blister your budget, and avoid crowds. When you're done, I won't be the least bit surprised if you share my enthusiasm for this, marble-coated, scandal-ridden, front-page city.

Conventions Used in This Book

Forget what you learned in elementary school. You don't need to start on page one and read the chapters of this book consecutively. *Washington, D.C. For Dummies, 1st Edition* is a reference guide. Like any...*For Dummies* book, think of this book as a friend you can turn to when you need help in a hurry. By the way, you aren't tested at the end. No gold stars or failing grades. Just refer to the section you need when you need it. It's as easy as ABC, no?

Hotels and restaurants in the book are listed alphabetically with prices and frank evaluations. In addition, some abbreviations are used for credit cards.

- AE: American Express
- CB: Carte Blanche
- DC: Diners Club
- DISC: Discover
- JCB: Japan Credit Bank
- MC: MasterCard
- V: Visa

I divide the hotels into two categories — my personal favorites and those that don't quite make the preferred list, but still get my hearty seal of approval. Don't be shy about considering the runner-up hotels if you're unable to get a room from my "favorites" list. D.C. has relatively few hotel rooms for a city of its magnitude, but all my runner-ups offer amenities and services that make them good choices to consider as you determine where to spend the night.

I also include some general pricing information to help you decide where to unpack your bags or dine. I use a system of dollar signs to show a range of costs for one night in a hotel or a meal at a restaurant. Unless I say otherwise, the lodging rates are for a standard double room during high season. (Chapter 7 explains when high season takes place.) Included in the cost of each meal is soup or salad, an entrée, dessert, an alcoholic drink, taxes, and tip. Prices, of course, are subject to change; call to confirm restaurant prices and hotel rates. Check out the following table to decipher the dollar signs.

Cost	Hotel	Restaurant
$	$100 and under	Less than $15
$$	$100–$150	$15–$25
$$$	$150–$225	$25–$35
$$$$	$225–$300	$35–$50
$$$$$	$300 and up per night	$50 and up, up, and away

Another helpful feature of this book is the use of bold type. All hotels, restaurants, attractions, and important resources are in bold type so that you can find essential information in this guide with a minimum of fuss.

Also, in researching this book, I discovered many wonderful places — hotels, restaurants, shops, and more. I'm sure you'll find others. Please tell me about them, so I can share the information with your fellow travelers in upcoming editions. If you were disappointed with a recommendation, I'd love to know that, too. Please write to

Washington, D.C. For Dummies
Dummies Travel Guides
909 Third Avenue
New York, NY 10022

Foolish Assumptions

As I wrote this book, I made some assumptions about you and what your needs might be as a traveler. Here's what I assume about you:

- You may be an inexperienced traveler trying to determine whether or not to take a trip to Washington, D.C. or looking for guidance to determine when and how to make this trip.

- You may be an experienced traveler, but you don't have much time to devote to trip planning or you don't have much time to spend in Washington, D.C. when you get there. You want expert advice on how to maximize your time and enjoy a hassle-free trip.

- You're not looking for a book that provides all the information available on Washington, D.C. or one that lists every hotel, restaurant, or attraction available to you. Instead, you want a book that focuses on places that give you the best or most unique experiences in Washington.

If you fit any of these criteria, *Washington, D.C. For Dummies, 1st Edition,* gives you the information you're looking for!

How This Book Is Organized

Washington, D.C. For Dummies is divided into seven parts. The chapters in each part lay out the specifics within each part's topic. Likewise, each chapter is written so that you don't have to read what came before or after, though I sometimes refer you to other areas for more information.

Part 1: Getting Started

Here I provide you with an overview and give you a taste of the nation's capital. I answer all your major questions about the weather, special events, planning your vacation budget, and cutting costs. I also provide special tips for families, seniors, travelers with disabilities, and gay and lesbian travelers.

Part II: Ironing Out the Details

Should you use a travel agent? How about buying a package tour? Where can you find the best airfare? I answer those questions, and then talk about booking tips and online sources in this part. I also give you a menu of area hotels and motels, and talk about travel insurance, renting a car, and packing tips.

Part III: Settling In to Washington, D.C.

In this section, I tell you how to get around and get along. I discuss the three airports serving Washington, finding your way around after you arrive, your transportation options, and that most important of matters — money.

Part IV: Dining in Washington, D.C.

In this part, you find out where the locals eat, how to dress and make reservations for dinner, tips for saving money at mealtime, and the city's best restaurants. To make your life easier, I index the restaurants by price, location and cuisine. And, in case you get a serious attack of the munchies, I also tell you the best places to grab a quick bite, some street food, a cup of coffee, or a scoop of ice cream.

Part V: Exploring Washington, D.C.

This section dishes the dirt on the top sights (and some lesser-known attractions too), and gives you the skinny on tours and shopping. I toss in some itineraries at no extra charge — you're welcome — and suggestions for day trips.

Part VI: Living It Up after the Sun Goes Down: D.C. Nightlife

Here's where you find out what's doing after the museums close and the government goes to sleep for the night. I tell you about the theater and performing arts scene, how to get tickets, where to grab a pre- or post-theater meal, and where to kick back with a cocktail or boogie the night away.

Part VII: The Part of Tens

Not, perhaps, as famous as the FBI's Ten Most Wanted list, the Part of Tens nevertheless is full of cool information. In this section, I dish up some scandalous Washington history and let you know the best places to view the city's breathtaking skyline.

You can also find two other elements near the back of this book. I include an appendix — your Quick Concierge — containing plenty of handy information you may need when traveling in Washington. In it, you can find such items as phone numbers and addresses for area hospitals and pharmacies, contact information for baby-sitters, lists of local newspapers and magazines, the protocol for sending mail or finding taxis, and more. Check out this appendix when searching for answers to many little questions that may come up as you travel. I've also included a bunch of worksheets to make your travel planning easier. Among other things, you can determine your travel budget, create specific itineraries, and keep a log of your favorite restaurants so that you can hit them again next time you're in town. You can find these worksheets easily because they're printed on yellow paper. Feel free to tear them out and take them along with you as you trek through Washington.

Icons Used in This Book

You'll find several icons (those little pictures in the margins) scattered throughout this guide. Consider them your roadmap for finding the information you need.

The Tip icon tells you how to save time (including ways to beat the lines), and it highlights other handy facts.

Watch for the Heads Up icon to identify annoying or potentially danger-ous situations such as tourist traps, unsafe neighborhoods, budgetary rip-offs, and other items to be aware of.

I use this icon to identify particularly kid-friendly hotels, restaurants, and attractions. Washington, D.C. is a city that goes all out for children, so it's an ideal spot for a family vacation.

Keep an eye out for the Bargain Alert icon as you hunt for money-saving tips and/or great deals. Congress may spend your money like crazy on the House floor, but the majority of the city's attractions don't cost you a cent. (Of course, that leaves more cash for the IRS — Uncle Sam gets you no matter what.)

The Remember icon highlights information that bears repeating. Bears repeating.

Look for the Capital Idea icon, which denotes places or attractions that feature perspectives unique to D.C. and its people.

Where to Go from Here

Now that you know what to expect from this book, you can plan a successful vacation to Washington, D.C. Sit back and start reading. You have plenty to do before you arrive — from arranging a hotel room where you can snatch a few hours of sleep between museum visits to locating the best shops where you can increase your contribution to the national debt. Like the Boy Scouts' creed, the successful Washington traveler needs to "be prepared." Follow the advice in this book and you'll likely vote your D.C. vacation as one of your best ever. And, last but not least, have fun — this is, after all, the spot where all your tax dollars eventually end up; you paid for it, so you might as well enjoy it!

Part I

Getting Started

The 5th Wave   By Rich Tennant

In this part . . .

To get the most enjoyment out of a vacation — with the fewest number of hassles — it helps to know what awaits you in your chosen paradise before the landing gear lowers. If you want your Washington, D.C. vacation to receive a high approval rating, you need to plan it as far in advance as possible. In this part, I highlight the joys of a trip to D.C. and help you sort out the logistics of planning your trip — from choosing the best times to go, to planning your vacation budget.

But before I get into the nitty-gritty details, I take a look at some of the best things Washington, D.C. has to offer.

Chapter 1

Uncovering Washington, D.C.'s Many Faces

● ●

In This Chapter

▶ Checking out great activities — for free

▶ Staying at the best places

▶ Dining at the premier spots

▶ Experiencing the city's nightlife

● ●

*W*hen you hear the words Washington, D.C., what comes to mind? I bet your list includes some of the following: Cherry blossoms. Washington Monument. Hearings. Arlington Cemetery. Interviews. Smithsonian. Investigations. Tourists. U.S. Capitol. Stars and Stripes. White House. Hail to the chief. Scandal. Oval Office. No comment.

Like me, you may have a carpetbag of notions about the nation's capital. I arrived in Washington, D.C. nearly 40 years ago, and today, I still sort through my views of the city. But some of my feelings for the nation's capital haven't changed since I first stepped foot on the National Mall.

I still get a thrill every time I enter a Smithsonian museum, stroll through Georgetown, glimpse the Capitol dome, catch a free concert downtown, or wave as the President's motorcade whizzes by.

Washington has it all: A wealth of free attractions bunched together on the National Mall, historic and glitzy hotels in all price categories, restaurants of every ethnic persuasion, wide-ranging cultural offerings, and easy accessibility on foot and via Metrorail, the city's subway system. (See the helpful map in this chapter for more on the layout of the city.)

In many respects, Washington is Anywhere, U.S.A. — home to citizens of all ages, races, and backgrounds, and prey to the vagaries of weather, mass transportation foul-ups, traffic, and local politics. Washington, D.C. is just another place on the map. And yet it's like nowhere else on the planet. So buckle your red-white-and-blue seatbelts and get ready for an exciting ride.

D.C. Metropolitan Area

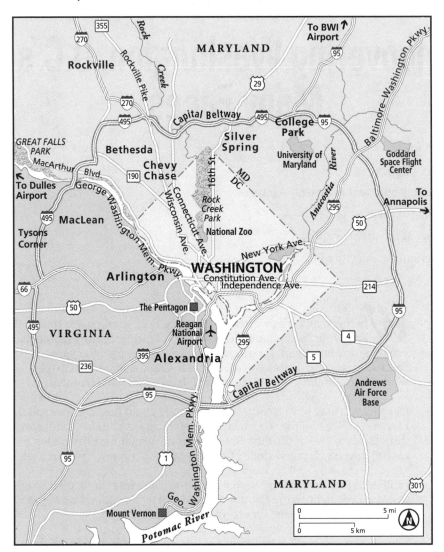

Spin City

Call the city what you will — Center of the free world, District of Columbia, D.C., the District, Sodom and Gomorrah on the Potomac — the nation's capital is an exciting, cosmopolitan city.

Lookin' for history? History is made here. Last night's rumor is this morning's headline. You want museums? It would take 2½ years of round-the-clock viewing to take in everything housed in the Smithsonian

Institution's museums. Walk down any street and you hear more foreign languages than at the United Nations. Visit any museum and you absorb more information than comparable time spent in a classroom. Sweep by majestic marble monuments and memorials and you feel more national pride than you ever thought imaginable.

The Land of the Free (Attractions)

Washington, D.C. is the only city in the world where most of the attractions — including the really cool ones — are free. You can visit all the Smithsonian museums, the National Zoological Park, and many private museums and galleries and never whip out your wallet.

Just a few of the better freebies include

- ✔ **The Smithsonian Institution.** This world-famous collection of museums keeps you busy for days without costing you a dime. Watch a group of weavers restore the original Star Spangled Banner at the National Museum of American History or let your kids swarm the Museum of Natural History's Insect Zoo to watch a tarantula chow down. You have 14 museums to choose from, so you're bound to find something that interests you.

- ✔ **The Federal Bureau of Investigation.** Kids love touring the house that Hoover built. Here you can find *the* Ten Most Wanted List, explore the FBI's renowned criminal investigation labs, see Mulder and Scully in the basement (Okay, I'm kidding on that one), and witness a bang-up weapons demonstration.

- ✔ **Congress.** Thanks to C-SPAN, some people call the action on the floors of the House and Senate the longest running comedy (or drama, depending on the day) in the United States. Watching lawmakers debate a bill can be either fascinating or a yawner, but the setting is definitely inspiring, the price is right, and better yet — no commercials!

And aside from the various attractions, you find numerous priceless — but not pricey — experiences waiting to be savored in Washington.

You don't pay a cent to stroll the Tidal Basin, ogle the cherry blossoms, get a bird's-eye view from the Old Post Office Pavilion, fly a kite on the Mall, take a hike on Theodore Roosevelt Island, or watch the President's helicopter touch down on the White House lawn.

Where Are the Skyscrapers?

Don't expect to find any clones of the Empire State or John Hancock buildings in the capital city. Washington's skyline is uncluttered for a good reason. The founding fathers laid down the law that no structure could be higher than the U.S. Capitol. To this day, the height of public buildings is strictly regulated. Most visitors find this restriction refreshing. If you want to get high (so to speak), ride 555 feet and 5 inches to the top of the Washington Monument.

Nevertheless, some rather famous buildings — if not for their height then certainly for their design — can be found in the city. Some examples include

- ✔ **The Pentagon.** This five-sided monstrosity, headquarters for the Department of Defense, is the largest office building in the world. The Pentagon covers 3.7 million square feet and has 17.5 miles of corridors.

- ✔ **The National Building Museum.** Fittingly dedicated to the building arts, this structure's interior resembles a Renaissance palace. Its Great Hall measures 15 stories (pretty impressive, I'd say), and contains magnificent Corinthian columns.

- ✔ **The U.S. Capitol.** The building that set the standard (height-wise anyway) for D.C. features one of the most famous landmarks in America — the rotunda and its dome. The dome has a diameter of 900 feet and weighs 9 million pounds.

And the city is pretty impressive on the outside as well. Everywhere you turn, trees and flowers flourish along city streets and in the public squares peppering the downtown area. The nation's largest wall-to-wall lawn carpets the National Mall for two miles — from the Lincoln Memorial east to the U.S. Capitol. You can catch polo and cricket matches near the Lincoln Memorial, or take a guided bike tour of the city. Try doing that in Times Square.

And if you prefer water-based recreation, the Potomac River and adjacent parks and trails provide recreation for hikers, bikers, boaters, anglers, and other sports enthusiasts. Cruises on the Potomac and the C&O Canal in season should be included on every visitor's itinerary.

When the Lincoln Bedroom Is Booked

You won't be left out in the cold if the postal service loses your invitation to stay in the Lincoln Bedroom, but you definitely need to plan ahead. Because lobbyists, media types, tour groups, and conventioneers sometimes fill D.C.'s 24,000 hotel rooms to near capacity, advance reservations are a must (but more about that in Chapters 6, 7, and 8).

Exercise your right and vote for your favorite accommodation. Stay near the White House in a deluxe presidential suite (Secret Service agents extra), in a double room with your kids (at no additional cost for them), a suite with a kitchen, a gracious historic inn, a bed-and-breakfast, or in a dorm-style hostel. Or head for the hills of suburban Maryland or Virginia and save bucks. (For whatever it's worth, my Deep Throats tell me the mattress in the Lincoln Bedroom is as lumpy as an overfed lobbyist.)

Here are a few great hotels that will accommodate special needs or interests:

- ✔ **Business.** If you're expensing the trip, the **Jefferson** offers a wealth of business-friendly amenities, including in-room fax machines, 24-hour concierge service, meeting rooms, and a business center. **Swissotel Washington: The Watergate** is another good choice; it features writing desks and fax machines in every room, plus a full range of business services. If you have business on the Hill, stay at the hip **Hotel George** and do your patriotic duty by paying homage to G. W.'s likeness while plugged into a high-speed data port.

- ✔ **Family.** This hotel is exceptionally pricey, but those traveling with tots will appreciate the **Four Seasons,** which offers children's programs, baby-sitting, games, a special children's menu in the restaurant, and evening turndown service that includes milk and cookies for the kids.

- ✔ **Romantic.** Experience a touch of Paris in the heart of Washington at the elegant **Hotel Sofitel,** which offers evening turndown service that includes chocolates and a single rose. Romantic Weekend packages are available and include a room, champagne, roses, and breakfast in bed.

- ✔ **Location.** The **J.W. Marriott** is within walking distance of most of the major attractions and only a block away from Metro Center. **Loews L'Enfant Plaza** is just a few blocks from the Mall, but if you feel really lazy, you can walk down to the basement and take the Metro.

Capital Dining

With more than 1,700 restaurants to choose from, your stomach will have no reason to growl when you arrive in Washington, and prices compare favorably with other major tourist meccas. Whatever type of cuisine you prefer, you're bound to find several restaurants that cater to your tastes. Menus here feature everything from grits to gnocchi, crab cakes to chateaubriand, rice pudding to rice noodles.

If you want a romantic evening out, try dining at the genteel **Morrison Clark Inn,** where the menu features regional American fare with a southern accent. Or take in a meal at **701,** where you dine on excellent American cuisine as piano music plays softly in the background. If you like a view with your meal, head for **Le Rivage,** which serves up a scenic view of the city's waterfront and superb fish dishes.

Some of the area's other best bets include

- ✔ **Italian cuisine.** No restaurant in D.C. does northern Italian better than **Obelisk.**

- ✔ **Seafood.** Even New Englanders don't find fault with **Kinkead's** clam chowder or fried clams and the rest of the menu is superb too.

- ✔ **Southern cooking.** If you can't go without pecan pie, try the mouthwatering dishes at **Georgia Brown's** or **B. Smith's.**

D.C. after Dark

Washington has never had a reputation as an exciting late-night town — except behind closed doors. But, rest assured, the sidewalks don't roll up when the lights go off in the Capitol. When it comes to the performing arts, the city more than holds its own when compared to other capitals of culture. And if you prefer bar-hopping and clubbing to Bach and Chekhov, you'll find a number of excellent places to go.

Some cool ways to spend your after-dark time include

- ✔ **An Evening of Theater.** Broadway-caliber performances take center stage at the **Kennedy Center** and the **Arena, National, Warner, Ford's,** and **Shakespeare theaters.** You also find more avant-garde offerings at venues all over the city.

- ✔ **A Little Night Music.** The **National Symphony Orchestra,** the **Washington Opera,** and the **Washington Ballet** perform most of the year — sometimes for free. And free outdoor concerts take place throughout the summer.

- ✔ **A Twilight Tour.** If the play's not your thing, take an after-dark city tour. Washington shines when the sun goes down and visiting the monuments when they are illuminated can be a far more moving experience.

- ✔ **Drinking and Dancing.** Kick back with a cocktail in a sophisticated supper club, shake your booty in Adams-Morgan, or sing your heart out in an Irish pub.

Chapter 2

Deciding When to Go

· ·

In This Chapter

▶ Joining (or avoiding) the crowds — understanding D.C.'s weather and activities

▶ Choosing a season to visit

▶ Exploring D.C's unique yearly happenings

· ·

*A*lthough, by most standards, Washington, D.C. remains a busy town throughout the year, some seasons are definitely busier than others. Deciding when to take your trip may affect what you see, how much you pay, and how crowded the museums and attractions are. In this chapter, I analyze the advantages and disadvantages of visiting during various times of the year so that you can decide on the time of year that works best for your dream vacation plans.

The Secret of the Seasons

Anytime is the right time to visit Washington, which enjoys a moderate climate *most* of the year. During the summer you may think you're in a Brazilian rain forest. And once in a while, Washington, D.C. has a major snowstorm (not an annual event, thank heavens). Natives, past visitors, and yours truly can tell you that spring and fall — April through mid-June and September through mid-November — are close to ideal. That's when Mother Nature is kindest, as evidenced by moderate temperatures and lower-than-normal humidity.

Unfortunately, the best weather in D.C. arrives at the same time the crowds do. You aren't the only one who wants to see the cherry blossoms in the spring or the fall foliage, so hotels and restaurants are booked solid and the traffic in town falls into the "don't even think of driving here," category. In order to help you decide the best time for your visit, I break down the pros and cons of the various seasons in the next section.

Spring: Excitement blooms in the nation's capital

Spring is a popular vacation time for most travelers. Some of the best reasons to visit D.C. in spring are:

- ✔ The days are clear and comfortable, and Washington is at its most lush and beautiful.

- ✔ Gardens in and around the Mall and monuments (and the entire city, for that matter!) bloom with tulips, daffodils, cherry blossoms, and dogwoods.

But keep in mind the following springtime pitfalls:

- ✔ The weather is fickle. One day feels like summer, the next winter. Think layers and bring a raincoat.

- ✔ Tourists, especially busloads of schoolchildren, pour in like a monsoon. Expect crowds, longer lines, and more traffic (which is sort of like saying "more" dead).

Summer: Having fun in the D.C. sun

Summer is another popular time to visit Washington, D.C. because:

- ✔ Hotels offer money-saving deals (they do almost anything to fill rooms when Congress is in recess).

- ✔ Public buildings are air-conditioned.

- ✔ Many museums offer extended hours.

- ✔ Free events, such as outdoor evening concerts, are plentiful.

But, again, keep in mind the following:

- ✔ Summer means major heat, folks. And humidity. The 3Hs — heat, humidity, and haze — may hang around until well after Labor Day. (See Table 2-1 for a month-by-month breakdown of Washington, D.C.'s temperatures.)

- ✔ The influx of summer vacationers can mean longer-than-usual lines at attractions and cold-drink vendors.

- ✔ Some theaters are dark (or at least darker) in July and August.

Fall: Harvest good times in Washington, D.C.

In my opinion, fall is a beautiful time of year — no matter where you are. Here are some autumn bonuses for those visiting D.C.:

- ✔ The weather is close to idyllic.
- ✔ Lines are shorter; crowds are smaller.
- ✔ The performing arts scene is in full gear.

Some things to look out for, however:

- ✔ Congress reconvenes and the convention scene heats up; finding a hotel room during the week may be difficult or impossible.
- ✔ Although summer traffic is heavy, traffic during the fall is brutal and remains so until June.

Winter: Celebrate the holidays in Washington, D.C.

Winter brings visions of softly falling snowflakes and holiday cheer to most travelers. You should consider the following when planning a winter vacation to D.C.:

- ✔ No need to worry about heat and humidity.
- ✔ Lines at museums and other sights are short or nonexistent.
- ✔ Colorful, often free, holiday events are plentiful from mid-December to early January.
- ✔ Airlines and tour operators offer good deals.

Winter does have its downside, however. Consider the following:

- ✔ The average temperatures look good on paper, but extremes are common. A damp, windy, 40-degree day on the Mall can feel colder than zero in Nome, Alaska.
- ✔ Fewer opportunities to take advantage of outdoor activities are available.

Table 2-1: Washington, D.C.'s Average Temperatures

	Jan	Feb	Mar	Apr	May	June	July	Aug	Sept	Oct	Nov	Dec
Avg. High	42°F	46°F	57°F	67°F	76°F	85°F	89°F	87°F	80°F	70°F	59°F	47°F
	(6°C)	(8°C)	(14°C)	(19°C)	(24°C)	(29°C)	(32°C)	(31°C)	(27°C)	(21°C)	(15°C)	(8°C)
Avg. Low	27°F	29°F	38°F	46°F	57°F	67°F	71°F	70°F	63°F	50°F	41°F	32°F
	(–3°C)	(–2°C)	(3°C)	(8°C)	(14°C)	(19°C)	(22°C)	(21°C)	(17°C)	(10°C)	(5°C)	(0°C)

Washington, D.C.'s Calendar of Capital Events

In this section, I list (by month) just a few of Washington's many exciting festivals and special events. Please double check festival contacts before planning your vacation around any of these events, because event dates are subject to change. Also, see the "Weekend" section of the *Washington Post* every Friday for a comprehensive listing of events. Because the easiest way to get anywhere in Washington is to use Metro — the local subway — the event listings below include the Metro stops closest to them. Unless otherwise noted, the events are free.

January

Martin Luther King Jr.'s Birthday, Lincoln Memorial (☎ 202-619-7222; Internet: www.nps.gov; Metro: Foggy Bottom). King's birthday is celebrated in word and music on the third Monday in January at the Lincoln Memorial, site of King's "I have a dream" speech.

Inauguration Day, U.S. Capitol (☎ 202-456-7041; Internet: www.whitehouse.gov; Metro: McPherson Square, Federal Triangle, Archives-Navy Memorial, Capitol South). On January 20 of every fourth year, the president is sworn in at the West Front end. A colorful — and endless — parade from the Capitol to the White House follows the swearing in. You need to call and reserve/purchase a bleacher seat (a bureaucratic perk that's tough to snag if your name doesn't have Sen., Rep., or VIP attached to it). Otherwise, just show up and stand in the crowd. The next presidential inauguration is scheduled for January 20, 2005. Check the *Washington Post* for parade information.

February

Black History Month, various locations (☎ 202-357-2700; Internet: www.si.edu). African Americans' contributions are recognized — through readings, speeches, and musical performances — at museums, libraries, and recreation centers throughout the area.

Abraham Lincoln's Birthday, Lincoln Memorial (☎ 202-619-7222; Internet: www.nps.gov; Metro: Foggy Bottom). On February 12 at the Lincoln Memorial (you were expecting Jefferson?), a wreath-laying ceremony and reading of the Gettysburg Address marks our 16th president's natal day.

George Washington's Birthday, Washington Monument (☎ 202-426-6839; Metro: Smithsonian). Don your knee britches, white stockings, and powdered wigs on February 22 and come ye to the celebration. The event features a wreath-laying ceremony, music by a military band, and a speech or two by some political figures. You may even see a streaker or two if the weather isn't too cold.

March

St. Patrick's Day Parade, Constitution Avenue from 7th to 17th Streets (☎ 202-637-2474; Metro: Federal Triangle, Smithsonian, Archives-Navy Memorial). On the Sunday closest to St. Paddy's Day, after an Irish coffee or two, you can sing "Top o' the Morning" at the annual wearing-of-the-green parade.

Smithsonian Kite Festival, Washington Monument (☎ 202-357-2700; Internet: www.si.edu; Metro: Smithsonian). Kite lovers fly over to the Washington Monument seeking prizes for their homemade creations. Store-bought kites are welcome, but can't be entered in the competitions.

April

National Cherry Blossom Festival, Tidal Basin (☎ 202-619-7222; Internet: www.nps.gov; Metro: Smithsonian). The festival is scheduled during the first two weeks in April, but timing a D.C. visit around the cherry blossom season is a crapshoot, owing to the area's unpredictable weather. Don't lose sleep over missing the blossoms' peak; you can always buy postcards. In my humble opinion, they can keep the blossom hoopla — parades, concerts, and the like — and just drop me and my camera at the Tidal Basin. Pick up any newspaper or turn on the TV news for a blossom update.

White House Easter Egg Roll, White House (☎ 202-456-2200; Metro: McPherson Square or Federal Triangle). Bodies scramble when kids roll eggs across the lawn of the White House. Some call this activity fun. Line up early and take a sedative — I'm not yolking. All participants should gather at the Visitors Entrance along East Executive Avenue, between Pennsylvania Avenue and E St. NW.

Note: The age limit for the event changes with each new administration, so call before you go to find out the current administration's policy.

Thomas Jefferson's Birthday, Tidal Basin, south end between Raoul Wallenberg Place (15th St.) SW and West Potomac Park (☎ 202-619-7222; Internet: www.nps.gov; **Metro:** Smithsonian or L'Enfant Plaza). Jefferson groupies (not the Jefferson Starship; the *other* Jefferson) gather April 13 to view drills and a wreath-laying ceremony at the memorial honoring the third U.S. president.

Smithsonian Craft Show, National Building Museum (☎ 202-357-2700; Internet: www.si.edu; **Metro:** Judiciary Square). More than 100 artisans show and sell their crafts at this juried show at the National Building Museum. Admission costs $12 to drool and/or buy. The show takes place April 26–29 in 2001.

May

Memorial Day, Arlington National Cemetery (☎ 202-685-2851; **Metro:** Smithsonian, Federal Triangle, Archives-Navy Memorial). Honor armed forces veterans at a wreath-laying ceremony with a military band at the Tomb of the Unknowns.

On the Sunday of Memorial Day weekend, "borrow" a blanket or folding chair for the **National Symphony** (☎ 202-416-8100; **Metro:** Federal Center SW or Capitol South). The celebration features recording stars in an awesome setting — the West Lawn of the Capitol, facing the National Mall.

June

Smithsonian Festival of American Folklife, the National Mall (☎ 202-357-2700; Internet: www.si.edu; **Metro:** Smithsonian, Federal Triangle, Archives-Navy Memorial). Traditional American music, crafts, and ethnic foods reflecting our nation's folk heritage fill the Mall with heady sounds, sights, and scents from late June through July 4th.

July

Independence Day Celebration, the National Mall (☎ 202-619-7222; Internet: www.nps.gov; **Metro:** Federal Triangle, Judiciary Square, Smithsonian, Archives-Navy Memorial, L'Enfant Plaza, Federal Center SW, Capitol South). Is there a more fitting place to sing "Happy Birthday" to the U.S.? Not that I know of. A parade along Constitution Avenue, beginning around noon, from 7th to 17th Streets NW, kicks off the day, followed by a picnic (BYO), concerts, and a dazzling fireworks extravaganza.

August

U.S. Army Band's 1812 Overture, Washington Monument (☎ 202-619-7222; Internet: www.nps.gov; Metro: Federal Triangle, Smithsonian). The U.S. Army Band plays a high-spirited version of Tchaikovsky's patriotic classic. The piece is punctuated with a round from the Salute Gun Platoon of the 3rd U.S. Infantry at the Sylvan Theatre.

September

Labor Day Concert, U.S. Capitol (☎ 202-619-7222; Internet: www.nps.gov; Metro: Federal Center SW, Capitol South). Even with the mercury hovering around 90°, the National Symphony plays a farewell-to-summer concert on the West Lawn.

Kennedy Center Open House Arts Festival, Kennedy Center (☎ 800-444-1324 or 202-467-4600; Internet: www.kennedy-center.org; Metro: Foggy Bottom). Local and national talent salute the performing arts in every nook and cranny of the Kennedy Center. This festival is popular; lines form for the inside events.

October

U.S. Navy Birthday Concert, Kennedy Center (☎ 202-433-6090; Metro: Foggy Bottom). On the second Monday in October, get out your dress blue denims for the U.S. Navy Band's annual birthday concert. The Navy celebrated its 225th birthday in 2000 (and I forgot to send a card). Call in September about free tickets. You know the drill: First come, first served.

Theodore Roosevelt's Birthday, Theodore Roosevelt Island (☎ 703-285-2225). Celebrate the old Rough Rider's birthday with nature programs and island tours on the Saturday closest to his actual birth date (October 27, 1858). The island is off the G.W. Parkway, north of Roosevelt Bridge.

Marine Corps Marathon, Arlington National Cemetery (☎ 800-RUN-USMC). The annual 26-mile marathon hosts about 16,000 runners on the fourth Sunday of the month. The race starts at the Iwo Jima statue of the Marine Corps Memorial in the cemetery.

November

Veterans' Day Ceremonies, Arlington National Cemetery (☎ 202-619-7222). A wreath-laying ceremony is performed by the president or another high-ranking government official at the Tomb of the Unknowns on November 11th. The solemn occasion honors the soldiers who gave their lives in war.

December

National Christmas Tree Lighting and Pageant of Peace, White House (☎ 202-619-7222). You can see the president light the national Christmas tree early in the month during the yearly traditional ceremony. Fifty-seven trees representing the 50 states, the District of Columbia, and the six U.S. territories are also part of the three-week Pageant of Peace that includes holiday music during most evenings from 6 to 9 p.m.

Kennedy Center Holiday Celebrations, Kennedy Center (☎ 202-467-4600). Many of the events are free during the Center's seasonal festivities. The programs include a "Messiah" Sing-Along, Hanukkah Festival, Christmas Eve and New Year's Eve celebrations, and concerts by local children's choruses.

White House Christmas Candlelight Tours, White House (☎ 202-208-1631). Candlelight tours are given for three evenings following Christmas; you can delight in the decorations of the White House holiday decorations from 5 to 7 p.m. This event is popular, so arrive early to ensure entry.

Chapter 3

Planning Your Budget

● ●

In This Chapter

▶ Managing your dollars and cents

▶ Avoiding surprise expenses

▶ Debating the use of traveler's checks, credit cards, ATMs, and cash

▶ Sharpening your cost-cutting skills

● ●

*Y*ou don't need a degree in accounting to budget for a D.C. vacation. (And you should definitely not look to Congress for guidance; making and sticking to budgets is not exactly Congress's forte.) To determine your expenses, all you need is the sense you were born with and maybe a calculator. The worksheets in the back of this book should also help you arrive at a pretty accurate estimate of your vacation's cost.

Adding Up the Elements

Several factors come into play when budgeting for your trip. To get started, I suggest visualizing your journey, making sure to include the following expenses:

 ✔ Flight/train costs, or driving costs if you're feeling especially masochistic (See Chapter 5 for tips on finding the lowest fares.)

 ✔ Transportation inside the city (See Chapters 10 and 11 for transportation options.)

 ✔ Your per-day hotel rate (See Chapter 7 for tips for finding the best deal.)

 ✔ Meals (excluding breakfast, of course, if it's included in your hotel rate)

 ✔ Admission to museums (You're in luck here, as most D.C. museums are free.)

✔ Theater/entertainment (See Chapters 22 and 23 for tips on cutting these costs down to size.)

✔ Miscellaneous charges (For example: Add 15–20 percent for incidentals, souvenirs.)

To further help you budget your expenses, here's a breakdown of the areas where you can expect to spend most of your vacation dollars.

Lodging

Choosing your accommodations in Washington, D.C. will be the biggest financial decision you make on your vacation. Rates vary considerably according to location, amenities, and a property's cache. Followers of the "less is more" philosophy may do the dorm bit at a hostel for under $50. If you make like Sherlock Holmes, you may be able to sleuth your way to a room for under $100 at a no-frills hotel or a B&B. If your tastes run toward caviar, champagne, and a massage at 3 a.m., prepare to plunk down between $300 and $400 a night. Somewhere among these extremes, however, are many well-appointed and well-located hotels charging an average $150 to $200 per night. By taking advantage of special packages and discounts, you can keep your lodging costs down.

Restaurants

You may dine at the Golden Arches or on prime steaks, tapas or Thai, and tortillas or tofu. You can find *almost* as many inexpensive and moderately priced restaurants in Washington as you can pencil pushers.

By dining early, opting for the early-bird specials or fixed-price deals, or eating your main meal at lunch when prices are lower, you can save big bucks.

Transportation

Several options for getting around Washington, D.C. are available. Some choices definitely are easier on your pocketbook than others.

Driving yourself

No one in his or her right mind should use a car to sightsee in Washington. Here's why:

✔ Too many vehicles on too few streets

✔ Weird traffic patterns that change faster than the headlines

✔ Drivers (and I use the term *drivers* loosely) who learned to parallel park in their native states, countries, galaxies, or not at all

✔ Scanty on-street parking

✔ Outrageous parking fees

Are you masochistic? If not, don't drive in D.C. If necessity dictates your arriving in the family buggy, I urge you to garage it (or go buggy in no time at all). Be sure to inquire about your hotel's parking charges; some hotels charge up to $20 a day for the privilege.

Using public subways and trams

Why drive when the **Metro** (the D.C. subway) is clean, efficient, and reasonably priced? Although the Metro may have a few wrinkles due to its age, you can find stations near all the major attractions. Figure $3 to $5 per day, per person to ride the Metrorail (see Chapter 11 for cost-saving tips). Metrobus is the other arm of Metro, but thanks to complicated routing and heavy traffic, it is not nearly as useful for getting around the city.

Another transportation option is to sit back and relax on **Tourmobile,** an open-sided tram that makes more than 20 stops around the National Mall and Arlington National Cemetery. The Tourmobile is a wonderful way to get an overview of the top attractions and is especially attractive to families, the elderly, travelers with disabilities, and the weary of all ages. For one fare, you can get off and reboard as many times as you want during the course of a day. (See Chapter 11 for more details.)

The good news for travelers watching their wallets is that D.C. is pedestrian friendly. Because many of the top sights are close to each other, walking, in my mind, is the best and most efficient way to navigate the District.

Attractions

You can definitely save money without sacrificing a fantastic time when calculating your attractions' budget. Aside from a handful of private galleries and museums, admission is f-r-e-e to most attractions, including *all* the **Smithsonian museums.** Try that in New York or Chicago.

Shopping

Unlike many other major U.S. cities, Washington is not a shopper's nirvana. If you are searching for more than souvenir T-shirts and postcards (and the occasional hotel towel) you need to trek to the 'burbs. Although, in tourist areas, you can find branches of many national stores (such as Gap or Foot Locker). What this basically means is that you don't feel the need to spend big bucks. (If you're good though, I'll tell you about my favorite local shopping haunts — the museum stores — in Chapter 19.)

Nightlife

If you want to catch a show, concert, or major dance performance, expect to pay $25 to $80 for a seat. If your budget won't stretch enough for a show ticket, don't fret; Washington offers an abundance of free nighttime entertainment. **The Kennedy Center's Millennium Stage** serves up free entertainment nightly throughout the year. (Much to my pleasure, I wandered in one evening on Melissa Manchester.) The **National Symphony** and military bands give free concerts at several sites throughout the summer. Otherwise, licking an ice cream cone while people watching in **Georgetown** or **Adams-Morgan** provides entertainment enough. See Table 3-1 for more about the average prices in D.C.

Table 3-1	What Things Cost in Washington, D.C.
Expense	**Cost**
Taxi from Reagan National Airport to Hotel Washington (15th and Pennsylvania)	$20
Taxi from Dulles Airport to downtown	$45–$50
Super Shuttle from Baltimore-Washington International Airport to any downtown D.C. hotel	$30 for first passenger, $8 each additional up to 4. (More than 5, call and reserve "exclusive van" nonstop service for $80)
Telephone call (local)	35¢
Metro	$1.10–$3.25
Taxi	$4 (within same zone)
Admission to movie theater (adult/child)	$8/$5 (after 6 p.m.)
Admission to all Smithsonian museums	Free
Glass of wine	$5–$9
Medium-sized coffee at Starbucks	$1.60
Medium-sized coffee at McDonald's	$1.25
Soft drink from vendor (12 oz. can)	$1–$1.50
Medium-sized soft drink at restaurant	$1.50–$2
Roll of 100-speed film, 36 exposures, at CVS drugstore	$6
Roll of 100-speed film, 36 exposures, in hotel	$7–$10

Keeping a Lid on Hidden Expenses

Someone once said that travelers should pack half the clothes they think they need and twice as much money. Smart Someone. I still haven't mastered this concept and usually arrive home with clean clothing and empty pockets. Vacationers easily get into trouble if they forget about a trip's hidden costs — the surcharges, taxes, and tips (and earrings you can't live without).

Here's how the extras can add up and why I advise factoring in 15 to 20 percent for incidentals when budgeting.

 The Biggest Ouch Award goes to the District for its 14.5 percent tax on hotel rooms. On a $150-per-night room, that charge translates to an additional $21.

Other hotel-related costs to watch out for include

- ✔ **Room service blues.** Enjoying that little breakfast or late-night snack — delivered to your door — does not come cheaply. A small glass of juice, half a grapefruit, and small pot of coffee in a moderately priced hotel once cost me $13 and change.

- ✔ **Phone home from the lobby.** Some hotels charge up to $1 for making a local phone call from your room. If you put on your slippers and shuffle to a lobby pay phone you can make the same call for 35 cents.

- ✔ **Minibar mania.** Unsuspecting tourists may think the cute little bottles and snacks stocking the minibar are gifts from the hotel. Wrong. You pay dearly for every nip and pretzel. Also, keep in mind that some minibars house sensors that automatically deduct the price of an item when you remove it, even if you put it back later on. Ask if this is the case before you start rummaging through the minibar in your room.

- ✔ **Where's the bacon?** The "free Continental breakfast" offered by some hotels may not be the pancakes, eggs, and bacon you're used to at home. Often the meal consists of juice, a muffin or bagel, and a hot beverage. It may save you a few dollars, but could still leave you hungry.

Cabbing costs

An unscheduled taxi ride can set you back, too. For your reading pleasure, here's a short course in D.C.'s cockamamie taxicab zone system:

- ✔ A cab ride to a destination within the same zone is $4. (For more on taxicab zones, check out Chapter 11.)

✔ Add an extra $1.50 if you brought a spouse, friend, relative, or significant other with you.

✔ Add 50 cents if you are carrying a suitcase (for a really big suitcase or trunk, add $2).

✔ Add a $1 penalty for riding during rush hour (7 to 9:30 a.m. and 4 to 6:30 p.m.).

Given a taxi's budget-busting potential you're much better off doing as I've advised and sticking with the Metro and your own two feet when you go sightseeing.

Tacking on for tickets

Brokers tack on a 10- to 20-percent service charge to secure you orchestra seats for a hot show or basketball game. Be sure to ask about this charge before you hand over your credit card.

Untangling tipping etiquette

A tip says thank you more eloquently than words can. This is not front-page news. Although tipping is not obligatory, in polite society (and we're all practicing members, right?) it is expected and appropriate. When dining out, tip 15 percent for average service. Dig deeper and give 18 to 20 percent or more for really good service. Do as the locals do: Double the 10 percent sales tax to arrive at a tip. See Table 3-2 for other tipping suggestions.

Table 3-2	Tipping in D.C.
Worker	**Amount**
Bartenders	10–15%
Bellhops/porters	$1 per bag
Taxi drivers	15% of fare
Hotel maids	$1 a day
Coatroom attendants	$1 per garment
Concierge	$5 (minimum, for securing tickets and other services)
Doormen (for hailing a taxi)	$1
Parking attendants	$1

Some restaurants add a gratuity to the bill, especially for large parties. The restaurant doesn't always tell you if this is the case, so don't be shy — ask whether a gratuity is included. Let the diner beware! If a gratuity isn't added, figure a tip of 15 to 20 percent of the bill *before* the 10 percent food tax has been added.

Paper, Plastic, or Pocket Change?

You decide to finalize your travel plans to Washington, D.C. How do you pay for meals, souvenirs, lodging, and so forth? You can choose from a number of methods of payment to cover your vacation expenses. In this section, I explore the available alternatives to help you determine the one that's right for you.

Traveling with traveler's checks

Traveler's checks are a throwback to the days before ATM machines gave you easy access to your money. Because you can replace traveler's checks if they're lost or stolen, they are a sound alternative to stuffing your wallet with cash. Although these checks are safe, they can be a hassle to exchange. If you insist on carrying traveler's checks, rest assured, most banks buy and sell them. Also, American Express has a downtown office near the Farragut North Metro station at 1150 Connecticut Ave. NW ☎ **202-457-1300** and another location near the Friendship Heights Metro and Mazza Gallerie, 5300 Wisconsin Ave. NW ☎ **202-362-4000.** (See Chapter 9 for more information on acquiring traveler's checks.)

Relying on ATMs

You can find 24-hour ATMs on nearly every street corner in D.C., as well as in hotel lobbies, many public buildings, and some restaurants. To find out which network your bank belongs to, check the back of your ATM card. Cirrus ☎ **800-424-7787** and Plus ☎ **800-843-7587** are the most popular networks. The 800 numbers give you the locations of the closest ATMs or you can go to the Web sites for Visa (www.visa.com) and MasterCard/Cirrus (www.mastercard.com).

 Keep in mind that many non-bank ATMs tack on an extra withdrawal charge, and your bank may assess yet another charge if you withdraw cash from an ATM that isn't affiliated with it. Therefore, I advise you to withdraw only the cash you need for 2 or 3 days. Carrying a lot of cash is an invitation for trouble.

Regarding the green stuff: Leave it in the coffee can buried in your backyard. It's safer there. Whipping out a wad on a crowded street is a liability. For a 3- or 4-day visit, I suggest bringing no more than $200 for incidentals (Metro, film, and floss) and emergencies.

Charge! Carrying the cards

What did we do before plastic? Common wisdom dictates using credit cards, rather than cash or traveler's checks. Plastic doesn't take up much room and is a whole lot safer than a pocket bulging with cash. Credit cards are good in hotels, restaurants, and retail stores. Foreign travelers get a better exchange rate with a credit card than with cash or traveler's checks. In addition, you may need a cash advance; you can get one at any bank *if* you have a credit card.

Interest rates for cash advances are often significantly higher than rates for credit-card purchases. More importantly, you start to pay interest on the advance *the moment you receive the cash.* (FYI: If you use an airline-affiliated credit card to secure a cash advance, you won't earn frequent-flyer miles.)

Please, please don't leave home without your personal identification number (PIN). Commit it to memory and/or hide it somewhere, like in your toothbrush case. You may call the number on the back of your credit card for assistance if you forget your PIN. Your card's issuer may give it to you on the spot or take up to a week when you hand over a bit of privileged information — like your mother's maiden name. (Be suspicious, however, if they ask you to hand over your mother.)

Tips for Cutting Costs

You can conserve your cash in more than just a couple of ways when you vacation in D.C. Use these tips to keep your vacation costs manageable:

✔ **Travel off-season.** In Washington, off-season usually refers to winter or summer. Winter — even during the holidays — is the least popular time to visit Washington. Because the hotels hate empty beds, visitors benefit. Good deals also abound in summer, which helps explain why downtown crawls with families from mid-June through August. Things die down in late August when the politicians are chatting up their constituents or taking exotic vacations until Congress reconvenes in September.

✔ **Package it.** You can book a package that includes, in many instances, airfare, hotel, sightseeing and/or restaurant perks, maybe even ground transportation for a whole lot less than if you put the trip together yourself. For particulars, call your friendly travel agent or visit Travelocity's Web site at `www.travelocity.com`. (See Chapter 5 for more on package tours.)

✔ **Stay in a suite hotel.** Dining out three times a day adds up, even if you take all your meals at Mickey D's or eat pizza on your laptop. Opt for a hotel room/suite with a kitchen where you can make breakfast and the occasional snack or hors d'oeuvres; then splurge on dinner without breaking your piggybank. If you travel with kids, a room with a refrigerator and microwave, in my humble experience, is a necessity.

You should also determine whether your children can stay in your room with you for free or a modest charge. Check to see if two double beds or a sofa bed or rollaway are available.

✔ **Be aware that convenience costs.** Show up at a popular restaurant without a reservation an hour before a show and you'll find yourself at the mercy of the more expensive restaurant next door. Starvation and a tight schedule may result in your eating at a less popular restaurant and spending double for dinner. Get my drift?

✔ **Feed your faces for less.** Dining can take a bite (excuse the pun) out of any travel budget. Here are some ideas for trimming the fat off your chowing expenses. (See Chapter 13 for more ways to save money on dining expenses.)

  • **Bring Munchies.** Toss snacks into your bag or backpack for emergencies. (That little bag of pretzels can prove nearly as indispensable as this book, especially if you're traveling with kids.) Vending machines in most hotels dispense the 3 Ss: snacks, sweets, and sodas.

  • **Bring a bottle of water.** Refill with water as you trek around the town — this way, you avoid paying for pricey sodas or little bottles of imported H_2O.

✔ **Take the Metro or hoof it.** You can get around D.C. on the cheap utilizing the subway and your feet. Purchase a $5 all-day Metro fare card. These cards enable you to get on and off the subway as many times as you like for a day. And when you are not taking the Metro, walk whenever possible — especially during peak Metro hours.

✔ **Abstain from some luxuries.** Skip the pricey souvenirs. Photographs and memories are your best mementos.

Chapter 4

Tips for Travelers with Special Needs

* *

In This Chapter

▶ Making your vacation fun for your kids

▶ Reaping the benefits of age (finally!)

▶ Dealing with disabilites

▶ Traveling tips for gays and lesbians

* *

*W*orried that your kids are too young or that you're too old to enjoy the best that Washington, D.C. has to offer? Afraid that you may experience barriers blocking your access or lifestyle? In this chapter, I dispense a little advice for travelers with specific needs.

Enjoying Family-Friendly Fun in D.C.

Washington, D.C. is one of the most family-friendly destinations in the galaxy. Those yellow school buses migrate to the Mall year-round for good reasons, and class trips to Washington are rites of passage for youngsters, like braces and pimples.

D.C. tourism for families is hot, almost as hot as the latest scandalous liaison. Those professionals in the travel industry aren't idiots. Hotels offer special rates to families and perks like free or lower-priced food in on-site restaurants. (See Chapter 8 for more hotel information.) Most hotels also arrange baby-sitting so that you can enjoy a quiet dinner. Just ask the concierge.

Speaking of hotels, if you travel with kids over the age of 2 to 3 years, I suggest staying in an all-suite hotel. Most have a bedroom, a kitchenette with a refrigerator and a microwave, and a separate living room with a pullout sofa. Your kids enjoy their own space (and TV), and you can relish some peace. Bring some snacks (cardboard containers of juice and microwave popcorn are easy to pack).

Restaurants entice your young and restless with kids' menus or half-portions, boosters and high chairs, crayons and other pacifiers. (See Chapters 14 and 15 for kid-friendly restaurants and snackeries.) Even previously ultra-elegant, adult-only restaurants are adding peanut butter and jelly to their menus. (I guess the changes are a sign of the times, but I long for the days when grown-ups could dine out without a kvetchy 2-year-old in the next booth.)

Many Washington, D.C. museums appeal to your kids and offer colorful age-appropriate workbooks that enhance your youngster's visit. Some host family film sessions, workshops, and educational programs. Kid-friendly food is on the menu at all the museum restaurants, too (see Chapters 16 and 17 for kid-friendly sights and activities). Making your children feel welcome is good P.R. — today's toddler may become tomorrow's benefactor.

Learning the hands-on way

Young minds absorb and retain more by viewing and doing than learning by rote. In Washington, kids can

- ✔ Gin raw cotton (**National Museum of American History**).
- ✔ Crawl through a replicated African termites mound (**National Museum of Natural History**).
- ✔ Touch a moon rock and enter the Skylab Orbital Workshop (**National Air and Space Museum**).
- ✔ Attend a family concert (**Kennedy Center**) or children's theater performance (**Kennedy Center, National Theatre, Smithsonian's Baird Auditorium**). The National Symphony Orchestra Concerts at the Kennedy Center are geared to kids 6 and older and their families. Thematic concerts (*The Mozart Experience* or *The Bernstein Beat*) run an hour and contain excerpts of classical and/or popular music mixed with dialogue. Tickets usually run from $10 to $20.
- ✔ Create oriental art (**Freer Gallery**).

And that list is a teeny-tiny sampling, Mom and Dad. Anything you can do in D.C., they can do too (except buy booze and go to a club, of course).

Frolicking in wide, open spaces

Washington's lush city parks are an open invitation to let your kids behave like, well, kids. Your children can run around, ride a carousel, or fly a kite on the 2-mile-long carpet known as the **National Mall.** For a more strenuous workout, you and your tykes can pedal a boat under Mr. Jefferson's gaze (**Tidal Basin**), take a hike in the middle of the Potomac River **(Theodore Roosevelt Island)**, or join a guided bike tour of downtown **(Bike the Sites)**. For more detailed information on the best of the nation's capital for families, check out *Frommer's Washington, D.C. with Kids.* (IDG Books Worldwide, Inc.)

Drafting a plan for your clan

To start your family vacation off right, let your kids get involved in the planning. They can start by contacting the **Washington, D.C. Convention and Visitors Association,** 1212 New York Ave. NW, Suite 600, Washington, D.C. 20005, or they can visit its Web site at www. washington.org for general information.

The computer literate may visit the following Web sites for information:

  ✔ National Park Service: www.nps.gov

  ✔ Smithsonian Institution: www.si.edu

  ✔ Washington Web: www.washweb.net

  ✔ Info on museums, sights, arts: www.governmentguide.com

After your children toss in their two cents, pencil in your itinerary using the worksheets at the back of this book. Be flexible. (After I deep-sixed the "I'm the Mom, that's why" attitude, my family vacations were more fun and less stressful.)

Savings for the Senior Set

Seniors can take advantage of their advanced years by cashing in on all the travel benefits offered to their age group. If you're a senior, you may want to join the **American Association of Retired Persons,** also known as the **AARP** (601 E St. NW, Washington, DC 20049; ☎ **800-424-3410** or 202-434-AARP; Internet: www.aarp.org). Members enjoy car rental and hotel discounts.

In addition, members of **Mature Outlook** (P.O. Box 9390, Des Moines, IA 50322; ☎ **800-336-6330**) receive discounts on car rentals. Mature Outlook members also pay lower rates at some chain hotels such as Holiday Inn, Howard Johnson, and Best Western. The annual membership fee is $19.95 and includes a bimonthly magazine and Sears' coupons worth more than $200. If you are age 18 or over, you are eligible to join, although the focus of the organization is geared toward the senior crowd.

101 Tips for the Mature Traveler is a valuable book available from **Grand Circle Travel,** 347 Congress St., Suite 3A, Boston, MA 02210 (☎ **800-221-2610;** Internet: www.gct.com). Grand Circle Travel is also one of the literally hundreds of travel agencies that specialize in vacations for seniors.

Many tours designed for senior citizens are of the tour-bus variety; those travelers who organize groups of 20 or more often receive a free trip. If you prefer to travel independently, advise your travel agent accordingly. One agency that specializes in tours and cruises for seniors is **SAGA International Holidays,** 222 Berkeley St., Boston, MA 02116 (☎ **800-343-0273**).

If you're a senior, here are some additional ways for you to save money:

- **Hilton's Senior Honors Program,** available to people 60 and older, provides discounts up to 50 percent off hotel rooms. The annual membership is $50 per person, but because spouses stay for free, only one of you needs to join if you travel together. Call ☎ **800-432-3600** 7 a.m. to 7 p.m. CST, Monday through Friday.

- The **Choice Hotels** group (**Comfort, Clarion, Sleep, Rodeway, Econo Lodge,** and **Friendship**) gives travelers ages 50 and older 30 percent off regular rates if they reserve in advance (10 percent discount for walk-ins). The hotels set aside only a few rooms for these Senior Saver Discounts, so book early. Call ☎ **800-424-4777** for Econo Lodge, Rodeway, and Friendship inns, and ☎ **800-221-2222** for Comfort, Clarion, and Sleep hotels.

- Most U.S. airlines, including American, United, Continental, US Airways, and TWA, offer discount programs for travelers 62 and older — be sure to ask whenever you book a flight.

- **Amtrak** (☎ **800-872-7245**) offers a 15 percent discount on the lowest available coach fare (with certain travel restrictions) to people 62 and over.

- Seniors 65 and older can pay half the rush-hour fare on **Metro,** with a reduced-rate rail card ($3 or $10). You can purchase reduced-rate cards at Metro Center, 12th and F St. NW (upper level), provided you show a valid ID. (A Medicare card is considered acceptable proof of age, but not a driver's license!) Locals can get a Senior Citizen ID at D.C. public libraries.

Entrance to most museums and attractions is free. And many private art galleries/museums, sightseeing tours, theaters, and movie theaters offer discounts to seniors. Aging has some rewards and this is one (maybe one of the few?). Set your vanity aside and ask if you qualify for a discount wherever you're required to hand over your greenbacks. The age requirement varies widely. Some establishments give you a break if you're 55 or older; at others you have to be at least 62 to 65 years of age. And if you look younger than your years, consider yourself blessed and always carry some form of photo ID so you may take advantage of discounts wherever they're offered.

Traveling without Barriers

A disability shouldn't stop you from traveling. There are more options and resources out there than ever before. *A World of Options,* a 658-page book of resources for disabled travelers, covers everything from biking trips to scuba outfitters. The publication costs $35 and is available from **Mobility International USA,** P.O. Box 10767, Eugene, OR 97440 (☎ **541-343-1284** voice and TTY; Internet: www.miusa.org). Another place to try is **Access-Able Travel Source** (Internet: www.access-able.com), a comprehensive database of travel agents who specialize in travel for the disabled; it's also a clearinghouse for information about accessible destinations around the world.

Transportation choices

Although I don't recommend driving in D.C., if you are disabled and you prefer to drive, you may find that many of the major car rental companies now offer hand-controlled cars. With at least 48 hours notice, Avis provides such a vehicle at any of its locations in the United States; Hertz requires between 24 and 72 hours of advance reservation at most of its locations. **Wheelchair Getaways** (☎ **800-536-5518** or 606-873-4973; Internet: www.wheelchair-getaways.com) rents specialized vans with wheelchair lifts and other features for the disabled in more than 35 states. Each of these rental agencies offers service in D.C.

Greyhound (☎ **800-752-4841;** Internet: www.greyhound.com) allows a physically challenged passenger to travel with a companion for a single fare. If you call 48 hours in advance, the bus line also may arrange assistance along the route of your trip.

One of the best operators of tours designed specifically for travelers with disabilities is **Flying Wheels Travel,** P.O. Box 382, Owatonna, MN 55060 (☎ **800-535-6790;** Fax: 507-451-1685). Escorted tours and cruises are offered and the company provides minivans with lifts. Another company worth mentioning is **FEDCAP Rehabilitation Services,** 211 W. 14th St., New York, NY 10011 (☎ **212-727-4200;** Fax: 212-727-4373). This company offers summer tours; contact them for more information.

If you are a vision-impaired traveler, you may want to contact the **American Foundation for the Blind,** 11 Penn Plaza, Suite 300, New York, NY 10001 (☎ **800-232-5463**), for information on traveling with a Seeing Eye dog.

Building accessibility

A wheelchair-bound friend of mine who travels a great deal considers Washington, D.C. very accessible. Travelers with special accessibility needs may breeze through the city. Every Metro station has an elevator. Blinking lights announce the arrival of trains for the hearing-impaired. Bells chime when the doors are about to open or close and a bumpy rubber guard covers platform edges to aid the vision-impaired. In addition, columns feature Braille lettering for station identification. The TDD number for Metro information is ☎ **202-628-8973.** The **Tourmobile** company offers trams that are accessible to disabled passengers; the company also offers vans with wheelchair lifts. Call ☎ **202-554-5100** for more information.

The Smithsonian Institution's museums as well as all other public museums and attractions are accessible. Many of the films aired in museum theaters offer narrated audio tapes for the vision-impaired that have been provided by the Washington Ear. Also, most live theaters have infrared headsets for the vision- and hearing-impaired. A number of live productions also feature at least one signed performance. Call the individual theater for the exact times of these signed performances.

Every once in a while, you may be slightly inconvenienced. For example, the wheelchair accessible entrance to the Archives is located on the Pennsylvania Avenue side of the building, while the main entrance is on Constitution. Some of the older galleries and shops are less accessible than the newer ones but, across the board, D.C. is user-friendly to the disabled. The best advice I can give is to call ahead in order to ensure that your needs are accommodated.

You may find that some old properties, historic inns, and bed-and-breakfasts are inaccessible, but these are the few exceptions. Most D.C. hotels are accessible. Ask when you make a reservation. If you book through a travel agency or tour group, be sure to make your special needs known.

Advice for Gay and Lesbian Travelers

Washington's active gay and lesbian population is focused around the Dupont Circle and Adams-Morgan neighborhoods. But gays and lesbians live, work, and recreate in every neighborhood in the city.

Perusing publications and reviewing resources

Turn to the weekly newspaper, the *Washington Blade* (Internet: www. washblade.com), for religious and spiritual activities, sports, entertainment, as well as politics and community news. Another good resource on the Web is www.gayscape.com. It has links to numerous sites covering topics ranging from herbal medicine to personal ads to a gay bar guide. Another good Web site is Gaybazaar.com, which lists upcoming events, personal ads, and reader comments on bars and clubs.

The Washington (and national) office of **PFLAG** (Parents, Families, and Friends of Lesbians and Gays) is at 1101 14th St. NW, Suite 1030, Washington, D.C. (☎ **202-638-4200**). In addition to its headquarters, PFLAG maintains a comprehensive Web site at www.pflag.com. You can tap into information on homosexuality-related topics, professional organizations, support groups, and national organizations. **Lambda Rising Book Store,** 1625 Connecticut Ave. NW (☎ **202-462-6969**), carries a wide selection of gay and lesbian literature and gift items. Another resource is the women's bookstore, **Lammas,** 1607 17th St. NW (between L and M; ☎ **202-775-8218**).

Finding hotels

The Gay Hotel Network (☎ **800-373-8880**; Internet: www.gayhotelnetwork.com) classifies the following properties as gay-friendly; you may contact the GHN for more information or to make reservations.

- ✔ **Carlyle Suites,** 1731 New Hampshire Ave. NW (Metro: Dupont Circle)

- ✔ **Henley Park,** 926 Massachusetts Ave. NW (Metro: Mt. Vernon Square)

- ✔ **Omni Shoreham,** 2500 Calvert St. NW at Connecticut Ave. NW (Metro: Woodley Park)

- ✔ **Radisson Barcelo,** 2121 P St. NW (Metro: Dupont Circle)

Dancing after dark: D.C.'s gay nightlife

The greatest concentration of gay bars is in the Dupont Circle neighborhood (centered around 17th and P Streets, NW, and 21st and P). The **Circle Bar & Tavern,** 1629 Connecticut Ave. NW, (between Q and R; ☎ **202-462-5575**), packs in a clientele of under-40 gays and lesbians. Shoot pool, play your favorite oldies on the jukebox, or dance up a storm at this Dupont Circle institution.

Around the corner, **J.R.'s,** 1519 17th St. NW (between P and Q; ☎ **202-328-0090**), is an upscale all-guys kinda place known far beyond the gay community for the 'hood Drag Race it sponsors every year.

You can find more information on gay bars and clubs at Gayscape.com and Gaybazaar.com. (See "Perusing publications and reviewing resources," in this chapter for information on these Web sites.)

Part II
Ironing Out the Details

The 5th Wave   By Rich Tennant

In this part . . .

Okay, it's nitty-gritty time. In this part, I chat a little about travel agents, package tours, and how you can get the best airfare. I also help you search for a place to rest your bones: I explore Washington's neighborhoods, zero in on a room that's right for you, book it, and send you packing.

Chapter 5

Planes, Trains, and Automobiles: Getting to Washington, D.C.

. . . .

In This Chapter

▶ Utilizing a travel agent — or not

▶ Checking out package tours: the pros, the cons, and where to get them

▶ Clinching the best airfares

▶ Arriving in Washington

. . . .

*Y*ou can get to Washington, D.C. in a number of ways and choosing a method of transportation may seem overwhelming at first. You may want to consult a travel agent or you may prefer to make your own arrangements. After you get to the city, do you want to travel on your own, or do you want the company and convenience of an escorted tour? In this chapter, I give you the lowdown on all your transportation options so that you can make an informed decision.

Travel Agent: Friend or Foe?

A good travel agent is like a good friend. Maybe better. A good friend may not be interested in saving you money. I prefer to research all my vacation options before calling Jane, my friendly and competent travel agent. She will tell me, "If you fly into Reagan National at 7 p.m., you can save $80 and miss rush hour." Or Jane may advise that "the Dew Drop Inn gives grandmothers a 15 percent discount." Now that's a friend. Although you can unearth much of this information on the Internet, you may spend *hours* locating it. Time is money; I'd rather spend both at my destination.

The best way to find a good travel agent is the same way you find a good plumber or mechanic or doctor — through word of mouth. Pick the brains of friends who utilize travel agents. Also, note that most travel agents work on commission, although some charge for their services.

Well-informed travelers benefit the most from a travel agent and are less apt to get duped. You need not study world geography, international cuisine, and hotel management, but you should invest some time researching your destination. If you have access to the Internet, check prices on the Web yourself in advance to gather some ballpark prices. (see "Tips for Getting the Best Airfare" later in this chapter for ideas.) Take your research to your travel agent and ask him or her to make the arrangements for you. Agents may access more information via their fingertips than you could in a month of Sundays. They can book your hotel room, issue tickets and vouchers, and secure better prices in most cases.

Joining an Escorted Tour or Traveling on Your Own

Some people love *escorted tours.* The tour company takes care of all the details and tells you what to expect at each attraction. You know your costs up front, and you don't experience many surprises. Escorted tours can take you to the maximum number of sights in the minimum amount of time with the least amount of hassle.

Other people need more freedom and spontaneity. These folks prefer to discover a destination by themselves and don't mind getting lost on the way or finding that a recommended restaurant is no longer in business. They consider these surprises just parts of their adventures.

If you decide you want an escorted tour, think strongly about purchasing travel insurance, especially if the tour operator asks to you pay up front. *Note:* Don't buy insurance from the tour operator! If the tour company doesn't fulfill its obligation to provide you with the vacation you paid for, it may not fulfill its insurance obligations either. Purchase travel insurance through an independent agency. (See Chapter 9 for more information on the pros and cons of travel insurance.)

When choosing an escorted tour, make sure to find out if you need to put down a deposit and when you have to make final payment. Other questions you should ask include:

1. **What is the cancellation policy?** Can the tour operators cancel the trip if they don't get enough people? How late can you cancel if you are unable to travel? Do you get a refund if you cancel? If

they cancel? You may rethink your choice of tour operators based on their cancellation policies.

2. **How jam-packed is the schedule?** Do they try to fit 25 hours into a 24-hour day or do you have ample time to relax by the pool or shop? If waking up at 7 a.m. every day and not returning to your hotel until 6 or 7 p.m. sounds like a grind, certain escorted tours may not be for you.

3. **How big is the group?** The smaller the group, the less time you spend waiting for people to get on and off the bus. Tour operators may evade this issue, because they may not know the exact size of the group until everybody confirms their reservations. But they should give you a rough estimate. Some tour operators require a minimum group size and may cancel a tour if they don't book enough people.

4. **What exactly is included?** Don't assume anything. You may need to pay for your transportation to and from the airport. A box lunch may be included in an excursion but drinks may cost extra. Beer may be included but not wine. How much flexibility do you have? Can you opt out of certain activities or does the bus leave once a day, with no exceptions? Are all your meals planned in advance? Can you choose your entree at dinner or does everybody get the same chicken cutlets? Knowing exactly what is included in your tour may help you decide if the plan is right for you.

Choosing a Package Tour

Package tours aren't the same as escorted tours. They're simply a way of buying your airfare and accommodations at the same time — hopefully, at a good deal.

For popular destinations like Washington, D.C., package tours are a smart way to go. In many cases, a package that includes airfare, hotel, and transportation to and from the airport costs less than just the hotel charge alone when you book the hotel room yourself. The rates are cheaper because packages are sold in bulk to tour operators, who resell them to the public. It's kind of like buying your vacation at a buy-in-bulk store — except the tour operator is the one who buys the 1,000-count box of garbage bags and resells them ten at a time at a cost that undercuts what you'd pay at your average neighborhood supermarket.

Package tours can vary in price as much as those garbage bags, too. Some offer a better class of hotels than others. Some offer the same hotels for lower prices. Some offer flights on scheduled airlines; others book charters. In some packages, your choice of accommodations and travel days may be limited. Some let you choose between escorted vacations and independent vacations; others allow you to add on just a few excursions or escorted day trips (also at discounted prices) without booking an entirely escorted tour.

Each destination usually has one or two packagers that are better than the rest, because they buy in even bigger bulk. The time you spend shopping around will be well rewarded.

The best place to start looking is the travel section of your local Sunday newspaper. **Liberty Travel** (☎ **888-271-1584** to find the store nearest you; Internet: www.libertytravel.com) is one of the biggest packagers in the Northeast and usually boasts a full-page ad in Sunday papers. **American Express Vacations** (☎ **800-346-3607;** Internet: http://travel.americanexpress.com/travel/) is another option.

The best source of packages to Washington, D.C. is the airlines themselves, which often package their flights together with accommodations. When you pick the airline, choose one that has frequent service to your hometown and the one on which you accumulate frequent flyer miles. Among the airline packages, your options include:

- ✔ **American Airlines Vacations** (☎ **800-321-2121;** Internet: www.aavacations.com)

- ✔ **Continental Airlines Vacations** (☎ **888-898-9255;** Internet: www.coolvacations.com)

- ✔ **Delta Vacations** (☎ **800-872-7786;** Internet: www.deltavacations.com)

- ✔ **US Airways Vacations** (☎ **800-455-0123;** Internet: www.usairwaysvacations.com)

The biggest hotel chains also offer packages. If you already know where you want to stay, call the hotel or resort itself and ask if they offer land/air packages.

National tour companies

More than a million people visit Washington annually as part of group tours. Some companies provide fully escorted tours, which means the tour guide or leader is with you from beginning to end to make sure everything runs smoothly. An escorted tour is for those who like the comfort of being with other people and having someone else at the helm, especially on a first visit.

Other tour companies make all the arrangements for you; then you're on your own. Many people prefer the convenience of someone else booking airline seats, hotel rooms, rental cars, and sightseeing excursions. If you don't want to travel with a large group and prefer more flexibility during your visit, an unescorted (also known as an independent or package) tour is probably a good fit for you.

Some companies offer you a choice of escorted or independent tours. Here are a few Washington tour providers: (***Note:*** The tour prices quoted are ballpark figures and are subject to change.)

- ✔ **Contiki,** with vacations for 18- to 35-year-olds, has offered tour packages for more than 38 years. Washington is in a couple of its tour itineraries. If you travel alone but want the companionship and price advantage that comes with sharing a room, Contiki can arrange for you to share a room with twin beds (same sex, sorry) at no extra cost. You can reach Contiki at ☎ **800-CONTIKI** or via the Web at www.contiki.com. You can also book a tour with this company through your travel agent.

- ✔ **Globus** and **Cosmos** repeatedly garner awards to lead the pack of tour operators. Both balance scheduled sightseeing with leisure time and offer escorted and independent tours. In the D.C. area, however, they primarily schedule escorted tours. Globus offers visits to Washington in conjunction with other stops, such as an 8-day Civil War tour. Other 8-day tours feature stops in Philadelphia, Williamsburg, Charlottesville, and Gettysburg, with Washington serving as the departure and return city. These trips run from about $950 to $1,000. A 6-day Cosmos tour of Niagara Falls and Washington starts at $389 and an 8-day tour starts at $650.

To induce adults to bring their kiddies along, Globus grants a 10 percent discount on the land-only price to tour members under 18 accompanied by an adult. This company doesn't accept children under 8 for escorted tours, but kids of all ages are welcome on independent tours. For more information on Globus or Cosmos tours, contact your travel agent or check their Web sites at www.globustours.com and www.cosmostours.com.

- ✔ Many travelers swear by **Tauck Tours.** This tour company's attention to detail is legendary, and Tauck Tours has been in business for close to 80 years. For example, Tauck's policy is for passengers to change seats twice a day. So, if the person next to you talks your ear off in the morning, you can look forward to a reprieve. Tauck includes most meals, a tour director, lodging, air-conditioned (nonsmoking) motorcoach transportation, gratuities (for bellhops, door attendants, housekeepers, dining room servers and local guides, but not the driver or tour director), entertainment, and sightseeing in its tours. Individuals with special needs must travel with an able-bodied companion. For more information, call your travel agent or contact Tauck Tours (☎ **800-468-2825;** Internet: www.tauck.com).

- ✔ For more than a quarter of a century, **Yankee Holidays** has offered individual city packages and customized group tour packages. Its trips, featuring a variety of hotels, restaurants, attractions, and entertainment, emphasize theater packages. The 3-day Capitol Experience includes 2 nights lodging, from around $139 to $255 per night depending on the hotel, and a 1-day sightseeing pass. Its Washington Diplomat tour (4 days and 3 nights) includes lodging, dinner at a big-name downtown restaurant, a day of sightseeing, and a choice of tours for about $280 to $454. Prices are lowest during July and August. For other tours, call ☎ **800-225-2550** or your travel agent, or go to its Web site at www.yankee-holidays.com.

✔ **Globetrotter Corporate Travel** offers 2-, 3-, 4-, and 5-night packages to Washington, with eight different categories of hotels (from Quality Suites to Willard Inter-Continental). Prices for 2 nights at the lowest category start at around $147 per person based on double occupancy and rise to about $937 for 5 nights at the upper category during prime season. Prices include all hotel taxes and service charges and some sightseeing fees, depending on the package purchased. The company's Price Match Guarantee says it honors any competitor's published price offering the same hotel, same room category, same length of stay, same travel dates, and comparable flights. Contact your travel agent for additional information or call ☎ **800-999-9696.** You can also take a look at the company's Web site at www.globetrotters.com.

✔ **Peter Pan,** another trooper, has been in business for 65 years. The company features wide-bodied coaches equipped with video cassette players, climate control, and plenty of overhead airline-style storage compartments. Peter Pan's motorcoaches have two-way radios and 24-hour dispatching in case of any emergency. For additional information, call ☎ **800-237-8747** or your travel agent. The company also has a Web site at www.peterpan-bus.com.

Local tour companies

For sightseeing D.C.'s major attractions, you can't beat **Tourmobile,** operated by the National Park Service. (See Chapter 11 for more on Tourmobile and Chapter 18 for information on other local tours.) If you want to do some specific sightseeing when you're in town, contact the following local tour bus companies.

✔ **Atlantic Coast Charters,** out of Hagerstown, Maryland, conducts tours through Civil War historical areas as well as shopping trips to Potomac Mills, the most visited attraction in Virginia (located less than an hour from D.C.). For more information, call ☎ **800-548-8584** or your travel agent.

✔ Passengers are said to travel on "air" with **Eyre Bus Service** and **Eyre Tour and Travel.** These companies offer mostly group charters, but their loss can be your gain. Depending on availability, you may be able to join a group. Eyre can assist you with your travel plans via motorcoach, train, air, or ship. In addition, if you gather a group to travel, you may receive one complimentary fare; this option is offered on most coaches with a group of 38 to 46 passengers. For more information, call your travel agent or ☎ **800-321-EYRE.** You can also check out the company's Web site at www.eyre.com.

✔ **The Smithsonian Associates,** with day and overnight bus trips to nearby areas, has gained esteem far and wide for its guides' expertise. Although this company is more expensive than most tour operators, you get what you pay for. For those with an interest in a specific locale or subject (Civil War history or famous military battlefields, for example), this company is an excellent choice. Call ☎ **202-357-3030** or surf over to www.si.edu/tsa/rap/tours-dc.htm.

For Independent Types: Making Your Own Arrangements

For those who prefer making their own travel arrangements, here are the pros and cons of Washington's three airports, tips on getting good fares, and suggestions for alternative ways of getting to D.C.

Finding out who flies there

Three major airports serve Washington, D.C.: **Ronald Reagan Washington National Airport** (Reagan National), **Washington-Dulles International Airport** (Dulles), and **Baltimore-Washington International Airport** (BWI). All three feature public transportation, fast-food outlets, and shopping. All the major airlines fly into at least one of the three. (See the specific airport sections later in the chapter for the airlines serving each one.) As their names suggest, Dulles and BWI handle domestic *and* international flights.

For a quarterly guide to flights in and out of National and Dulles, write to **Metropolitan Washington Airports Authority,** P.O. Box 17045, Washington Dulles International Airport, Washington, D.C. 20041; or check the Web site at www.metwashairports.com.

To receive a similar guide for BWI, write to **Maryland Aviation Administration,** Marketing and Development, P.O. Box 8766, BWI Airport, MD 21240-0766; or head on the Web to www.bwiairport.com.

So many choices! So little time! I look at the airports one at a time. Where you land can affect your travel plans and pleasure.

Ronald Reagan Washington National Airport (Reagan National)

Just call it **Reagan National.** If you take the time to spit out the full name, you'll miss your flight. The airport lies on the Virginia side of the Potomac River, within sight of downtown D.C. However, the short distance between the two places can be deceiving.

You're probably thinking, "It's so close, you can catch a taxi into town and arrive at the hotel in a flash." I hate to burst your bubble. On the two occasions in the past few years that I have flown into Reagan National, I waited more than an hour for a taxi in a line that snaked to the Lincoln Memorial. And the traffic . . . don't ask!

The **Metro** (subway) stop is a short walk away, but if you're saddled with luggage, children, pets, gifts, or your in-laws it will seem like an Olympic marathon.

The runways are shorter than the aisle I taxied down to say "I do." (Rent the video *Pushing Tin* and you'll get the picture.) Thank Congress and the diplomatic community who like the convenience and the perk of free VIP parking *close* to the terminals for this airport's popularity. If you opt for Reagan National and need a taxi, try to arrive midday when road traffic is less congested.

The following airlines serve Reagan National: Air Canada, America West, American, Continental, Delta, Midway, Northwest Airlines, TWA, United, and US Airways. (See the Quick Concierge at the back of the book for phone numbers and Web sites.)

As you may guess, I dislike this airport. I disliked it since I first landed here in 1963. Despite a major facelift ($1 billion) and the addition of stunning art, this airport is overused, overcrowded, and overstressed. Maybe that's why there's a Meditation Room, near Baggage Claim.

Washington-Dulles International Airport (Dulles)

Dulles, on the other hand, is majestic. An awesome sight. Saarinen's soaring winged design gives me goosebumps. But the airport's overall functionality elicits a rash. Travelers must contend with a main terminal, infield terminal, and — straight out of *Mad Max Beyond Thunderdome* — shuttle vans to the planes.

Be sure to factor in extra half-hours to your arrival and departure times for the shuttle. Getting to Dulles is no picnic during rush hour (roughly 6 to 10 a.m. and 3 to 8 p.m.). The 45-minute ride between the airport and downtown D.C. may take twice as long during these busy time periods.

Dulles offers domestic and international service on the following airlines: Aeroflot, Air Canada, Air France, Air Tran, ANA, American, Atlantic Coast Air, Austrian Airlines, British Airways, BWIA, Continental, Delta,

Ethiopian, KLM Royal Dutch, Korean Air, Legend, Lufthansa, Midwest Express, Northwest, Sabena, Saudi Arabian, Spanair, Swissair, TWA, United, US Airways, Virgin. Check out the Quick Concierge for phone numbers and Web sites for these airlines.

Baltimore-Washington International Airport (BWI)

BWI is the easiest airport to negotiate because five fingerlike piers fan out from a single check-in area. BWI has grown explosively in recent years. (I hope it doesn't self-destruct.) Despite some growing pains, BWI is my airport of choice.

Southwest Airlines, with its low fares and a record of efficient, on-time service, is reason enough to use BWI. (Southwest doesn't fly into either of the other two D.C. airports.) The ride into Washington from BWI takes 45 minutes under primo conditions, longer in rush hour and bad weather. If you arrive late at night or depart early in the morning, think about staying in one of the many hotels and motels within 5 minutes of the airport. Most offer complimentary shuttle service.

The following airlines serve BWI: Aer Lingus, Air Aruba, Air Canada, Air Jamaica, America West, British Airways, Continental, Delta, Icelandair, Metro Jet, Northwest, Southwest, TWA, United, US Airways. The Quick Concierge at the back of the book has phone numbers and Web site information for these airlines.

Getting the best deals on airfares — plane and simple

Thank God I was too small to help push the DC-3 down the runway when I took my first flight. Ah, for the good old days. Everyone paid the same price, regardless of the day of the week, their age, religion, hair color, or political persuasion. Today, the number of fare rules, restrictions, and pricing schedules could fill the Gutenberg Bible.

For now, all you need to remember is that for every flight several fares are usually available under three main categories: first class, coach, and discount. Although visitors to Washington benefit from a wide choice of flights, their heads may spin deciphering the fare structure — another reason to seek help from a travel agent.

Generally, midweek fares ticketed 21 days or more in advance are the lowest. Holidays are often subject to blackout restrictions, as in "no bargains, sucker." Winter fares are usually lowest and summer fares are highest, but this rule isn't written in stone. Check your daily newspaper and the airline and travel Web sites for special promotions to save big time. (Recently, I missed a midnight deadline for purchasing a discounted ticket over the Internet. The very next morning, I had to pay an extra $100. Ouch!)

The comfort zone

Flying is fun for some folks, but if you're like me, you consider flying a necessary evil for getting to the real party. Some airlines added an inch or so of legroom, but tourist class remains cramped, the cabin temperature is often too hot or too cold, and the air is dry enough to suck the spit out of a Saint Bernard. However, here are a few things you can do — some while you book your flight — to make your trip more tolerable.

✔ **Bulkhead seats** (the front row of each cabin compartment) allow a little more legroom than the other rows. However, sitting in the bulkhead also has some drawbacks. For example, bulkhead seats don't provide you with a place to put your carry-on luggage (except in the overhead bin), because you can't place your bag under a seat in front of you. Likewise, you may find that the bulkhead seat isn't the best place to see an in-flight movie (unless the video screen is connected to the armrest).

✔ **Emergency exit row seats** also offer extra room. Airlines usually assign these seats at the airport on a first-come, first-served basis, so ask when you check in whether you can sit in one of these rows. Remember though, that in the unlikely event of an emergency, you're expected to open the emergency exit door and help direct traffic. This requirement, of course, doesn't count in-air emergencies. (You'll be jeered or even wrestled to the ground by fellow passengers if you try to open the emergency door in midflight.)

✔ **Wear comfortable clothes.** Be sure to dress in layers, because "climate controlled" aircraft cabins vary greatly in temperature and comfort levels. You won't regret taking a sweater or jacket that you can put on or take off as your onboard temperature dictates.

✔ **Bring some toiletries on long flights.** Cabins are notoriously dry places. If you don't want to land in D.C. with the complexion of King Tut, take a travel-size bottle of moisturizer or lotion to refresh your face and hands at the end of your flight. If you're taking an overnight flight (the red-eye), don't forget to pack a toothbrush to combat your morning breath upon arrival.

Although some toiletries are helpful on airplane trips, some are dangerous. *Never* bring an unsealed container of nail polish remover into an airline cabin, because the cabin pressure causes the remover to evaporate and damage your luggage; the resulting smell doesn't help you gain any friends on your flight either. Likewise, if you wear contact lenses, wear your glasses for the flight or at least bring some eye drops. Your don't want to spend your hard-earned cash to have your "soft" lenses surgically removed at a Washington hospital due to cabin dryness.

✔ **Jet lag** usually isn't a problem for flights within the United States, but some people coming from the West Coast are affected by the 3-hour time change. The best way to combat this time warp is to acclimate yourself to local time as quickly as possible. Stay up as long as you can the first day; then try to wake up at a normal time the second day. Likewise, drink plenty of water during your first few days in town, as well as on the plane, to avoid dehydration.

✔ **If you're flying with kids,** don't forget chewing gum for ear-pressure problems (adults with sinus problems should chew as well), some toys to keep your angels entertained, extra bottles or pacifiers, and diapers.

If you don't qualify for a promotional or other reduced fare, you may end up paying substantially more. To stretch your travel dollar, plan well in advance whenever possible. Comparison shop by calling the airlines, visiting travel Web sites (see the "Booking your ticket online" section later in this chapter), or consulting an accredited travel agent. And inquire about money-saving packages that include hotel accommodations, car rentals, tours, and so forth, with your airfare.

The airlines frequently offer special family fares whereby kids under the age of 2 (who do not occupy a seat) travel free. Depending on the airline, various discounts apply to kids between the ages of 2 and 12. If you travel with an infant, toddler, or active preschooler, request the seats behind the bulkhead. You have more legroom, and your kids have more play room. (However, if the row behind the bulkhead accesses the emergency exit, you aren't allowed to occupy these seats with infants.)

Many planes are equipped with special fittings for bassinets. Some allow you to use your child's car seat. To find out if your particular brand of car seat is approved by the Federal Aviation Administration, request *Child/Infant Safety Seats Acceptable for Use in Aircraft* from the **Community and Consumer Liaison Division,** APA-400 Federal Aviation Administration, 800 Independence Ave. SW, Washington, D.C. 20591; ☎ **202-267-3479.**

Also known as bucket shops, consolidators are a good place to check for the lowest fares. These companies buy large blocks of seats from the airlines at a substantial discount and then resell those seats to travelers. Their prices are much better than the fares you can get yourself and are often even lower than what your travel agent can get you. You see their ads in the small boxes at the bottom of the page in your Sunday travel section. Some of the most reliable consolidators include **Cheap Tickets** (☎ **800-377-1000;** Internet: www.cheaptickets.com), **1-800-FLY-CHEAP** (Internet: www.flycheap.com), and **Travac Tours & Charters** (☎ **877-872-8221;** Internet: www.thetravelsite.com). Another good choice, **Council Travel** (☎ **800-226-8624;** Internet: www.counciltravel.com), caters especially to young travelers, but its bargain-basement prices are available to people of all ages.

Booking your ticket online

Another way to find the cheapest fare is to scour the Internet. This task is what computers do best — search through millions of pieces of data and return information in rank order. The number of virtual travel agents on the Internet has increased exponentially in recent years.

Too many travel sites exist to mention them all, but a few of the better respected (and more comprehensive) ones are Travelocity (www.travelocity.com), Microsoft Expedia (www.expedia.com), and

Yahoo! Travel (http://travel.yahoo.com). Each has its own little quirks, but all provide variations of the same service. Just enter the dates you want to fly and the cities you want to visit, and the computer looks for the lowest fares. Several other features are standard to these sites: the ability to check flights at different times or dates in hopes of finding a cheaper fare, e-mail alerts when fares drop on a route you have specified, and a database of last-minute deals that advertises super-cheap vacation packages or airfares for those people who can get away at a moment's notice.

Great last-minute deals are also available directly from the airlines themselves through a free e-mail service called *E-savers*. Each week, the airline sends you a list of discounted flights, usually leaving the upcoming Friday or Saturday and returning the following Monday or Tuesday. You may sign up for all the major airlines at one time by logging on to Smarter Living (www.smarterliving.com) or go to each individual airline's Web site. These sites offer schedules, flight bookings, and information on late-breaking bargains. (For a list of airline Web sites, see the Quick Concierge in the back of this book.)

Using Other Methods to Get to Washington, D.C.

If you live near Washington, D.C. or you can't stand to fly, several alternatives to air travel are available; some of them may even be cheaper than air travel.

Riding the rails

For travelers arriving from New York, Philadelphia, and Wilmington, I think Amtrak is the *only* way to go. In the long run, a train is faster than an airplane because you don't need to check in an hour early and you're not at the mercy of the weather and unexpected flight delays. (And you don't hear "Your plane will be here in a few minutes," even though it hasn't left Minneapolis — 3 hours away.)

Amtrak runs dozens of trains daily to Boston, New York, and Washington (fewer trains run on weekends). The **Metroliner** has roomier seats, makes the New York to D.C. run in 3 hours, and costs $100 each way. Regular **Amtrak** trains take about 3 hours and 30 minutes, depending on the number of stops. The one-way cost is $68 except Friday and Sunday afternoons, and some holidays when the fare jumps to $84. If possible, I advise calling ahead for a guaranteed reserved seat (no extra charge) rather than just showing up at the station. Sometime in the near future, Amtrak will begin phasing in the high-speed **Acela Express,** which will make the New York to D.C. run in 2 hours and

45 minutes versus 3 hours on the Metroliner. Big Deal. Then the old Metroliners will be spruced up and incorporated into the Acela Regional system.

All rates quoted here were accurate at the time of this book's publishing. But, because rates are subject to change, make sure to inquire about them again when booking your trip.

From the southern and southwestern United States, Amtrak trains are less plentiful. All trains arrive at Union Station on Capitol Hill with a Metro station and plenty of cabs out front, as well as a food court, dozens of restaurants, shops, and a multiplex theater.

Amtrak Vacations offers package tours, which include round-trip coach rail passes from New York, Philadelphia, Wilmington, or Baltimore, plus two nights lodging, and other perks. You can count on Amtrak for summer deals for families, too. Call your travel agent or ☎ **888-AMTRAK-1,** or go to Amtrak's Web site at `www.northeast.amtrak.com/bestbuys` for more information.

Taking a car

If you must drive to Washington, you must. Those of us who hate needless suffering keep D.C. driving to a minimum. If you do arrive by car, be prepared to garage it at an average cost of $15 to $20 per day.

Easily accessible on foot and by the **Metro** (subway), Washington is your worst driving nightmare: confusing traffic circles, poor signage, one-way streets that dead end and continue several blocks away, and craters deeper than the moon's. Traffic is heavy from predawn to post-sunset. One wrong turn and you may end up in Virginia or one of the less desirable neighborhoods. If, despite my warnings, you insist on driving, cruise down to the next paragraph so you can figure out how to get here.

All roads lead to the Capital Beltway (I-95/I-495), a wheel (or noose) around the District with spokes leading into the city. When you make your reservation, ask which "spoke" to take to your hotel. From the north, I-270, I-95, and I-295 are the main links. From the south, I-95 and I-395 are the most direct routes. Route 50, known as New York Avenue in D.C., is the road of choice from Annapolis and the Eastern Shore of Maryland. From the west, take Route 66, which leads into Constitution Avenue and Rock Creek Parkway. (See the "Driving to D.C." map in this chapter for clarification.)

AAA (☎ **800-222-4357**) and some other automobile clubs offer free maps and optimum driving directions to their members. If you're a club member and you have no sense of direction, give them a call.

Driving to D.C.

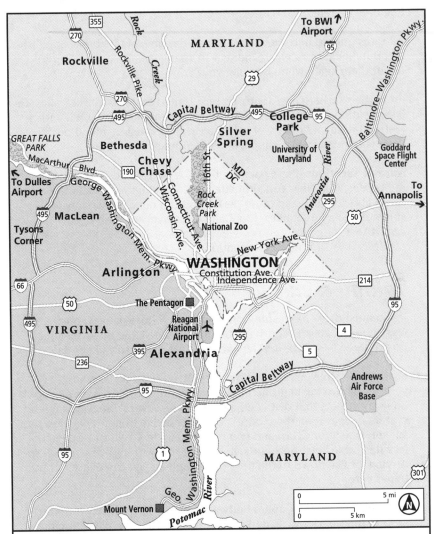

Driving into D.C.
Note that all of the following highways lead to the **Capital Beltway (I-95/I-495)**, which is a wheel (or noose) around the D.C. area, with spokes leading into the city. Talk to your hotel to find out which spoke is right for you.

- If you're driving into D.C. from the north, **I-270**, **I-95**, and **I-295** are the main links to the Washington metropolitan area.

- From the south, **I-95** and **I-395** are the most direct and quickest routes.

- From points east, such as Annapolis and the Eastern Shore of Maryland, the road of choice is **Route 50**, which becomes New York Avenue in the District.

- West of D.C., coming from Virginia, motorists should cruise down **I-66**, which leads into both Constitution Avenue and Rock Creek Parkway.

Chapter 6

Deciding Where to Bed Down

In This Chapter

▶ Finding a hotel room that meets your needs

▶ Choosing the neighborhood in which you want to stay

▶ Selecting a hotel that falls in your price range

*W*here you plant yourself during your vacation helps determine many things about your trip, including your itineraries and how much money you spend.

The factors that decide where you rest your head for the night boil down to location and price. Although you pay more for the best locations, you may find these hotels are worth the extra bucks for their convenience. The closer your hotel is to the things you want to do and see, the less time you waste getting to these attractions.

In this chapter — and in Chapters 7 and 8 — I help you map out the best Washington accommodations, so sharpen your pencil and read on.

Finding Your Hotel Flavor

Accommodations come in nearly as many flavors as ice cream. Options include chain hotels (vanilla), independent hotels (mocha), hotels that cater to business travelers (strawberry), hotels suited to families (tutti-frutti), motels (chocolate chip), B&Bs (mango), and campgrounds (grape Popsicle). The next section samples all of them.

Comparing chain gangs to independent types

Almost all the major hotel chains are represented in the Washington, D.C., area including Best Western, Clarion, Doubletree, Embassy Suites, Hilton, Holiday Inn, Hyatt, Intercontinental, Loews, Marriott, Radisson,

Sheraton, Westin, and Wyndham. Conventioneers and other business types favor these hotels. When the briefcases check out on Fridays, travelers (especially families) fill the void, drawn to special weekend prices and perks.

Face it, vanilla is vanilla. It tastes pretty much the same regardless of the brand. Similarly, the appearances, prices, amenities, and services of the big chain hotels imperceptibly vary. Nothing's wrong with vanilla. It's reliable. You know what vanilla will taste like before you take your first lick. For those who prefer familiarity when they travel — a flavor and brand name you can count on — a chain is the way to go. The Quick Concierge at the back of this book contains a list of toll-free telephone numbers for the major ice cream producers, er, chain hotels in Washington, D.C.

Independent hotels generally fall into one of two categories; they belong to a group of properties managed by a private company, or they are single-owner establishments. These lodgings tend to exhibit more personality and charm. Their lobbies may be less opulent, but their staff tends to be more personable, less harried, and more detail-oriented. (The big chains would probably argue the last point, but that has been my experience.) It's the difference between living in a big city as a face in the crowd, and a small town where everyone knows your name. Independents are often called *boutique hotels* and tend to target a specific type of traveler. People who are bored by vanilla and prefer more intimate surroundings are happier in an independent hotel.

Weighing hotels versus motels

While chain and independent hotels offer service and amenities (at a price, of course), motels are typically no-frills and, therefore, friendlier to your pocketbook. Usually these lodgings are one- to three-story structures of nondescript design with thin walls. Motels typically offer free parking (a big plus when you consider downtown parking costs up to $20 a day), a coffee maker, soda, snack and ice vending machines, and sometimes a swimming pool. Other than that, you're pretty much on your own. Don't look for a crystal chandelier in the registration area, plush terry robes, or phones in the bathroom. You can't call the manager for theater tickets or a club sandwich at midnight.

Motels are a good choice for budget-conscious travelers (especially families) willing to trade location for savings. No motels are within walking distance of the major downtown sights, such as the Air and Space and American History museums. If you want to stay in a motel during your Washington visit (see the Quick Concierge at the end of the book), head for the hills, in this case the Maryland and Virginia suburbs. From either 'burb, you have a 10- to 30-minute Metro ride to the Senate floor or the White House.

Evaluating bed-and-breakfast inns

Bed-and-breakfast or B&B accommodations run the gamut from a closet-sized bedroom with a shared bathroom to an antiques-filled site oozing antebellum charm. The prices run the gamut, too. Although I enjoy staying in B&Bs, I can't recommend them across the board as most are not easily accessible via Metro to the major sights. If you come to town for an intense, two-day Mall crawl, B&Bs are probably not your best choice. But if you can spend more time, wish to soak up the city's culture, and enjoy interacting with the locals, a B&B may suit you well. Having said that, I do recommend an exceptional B&B (in my mind, a "crossover" between an inn and a boutique hotel) in Chapter 8.

If you want more information on the B&B scene in D.C., you can look up two very helpful B&B groups that have been around forever. Both act as reservation services, screening the inns and booking rooms from $65 to $250 per night. You can contact the **Bed and Breakfast League/ Sweet Dreams & Toast** at P.O. Box 9490, Washington, D.C. 20016; (☎ **202-363-7767**). To get in touch with **Bed & Breakfast Accommodations Ltd.,** write to P.O. Box 12011, Washington, D.C. 20005, call (☎ **202-328-3510;** Fax: 202-332-3885), or check out the company's Web site at www.bedandbreakfastdc.com.

Finding the Perfect Location

Maybe you're visiting Washington with your college roommate. You want to sightsee for a couple of hours, and then catch up on the past 20 years. You want a convenient location, but in a residential neighborhood that's relatively quiet. You'll get your way in **Foggy Bottom.** Perhaps you're bringing the kids and can spend the bucks to stay in a large hotel within walking distance of the major sights. If so, **Downtown** has your name on it. Or, if after the museums close, you and your significant other want to trip the night fantastic, try **Georgetown** on for size.

Each Washington, D.C. neighborhood has its own distinctive character. You couldn't stay Downtown, near the White House, and mistake the area for Dupont Circle or Georgetown. To help you choose, check out Chapter 10 for a map of the major D.C. neighborhoods described in this section.

Please note that **Adams-Morgan,** a favorite neighborhood for dining, browsing, and people-watching is not discussed in this section because this area offers few places to stay and is not easily accessible via the Metro. (See Chapter 10 for more on Adams-Morgan.) A shuttle currently runs between the Woodley Park station and 18th St. NW from 6 p.m. to midnight, later on weekends. Unfortunately, this shuttle is no help to visitors during daytime sightseeing hours. (One hopes that the service will be expanded in the future.)

Capitol Hill

"The Hill" extends from the U.S. Capitol in three directions: north, south and east. In addition to the Capitol, staying in this neighborhood means you can walk to the Supreme Court, the Library of Congress, Union Station, the Capital Children's Museum, and the National Postal Museum. The area, with its distinctive brick row houses, local watering holes, and mom-and-pop businesses, brims with vitality and a persona uniquely its own.

The perks of staying on Capitol Hill are . . .

✔ You're a hop, skip, and a jump from the Mall.

✔ If you arrive and depart by train, your lodging is conveniently close to Union Station and the Metro.

✔ This area is easier on your pocketbook than many other D.C. neighborhoods.

On the downside . . .

✔ Although there are pocket parks in the area, you'll find less elbow room than in other sections of the city.

✔ You won't encounter many problems in the immediate vicinity of the major hotels and attractions, but this neighborhood is not the safest at night.

Downtown/Convention Center

Office buildings, shops, hotels, and restaurants vie for space in this central area that encompasses the White House, Chinatown, the Convention Center, the MCI Center (for sports events and concerts), the theater district, and the 7th Street arts corridor. Once as scintillating as white bread, the area is now a prime destination on evenings and weekends thanks to redevelopment along Pennsylvania Avenue and the addition of the MCI Center.

The perks of staying Downtown are . . .

✔ You're within walking distance of all D.C.'s major attractions, theaters, restaurants, and shops.

✔ The area pulses with action, and you're in the heart of it.

On the other hand . . .

✔ You pay a very high price for the convenient location.

Dupont Circle

A melting pot known for its bookstores, boutiques, galleries, restaurants, and hospitable climate to gays, **Dupont Circle** is an insomniac's dream long after most of D.C. has rolled up the sidewalks. Although you are a Metro stop or two farther away from the National Mall attractions, the hotel rates are more reasonable than in the Downtown sector. Dupont Circle's free spirit is reminiscent of New York City's Greenwich Village, but with less grunge.

On the upside . . .

- ✔ This area is hip, trendy, lively, colorful, more interesting, and less homogenized than most of the other neighborhoods in the city.
- ✔ You can easily access some of the city's best nightlife and dining.
- ✔ Prices here are pretty reasonable.

The drawbacks include . . .

- ✔ All that after-dark partying means the area can get very noisy at night.
- ✔ In a city full of traffic horrors, this neighborhood can be particularly nightmarish.

Foggy Bottom/West End

A hamlet within the city, this former industrial area west of the White House was once known as Funkstown. (Put that in your trivia pipe and smoke it.) Dollhouse-sized row houses line up along bricked sidewalks in the shadow of the Kennedy Center, the State Department, George Washington University, and the infamous Watergate. A very pleasing European ambiance pervades the neighborhood. You can walk to the White House and Georgetown from **Foggy Bottom.** Otherwise, the major sights are a long walk or a 10-minute Metro ride away from the Foggy Bottom station.

The pros . . .

- ✔ You're close to the Kennedy Center and Georgetown.
- ✔ The atmosphere is urban, but Foggy Bottom is quieter than other sections of town.

The cons . . .

- ✔ Although the selection of hotels in the West End is growing, the closest Metro stop (Foggy Bottom) is not convenient to them.
- ✔ You need to take the Metro to get to most of the popular sights and attractions.

Georgetown

An instantly recognizable address for eons, **Georgetown** was a colonial tobacco port situated due west of Foggy Bottom. Georgetown dances to a beat all its own. A rainbow of visitors — from D.C., the suburbs, local universities, and all over the world — frequent the restaurants, pubs, and boutiques along Wisconsin Avenue, M Street, and the K Street waterfront.

Staying here is great because . . .

- ✔ An abundance of great shopping, dining, and nightlife is within walking distance.
- ✔ You're close to Dumbarton Oaks, the waterfront, and the recreation of the C&O Canal. See Chapter 16 for more on these attractions.

On the other hand . . .

- ✔ If you seek tranquility, especially at night, stay elsewhere. The noise on weekends (when the student population comes out to party) can grow very loud.
- ✔ The nearest Metro station, Foggy Bottom, is about a 20-minute walk or a 10-minute bus ride. If you stay here, you need to walk a lot and/or take more taxis.
- ✔ Georgetown can get very crowded. Traffic is bad at all times, and is particularly horrendous during rush hour and on weeknights and weekends. That basically leaves you weekdays between 10 a.m. and 2 p.m, when traffic is only semi-nightmarish.

Uptown

This largely residential area has several hotels along upper Connecticut and Wisconsin Avenues in all price ranges. The biggest drawing card here is the **National Zoo,** a must with children in tow. You find the city's greatest concentration of upscale shopping at **Mazza Gallerie, Chevy Chase Pavilion,** and numerous designer and specialty stores. Heavy traffic aside, **Uptown** is much less citified than Downtown. The downside of staying here is that you spend more time and money commuting, via Metrorail, taxi, or bus to the downtown sights.

The good . . .

- ✔ Families appreciate the area's proximity to the National Zoo, a major child-pleaser.

> ✔ You get more bang for your hotel buck here, especially on weekends, when hotels usually offer special deals.

The bad . . .

> ✔ You're a long way — at least several Metro stops — from the major attractions.

> ✔ Due to the distance from most of the major attractions, commuting times and expenses are significantly higher.

Getting Your Money's Worth

To help you budget for your hotel room, I've assigned a $ symbol to each hotel. The $ symbols are based on the rack rate (standard rate without any discounts applied), and the dollar amounts reflect the *average* of the hotel's high- and low-end rates. The rates quoted may be different from the rate you receive. (Hey, I only write about this stuff. I don't set policy.) Price changes are inevitable in this business, so you may be offered a rate that is lower (Yeah!) or slightly higher (Boo!) than the rates listed here.

Keep in mind that unless I note otherwise, all hotel rooms in this book include private bathrooms and air-conditioning, so even if you get hot under the collar about the price you end up paying for your room, you have the opportunity to cool down. You can also expect a radio, TV, and at least one phone (some phone systems come with modem access and voice mail capability). Data ports, once a rarity, are fast approaching standard, as are designated business suites and/or business centers with all the electronic doodads. Not long ago, you had to request irons and ironing boards from housekeeping. Now these aids are as common as pillows in many rooms. When you're done ironing (or maybe while you're ironing), you can tune in to your favorite network show and, in most instances, cable channels (HBO, CNN, ESPN), as well as pay-per-view movies. The list of amenities only grows larger as you climb the hotel ladder.

For an idea of what you get for your money, here's the lowdown on my hotel price ratings:

> ✔ **$ ($100 and under).** In this category, you may share a room (and bathroom) at the International Hostel, stay in a smallish room (with a private bathroom) in an older, no-frills hotel, stay at a B&B (perhaps with a shared bathroom), or check into a motel in the suburbs. Your room will be clean and probably include a TV and phone. Don't expect room service or chocolates on the pillows.

✔ **$$ ($100–$150).** The rooms in this category may be smallish, but you can count on a TV (most likely with cable hook-up) and other amenities (coffee maker, soaps, and shampoos). You're apt to find more uniformed men and women offering their services. (Don't forget to tip.)

✔ **$$$ ($150–$225).** Amenities such as hair dryers; irons; coffee makers; on-site restaurants; health clubs (on- or off-site); cable TV; and larger bedrooms, bathrooms, and closets are standard in this category. You will probably find more than one phone and a modem jack for your PC in this category. Room service may or may not be standard.

✔ **$$$$ ($225–$300).** Besides a large, well-decorated room, you can count on a larger-than-a-closet bathroom with ample towels and a terry robe — as a loaner, so don't pack it as a souvenir. Expect a full range of amenities, multiple phones (some people like this; I travel to get away from phones), a data port, minibars, on-site restaurant(s), a health club, and room service (either 24-hour or early morning to late night).

✔ **$$$$$ ($300 and up).** You pay for the prestigious name, location, and service. Expect round-the-clock concierge and room service; sumptuous lobbies and room furnishings (entertainment centers, heated towel racks, in-room safes); one or more restaurants for fine dining; a bar and/or lobby cocktail lounge; an on-site spa/ health club; shuttle or van service; staff members who trip over themselves to serve you; and, most blessed of all, chocolates at evening turndown.

Chapter 7

Booking the Best Hotel Room Your Money Can Buy

In This Chapter

▶ Getting a good deal on your hotel room

▶ Shopping for a hotel on the Internet

▶ Arriving in town without a reservation

Some folks call a hotel, ask for a rate, and pay it — no questions asked. These people are the same folks who go to a car lot and pay sticker price. You, however, aren't going to mimic these people by paying the first price you're quoted, because I show you how to find the best hotel rates.

The Truth about Rack Rates (And Why You Don't Have to Pay Them)

If you walk in off the street and ask for a room for the night, you receive the hotel's maximum charge for that room or its *rack rate*. (During your next overnight stay in a hotel, take a peek at the fire and/or emergency exit signs posted on the back of your door; the rack rates are usually posted on these notices.) If a hotel can get away with collecting its rack rate for a room, the management is very happy. But here's the scoop — hardly anyone forks over the rack rate. The step you need to take to avoid being charged the rack rate is surprisingly simple: Ask if there is a cheaper or discounted rate. You almost always will get it!

Getting the Best Room at the Best Rate

Room rates change with the season, as occupancy rates rise and fall. If a hotel is close to full, it is less likely to extend discount rates; if a hotel is close to empty, it may be willing to negotiate. D.C. hotels are more likely to negotiate with you on weekends and during low season. Room prices are subject to change without notice; therefore, the rates quoted in this book may be different than the actual rate you receive when you make your reservation.

A short course in D.C. hotelnomics

To everything there is a season — and hotel rates are no exception. Here's a short course on how the changing seasons affect hotel rates in D.C. A passing grade to all who avoid the worst times to visit Washington. Go to the head of the class!

Low season — low rates

The three best times of year to find deals on hotel rooms are

- ✔ **Thanksgiving through New Year's.** Fewer travelers leave home and hearth.

- ✔ **July and August.** Congress is in recess, and the city is in siesta mode.

- ✔ **Weekends throughout the year.** Politicians (and all the folks who follow them) get outta town on the weekends leaving space for the rest of us.

Between Thanksgiving and early January, the pace slows down. Many of our congressional representatives take very long breaks — hence, lower hotel rates. (Someday Thankmas may become a national holiday.) During July and August, when the Senate and House office buildings are morgue-like because our elected officials are vacationing, hotels woo visitors with lower rates. (For more on the District's high and low seasons, see Chapter 2.) And on the weekends, the gang on the Hill takes to the highway, and the rates at the hotels take a dip.

High season — high prices

High season in Washington is

- ✔ **Mid-March through June.** Everyone wants to visit D.C. in spring, and who can blame them? The city blossoms in the warm weather, but, alas, so do hotel prices.

✔ **September through mid-November.** Congress is back in session, and Capitol Hill is hopping in fall. The weather outside may be delightful, but it's a safe bet that hotel prices will be frightful.

In spring, the Cherry Blossom Festival, good weather, and kids' vacations historically draw visitors to the city in huge numbers. The weather is mild through June and that keeps the crowds coming. High season is also when Congress is in session. When the Capitol is a beehive of activity, influence peddlers, soothsayers, journalists, state politicians, diplomats, media personalities, party organizers, and political wannabes (did I leave anyone out?) converge on Washington like flies to cow pies. During this period, the hotels can and do charge higher prices.

Planning strategically for savings

The amount you spend to bed down eats the biggest chunk of your travel dollars. In all but the smallest accommodations, the rate you pay for a room depends on many factors — chief among them being how you make your reservation. Prices change, sometimes faster than room service can deliver coffee and a bagel.

Calling your friendly travel agent

A travel agent may be able to negotiate a better price with certain hotels than you can get yourself. Often the hotel gives the agent a discount in exchange for steering his or her business toward that hotel.

Your travel agent may suggest a package deal (with airfare) and/or traveling with a group. (See Chapter 5 for more on package tours.) Booking with a group is often the best way to get the best deal. Not only do you hand over the responsibility of planning a trip to someone else — the tour operator — you also often get a better rate. Hotels, joyful at the prospect of booking 10 rooms instead of one or two, give tour operators a discount that's passed on to you. It's the American way. Why fight it?

Making your own hotel reservations

Most hotels have a central reservations number and a toll-free number. Sometimes these numbers will have different rate information. Your best bet is to call both the local and toll-free numbers to see which reservations agent gives you a better deal.

Be sure to mention membership in AAA, AARP, frequent flyer programs, and any other corporate rewards programs when you make your reservation. You never know when doing so may be worth a few dollars off your room rate.

After you make your reservation, ask one or two more pointed questions. These inquiries can go a long way toward making sure you secure the best room in the house.

- ✔ **Always ask for a corner room.** At the same cost as a standard room, sometimes corner rooms offer more space and windows (with views). And the corner location may mean a quieter environment (if you are located at the end of the hall, you don't hear your neighbors passing your room or using the elevator all night).

- ✔ **Steer clear of construction zones.** Be sure to ask if the hotel is renovating; if it is, request a room *away from the renovation site.* The noise and activity may be a bit more than you want to deal with on your vacation.

- ✔ **Request smoking or nonsmoking rooms.** Be sure to indicate your preference. Otherwise, you may get stuck with a room that doesn't meet your needs.

- ✔ **Inquire about the location of the restaurants, bars, and discos.** These areas of the hotel can all be a source of irritating noises. On the other hand, if you want to be close to the action, or if you have a disability that prohibits you from venturing too far very often, you may choose to be close to these amenities.

Even if you secure a relatively quiet room, strange noises, loud TVs, and snoring partners can wreak havoc with your sleep. Carry earplugs whenever you travel. If you forget, substitute cotton balls or wadded-up tissue. When all else fails, I make a salami sandwich of my head with two pillows.

Taxing matters

Another important factor to remember when booking your hotel room is Washington's hotel tax. The District tacks a hefty 14.5 percent tax onto your hotel bill. So if your hotel room costs $125 a night, it actually runs you $144 a night after the tax is added. Make sure to ask whether the hotel tax is included in the price when you are quoted a room rate.

Surfing the Web for Hotel Deals

Although the major travel booking sites (Travelocity, Expedia, Yahoo! Travel, and Cheap Tickets; see Chapter 5 for more details) offer hotel booking services, using a site devoted primarily to lodgings may be best; you may find properties that aren't listed on more general online travel agencies. Some lodging sites specialize in a particular type of accommodations, such as bed-and-breakfasts, which you won't find on the more mainstream booking services. Others, such as TravelWeb (keep reading for more details about it), offer weekend deals on major chain properties.

Here's a look at some of the best accommodations-oriented booking sites on the Web.

- ✔ Although the name **All Hotels on the Web** (www.all-hotels. com) is something of a misnomer, the site *does* have tens of thousands of listings of hotels throughout the world. Bear in mind each hotel pays a small fee ($25 and up) to be listed, so the list is less objective and more like a book of online brochures.

- ✔ **hoteldiscount!com** (www.180096hotel.com) lists bargain room rates at hotels in more than 50 U.S. and international cities. The cool thing is that hoteldiscount!com pre-books blocks of rooms in advance, so sometimes it has rooms — at discount rates — at hotels that are "sold out." Select a city, input your dates and you receive a list of the best prices for a selection of hotels. This site is notable for delivering deep discounts in cities where hotel rooms are expensive. The toll-free number is printed all over this site (☎ 800-96-HOTEL); call it if you want more options than are listed online.

- ✔ **TravelWeb** (www.travelweb.com) lists more than 26,000 hotels in 170 countries, focusing on chains such as Hyatt and Hilton. You can book almost 90 percent of these hotels online. TravelWeb's Click-It Weekends, updated each Monday, offers weekend deals at many leading hotel chains.

Washington also has several local online reservation services. Let your fingers do the clicking to the following Web sites or e-mail addresses for information on accommodations:

- ✔ **Washington, D.C. Convention and Visitors Association:** www.washington.org

- ✔ **Washington, D.C. Reservations:** www.dcaccommodations.com

- ✔ **Bed and Breakfast Accommodations Ltd.:** www.bedandbreakfastdc.com

- ✔ **Bed and Breakfast League/Sweet Dreams & Toast:** E-mail: bedandbreakfast-WashingtonDC@erols.com

Showing Up without a Reservation

Unless you come on short notice to claim a very large inheritance, don't arrive in Washington without a reservation. If your idea of fun is spending a night in an airport lounge or all-night fast-food joint, be my guest. There's a slim chance that you *may* get a room by calling a reservation service, which buys rooms in bulk and resells them. Call (or boot up your laptop) as soon as you touch down at the airport or arrive at Union Station. Try Capitol Reservations (☎ **800-VISIT-DC** or 202-452-1270; Internet: www.hotelsdc.com) and/or Washington, D.C. Accommodations (☎ **800-554-2220** or 202-289-2220; Internet: www.dcaccommodations.com).

Chapter 8

Washington, D.C.'s Best Hotels

● ●

In This Chapter

▶ Showcasing Washington's best hotels

▶ Discovering some additional lodging choices.

● ●

*O*kay, you need to find a hotel, the place where you drop your dirty laundry and read *Goodnight Moon,* at the end of a busy day. The good news is that I scoured the city for the best hotels so that you don't need to pound the pavement when you get here. I follow the KISS (Keep it simple, stupid) philosophy; I start off with indexes of D.C.'s hotels by neighborhood and price. The dollar signs translate into price categories as follows:

$	$100 and under
$$	$100–$150
$$$	$150–$225
$$$$	$225–$300
$$$$$	$300 and up

Later in this chapter, the reviews appear in alphabetical order with the hotel's neighborhood beneath its name. You can also check out the map in this chapter to get a better idea of the hotel's location.

If you're traveling with kids, note the "Kid Friendly" icons. These hotels feature amenities that are especially attractive to families.

Hotel Index by Price

$

Hosteling International —
    Washington, D.C. — Downtown
Hotel Harrington — Downtown
Hotel Tabard Inn — Dupont Circle

$$

Hotel Washington — Downtown
Lincoln Suites Hotel — Downtown
Red Roof Inn — Downtown

$$$

Canterbury Hotel — Dupont Circle
Holiday Inn on the Hill — Capitol
    Hill
Hotel Sofitel — Dupont Circle
State Plaza Hotel — Foggy Bottom

$$$$

George Washington University Inn
— Foggy Bottom

Grand Hyatt Washington at
Washington Center —
Downtown

Hotel George — Capitol Hill

Hotel Sofitel — Dupont Circle

Hyatt Regency Washington —
Capitol Hill

J.W. Marriott — Downtown

Loews L'Enfant Plaza — Downtown

Morrison-Clark Historic Inn —
Downtown

Omni Shoreham — Uptown

Renaissance Washington, D.C.
Hotel — Downtown

State Plaza Hotel — Foggy Bottom

$$$$$

Four Seasons — Georgetown

Jefferson Hotel — Downtown

Swissotel Washington: The
Watergate Hotel — Foggy
Bottom

Willard Inter-Continental —
Downtown

Hotel Index by Location

Capitol Hill

Holiday Inn on the Hill — $$$

Hotel George — $$$$

Hyatt Regency Washington — $$$$

Downtown

Grand Hyatt Washington at
Washington Center — $$$$

Hosteling International —
Washington, D.C. — $

Hotel Harrington — $

Hotel Washington — $$

J.W. Marriott — $$$$

Jefferson Hotel — $$$$$

Lincoln Suites — $$

Loews L'Enfant Plaza — $$$$

Morrison-Clark Historic Inn
— $$$$

Red Roof Inn — $$

Renaissance Washington, D.C.
Hotel — $$$$

Willard Inter-Continental — $$$$$

Dupont Circle

Canterbury Hotel — $$$

Hotel Sofitel — $$$ — $$$$

Hotel Tabard Inn — $

Foggy Bottom

George Washington University Inn
— $$$$

State Plaza Hotel — $$$–$$$$

Swissotel Washington: The
Watergate Hotel — $$$$$

Georgetown

Four Seasons — $$$$$

Uptown

Omni Shoreham — $$$$

Washington, D.C. Hotels from A to Z

Canterbury Hotel

$$$ Dupont Circle

This hotel sits on one of the neighborhood's quieter blocks and features 99 suites equipped with queen, double queen, or king beds.

Each suite has a separate dressing area and kitchenette. Friends tell me they receive top-notch service here and, as long as the requests are legal, the staff bends over backward to please guests. Slip into the Canterbury's restaurant for breakfast (a continental version is included in the room rate; a la carte is extra), lunch, or dinner. Quaff a pint in the cozy **Union Jack Pub.** The world-renowned Phillips Collection of 19th and 20th century art is within walking distance, as is the Connecticut Avenue business district. Between museum visits and meetings, browse Dupont Circle's galleries, boutiques, and bookstores. Walk 2.5 blocks to the Dupont Circle Metro station; then ride about 10 minutes to Metro Center. From there, you can walk 5 blocks to the Mall or hop another train. Guests receive complimentary passes for the YMCA (indoor pool and track) around the corner.

1733 N St., NW, between 17th and 18th Sts. ☎ *800-424-2950 or 202-393-3000. Fax: 202-785-9581. Internet:* www.canterburydc.com. *Metro: Dupont Circle. Take escalator out of south entrance, left onto Connecticut Ave., and left at N St., cross 18th St. to the hotel (in the middle of the block). Parking: $14. Rack rates: $165–$215 double. AE, DC, DISC, MC, V.*

Four Seasons

$$$$$ Georgetown

Straddling Foggy Bottom and Georgetown, the Four Seasons' hallmark is impeccable service. This place is for hedonists with deep pockets. Many of the luxurious rooms and public areas overlook Rock Creek Park and the C&O Canal. (You can read more about those attractions in Chapter 16.) At any time of the day or night the concierge can rent you a tuxedo, find you a toothbrush or theater tickets, or send roses to your sweetie back home. VICs (Very Important Children) receive gifts and snacks at check-in. A bone and water, served on a silver tray, no less, welcome Fido. Deals are sealed and love affairs ignite over high tea or cocktails in the **Garden Terrace,** one of my favorite spots for a sundowner. Enjoy the indoor pool, health club (Vichy shower, hydrotherapy, aerobics studio, quiet rooms, whirlpool, steam, and sauna), and multiple phones in every room (my fantasy is a room with no phones). Tom Hanks, Sheryl Crow, and Nicolas Cage have sawed logs in the triple-sheeted beds. Kids under 16 stay free with an adult, and the Four Seasons spoils them rotten with snacks, games, magazines, terry robes, and colorful pillow covers. The hotel provides older children with a Sony PlayStation, board games, video games, and coloring books. A children's menu is available in the restaurant and at tea. The closest Metro (Foggy Bottom) is a good 15-minute walk, or a short bus or taxi ride. The hotel makes amends by offering complimentary shuttle service but can't guarantee availability every time you need a lift. Walk 5 minutes in the opposite direction (west along M Street) and you're in the heart of Georgetown. The Four Seasons creates such a cushy, nurturing environment you may want to skip the monuments altogether. I can think of worse ways to while away a weekend.

Hotels in Washington, D.C.

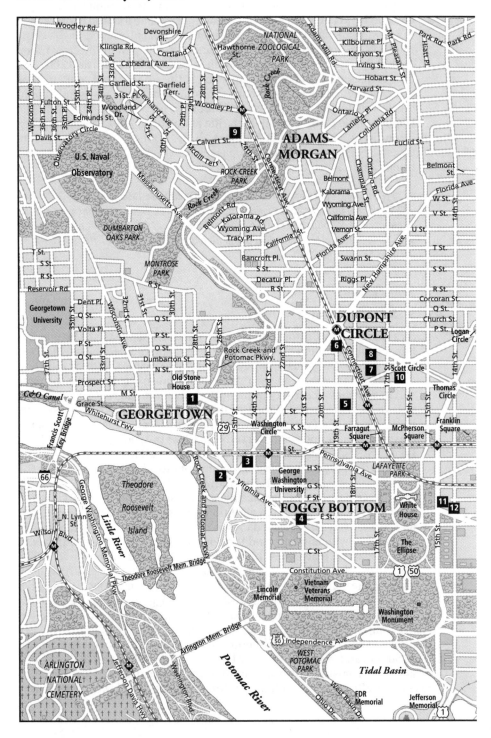

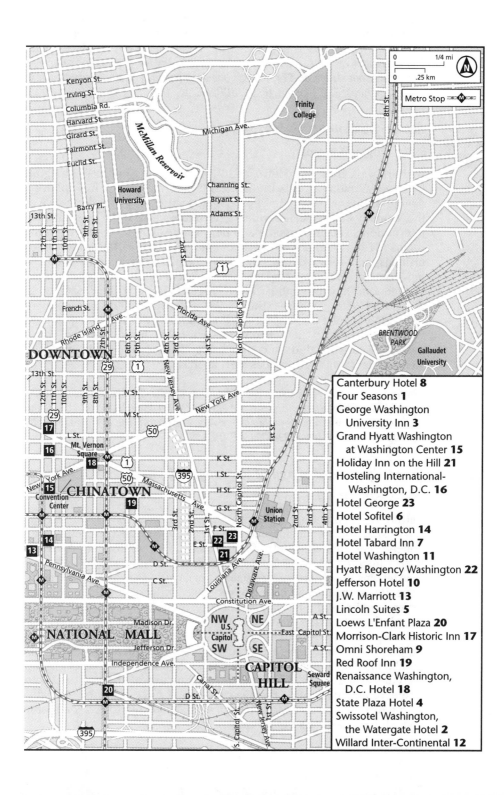

Canterbury Hotel **8**
Four Seasons **1**
George Washington
   University Inn **3**
Grand Hyatt Washington
   at Washington Center **15**
Holiday Inn on the Hill **21**
Hosteling International-
   Washington, D.C. **16**
Hotel George **23**
Hotel Sofitel **6**
Hotel Harrington **14**
Hotel Tabard Inn **7**
Hotel Washington **11**
Hyatt Regency Washington **22**
Jefferson Hotel **10**
J.W. Marriott **13**
Lincoln Suites **5**
Loews L'Enfant Plaza **20**
Morrison-Clark Historic Inn **17**
Omni Shoreham **9**
Red Roof Inn **19**
Renaissance Washington,
   D.C. Hotel **18**
State Plaza Hotel **4**
Swissotel Washington,
   the Watergate Hotel **2**
Willard Inter-Continental **12**

2800 Pennsylvania Ave. NW, at 28th St. ☎ **800-332-3442** *or 202-342-0444. Fax: 202-944-2076. Internet:* www.fourseasons.com. *Metro: Foggy Bottom station. Up the escalator, take a left at 23rd St., left at the traffic circle, left onto Pennsylvania Ave., and continue 4 blocks to hotel. Ask about weekend rates and special packages. Parking: $24 per night (inquire if parking is included in your package). Rack rates: $355 and up. AE, DC, JCB, MC, V.*

George Washington University Inn

$$$$ **Foggy Bottom**

A short walk from the Metro and 2 blocks from George Washington University's campus, this inn is ideal if you're checking out colleges, doing business at the State Department, or attending a performance at the Kennedy Center. All are within a 10-minute walk, so the hotel attracts international businesspeople and performing artists. The 95 spacious rooms (31 of which are one-bedroom suites) come with traditional furnishings, mini-refrigerators, microwaves, coffee makers, irons and ironing boards. You may also request a room with a fully equipped kitchenette. Fill your cupboard with groceries from the small Safeway in the nearby Watergate where there's also a pharmacy. The inn has secure underground valet parking. Stay in this charming neighborhood and use your complimentary passes to the nearby GWU fitness facilities. If you need to wash your duds, a coin-operated laundry facility is available. Weekend and holiday packages start at $89.

824 New Hampshire Ave., between H and I Sts. ☎ **800-426-4455** *or 202-337-6620. Fax: 202-337 254. Internet:* www.gwuinn.com. *Metro: Foggy Bottom/GWU. Exit the station; make a U-turn to New Hampshire Ave. and go left. The inn is on the right. Parking: $15. Rack rates: $239–$350. AE, DC, MC, V.*

Grand Hyatt Washington at Washington Center

$$$$–$$$$$ **Downtown**

Getting to Washington's sights from this hotel is as easy as identifying the Washington Monument, because the Grand Hyatt is connected by an underground tunnel to Metro Center, the transfer station for all five rail lines. Kids under 18 stay free in their parents' room (which is cheaper than leaving them home with a babysitter). Large, well-appointed rooms and suites surround a 12-floor glass-enclosed atrium; they come with hair dryers and irons and ironing boards. Conventioneers pack this place, a stone's throw from the Convention Center, on weekdays. A different clientele surfaces on weekends — couples, families, and business travelers tacking on downtime before or after meetings. A heated indoor pool (adults must accompany kids under 16), steam room, sauna, and health club are available for a fee, which includes use of the hot tub, exercise/aerobics room, and massage room. You can arrange bonded babysitting through the concierge. Sip a martini and listen to jazz, or chomp your stogie at **Butler's Cigar Bar.**

1000 H St. NW, at 11th St. ☎ *800-233-1234 or 202-582-1234. Fax: 202-637-4781. Internet:* www.hyatt.com. *Metro: Metro Center, Washington Center/Grand Hyatt exit. Walk through the tunnel and up the escalator to the hotel. Parking: $12 (self), $15 (valet). Rack rates: $285–$310. AE, CB, DC, DISC, MC, V.*

Holiday Inn on the Hill

$$$ Capitol Hill

This Holiday Inn enjoys a choice location within sight of the Capitol 2 blocks away. The rooms were refurbished in 1999 and, if not worthy of *Architectural Digest,* are large and comfortable. Each room has a coffee maker, a hair dryer, an iron and ironing board, and a large bathroom. If you desire a separate workspace or your family is travelling with you, request a room with an adjoining parlor. The parlor includes a Murphy bed (a bed that can be folded or swung into a closet). Eight of the hotel's rooms are equipped for disabled guests. A large rooftop pool, which enjoys a great view of the area, is open in summer. Many of the hotel's employees have been here long-term, and that translates into staff and visitor satisfaction. Open daily from Memorial Day weekend until Labor Day, the **Kids' Discovery Zone** offers supervised children's programs from 4 to 7 p.m. for kids 4 to 14. The cost is $5 per child, per session. Drop your children off and enjoy a drink or quiet meal all by your lonesome! Children 18 and under stay free with their parents.

415 New Jersey Ave. NW, between D and E Sts. ☎ *800-638-1116 or 202-638-1616. Fax: 202-638-0707.* Internet: www.holidayinn.com.ru/hotels/wasch. *Metro: Union Station. Cross 1st St. and Massachusetts Ave. to E St.; turn right. Walk down E St. 2 blocks; turn left onto New Jersey Ave. The hotel is on the left. Ask for seasonal packages, weekend rates.. Parking: $15. Rack rates: $189 and up. AE, DC, DISC, MC, V.*

Hosteling International — Washington, D.C.

$ Downtown

If you want candy, you better bring it with you because you don't get Godiva on your pillow here. And the only TV is in the recreation area. Whaddaya expect at these prices? Early Spartan describes this 250-bed facility. It is, however, clean and comfortable, with dorm-style rooms (all air-conditioned) in an historic building 3 blocks from Metro Center and all five subway lines. The rooms are segregated by sex, 4 to 18 beds to a room, and bathrooms are down the hall. Families with foresight opt for the 4-person family rooms, but you have to act fast because they are booked very early during spring and summer. You snooze, you lose. BYO soap and towels. Linens, blankets, and pillows are provided. The HI organizes walking tours, concerts, movies, and other events. The savvy staff can help you with your itinerary. You may shop for groceries at the Giant, at 9th and P Streets NW (cab it, as the neighborhood is iffy). The large kitchen and dining room are available for guests' use.

1009 11th St. NW, at K St. ☎ *202-737-2333. Fax: 202-737-1508. Internet: www.hiwashingtondc.org. Metro: Metro Center. Walk north on 11th St. 3 blocks. Parking: Are you kidding? Rack rates: $22–$25 (per person). MC, V.*

Hotel George

$$$$ Capitol Hill

Warhol-ish posters of the Big Daddy of our Country adorn the hotel, which attracts lobbyists and other Hill business types. The hotel is a hop, skip, and a jump from Union Station (Amtrak and Metro) and the Capitol. The handsome, minimalist décor of the guest rooms is refreshing if you're weary of imitation mahogany, swags, and antiques. The amenities — all the top level gadgets and gizmos you can expect — are tucked away, adding to the spare, uncluttered look. BYL (Bring your laptop) as rooms have 2-line cordless phones, executive desks, and electronic hook-ups. The CD/clock radios with nature sound waves soothe jangled nerves. Award-winning chef/owner Jeff Buben wields his whisk at **bis,** the hotel's French bistro. Now that the United States is playing footsy with Cuba again, you can puff your Havana cigar in the billiard room without fear. Not just for big wigs or powdered wigs, the George is a good choice for families as kids under 14 stay free.

15 E St. NW. ☎ *800-576-8331 or 202-347-4200. Fax: 202-347-4213. Internet: www.hotelgeorge.com. Metro: Union Station. Walk 1 block west on Massachusetts Ave., left (south) 1 block at N. Capitol St. (Post Office), and right ½ block at E St. Parking: $24. Rack rates: $245–265. AE, CB, DC, DISC, MC, V.*

Hotel Harrington

$ Downtown

When you think bargain and no frills, think Hotel Harrington. Family-owned for more than 75 years, the Harrington caters to groups, families, and others looking for good value. Nearby, you'll find the FBI headquarters, Ford's theatre, the National theater, the MCI Center, the Pavilion at the Old Post Office, and the Shops at National Place. In addition, the Metro Center is conveniently located 2 blocks away; the Museum of Natural History is less than 6 blocks away. Planet Hollywood is within easy orbit or you can boogie over to the Hard Rock Cafe. If you're travelling with your tribe, a family suite is a good idea. These suites include two rooms (queen bed in one room, twin beds in the other) and two bathrooms. You can request a crib and a refrigerator at no charge. Toss in a load at the self-service laundry on the premises. A few late-summer visitors have said the rooms looked tired. The owners paint and refurbish every winter, but the rooms (like your favorite shoes) take a beating sometimes. The hotel has three on-site restaurants, all reasonable, and plenty of other food options nearby.

11th and E Sts. NW. ☎ *800-424-8532 or 202-628-8140. Fax: 202-347-3924. Internet: www.hotel-harrington.com. Metro: Metro Center, 11th St. exit to the corner of G St. Walk 2 blocks to E St. and the hotel. Parking: $8.50. Rack rates: From $85. AE, DC, DISC, MC, V.*

Hotel Sofitel

$$$–$$$$ Dupont Circle

Question: Where can you find first-class European-style service? Answer: At the Sofitel, where a rose and chocolate accompany evening turndown and you hear "Bonjour" when checking in. The Embassy Row location adds a bit of class as well. The 144 spacious rooms (including 38 suites equipped with kitchenettes) are elegantly appointed and also designed for today's business traveler with telephones and computer- and fax-line access. When you enter your room, you find a bottle of Evian and French soaps and toiletries in the bathrooms. At the Sofitel you can habla whatever with the multilingual concierge and order from room service around the clock. Enjoy fine dining in the **Trocadero** restaurant; then work it off in the on-site health facility and sports complex.

1914 Connecticut Ave., NW, at 19th St. ☎ 800-424-2464 or 202-797-2000. Fax: 202-462-0944. Internet: www.sofitel.com. Metro: Dupont Circle, north exit. Walk up Connecticut Ave. 3 blocks to the hotel on the left. Parking: $17. Rack rates: $199–$259. AE, DC, DISC, MC, V.

Hotel Tabard Inn

$$ Dupont Circle

This inn, composed of three combined town houses and furnished with Victorian and American Empire antiques, is an ideal place to rest your feet after a day of touring. Although the 40 rooms are decorated in a similar colors and styles, they are of different sizes — those facing N Street are the largest. Some rooms include shared bathrooms and are an exceptional deal ($67 to $95). Enjoy a complimentary breakfast in the hotel restaurant. (The restaurant also serves a good lunch and dinner, but these meals are not complimentary.). The Tabard Inn's paneled lounge is a favorite local drinking spot.

1739 N St. NW, between 17th and 18th Sts. ☎ 202-785-1277. Fax: 202-785-6173. Metro: Dupont Circle. Leave the station via the south exit, onto Connecticut Ave.; turn left on N St. and walk about 3 blocks to the hotel. Parking: Garage $15 per day. Rack rates: $99–$155. MC, V.

Hotel Washington

$$$–$$$$ Downtown

Just a block from the White House and convenient to the Smithsonian museums, theaters, and the downtown business district, this hotel holds the honor of being D.C.'s oldest continuously operated hotel. Antique reproductions help to create an atmosphere of old-world charm that is both comfortable and comforting. Request a room with a view and count how many pizza trucks make late-night deliveries to 1600 Pennsylvania Avenue. The **Sky Terrace** crowns the hotel as its rooftop bar. Enjoy cocktails and light fare while glimpsing the Washington Monument, White House, and planes approaching Reagan National. A full-service restaurant,

Two Continents, is open for breakfast, lunch, and dinner in winter; breakfast only in summer, when lunch and dinner are served in the Sky Room, located just across from the Sky Terrace bar. Stop by the hotel's fitness center if the exercise bug bites you.

515 15th St. NW, at Pennsylvania Ave. ☎ *800-424-9540 or 202-638-5900. Fax: 202-638-1594. Internet:* www.hotelwashington.com. *Metro: Metro Center. Leave 12th and F Sts. exit; walk 3 blocks on F St. to 15th St. The hotel is on the corner. Parking: $20. Rack rates: $145–$275. AE, DC, MC, V.*

Hyatt Regency Washington

$$$$ Capitol Hill

About as close as you can get to Congress without running for office, the Hyatt Regency is popular with conventioneers, lobbyists, and travelers from Keokuk to Kyoto. Surrounding the Hyatt's signature five-story atrium lobby are 834 rooms and 31 suites. After an $11 million renovation of the guest rooms and public areas in 1999, the hotel is looking mighty spiffy. The décor of the spacious guest rooms — enhanced by a comfortable club chair, a desk and chair, and plenty of good reading light — invites travelers to relax. Hair dryers, irons and ironing boards, computer and modem hookups are standard. However, you still pay for drinks from the so-called "honor bar." Another two-story glass atrium covers the pool and features a snack bar. Guests can use the hotel's health club, but must pay a fee. Children under 18 always stay free in their parents' room. Ask about the Camp Hyatt program, with a second room at half-price for the kiddies and other perks, such as special menus in the Hyatt's restaurant and for room service. The **Capitol View Club** offers a bird's-eye view of the Capitol.

400 New Jersey Ave. NW, at E St. ☎ *800-233-1234 or 202-737-1234. Fax: 202-737-5773. Internet:* www.hyatt.com. *Metro: Union Station. Walk down E St. 3 blocks; the hotel is on the left. Parking: $24. Rack rates: $260–290. AE, DC, DISC, MC, V.*

Jefferson Hotel

$$$$$ Downtown

Quiet, elegant, and expensive, with a top-notch staff that remembers return guests by name. That's the Jefferson. Antiques, reproductions, and original art fill the gracious 68 rooms and 32 suites — many with balconies. (No wonder so many politicos meet their amours of the moment at this hotel.) Some rooms include canopied beds, and all rooms feature 2-line telephones, private fax lines, VCRs, CD players, hair dryers, and bathrobes. Double-glazed windows mute the traffic noise from 16th and M Streets. Laundry is hand-ironed and delivered in wicker baskets, just like home. LOL. The hotel has a 24-hour butler and multilingual concierge service. The Jeff is a member of the Small Luxury Hotels group, so standards are top-flight. Dip your toes in the indoor pool or define your pecs in the fitness center, which is equipped with a sauna and Jacuzzi.

*1200 16th St. NW, at M St. ☎ **800-368-5966** or 202-347-2200. Fax: 202-785-1505. Internet: www.slh.com. Metro: Farragut North. Leave via Connecticut and L Sts. Follow L St. to 16th St. and turn left for 1 block to M St; the hotel's on the left side. Parking: $20. Rack rates: From $300. AE, DC, MC, V.*

J.W. Marriott Hotel

$$$–$$$$ Downtown

With a downtown address that is synonymous with convenience (to sightseeing, restaurants, shopping, and Metro), the J.W. has 772 rooms and 34 suites. The Shops at National Place (souvenir shops, boutiques, and eateries) and the National Press Club share the same building. Stay here if you like to walk to attractions and restaurants. It's a 10-minute stroll, tops, to the Mall. Several theaters and the Old Post Office Pavilion are also within walking distance. The spacious rooms, redecorated in 2000, have cherry-wood furnishings and come with all the electronic connections and doohickeys travelers come to expect. Children under 18 stay free in their parents' room. To capitalize on your experience, shell out a few extra bucks for a view and reserve a room overlooking Pennsylvania Avenue or the Washington Monument. While older kids visit the game room or Food Hall in the Shops at National Place, you can tone up in the health club and/or indoor pool. Four restaurants offer a range of menus and prices. The J.W. is a hub of conferences and meetings, and all the suits may have you thinking you're seeing double. Ask about weekend deals and other packages.

*1331 Pennsylvania Ave. NW, at 13th St. ☎ **800-228-9290** or 202-393-2000. Fax: 202-626-6991. Internet: www.Marriotthotels.com. Metro: Metro Center. Take the 13th & F exit. At the top of the escalator, take a left at F St. toward the Shops at National Place. Enter the shopping mall and go down one level; turn right at Boston Seafood. Walk straight ahead to the hotel. Parking: $25. Rack rates: $179–$279. Ask for seasonal weekend rate and the Marriott Awards programs. AE, CB, DC, DISC, JCB, MC, V.*

Lincoln Suites

$$–$$$ Downtown

The all-suite property, just 2 blocks from the Connecticut Avenue business corridor, features 99 studio suites, most equipped with wet bars, microwaves, and refrigerators; some suites (27) feature fully equipped kitchens. The king suites offer the comforts of a home office — desks, second phones, and computer jacks. Children under 16 stay free in their parents' room. The service here is great; the employee to suite ratio is one to three. Would you believe cookies and milk every evening? Julius, a former Park Service ranger, oversees the front desk and will tell you everything you want to know about the Washington Monument. Guests receive a complimentary *Washington Post* weekdays and full privileges at the nearby Bally Total Fitness center. Complimentary continental breakfast is served in the lobby on weekends. On site is **Mackey's Public House,** which offers great fish and chips, other light fare, and your favorite brews in a pared-down pub setting.

1823 L St. NW, between 18th and 19th Sts. ☎ 800-424-2970 or 202-223-4320. Fax: 202-223-8546. Internet: www.lincolnhotels.com. *Metro: Farragut North or Farragut West. Exit onto 18th Street. Turn left and go 2 blocks; then left on L for half a block. Parking: $16. Rack rates: $109–$209. Seasonal and weekend packages. AE, CB, DC, DISC, MC, V.*

Loews L'Enfant Plaza

$$$–$$$$ Downtown.

The neighborhood isn't sexy (major traffic arteries and government build-ings for the most part), but this hotel's lavishly appointed rooms are quiet because they occupy the top four floors of an office building. If you want a room with a balcony, ask for one on the 14th or 15th floors. You may request a room near the pool or one with a view of either the presidential monuments or Potomac riverfront. Loews is très convenient to the Air and Space Museum (2 blocks away), Hirshhorn, and other Mall museums. The L'Enfant Plaza Metro station is beneath the building and a pedestrian walkway leads to the Maine Avenue/Water Street waterfront, with restau-rants, theaters, and cruises. The resortlike outdoor pool (covered in the winter) has a snack bar. Children under 18 stay free in parents' room and receive a gift at check-in, and **The Lobby Café** and **American Grill** have a Kid Cuisine menu. Loews lends games, organizes tours, and offers super-vised recreational programs. Amenities include the 11th floor health club, gift shop, express check-in and business-class rooms with three phones (one in the bathroom so you can talk and blow-dry your hair at the same time) and electronics up the ying-yang. Pets, always welcome at Loews, are invited to the local SPCA's annual Doggy Ball.

480 L'Enfant Plaza, 7th & D Sts. SW. ☎ 800-23-LOEWS or 202-484-1000. Fax: 202-646-4456. Internet: www.loewshotels.com. *Metro: L'Enfant Plaza station, exit at 9th & D Sts. Exit puts you in the underground shopping area; look for signs leading to the hotel. Parking: $16. Rack rates: $185–$299. AE, DC, DISC, MC, V.*

Morrison-Clark Historic Inn

$$$–$$$$ Downtown

Although billed as a B&B, the Morrison-Clark is a sumptuous and gra-cious inn, not some cutesy bed-and-breakfast with stamp-sized rooms. One of Classic Hospitality's Washington hotels, the Morrison-Clark exudes antebellum charm and shines at personal service. You can rest your psyche as well as your body at this elegant oasis. Enjoy twice-a-day maid visits and free overnight shoe shines. Trellised balconies overlook a fountained courtyard garden reminiscent of New Orleans. Choose from a Deluxe room (the least expensive), a Victorian (two of which include private balconies), or a Parlor Suite (with a sleep sofa in the sitting room, these suites are ideal for families). Enjoy drinks in the **Club Room,** which has two working fireplaces; then slip into the hotel's award-winning restaurant. Weather permitting, meals are served in the courtyard. Whatever you do, try the lemon chess pie; it was featured in *Gourmet* magazine. I don't recommend the neighborhood for a midnight stroll, but it's fine otherwise and convenient to Metro Center train on all five lines (but not at the same time). We times a fraction of the rack rates. The Morrison-Cla but if they break an antique, *you* pay.

1015 L St., NW, at Massachusetts Ave. and 11th St. NW. ☎ *800-332-7898 or 202-898-1200. Fax: 202-289-8576. Internet:* www.morrisonclark.com. *Metro: Metro Center. Exit right from the station; go up (north) on 11th St. 3 blocks to Massachusetts Ave. and the inn. Parking: $15 (self), $19 (valet). Rack rates: $149–$319. AE, CB, DC, DISC, MC, V.*

Omni Shoreham

$$$–$$$$ Uptown

Stay here if you think size counts and money is no object. Actually a 14-acre self-contained resort, the Omni Shoreham makes sense if you want to be near the **National Zoo** and/or prefer a residential location. Getting to the Mall via Metro takes about a half-hour. Truman played poker here, and "Hostess with the Mostess" Perle Mesta entertained royalty, politicos, and Washington's upper crust. Satirist Mark Russell cut his eyeteeth in the long-gone Blue Room. Upper floors look out on trees and those facing southeast have a panorama of Rock Creek Park and beyond. This place is jock heaven, with a huge outdoor pool and health club. Rock Creek Park, with a fitness course, hiking, biking, and horseback riding is just outside the back door. For the less active, the hotel gardens invite a leisurely stroll. **Robert's** is an upscale restaurant that serves classic American fare. Pick up a little something from **A Little Something,** a gourmet carryout, and eat in your room or tote your fare to the Zoo. The rooms and public spaces recently underwent a 3-year, $80 million restoration, but the players didn't change, mostly conventioneers and high rollers. The Omni gives new meaning to huge. The elegantly furnished rooms, large by any standards, include all the extras (marble baths, electronic hookups, multiphones). If you bring your kids, forget the extras; you can walk to the Zoo.

2500 Calvert St. NW, at Connecticut Avenue. ☎ *800-THE-OMNI or 202-234-0700. Fax: 202-332-1372. Internet:* www.omnihotels.com. *Metro: Woodley Park/Zoo. Walk ½ block south on Connecticut Ave. to hotel (in front of you as you get off the escalator). Parking: $18. Rack rates: $149–$319. AE, CB, DC, DISC, JCB, MC.*

Red Roof Inn Washington, D.C.

$$ Downtown

This hotel is not like the Red Roof Inns you breeze by on the interstate. Hardly. Close to the Convention Center, the MCI Center (sports and big-name entertainers), the 7th Street galleries and theaters, many restaurants, and on the edge of Chinatown, this inn houses 197 rooms on 10 floors. I'm talking value! A find for business travelers and families, the Red Roof doesn't raise the roof on your travel budget. King rooms include large desks with enhanced workspaces. All rooms feature coffee makers, irons and ironing boards, hair dryers, and large bathrooms. The kids can work off excess energy using the in-room Nintendo (hourly charge). Eight rooms are equipped for disabled guests. An exercise room and restaurant, open for breakfast and lunch, are on-site.

500 H St., NW, at 5th St. ☎ *800-843-7663 or 202-289-5959. Fax: 202-682-9152. Internet:* www.redroof.com. *Metro: Gallery Place/Chinatown. Take the 7th St. exit to H St. and walk 2 blocks to 5th St. Parking: (limited) $9.50. Rack rates: $89–$159 double. AE, DC, DISC, V.*

Renaissance Washington, D.C. Hotel

$$$–$$$$ Downtown

The 800-room Renaissance, mainly services the briefcases and pearls headed to the Convention Center across the street. Although you may find neighborhoods with more panache, the location is an excellent choice for sightseeing as it's convenient to all five subway lines at Metro Center. Children 18 and under stay free in their parents' room and eat free from the children's menu. (The value is worth the uninspiring neighborhood, I'd say.) The rooms, upgraded in 1997, are decorated in neutral tones and feature oak furnishings; amenities include voice mail and computer jacks. Sixteen rooms are designed to suit the needs of disabled travelers. Families save big-time on weekends while enjoying all the extras. You have to pay a fee for using the health club, with its lap pool, steam rooms, and whirlpool.

999 9th St. NW, between K and I Sts. ☎ *800-228-9898 or 202-898-9000. Fax: 202-789-4213. Internet:* www.rennaissancehotels.com. *Metro: Gallery Place. Turn right out of the station from 9th St. Exit (onto 9th St.); walk 2 blocks to the hotel. Parking: $15. Rack rates: From $209. AE, CB, DC, DISC, JCB, MC, V.*

State Plaza

$$$–$$$$ Foggy Bottom

The spacious rooms and suites at the State Plaza provide a home away from home for diplomats, business travelers, performing artists, and educators headed to the nearby World Bank, State Department, Kennedy Center, and George Washington University. The State Plaza is also a find for families too. Kids under 12 stay free in their parents' room, and you can save money by cooking meals in the suites' kitchens. On a quiet Foggy Bottom block, the hotel feels more like the private residence it once was than a downtown hotel. Spacious is the operative word here. The largest suite (Grand Plaza Suite) has a master bedroom and bathroom, living room (with queen sofa bed), a stylish and well-equipped kitchen, and a separate dining area. The Foggy Bottom Metro station is a short walk away. Hoof it to the Lincoln Memorial, Vietnam Veterans Memorial, Washington Monument, or White House with ease. Rooms include data ports and dual phone lines; complimentary shoeshine and room service are available. The on-site fitness center has a ballet barre for the dancers who stay here. (Go ahead, belly up to the barre.) The

Garden Café serves breakfast, lunch, and dinner, with outdoor dining in season. Two thumbs up for the exceptional Sunday brunch served, weather permitting, on the delightful plant-filled patio.

2117 E St. NW, between 21st and 22nd Sts. ☎ 800-424-2859 or 202-861-8200. Fax: 202-659-8601. Internet: www.stateplaza.com. *Metro: Foggy Bottom. Walk 3 blocks south on 23rd St. to left at F St.; walk 1 block on F St. to right at 22nd St. Continue 1 block on 22nd St. to left at E St; hotel is on the left. Parking: $15. Rack rates: $185–$245. Weekend and seasonal specials. AE, CB, DC, DISC, MC, V.*

Swissotel Washington: The Watergate Hotel

$$$$$ Foggy Bottom

Overlooking the Potomac River and across from the Kennedy Center, The Watergate has enjoyed a reputation for outstanding service for more than 30 years. The rooms and suites, many with river views, are among the largest in the city. Renovated in 1999, these rooms feature writing desks, fax machines, and bathrooms with separate showers and tubs; some include wet bars. Concierge service is available from 7 a.m. to 11 p.m. and some rooms include kitchenettes. The health club (indoor pool, sauna, Jacuzzi, aerobic classes, Nautilus, and other beneficial equipment) fills at lunchtime. Schedule a massage or make a hair appointment in the salon where "that woman," Monica, used to have her tresses trimmed. Complimentary limousine service is available, 7 to 10 a.m., Monday through Friday. You can shop till you drop — or until the money runs out — at Yves St. Laurent, Valentino, and Saks.

2650 Virginia Ave., NW. ☎ 800-424-2735 or 202-965-2300. Fax: 202-337-7915. Internet: www.watergatehotel.com. *Metro: Foggy Bottom/GWU. Turn right toward New Hampshire Ave., left onto New Hampshire, right on Virginia Ave. to hotel. Parking: $23. Rack rates: $400–$3,500 (Honest!). AE, DC, MC, V.*

Willard Inter-Continental

$$$$$ Downtown

Except for a 15-year period when this historic landmark closed for a top-to-bottom restoration, the Willard has always been a place to see or be seen in. It never shouts "class." It whispers. Around the corner from the White House, the Willard is also close to Washington's business district, theaters, and scores of restaurants. The Museum of American History is a 10-minute walk away. (Interesting tidbit: The Secret Service and State Department helped design the the secure "Heads of State" suites on the Willard's sixth floor.) Antique reproductions fill more than 300 rooms and three dozen suites. Rooms come equipped with dual-line phones, voice mail, data ports, in-room safes, and irons and ironing boards. The large bathrooms include hair dryers, scales, and phone lines. Ergonomic chairs and halide lighting are standard in business guest rooms. Restaurants include the **Willard Room** and **Cafe Espresso.** The hotel features a complete fitness center and a full business center.

1401 Pennsylvania Ave., NW, at 14th St. ☎ ***800-327-0200*** *or 202-628-9100. Fax: 202-637-7326. Internet:* www.interconti.com. *Metro: Metro Center. Take F St. exit, left off escalator onto F St. Walk less than 2 blocks to 14th St. and the hotel's rear entrance. Parking: $20. Rack rates: $425–$510. AE, DC, MC, V.*

No Room at the Inn?

Space limitations prevent me from publishing an encyclopedia of Washington's hotels. (Maybe next year.) If you're stuck and can't find a room, please see Chapter 7 and/or contact the following hotels, all tried and true (until readers of this book tell me otherwise). All offer lower weekend and off-peak rates. How low? Sometimes under $100 a night, depending on availability.

The Henley Park Hotel

$$$ Downtown

926 Massachusetts Ave. NW (2 blocks from Mt. Vernon Square-UDC Metro station; 8 blocks to Mall). ☎ ***800-222-8474*** *or 202-638-6600. Rack rates: $195–$235.*

Hotel Lombardy

$$$ Foggy Bottom/West End

2019 Pennsylvania Ave. NW (3 blocks to Foggy Bottom Metro station). ☎ ***800-424-5486*** *or 202-828-2600. Rack rates: $159–$179.*

Phoenix Park Hotel

$$$ Capitol Hill

520 N. Capitol St. NW (on Capitol Hill across from Union Station). ☎ ***800-824-5419*** *or 202-638-6900. Rack rates: $179–$219.*

Washington Monarch

$$$$ Foggy Bottom/West End

2401 M St. NW (4 blocks to Foggy Bottom Metro station). ☎ ***877-222-2266*** *or 202-429-2400. Rack rates: $279–$309.*

Washington Plaza Hotel

$$$ Downtown

10 Thomas Circle, (3 blocks to McPherson Square Metro station). ☎ ***800-424-1140*** *or 202-842-1300. Rack rates: $179–$199.*

Washington Suites Georgetown

$$$$ Foggy Bottom/West End

2500 Pennsylvania Ave. NW (3 blocks to Foggy Bottom Metro station). ☎ ***877-736-2500*** *or 202-333-8060. Rack rates: $219–$239.*

Chapter 9

Tying Up the Loose Ends: Last-Minute Details and Other Things to Keep in Mind

● ●

In This Chapter

▶ Buying travel and medical insurance

▶ Renting a car

▶ Making reservations, ordering tickets, and getting information in advance

▶ Acquiring traveler's checks

▶ Packing tips

● ●

*B*efore you leave for your vacation, you'll probably feel like you need to do a thousand things: make reservations, put the dog in the kennel, pack your bags, and so on. Trust me, if you organize everything ahead of time, you can save precious hours otherwise spent waiting in line, trying to get show tickets, buying the underwear you forgot to bring, and dealing with all the other annoyances that plague the unprepared traveler. In this chapter, I tell you how to take care of all the pesky details that you need to handle before you leave on your trip, right down to packing comfortable walking shoes.

Buying Travel Insurance: Good Idea or Bad?

Three primary kinds of travel insurance are available: *trip cancellation, lost luggage,* and *medical.* Trip cancellation insurance is a good idea for some, but lost luggage and additional medical insurance don't make sense for most travelers. Be sure to explore your options and consider the following insurance advice before you leave home:

- ✔ **Trip cancellation insurance.** If you pay a large portion of your vacation expenses up front, you should consider purchasing this type of insurance. If you've bought a package trip, cancellation insurance comes in handy if a member of your party becomes ill or (heaven forbid!) you experience a death in your family and aren't able to go on vacation.

   Trip cancellation insurance costs approximately 6 to 8 percent of your vacation's total value.

- ✔ **Lost luggage insurance.** Your homeowner's insurance should cover stolen luggage if your policy encompasses off-premises theft. Check your existing policies before you buy any additional coverage. Airlines are responsible for up to $2,500 on domestic flights, but that may not be enough to cover your sharkskin suit or wedding dress. My best advice: Either wear it on the plane or carry it on board (this idea goes for anything else of value, too).

- ✔ **Medical insurance.** If you get sick while on vacation, your existing health insurance should cover your expenses. But keep in mind that some HMOs may differ in policy in regard to your benefits when you travel. You may wish to review your policy before leaving home.

If you think you need additional insurance, make sure that you don't pay for more insurance than you need. For example, if you need only trip cancellation insurance, don't purchase coverage for lost or stolen property. Calling around to find a good deal on insurance is a good idea. Here's a list of some reputable issuers of travel insurance:

- ✔ **Access America.** 6600 W. Broad St., Richmond, VA 23230; ☎ **800-284-8300;** Fax: 800-346-9265; Internet: www.accessamerica.com.

- ✔ **Travelex Insurance Services.** 11717 Burt St., Suite 202, Omaha, NE 68154; ☎ **800-228-9792;** Internet: www.travelex-insurance.com.

- ✔ **Travel Guard International.** 1145 Clark St., Stevens Point, WI 54481; ☎ **800-826-1300;** Internet: www.travel-guard.com.

- ✔ **Travel Insured International, Inc.** P.O. Box 280568, 52-S Oakland Ave., East Hartford, CT 06128-0568; ☎ **800-243-3174;** Internet: www.travelinsured.com.

Deciding Whether or Not to Rent a Car

The answer is NOT. That's spelled N-O-T, as in uh-uh. Negative. That's my *final* answer, and I'm so sure it's correct, I don't have to ask the audience or call a friend. Driving in Washington is the pits. (See Chapter 5 for reasons you don't want to get behind the wheel.) Ask anyone who lives here. (And they know where they're going). Rely on a shuttle, taxi, or Metro from the airport or train station; use Metro and your own two feet for sightseeing.

This rule applies only to the city proper. If you want to take a side trip, say to Annapolis, or to visit your relatives in the boonies you probably need to rent a vehicle.

Getting the best rental rate

Okay, I warned you. If you insist on renting a car, keep in mind that car rental rates vary widely. The price depends on many factors: the size of the car, the length of time you keep it, where and when you pick it up and drop it off, where you go in it, and a host of other factors (like what kind of mood the agent happens to be in). Asking a few key questions can save you big bucks. The following are some questions that may help:

- ✔ **Is the weekend rate lower than the weekday rate?** Ask if the rate is the same for pickup Friday morning as it is for Thursday night. If you keep the car 5 or more days, a weekly rate may be cheaper than the daily rate.

- ✔ **Am I charged a drop-off fee if I return the car to a location that's different from where I picked it up?** Some companies may assess a drop-off charge, others, notably National, do not.

- ✔ **Is the rate cheaper if you pick up the car at the airport instead of a location in town?** The rates may vary depending upon where you pick up your car. One location may be more practical than the other, so don't forget to factor convenience into your decision.

- ✔ **Do I get a special rate for being a member of . . . ?** Don't forget to mention membership in AAA, AARP, frequent-flyer programs, and trade unions. Such memberships usually entitle you to decent discounts (ranging from 5 to 30 percent). Ask your travel agent to check any and all of these rates before booking your rental car.

- ✔ **May I have the discounted rate I saw advertised in the local newspaper?** Be sure to ask for that specific rate; otherwise you may be charged the standard (higher) rate.

Adding up the costs of renting a car

On top of the standard rental prices, other optional charges apply to most car rentals. The *Collision Damage Waiver (CDW)*, which requires you to pay for damage to the car in a collision, is charged on rentals in most states, but is covered by many credit card companies. Check with your credit card company before you go so that you can avoid paying this hefty fee (as much as $15 a day). Face it: An extra $15 in your pocket may mean a better seat at the theater.

Car rental companies also offer additional *liability insurance* (if you harm others in an accident), *personal accident insurance* (if you harm yourself or your passengers), and *personal effects insurance* (if your luggage is stolen from your car). If you have insurance on your car at home, you're probably covered for most of these unlikelihoods. Call your insurance company to find out exactly what you're covered for.

Some rental car companies also offer *refueling packages,* which means that you pay for an entire tank of gas up front. The price is often fairly competitive with local gas prices, but you don't get credit for any gas remaining in the tank when you drop off the vehicle. If you decide not to go with this option, you pay only for the gas you use; you need to return the car with a full tank or face charges of $3 to $4 a gallon for any shortfall. If you're worried that a stop at a gas station on the way to the airport may cause you to miss your plane, by all means take advantage of the fuel-purchase option. Otherwise, I suggest that you skip it.

Frequent fliers can cheer themselves up with the knowledge that most car rentals are worth at least 500 miles in their frequent-flyer accounts!

Booking a rental car on the Internet

As with other aspects of planning your trip, using the Internet can make comparison shopping and reserving a car rental much easier. All the major booking sites — **Travelocity** (www.travelocity.com), **Expedia** (www.expedia.com), **Yahoo! Travel** (www.travel.yahoo.com), **Cheap Tickets** (www.cheaptickets.com) — offer search engines that dig up discounted car rental rates. Enter the size of the car you want, the pickup and return dates, and the city where you want to rent, and the server returns a price. Find the best rate and make your reservation through these sites.

Making Reservations and Getting Tickets in Advance

I'm a firm believer in doing a little homework before a trip. It's a bummer to arrive and find out your favorite artist is featured at the National Gallery, but you need passes to get in and they're all gone. Wing it if you prefer, but a few minutes of phoning or Web surfing can ensure that you see that special exhibition or play.

To find out what's going on in D.C. during your visit (museum exhibitions, special events, performing arts, and the like) check out the following Web sites:

- ✔ **Washington, D.C. Convention and Visitors Association** (www.washington.org): You can easily make this your one-stop surfing site. This Web address features loads of information on hotels, packages (for vacationers, groups, and meeting planners), restaurants, attractions, shopping, and links to other sites. Especially good is the colorful and easy-to-read map of the National Mall.

- ✔ **The Washington Post** (www.washingtonpost.com): Log on to this site to bone up on local and, by extension, world news, or to check the president's schedule and the congressional and Supreme Court calendars. Entertainment listings are posted daily in the *Style* section. The Friday *Weekend* section is rich with listings, previews, and reviews of upcoming events, performing arts, movies, music/dance clubs, restaurants, and nightlife.

- ✔ **The Smithsonian Institution** (www.si.edu): Here you can find general visitor information and tips on planning your visit. Enter the portals for each of the Smithsonian museums and get the skinny on new exhibitions, on-site restaurants, museum stores, education programs, seminars, and workshops.

- ✔ **National Park Service** (www.nps.gov/ncro): The National Park Service oversees all the presidential monuments and memorials, including the annual Cherry Blossom watch. So, if you want the latest on the hours (regular and extended), location, and/or history of a particular monument, visit this site before you visit the real thing!

- ✔ **Washington, D.C. Reservations** (www.dcaccommodations.com): Many plan-aheads and last-minute visitors swear by this free reservation service for its good prices and ability to garner a room at the 11th hour. You can book online or browse to your heart's content.

- ✔ **Capitol Reservations** (www.capitolreservations.com): Another tried-and-true reservation service, Capitol Reservations lists more than 100 D.C. hotels by location, price, and amenities. The site also has links to attractions, dining, and entertainment.

Booking a capital tour

You need a special pass for a VIP tour (usually a group of 30 rather than the entire population of Texas) of the White House, U.S. Capitol, FBI, and for admittance to the Senate or House gallery when either is in session. You also need a pass to slurp Senate Bean Soup in the members' dining room. Send your request up to 6 months before your visit, *with the dates of your trip,* to your senator, U.S. Senate, Washington, D.C. 20510, or your congressional representative, U.S. House of Representatives, Washington, D.C. 20515. If you're not sure to whom you should write, surf over to www.capweb.net.

Reserving tickets for theater or symphony performances

If you want to attend a theatrical event during your stay and look forward to seeing a particular show, I strongly suggest ordering tickets ahead. You may be able to amble up to the box office 15 minutes before curtain times and purchase tickets for many events. But the odds are not in your favor. If you wait till the last minute for seats to pop concerts, major sports events, or ballyhooed Broadway-bound productions, you may be out of luck.

Several ticket companies allow you to order tickets before you leave home. You're in business simply by calling with the name and date of the performance and charging the tickets to your credit card. For this service, expect to pay a surcharge, usually of $1.50 per ticket. For tickets to most events, try Ticketmaster at ☎ 202-432-SEAT. You can also order tickets on the individual theaters' Web sites.

- ✔ **Arena Stage:** www.arenastage.com
- ✔ **Ford's Theatre:** www.fordstheatre.com
- ✔ **John F. Kennedy Center for the Performing Arts:** www.kennedy-center.org
- ✔ **National Theatre:** www.nationaltheatre.org
- ✔ **Shakespeare Theatre:** www.shakespearedc.org
- ✔ **Warner Theatre:** www.warnertheatre.com

The **National Symphony** (☎ **202-416-8100**), under the baton of Leonard Slatkin, plays in the Concert Hall (Where else — the cafeteria?) of the John F. Kennedy Center for the Performing Arts. Subscribers fill a majority of the seats during the September to June season, and many performances are sold out. But you may get lucky, so call ahead or show up at the box office a half-hour before curtain time.

The National Symphony gives free concerts on the West Lawn of the U.S. Capitol the Sunday of Memorial Day weekend, the 4th of July, and Labor Day weekend. Bring a picnic basket and something to sit on, relax, and enjoy the music.

Living the sporting life

If you want to catch a game at the **MCI Center,** try Ticketmaster ☎ **202-432-SEAT** or visit the center's Web site at www.mcicenter.com. **Great Seats,** an independent broker with tickets for concerts and sports events (Washington Redskins, Baltimore Ravens, Baltimore Orioles), can be reached at ☎ **1-877-478-SEAT,** or you can visit them on the Web at www.greatseats.com.

Getting a table at a trendy restaurant

If you hear about a trendy restaurant and are dying to try it out, make a reservation a week or more ahead. This suggestion is a good idea, especially for a Friday or Saturday night. Here's a list of long-popular establishments with a history of turning away the uninitiated.

- ✔ **Coco Loco:** ☎ 202-289-2626
- ✔ **Galileo:** ☎ 202-293-7191
- ✔ **Kinkead's:** ☎ 202-296-7700
- ✔ **Morton's:** ☎ 202-955-5997; Downtown location: ☎ 202-342-6258
- ✔ **Obelisk:** ☎ 202-872-1180
- ✔ **Pesce:** ☎ 202-466-3474
- ✔ **Prime Rib:** ☎ 202-466-8811

See Chapter 14 for more information on these restaurants.

Using ATMs and Traveler's Checks

Washington, D.C., like most cities, has an ample supply of 24-hour *ATMs* (automated teller machines) linked to national networks that almost always include your bank. Check the back of your ATM card to see which network your bank belongs to and look for ATMs that display your network's sign. You are probably connected to one of the two most popular networks: **Cirrus** (☎ 800-424-7787; Internet: www.mastercard.com/atm/) and **Plus** (☎ 800-843-7587; Internet: www.visa.com/atms). You may opt to call their toll-free numbers or look up their Web sites to obtain convenient D.C. locations.

The plus of using ATMs: You withdraw only as much cash as you need every couple of days and avoid carrying around a wallet full of cash.

One important reminder: Many banks now charge a fee that ranges from 50 cents to $3 whenever a non-account-holder uses their ATMs. Your own bank may also assess a fee for using an ATM that's not at one of their branch locations. In some cases, these fees mean you may get charged *twice* for using your bank card when you're in D.C.

With the convenience of ATMs, traveler's checks seem to be something from another era (when people wrote personal checks instead of going to ATMs). Because traveler's checks may be replaced if lost or stolen, they may still offer a sound alternative to filling your wallet with cash at the beginning of a trip.

Keep in mind that paying with traveler's checks may be time-consuming. You need to sign each check and present identification when cashing them.

If you prefer the security of traveler's checks, you can get them at almost any bank. **American Express** offers checks in denominations of $20, $50, $100, $500, and $1,000. You pay a service charge ranging from 1 to 4 percent. Call American Express (☎ **800-221-7282**) to purchase traveler's checks over the phone.

AAA members can get traveler's checks without a fee at most AAA offices. Members can call their local AAA offices for more information.

Visa (☎ **800-227-6811**) also offers traveler's checks, available at Citibank locations across the country and at several other banks. Call its toll-free number for other bank locations. Visa's traveler's checks come in denominations of $50, $100, $500, and $1,000 with service charges ranging from 1.5 to 2 percent. **MasterCard** also offers traveler's checks; call ☎ **800-223-9920** for a location near you.

For more on money matters while on vacation, see Chapters 3 and 12.

Packing Like a Pro

It's taken me most of my life to arrive at this simple truth: Successful packing means traveling light and arriving home with all your clothes dirty. The big mistake any traveler, experienced or otherwise, can make is to overpack. Why schlep all that extra stuff? Do you like suffering? Trust me, no one ever comes back from a trip saying "Boy, I wish I had brought more stuff with me." The good news is that, unless you reside in a nudist colony, you can dress in Washington pretty much as you do at home. Better to take half the clothing you think you need, an extra credit card, and a packet of soap powder. (You can always wash a shirt or shorts in the sink and dry your duds on a towel rack.) And if you get bored with your clothes, seize this excuse to treat yourself to something new.

Knowing what to pack

Like I said, the less you take, the better. Nevertheless, you need to bring along a few essential items. Here are some necessities:

- The single most important thing to pack for your visit is a pair of comfortable walking shoes, preferably broken in. You can always pick up toothpaste or Viagra. But you may be sorry if you try to break in a pair of brand new shoes while sightseeing. (I learned that one the hard way some years ago when I hobbled through Europe in stylish pumps.)

✔ Summers can be brutal, especially for those not used to heat and humidity. Because the mercury often climbs from bearable to uncomfortable by noon during the months of June through August, I urge you to bring breathable cotton clothing, not synthetics. If worse comes to worse, you can always buy an extra souvenir T-shirt.

During the other seasons of the year, Washington's climate can be fickle. You need to wear layered clothing, preferably in two colors or mix-and-match neutrals. Who wants to spend time coordinating T-shirts and shorts when you have to be at the White House for an 8:30 a.m. tour?

✔ A light sweater, sweatshirt, or windbreaker is a necessity in all seasons, even in summer when overly air-conditioned buildings may turn your lips blue.

✔ By all means, pack a raincoat to handle the precipitation that falls fairly evenly throughout the year.

✔ To find out what the weather may be like when you arrive, call the local weather hotline at ☎ **202-976-1212.** Other options include tuning in to the Weather Channel or visiting its Web site at www. weather.com.

✔ Don't leave home without a camera and film (these items are probably cheaper in your neighborhood), toiletries, and medications. Pack them, along with something to sleep in and a change of underwear, in a carry-on bag. That way you have them in case your luggage ends up in Alaska.

✔ Unless you're invited by the commander in chief to a black-tie event, you can leave your formal wear in mothballs. Men should pack a jacket and tie for the few restaurants that require such attire. Otherwise a collared shirt and khakis or dress slacks will work. A simple dress (perhaps in recyclable basic black), pantsuit, or skirt and jacket will get women into the finest restaurants.

Knowing how to pack

When choosing your suitcase for Washington, D.C., think wheels. Even with an abundance of bellhops, chances are you carry your suitcase at some point, and that sort of thing can wear you down. A foldover garment bag helps keep dressy clothes wrinkle-free, but can be a nuisance if you pack and unpack a lot. Keep in mind that hard-sided luggage may better protect breakable items, but weighs more than soft-sided bags.

Pack the largest, hardest items, like shoes, on the bottom. Put smaller items in and around them. Put breakables among several layers of clothes or keep them in your carry-on bag. Zip-seal bags are ideal for leaky items like shampoo and suntan lotion. Put white tissue paper or dry cleaning bags between items that wrinkle.

Limiting your carry-on luggage

Because lost-luggage rates have reached an all-time high, many consumers bring their possessions onboard to try to divert disaster. But airplanes are more crowded than ever, and overhead compartment space is at a premium. Because of these factors, some domestic airlines started cracking down, limiting you to a single carry-on for crowded flights and imposing size restrictions to the bags that you bring onboard. The dimensions vary, but the strictest airlines say carry-ons must measure no more than 22 x 14 x 9 inches, including wheels and handles, and weigh no more than 40 pounds. Many airports are already furnished with X-ray machines that literally block any carry-ons bigger than the posted size restrictions.

These measures may sound drastic, but they are often necessary to avoid overcrowding. Look on the bright side. For example, you may carry on only a small bag with your essentials, but your fellow traveler may try to carry on a bag big enough to hold a piano. Without the carry-on restrictions, the Liberace-wannabe may take up all the space in the overhead bin, leaving you to check your wee bag.

Keep in mind that many of these regulations are enforced only at the discretion of the gate attendants, so if your flight is empty, the attendants may let you exceed the carry-on limit. If you plan to bring more than one bag aboard a crowded flight, make sure that your medications, documents, and valuables are consolidated in one bag in case you must check your second bag.

The experts say to lock your suitcase with a small padlock (available at luggage and leather goods stores, if your bag isn't equipped with one). I think locking your baggage is a waste of time. I figure if someone wants to break into my bag, steal my floss and old socks, they'll find a way to break in. The choice is up to you. Do, however, secure an identification tag on the outside *and* the inside for easy identification. I also suggest affixing a bright-colored ribbon or tape to the handle for easy identification, especially if your luggage is black like 99 percent of the world's.

Before you pack, call your airline for the latest word on allowable carry-on items. Airline policies differ over whether you're allowed one or two pieces, but they concur on this: Carry-on bags must fit in the overhead compartment or under the seat in front of you. (See the sidebar, "Limiting your carry-on luggage" in this chapter.) Bring breakable items, a book or magazine, and vital documents (like return tickets, passport, and wallet) with you. And I suggest packing a snack, in case you don't like the airline food. (Does anyone like it?) You wait about an hour after lift-off for meal service to begin, and that meal may be a miniscule bag of not-very-good nuts. I always bring food along with me. (I was once offered a king's ransom for a sloppy homemade tuna sandwich.)

Part III
Settling In to Washington, D.C.

The 5th Wave   By Rich Tennant

"I want a lens that's heavy enough to counterbalance the weight on my back."

In this part . . .

Navigating your way through Washington, D.C. can seem quite overwhelming at first. The city's maze of poorly marked streets, traffic circles, and ever-present traffic can be quite intimidating. Don't worry, though — getting around is not as complicated as it looks. In this part, I walk you through the city's neighborhoods, tell you where to catch local transportation, and ease any apprehensions you may have about finding your way around the city.

Chapter 10

Orienting Yourself in Washington, D.C.

....

In This Chapter

▶ Landing at the airport

▶ Exploring Washington, D.C.'s neighborhoods

▶ Getting information when you arrive

....

*A*rriving in a strange city can be a daunting experience. That's why I'm here — to help relieve your angst. I hope your plane lands on time (a major miracle these days), your train chugs into Union Station on schedule, or you drive into D.C. without circling the Beltway half a dozen times. Those petty details aside, in this chapter, I tell you the best way to get to your hotel, describe Washington's diverse neighborhoods, and steer you to places for gathering maps, brochures, and other useful information. The camera dangling from your shoulder and the white socks and sandals may mark you as a tourist, but if you stick with me you can feel like an insider in no time at all.

Arriving in Washington, D.C.

The capital city is served by three major airports (see the map showing the airports' locations in this chapter), but none is within the boundaries of the federal district. Whaddaya expect in an itty-bitty place filled with monuments and bureaucrats? **Baltimore-Washington International** (BWI) is in Maryland, and **Ronald Reagan Washington National** (better known as Reagan National) and **Washington Dulles International** (Dulles) are located in Virginia. All the airports offer several options for getting you into town. (See Chapter 5 for more information on the individual airports.)

Washington, D.C. Airports

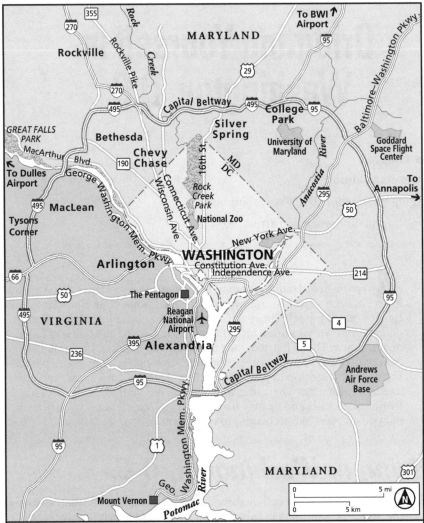

How To Get Into Town From The Airports

- **From Dulles International Airport:**
  Take the Dulles Airport access road (the only road out!) to I-66 east, through the Virginia suburbs and over the Theodore Roosevelt Bridge (still I-66), which will land you on Constitution Avenue and the western edge of the National Mall near the Lincoln Memorial.
- **From Baltimore Washington International Airport:**
  Take the airport access road to Highway 295 (Gladys Spellman Parkway; also known as the Baltimore-Washington Parkway) south to Route 50 west (New York Avenue).
- **From Reagan National Airport:**
  Take the George Washington Memorial Parkway north to I-395 north and continue over the Rochambeau Memorial Bridge (known as the 14th Street Bridge; and still I-395) into the District. Be sure you have specific directions to your hotel before you attempt this. It's tricky and still causes me palpitations.

Finding your way to your hotel

Signs for taxis, the Metro (at Reagan National *only*), and other ground transportation are posted in the Baggage Claim areas, as well as outside the terminals in all the airports serving Washington, D.C. If you experience difficulty finding a cab, ask at the information/transportation desks that are located inside or adjacent to the baggage claim areas. Now take a look at how you get from flying to sightseeing.

From Ronald Reagan Washington National Airport (Reagan National)

If you fly into **Reagan National,** you'll glimpse some major sights, but you won't touch down on the National Mall or the White House heliport. Reagan National is the closest of the three major airports to the hotels and attractions, but not by taxi during rush hour. Despite major physical improvements, the airport continues to be overutilized, overcrowded, and, many maintain, unsafe. The runways here are notoriously short and are too close to the Potomac; flight paths often get ominously close to office buildings in Rosslyn, Virginia, resulting in many unpublicized near-misses. Baggage handling is notoriously slow, and a wait of a half-hour or more to get a taxi is common.

Before you arrive, check to see if your hotel offers complimentary shuttle service. If not, you may choose from the following array of transportation choices:

✔ Your best bet is to hoof it 5 to 10 minutes, via covered walkway, to the airport Metro station. (Here's where a wheeled carry-on comes in handy.) A Yellow Line train will whisk you into D.C. in 15 to 20 minutes. In four stops, you arrive at L'Enfant Plaza where you can change to the Blue and Orange lines; in six stops, you reach Judiciary Square where you can switch to the Red Line. The fare, at nonpeak times (9:30 a.m. to 3:00 p.m.), is $1.10. Trains run from 5:30 a.m. to midnight weekdays, 8 a.m. to 1 or 2 a.m. (the transportation people are still deciding which time they like better) weekends and holidays. Because of traffic congestion between the airport and D.C., the Metro is more efficient and much cheaper than a taxi. For Metro information, call ☎ **202-637-7000** or check out www.wmata.com.

✔ Door-to-door taxi service is $15 to $20, plus a 10 to 15 percent tip, to most downtown locations. To avoid price gouging, ask for the fare before you get in. If you suspect the driver is pulling your chain, write down the company's name, the driver's name, and the cab number (on the door) and get a receipt. Report any problems to ☎ **202-331-1671.** Allow plenty of time to get to the airport for your return flight if you travel weekdays from 6 to 10 a.m. and 3 to 8 p.m. Saturday and Sunday traffic is relatively light.

✔ Another option is **SuperShuttle,** with vans departing every 15 to
20 minutes. Door-to-door service is on a shared-ride basis to
downtown and beyond. Expect to pay $9 per person to a down-
town address, more to points farther afield. If your driver gets
you to your destination in one piece, a 10 percent tip is in order.
Call ☎ **800-258-3826** 24 hours ahead to reserve your return ride
or visit www.supershuttle.com. For general airport information
call ☎ **703-419-8000.**

From Washington Dulles International Airport (Dulles)

Dulles is in suburban Chantilly, Virginia, about 26 miles from downtown
D.C. Expansion has been ongoing since I was in kindergarten and is
slated for completion in 2010. I hope I'm around to see it. The incon-
venient mobile lounges that carry passengers to and from the midfield
terminals (adding significant travel time) should be replaced by underground "people movers," similar to the ones used at Atlanta's Hartsfield
International Airport. Some call this progress.

To get into town from Dulles, pick from the following:

✔ The taxi ride between Dulles and downtown D.C. takes about 45
minutes in non–rush-hour traffic and a week or so during rush hour
(I'm joking, but not by much). If you stay at the White House or a
hotel near it, a cab ride sets you back about $50 plus a 10 to 15
percent tip.

✔ The **Washington Flyer Shuttle,** designed primarily for business
travelers, provides bus service between Dulles and the D.C.
Convention Center, 11th Street and New York Avenue NW, Monday
through Friday, twice an hour from 5:20 a.m. to 10:20 p.m. Service
is less frequent Saturday, Sunday, and holidays. The one-way fare
is $16, $26 round-trip. Call ☎ **703-685-1400.**

✔ You can also catch a SuperShuttle, with fares computed by zip code,
every 20 to 30 minutes to D.C. (see the Reagan National listing in
the previous section). To the Hotel Washington, 15th Street and
Pennsylvania Avenue NW, the fare is $20 for the first person, $10
for each additional passenger. For information, call ☎ **800-258-
3826** or visit the company's Web site at www.supershuttle.com.

From Baltimore-Washington International Airport (BWI)

Of the three airports, **BWI** is first in efficiency (relating to layout, on-time
take-offs and landings, and baggage claim) and in number of bargain
fares, thanks largely to Southwest Airlines. It's located a few miles south
of Baltimore, Maryland, and, like a gangling adolescent, BWI has been
experiencing some growing pains due to explosive growth in recent
years. Still, it's my airport of choice.

The lowdown on getting into the city from this airport is as follows:

- ✔ The ride from BWI to D.C. takes 45 minutes — and that's under optimal conditions — via taxi. Cab fare from BWI to a downtown D.C. hotel averages $50 to $60, plus a tip of 10 to 15 percent.

- ✔ By comparison, the SuperShuttle to the Hotel Washington, 15th Street and Pennsylvania Avenue NW, is $28; $5 for each additional passenger. Call ☎ **800-258-3826** or visit www.supershuttle.com for more information.

- ✔ A courtesy shuttle operates between BWI Airport and the **BWI Rail Station,** less than 10 minutes away. Here you can board a MARC commuter train (☎ **800-325-RAIL;** Internet: www.mta.com), on *weekdays only;* or an Amtrak train (☎ **800-USA-RAIL;** Internet: www.amtrak.com), on any day. The MARC train sets you back $5, taking Amtrak costs you $14. Both trains chug into D.C.'s Union Station on Capitol Hill. For BWI airport information, call ☎ **410-859-7111.**

Arriving by train

Amtrak serves the Northeast Corridor. In my experience, Amtrak is the most efficient way to arrive from New York and other points between, such as Metropark (New Jersey), Philadelphia, Trenton, and Wilmington. Trains arrive a few blocks from the U.S. Capitol at historic Union Station, a tourist attraction unto itself. Taxis are plentiful at the main (Massachusetts Avenue) entrance, and lines are usually short or nonexistent. The fare to most hotels, based on a nutty zone system, can run you anywhere from $4 to $10. See Chapter 11 for more on Washington's unique (to put it politely) taxi system.

Arriving by car

Driving *to* Washington is a walk in the park. Driving *in* Washington can evoke memories of *Nightmare on Elm Street.* I avoid it like a root canal. If you must drive, plan to arrive in the area before 3 p.m. or you'll face the country's second worst rush-hour scene (after Los Angeles).

How do you feel about confusing traffic circles and patterns, poor (or no) signage, and one-way streets that dead-end and, perhaps, re-emerge blocks away? Scary stuff, huh? One wrong turn and you may end up vacationing in Virginia. . . or Indiana. And the potholes are downright nasty. They'll swallow you whole.

Be prepared to fork over up to $25 per day to garage your wheels. If an attendant parks your car, inspect it for new dents and dings before exiting the garage. It's too late after you leave. (Would you like to hear about the time I retrieved my new car from a downtown garage, and the attendant said I had driven in with the broken taillight and dented right rear?) If you must drive, check out the next paragraph for a briefing on the major routes into D.C.

Regardless of the route you take, sooner or later you're bound to run into (sorry, poor choice of words) the Capital Beltway (I-95/I-495). Think of the Beltway as a bicycle wheel with spokes leading into Washington, the hub. Puhleeeze talk to your hotel concierge or someone at AAA, or visit MapQuest online at www.mapquest.com to find out the exit number from the Beltway, the number or name of the road, and in which direction you need to travel. Don't laugh. If you're not familiar with the area, you may end up in Pennsylvania or West Virginia. To help you visualize the territory, see the "Driving to D.C." map in Chapter 5.

Here are the roads you're most likely to travel by:

- ✔ From the north, I-270, I-95, and I-295 are the main links.
- ✔ From the south, I-95 and I-395 are the most direct routes.
- ✔ From Virginia and points west, get your kicks on I-66, which leads into Constitution Avenue and Rock Creek Parkway.
- ✔ From the east (Annapolis and Maryland's Eastern Shore), Route 50 is the road of choice.

Washington, D.C. by Neighborhood

Many first-time visitors are surprised to find that Washington is not all marble monoliths and memorials. Even in the most populated areas, you'll find grass, trees, flowers, and a place to chill. You can discover much more in Washington, D.C. than the White House, U.S. Capitol, and the other familiar places featured on the nightly news. In fact, the District has several distinct and distinctive neighborhoods. You may explore their different facets during your visit and will, no doubt, leave with a kaleidoscope of impressions. To get you started, here are thumbnail sketches (and a handy map) of D.C.'s major 'hoods.

Adams-Morgan

Vibrant and diverse — that's **Adams-Morgan,** whose crossroads are 18th Street and Columbia Road NW, roughly, north of Dupont Circle and south of Ontario Road. This neighborhood's ethnic restaurants, boutiques, and jumping nightlife draw fun-seekers of all ages and political and gender persuasions. Weekends and summer evenings, Adams-Morgan is packed, and parking is near impossible. The Dupont Circle and Woodley Park Metro stations are a hike, but are doable for the physically fit. After dark, however, take the shuttle from the Woodley Park station (6 p.m. to midnight, later on weekends) or a taxi and exercise your street smarts. It's a great place to visit, but you wouldn't want to stay here.

Capitol Hill

Despite occasional erosion and tremors, the government's judicial and legislative branches remain deeply rooted here — as do senators, influence peddlers, yuppies, creative types, and interns fresh from college. On the Hill, you find the U.S. Capitol, the Senate and House office buildings, the Supreme Court, the Library of Congress, and Union Station. Victorian houses with street-front gardens rub rooflines with restaurants, watering holes, and mom-and-pop businesses. The neighborhood extends 18 blocks eastward from the Capitol to the D.C. Armory, north to H Street NE, and south to the Southwest Freeway.

Downtown

This large central area actually encompasses several small neighborhoods. Chinatown, the theater district, MCI Center, various government offices, the White House, and the Connecticut Avenue/K Street business corridor are all located downtown. A heavy concentration of office buildings, hotels, restaurants, and retail businesses serve weekday worker bees, expense-account executives, and tourists. Downtown's perimeter is marked by 7th Street NW to the east, 22nd Street NW to the west, P Street NW to the north and Pennsylvania Avenue to the south. The area's proximity to the major sights, lodging, food, and shopping makes it a mecca for tourists.

Dupont Circle

If you are familiar with Greenwich Village in New York City, you may understand the climate of this neighborhood. All-night bookstores, movie houses, low- to high-class restaurants, galleries, and a liberal attitude reflect Dupont Circle's unconventional atmosphere. Sandwiched between the upper end of Downtown (south) and Adams-Morgan (north), the Dupont Circle neighborhood radiates from its namesake circle, roughly from along Connecticut Avenue between N and S Streets, west to 22nd Street and east to 16th Street.

Foggy Bottom

Brick row houses in a palate of pastels, Lilliputian gardens, and mature trees create an oasis in the urban landscape of **Foggy Bottom.** One of the city's most charming areas was a bustling port in bygone days and occupies a portion of the city's West End below Georgetown. Foggy Bottom stretches east to west between 17th and 28th Streets, north to Washington Circle, and south to Constitution Avenue. Foggy Bottom is home to the Kennedy Center, Watergate, George Washington University, the State Department, and various government and apartment buildings.

Washington, D.C. Neighborhoods

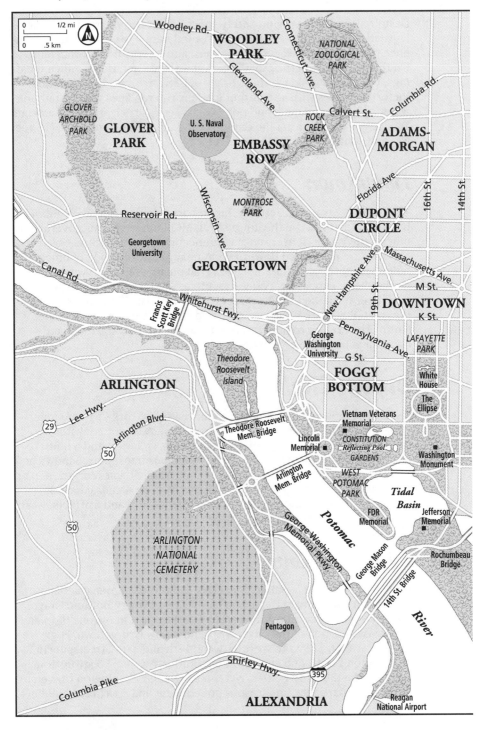

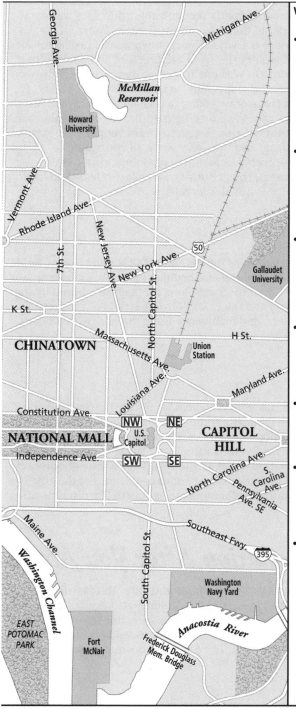

WHAT'S DOING WHERE?

- **ADAMS-MORGAN** This neighborhood gets its flavor from the large Latino and African-American populations that live here. It's a great place to wander around and explore the funky shops, cool bars, and culinary delights from around the world.

- **CAPITOL HILL** The Capitol is king of the hill in this neighbor- hood. Visit the Capitol, Supreme Court, Library of Congress, and enjoy restaurants that cater to those with business on the Hill.

- **CHINATOWN** Before or after an event at the MCI Center, this is the place to eat good Chinese food, buy some tea, or find that Chinese folk medicine that you can't get at your local pharmacy.

- **DUPONT CIRCLE** Day or night, there's always something to do in Dupont Circle. Just pop into one of the many galleries, restaurants, movie theaters, or boutiques that abound here.

- **FOGGY BOTTOM** Within walking distance of the White House, Foggy Bottom is home to the Kennedy Center and George Washington University.

- **GEORGETOWN** Here, in one of the oldest parts of town, you'll find Georgetown University, Dumbarton Oaks Gardens, historic homes, and great shopping and restaurants.

- **NATIONAL MALL** You can spend hours here exploring the Lincoln Memorial, Washington Monument, Air and Space Museum, National Museum of Natural History, (and numerous other Smithsonian museums), or just lounging in the 2-mile park-like space extending from the Capitol to the Lincoln Memorial.

Georgetown

One of Washington's most instantly recognizable addresses was established before the District of Columbia was a gleam in Pierre L'Enfant's eye. Fragments of a former era, when **Georgetown** was a bustling tobacco port, endure in the exemplary Georgian architecture and cobblestone streets off the main drag. On Wisconsin Avenue and M Street, however, the mood is far from genteel, especially on weekends. Here, shops, restaurants, bars, and clubs draw young people by the caravan. The sidewalks fill weekdays with local businesspeople, students, suburban matrons, and out-of-town visitors. Georgetown University, Dumbarton Oaks, the scenic riverfront and the C&O Canal, all contribute to Georgetown's enduring cache. Unfortunately, Georgetown has no Metro station. The nearest, Foggy Bottom, is a hike for less-than-avid walkers, and bus service is not always reliable.

The Mall

The 300-foot-wide lawn known as the **National Mall** is a sightseeing target for every D.C. visitor. Most of the Smithsonian Institution museums and major art galleries surround the 2-mile-long rectangle anchored by the Lincoln Memorial (west) and the U.S. Capitol (east). In-line skaters, bikers, joggers, kite fliers, and picnickers share the park with pigeons and squirrels year-round.

Uptown

Like Oz, you can't find this spot on a map, as it's part geographical and part state of mind. The far northwest corner of the city blurs at the Maryland line. Traffic, shopping centers, department stores, restaurants, expensive homes, and family-filled vans flavor the largely residential area of **Uptown.** The National Zoo, in the Woodley Park neighborhood, is worth the trek from the main tourist zones to this part of the city. The area's numerous hotels and restaurants are supported by discriminating locals and visitors.

Gathering Information After You Arrive

Several sources are available to you after you enter the District. The information desks in the airports and at Union Station can offer helpful advice about D.C. Most hotels display reams of visitor information in their lobbies. If you don't see any informative travel brochures about the city, ask when you check in. The following downtown sites also provide extensive visitor info.

✔ **The White House Visitors Center,** 1450 Pennsylvania Ave., NW (Herbert Hoover Building of the U.S. Department of Commerce, between 14th and 15th Streets); ☎ **202-208-1631.** The Visitors Center has brochures on the White House and other tourist attractions and also offers maps. The center also distributes White House passes. Open 7:30 a.m. to 4:00 p.m. daily, sometimes with extended summer hours; closed Thanksgiving, Christmas, and New Year's Day. Metro: Metro Center or Federal Triangle.

✔ **Smithsonian Information Center ("Castle"),** 1000 Jefferson Dr., SW (the Mall); ☎ **202-357-2700.** Stop here for information on the Smithsonian and other attractions. Watch a 20-minute video for details about the museums; peruse a layout of the Mall to help you locate your first stop. Find attractions and Metro and Tourmobile stops using an electronic map. (See Chapter 11 for information on Tourmobile.) This information center can also give you details regarding daily events in the city. Your kids can access information from the video-display monitors while you challenge the staff with your most esoteric questions. If you're on overload, ask one of the volunteers for help in planning your itinerary. On your way out, you may want to pay your respects to British subject James Smithson, whose bequest birthed the institution. His crypt is off the Jefferson Drive entrance. For more information about special events, consult the sources listed in the Appendix. Many are distributed free at newsstands, restaurants, and bookstores. Open 9:00 a.m. to 5:30 p.m. daily; closed Christmas.

Chapter 11

Getting around Washington, D.C.

● ●

In This Chapter

▶ Exploring Washington's transportation options

▶ Driving in Washington

▶ Strolling around the city

● ●

*W*ashington, D.C. is not the most user-friendly city in the United States. Forewarned is forearmed. If you don't know what you're doing when you move around Washington, you can easily end up lost, or in Virginia. Keeping that idea in mind, you may want to pay close attention as I take you on a brief orientation tour of the nation's capital. To help you visualize the areas I talk about in this chapter, see the "Washington, D.C. Neighborhoods" map in Chapter 10. This won't hurt. I promise.

The Key to the City — Getting from Here to There

D.C. is a diamond divided into four quadrants, northeast (NE), northwest (NW), southeast (SE), and southwest (SW). Most attractions are in the NW or SW regions, but the same address sometimes shows up in all four zones, so paying attention to the NW, NE, SW, or SE designation is important.

Understanding the District's directions

North Capitol Street and South Capitol Street run north and south, respectively, from the U.S. Capitol, the District's center or heart. East of the Capitol, East Capitol Street divides the city north and south.

West of the Capitol lies the National Mall with most of the Smithsonian museums. Constitution Avenue and Independence Avenue mark the north and south sides of the Mall. Pennsylvania Avenue NW runs between the Capitol and the White House and on into Georgetown.

The city is laid out in a grid. Lettered streets and streets with one- and two-syllable names run alphabetically east and west. Numbered streets run north-south.

The major arteries — Pennsylvania, Constitution, Independence, Massachusetts, Connecticut, and Wisconsin Avenues — cut through the lettered and numbered streets with abandon. Don't even try to figure out the logic (or lack thereof).

City planner Pierre L'Enfant also placed circles at strategic intersections to fend off robbers. I'm not sure his plan met its intended goal. I can tell you that today these traffic circles breed confusion and frustrate drivers, who find themselves circling endlessly in a loop, sometimes for days. (Okay, maybe I exaggerate a little, but just a little.)

Finding an address

To find an address on a lettered street, look at the first two digits. For example, 1850 M St. NW is on M Street, between 18th and 19th Streets in the northwest section of the city. To find an address on a numbered street, look at the first digit and start counting from A. For example, the 3 in 315 7th St. SE equals C, the third letter of the alphabet. So the address is on 7th Street, between C and D, in the southeast quadrant. Navigating the city like this is easy after you get the hang of this system.

 To stir things up, you won't find a B Street, but B is "counted" as the second letter of the alphabet. There's no J Street either. In this case, K becomes the 10th letter. Good luck.

The bottom line: If you're unsure, ask for directions. I still do.

Movin' Around on Metro

Washington's extensive public transportation system makes navigating the city a cinch. **Metrorail,** called Metro by locals, is the city's subway system. Trains travel more than 100 miles of track to 72 stations on five rainbow lines: Red, Blue, Orange, Yellow, and Green. The last five stations on the Green Line (opened in January 2001) complete the system. Metro operates Monday through Thursday, 5:30 a.m. to midnight; Friday, 5:30 a.m. to 2:00 a.m.; Saturday, 8:00 a.m. to 2:00 a.m.; Sunday, 8:00 a.m. to midnight. The 2:00 a.m. weekend closing is an experiment, part of a pilot program that lasts until some time in 2001. District residents hope the policy remains in effect for eternity because it gives them extra time to party. To be on the safe side, ask the station manager about weekend hours, and/or check the posted schedule as the last train may depart at 1:30 a.m.

Finding Metro stations

All Metro stations are situated within a few blocks of nearly all the sightseeing attractions, hotels, and restaurants recommended in this book. For transit information and to request *The Ride Guide,* call ☎ **202-637-7000** or visit www.wmata.com. To familiarize yourself with the subway's routes, use the Metro map on the Cheat Sheet in the front of this book or the Metro map in this chapter. Stations are marked with little circles.

To find a Metro station on Washington's streets, look for the brown pole topped by the letter M and the station name. You should see a *colored stripe* beneath the M to indicate the line or lines that stop there. The different Metrorail lines are named for colors rather than letters (A train), numbers (No. 5) or destinations (Oxford Circus, Times Square). As you've probably figured out, they run to and through different parts of the city. Trains are well marked, but sometimes trains from different lines (such as Yellow and Green) use the same tracks. If you're unsure, ask the station manager or another waiting passenger. Don't get caught doing what I did a few months ago. I was busy gabbing and boarded a Blue Line train when I wanted Orange. If this mistake happens to you, get off at the next stop and hop the next train in the opposite direction.

Metro's cars are air-conditioned, and the seats are upholstered. Stations are clean and well lit. Service is *usually* frequent and prompt. Metro trains run every 3 to 5 minutes (theoretically, at least) at peak times (5:30 to 9:30 a.m., 3:00 to 7:00 p.m.); less frequently at other times. I've never waited more than 15 minutes for a train, and that was late one night. Just go to the platform and people-watch with everyone else. You may be pleasantly surprised at how quickly the time passes.

Paying your way on Metro

Getting around via Metro is relatively inexpensive. Budget $3 to $5 per day per person, and use Metro during nonpeak times (9:30 a.m. to 3:00 p.m. and 7:00 p.m. to midnight weekdays; all day Saturday, Sunday, and holidays) to save money. Though Metro is showing its age (not unlike the rest of us), a major effort is underway to replace tired escalators and to repair cracks in the system.

Washington, D.C. Metro Stops

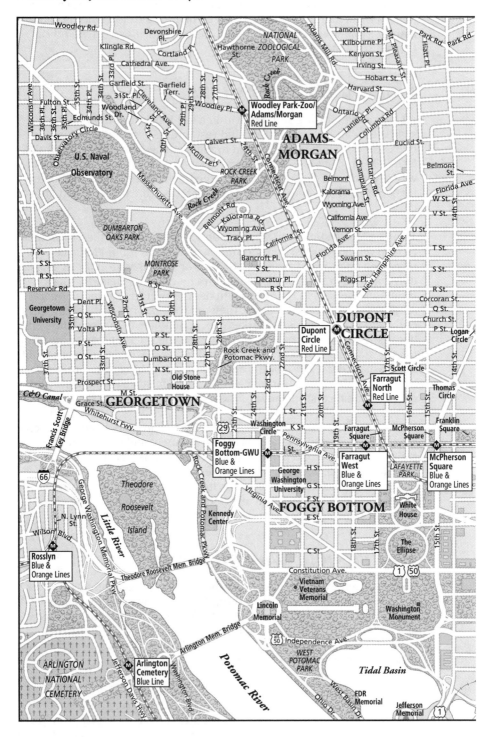

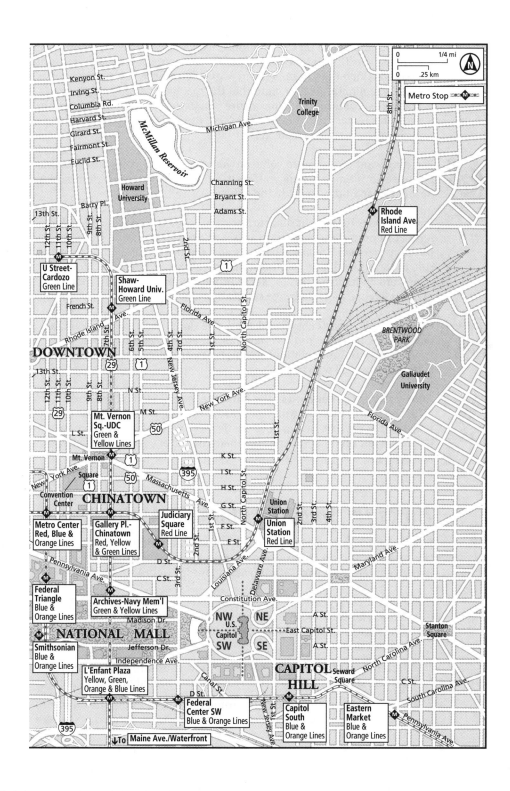

Fares are based on distance traveled and the time of day, so you pay considerably less during non-peak hours. At these times the minimum fare is $1.10. You can pick up computerized fare cards from vending machines near the station entrances. The machines accept coins (from nickels to quarters) and bills (from $1 to $20). These vending machines don't discriminate. Bear in mind that the machines regurgitate *up to $5 in change — coins only.* So, make sure you use small bills when you buy a fare card. Experiencing difficulty? Push the AUDIO button for instructions or ask the station manager for help.

You may want to put more value on your fare card if you plan on taking Metro several times during your visit. Otherwise, you must purchase a new card each time you ride the subway system.

You receive a 10 percent discount on fare cards with a value of $20 or more. Children (two maximum, ages 4 and under) can ride free with a paying passenger. Disabled persons and seniors (65 and older) can ride for a reduced fare, but they must possess valid proof — Metrorail considers a Medicare card or some other official ID valid, but *not* a driver's license — of their age or disability.

One-day rail passes cost $5 and allow you unlimited rides for a single day (after 9:30 a.m.). You can buy them at all the rail stations. If you travel to two or more stations in different parts of the city, this pass is the economical way to go.

After you insert your card in the entrance gate, it is stamped and returned. Don't walk off without it (as many people do). You need to reinsert it in the exit gate at your destination, where the card is returned if value is left on it. If you underestimate the fare, you can add what's necessary at the *Addfare* machines found near the exit and entrance gates.

Hints for smooth riding on Metro

First-time riders sometimes find the system intimidating. Follow these tips and you should enjoy a smooth ride. (But if you should start to hyperventilate, just ask a station attendant for help.)

✔ For your convenience, a wall-mounted map and the station-to-station fares are posted in Metro stations. Take your time in locating the station closest to your destination. When in doubt, ask the station manager.

✔ Don't forget that you need to hold onto your fare card when it's returned to you. Keep it handy for reinsertion at your destination.

✔ Don't make the mistake of boarding the wrong train. The minute (or two) that you take to note the station stops, listed on concrete columns and pillars inside the stations, is worth it.

✔ No eating, drinking, or smoking is allowed on Metro or in the stations. These activities are strictly prohibited and punishable by a fine. Conductors can throw passengers off the train or, worse, stick them with a juicy fine. (My son learned the hard way and ate a $25 banana one day.)

✔ You need to pick up your transfer to a Metrobus at the station where you enter the subway system, because these machines are only available on the mezzanines *before* you descend to the tracks. Your transfer is not bus-to-subway, but a means to obtain a discount on bus fares in Washington and Virginia. No bus-to-subway transfers are available.

✔ If you're in town for a special event, such as the Fourth of July or a rally on the Mall, call Metro's **Events Hotline** round-the-clock for updated information at ☎ **202-783-1070.**

Travelling by Bus

Metrobus covers a 1,500-square-mile route extending from D.C. into Maryland and Virginia. Because of heavy traffic and erratic scheduling most people rely on the rail, rather than the bus, portion of Metro to get around.

Look for the red, white, and blue signs with route numbers that mark bus stops. The route numbers are the only indications of where the buses go. (Take Metro.) Call ☎ **202-637-7000,** Monday through Friday from 6:00 a.m. to 10:30 p.m., weekends and holidays from 8:00 a.m. to 10:30 p.m. for routing information. Bus fare is $1.10; transfers cost 10 cents. Drivers don't make change so you need to carry exact fare. (Take Metro.) Most buses run daily around the clock (so they say). Service is less frequent on evenings and weekends. (Take Metro. Do you sense a theme here?) Children (two maximum, ages 4 and under) ride free with a paying passenger. Discount fares are available for seniors (☎ **202-962-7000**) and persons with disabilities (☎ **202-962-1245**). As with Metro, valid proof of age or disability must be presented when boarding.

Read my lips: Downtown traffic creeps, and bus service is inconsistent. You'll do better taking Metro and/or walking.

Yo, Taxi: Choosing to Go by Cab

With about 9,000 cabs on Washington's streets, hailing one is usually a snap (except when it's raining). Stand on a main street — those bearing state names and four-lane numbered and lettered streets — or in front of a hotel or large office building to better snag a taxi.

Taxicab Zones

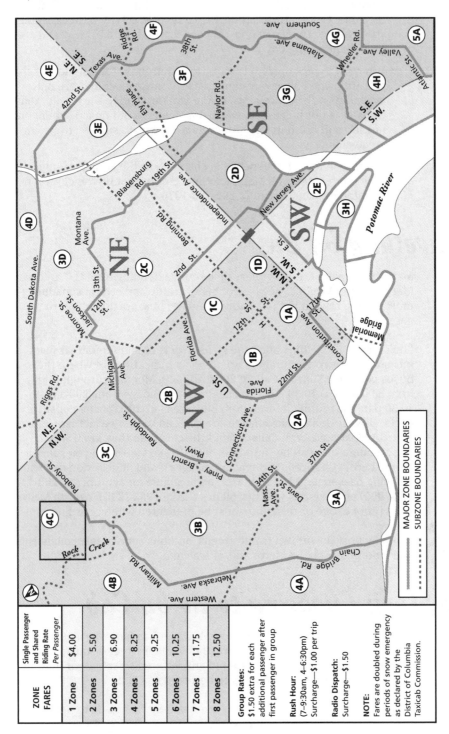

Strangers to D.C. may find the zone system baffling — as do the locals. When the politicos come up with a better system, I'll let you know. In the meantime, here's how the system works.

When traveling from Point A to Point B within the same zone your fare is $4. (Consult the map detailing taxicab zones in this chapter to see which zones you may be traveling through.) Many attractions are in Zone 1, so $4 is a good deal, right? Yes. But crossing into the second zone raises the fare to $5.50; you pay $6.90 for the entering the third zone, and so on. The going rate for a tip is 10 to 15 percent of the fare. To find out a fare ahead of time, call the D.C. Taxicab Commission, ☎ **202-645-6018.**

If that system sounds pretty easy to understand, here's how the craziness drives up fares:

- ✔ Zone lines sometimes go down the middle of the street. That means your fare can jump to the next level depending on which side of the street you enter or exit the cab. (Hey, this is Washington, where things don't always make sense.)

- ✔ A $1 rush-hour surcharge applies. Rush hour runs from 7:00 to 9:30 a.m. and from 4:00 to 6:30 p.m.

- ✔ For each additional passenger, you pay $1.50.

- ✔ You are charged another $1 if you stop en route to mail a letter (or for any other reason).

- ✔ A surcharge of between 50 cents and $2 is added for each large piece of luggage.

- ✔ You pay $1.50 extra if you call to order a taxi. (I wonder if Congress had anything to do with crafting this system?)

If you travel to a destination outside D.C., the fare is based on distance covered. You pay $2.25 to open the door and 75 cents additional for each half-mile. For information on fares to Maryland and Virginia from D.C. call ☎ **202-331-1671.**

I'm math-phobic and have trouble computing fares, so I take cabs infrequently. (I take comfort in the knowledge that even a mathematician would likely struggle to keep track of all the variables involved in Washington's system.) I suggest taking a cab when you're burdened with luggage, when it's pouring, when Metro has closed down for the night, or when you're on crutches. Otherwise, save yourself the headaches, and some cash, and take Metro or just hoof it.

Taking a Ride on Tourmobile

An excellent way to get an overview of the major sights is to board one of Tourmobile's (☎ **202-554-5100;** Internet: www.tourmobile.com)

red, white, and blue sightseeing trams. The National Park Service operates **Tourmobile,** the only tour licensed to stop on the Mall. On the
Heritage Tour ($16 adults, $7 kids 3 to 11, free for kids ages 2 and under),
you can get on and off the trams as often as you like at 25 stops on or
near the National Mall, along Pennsylvania Avenue, and in Arlington
National Cemetery. If you possess the stamina, go for it. Otherwise,
take the **Arlington Cemetery Tour** another time ($4.75 adults, $2.25
kids 3 to 11, free ages 2 and under). Trams stop every 15 to 20 minutes
at drop-off and pick-up points. Some visitors remain aboard for an entire
figure-eight loop on the Mall; then get off to visit sites on the second
go-round.

From June to Labor Day, the trams run from 9 a.m. to 6 p.m., from
September through May, from 9:30 a.m. to 4:30 p.m. Purchase tickets
from your driver, at ticket booths (For a list of ticket booths see the
"Tourmobile" map in Chapter 18 or surf over to `www.tourmobile.`
`com`), or from Ticketmaster (☎ **800-551-SEAT** or 202-432-SEAT).

Tourmobile also runs a twilight tour from Union Station and other sight-
specific tours. For more information on these tours, see Chapter 18.

Walking through Washington

Like Nancy Sinatra's "boots," Washington is made for walking. In these
health-and budget-conscious times, putting mileage on your feet instead
of your wallet, fare card, or car makes sense. On foot, you discover
things that you may otherwise miss, things that make a trip special.
(When you get home, please write and tell me what they are.)

Plan your itinerary wisely (I give you more tips about planning your
trip in Chapters 16 and 17), and you get a workout among museums.
On days when the humidity is below 80 percent, I suggest you try the
Mall crawl, a distance of nearly 2 miles between the U.S. Capitol and
the Lincoln Memorial. No sweat. Or stroll through the residential side
streets of Foggy Bottom and/or Georgetown. (For information on walking
tours, please see Chapter 18.)

Keep your wits about you when you walk. That's not to say that D.C.
isn't safe to walk around in, it is, provided you don't stray from the
major tourist zones. Stride with a sense of purpose. Dawdlers appear
vulnerable, which is just what professional pickpockets look for. Avoid
getting lost in crowds, where a bump from a pickpocket could easily be
missed. Be aware of your surroundings. Stow wallets, cash, and credit
cards in hard-to-reach pockets. Wear purses across one shoulder and
over the chest — bandolier style. (For more on safety in Washington,
D.C., see Chapter 12.)

Driving Your Car

I have yet to meet a person who enjoys driving in Washington. What makes you think you are different? The ever-changing traffic patterns, one-way streets, and circles are daunting. When you add drivers (I'm willing to bet most of them never took driver's ed), who seem to follow different or no rules of the road, to this mix, the result is chaos. Street parking is at a premium, and a garage extracts a pound of flesh.

 If you plan on arriving in the family buggy, ask about parking rates at your hotel when you make a reservation. For your own sanity, I urge you to garage your car for the duration of your stay.

Chapter 12

Keeping Your Cash in Check

*T*he good news for Washington visitors is that many of the city's best and most popular attractions are free. That said, the city is a major tourist center, so you may find yourself tempted to empty your wallet on numerous occasions. (Everyone else in the city is throwing away cash, why shouldn't you?) If you decide to indulge in a little spending, finding a place (and I'm not talking about the U.S. Mint) to replenish your money supply is not a problem.

Finding Funds in Washington, D.C.

Washington used to have more monuments than ATMs. Now, I think the reverse is true. Most, if not all, the major banks in the city house ATMs, so cash is as close as the next bank. In addition, ATMs can be found at many attractions, museums, supermarkets, and shopping malls, among other locations.

Before you leave home, I suggest finding out the location of an ATM or two close to your hotel and another that's near the National Mall/ Smithsonian Institution museums. That way you cover all the bases. With any luck, you can find ATMs that don't charge non–account-holders for their services. Go to the Web sites for Visa (www.visa.com) and MasterCard/Cirrus (www.mastercard.com) for the locations of their nearest machines. You may also want to call the major ATM networks, Cirrus (☎ 800-424-7787) and Plus (☎ 800-843-7587), for specific ATM locations where you can withdraw your money. If you access an ATM operated by your bank, you won't pay a cent. (In all other cases, you'll need to go to Europe to find ATMs that don't charge a fee.) The fee for withdrawing cash from an ATM not connected to your specific bank varies from $1 to $3. Every ATM should tell you, on a printed sign, how much the fee is. If there is no sign, a message will announce the fee *after* you punch in your PIN (personal identification number). At that point, you can change your mind about whether to continue or to cancel the transaction.

For more information on money matters, see Chapter 3.

Keeping Your Money Safe (And What to Do If It's Stolen)

Washington, D.C. is about as safe as any other major city in the United States, which means crime does exist, but if you stick to areas frequented by tourists, you should not have any problems. To reduce your chances of losing your cash to a thief, take the following precautions:

- ✔ Women should always keep their purses slung diagonally across their chests, preferably under a jacket. The best kind of purse to take is one that folds over, rather than one that has just a zipper on top. Do not sling your purse or camera over your chair when in a restaurant.

- ✔ Ladies: Try slipping a credit card and $20 in your bra. (If you can't spare the room, I don't want to hear about it.) I like to carry necessities in the zippered pockets of cargo-style pants and leave my wallet and purse at home. This move is positively freeing. Men should ideally use a money belt or a fanny pack to store cash, credit cards, and traveler's checks.

- ✔ If your hotel has an in-room safe, use it. Stash excess cash, traveler's checks, and any other valuables that you don't need for immediate use. If your hotel room doesn't have a safe, put your valuables and cash inside the hotel's safety deposit box. In general, I would say the best policy is to use an ATM machine and withdraw only the amount of money you need to cover your expenses for about 2 days at a time.

If you are robbed, however, keep the following in mind:

- ✔ Almost every credit-card company has a toll-free emergency number that you can call if your cards are lost or stolen. The credit-card company may be able to wire you a cash advance off your credit card immediately and send you an emergency credit card within a day or two.

- ✔ The issuing bank's toll-free number is usually printed on the back of the credit card. Make note of this number before you leave on your trip and stash it somewhere other than your wallet. If you forget to write down the number, you can call ☎ **800-555-1212** — that's 800 directory assistance — to get your issuing bank's toll-free number. And because thieves may not swipe this guidebook — though it's worth its weight in gold — Citicorp Visa's U.S. emergency number is ☎ **800-336-8472.** American Express cardholders and traveler's check users need to call ☎ **800-221-7282** for all money emergencies. MasterCard holders must call ☎ **800-307-7309.**

✔ If you opt to carry traveler's checks, make sure that you keep a record of their serial numbers in a safe, separate location from the checks in case they are lost or stolen. (As examples: Leave the numbers with a relative back home or in the hotel or room safe.) Traveler's checks can be somewhat cumbersome, and considering the number of ATM machines in Washington, they're probably unnecessary. Nevertheless, traveler's checks are the safest way to carry the equivalent of a large amount of cash (which, by the way, I do not recommend). Should your checks be stolen, call the issuer, give the serial numbers, and ask for instructions on replacing your checks.

 If your wallet is stolen, it probably won't be recovered by the police. However, you should head to the nearest phone to cancel your credit cards and inform the authorities. A police report number may come in handy for credit card or insurance purposes later.

Understanding Local Taxes

When you're budgeting for your trip, be sure to make allowances for the local taxes. They can add up, especially on an extended visit. The sales tax on merchandise is 5.75 percent. So that $45 painting of the Washington Monument on black velvet will actually set you back $47.59. For each meal you eat in a restaurant, you will pay a 10 percent tax, so it will cost you $55 for a $50 dinner check (*plus* tip). The tax on a hotel room is 14.5 percent — that's $29 for a $200 room. Yep, the taxes are high; you get no argument on that point. So if you can, you may want to stay with relatives, even your least favorite.

Part IV
Dining in Washington, D.C.

"Six of Jennifer's goldfish died today, and, well, I just don't think it's worth the three of us keeping our reservations at Takara's Sushi Restaurant tonight."

In this part . . .

Washington, D.C. may not be as renowned for its dining as New York and San Francisco are, but it is certainly no slouch in this department. After all, this is the city that put the "power" into power breakfast (all those lobbyists need some place to rack up their expense accounts). D.C.'s diverse population has resulted in an astonishing array of ethnic dining opportunities; no matter what kind of cuisine you like, you can find it here. Even the most particular foodies will find places to satisfy their palates.

In this part, I let you in on the hottest trends in D.C. dining, give you complete and detailed reviews of the city's best restaurants, and tell you about some great snacking opportunities.

Chapter 13

The Lowdown on Washington, D.C. Dining

*P*ity the poor Washington restaurateurs and chefs; their work is cut out for them. These hosts must please finicky foreign ambassadors, campaign donors from the Far East, lobbyists from Arizona, senators from the Corn and Bible Belts, little old ladies from Boca, and the local citizenry. Phew! I can think of easier ways to make a living. Because of Washington's diverse dining group, you find everything from couscous to Pad Thai to jicama to grits to gnocchi on menus.

In the nation's capital, the proof is not always in the pudding, excuse me, crème brûlée or mousse au chocolat. Ambiance, service, location, presentation and that ubiquitous X factor — word-of-mouth — can make or break a restaurant faster than a line veto.

Aside from the dining recommendations in this book and in specialized restaurant guides, I think you find the best restaurant suggestions come from locals — those you may know and those you meet during your visit. Having been burned more than once, I shy away from asking hotel staff for recommendations. (You never know if cousin Billy-Bob, fresh out of the slammer, has the know-how to prepare haute cuisine.) The word on the street is that hotel workers are sometimes in cahoots with nearby restaurants. It's your call, but don't say I didn't warn you.

What's Hot Now in D.C.

Because of the city's diverse population, no *single* favorite cuisine or cooking style exists in Washington. Residents can choose among a few thousand restaurants.

Here's a rundown of the latest and most popular culinary trends in the city:

- ✔ The Starr Report isn't the only spicy thing to come out of Washington in recent years. Fusion still enjoys immense popularity. This fare may sound like something undertaken in a laboratory, but *Fusion* marries ingredients from different types of cuisine, and then sprinkles them with Asian blessings. Think catfish with sweet-and-sour kumquat sauce, pork loin with rice noodles, vermicelli with lox and lemongrass, and the like.

- ✔ D.C.'s love for Italian and Oriental fare is ongoing and unconditional, having passed one-night-stand status eons ago. Mediterranean dishes — melding ingredients from southern France, Italy, Spain, Greece, and North Africa — are still hot. Washingtonians continue to toss cholesterol to the wind and devour steaks and roast beef, with Cuban cigars (shhh, don't tell) for dessert.

- ✔ For politicians, Washington is a piranha tank, and it's always feeding time. Maybe that's why seafood restaurants rival steakhouses in number. Fresh and farm-raised fish and shellfish anchor many menus. During your visit, I suggest you try crabmeat: crab cakes, sautéed soft-shell crabs, lump crabmeat cocktail, crab imperial, or crabmeat-stuffed fish. Maryland blue crabs are harvested from the nearby Chesapeake Bay from roughly May through October. When supplies dwindle, restaurants fish more distant waters for the delectable crustacean.

Let's Do Lunch

On weekdays, overworked Type-As prefer to grab quick salads or sandwiches from nearby carryouts than to take lengthy lunch breaks. They either wolf down their tuna fish sandwiches on the spot, in nearby parks, or while placing phone calls at their desks. Sexy, huh?

The suits dining on prime rib or crab cakes during midday are, for the most part, out to clinch the big deals. These folks are lawyers, lobbyists, media execs, and international bankers; or they're retirees and wannabes. Who else has the time to graze for the better part of an afternoon on the latest juicy scandal? On weekday evenings, most worker bees desert the city. If you hold any doubt about this, observe the rush-hour traffic leaving the city or the crush aboard outward-bound Metro cars.

On Friday and Saturday nights, many deserters return — looking a lot more relaxed — to dine leisurely with their spouses and SOs. That's why you need a reservation. (I talk more about reservations later in this chapter.)

Downtown, Foggy Bottom, and Capitol Hill restaurants generally attract a clientele of conventioneers, business types, pols, and lobbyists. A more diverse group fills the restaurants in Georgetown, Dupont Circle, and Adams-Morgan.

What's Cooking: Washington's Ethnic Eats

When I moved here, John F. Kennedy was rockin' in the White House, and Washington had two French restaurants of note; today there are scores of them. Some of my college pals had never seen a bagel back then, much less tasted one; now, vending machines dispense them in a variety of flavors such as blueberry tofu. Between bra burnings, my friends and I used to annihilate cartons of chicken chow mein and egg foo yong; today, Washingtonians have trouble deciding among Indonesian, Chinese, Japanese, Vietnamese, and Thai fare.

Although the city's palate has matured, its ethnic neighborhoods remain small (or nonexistent) by other cities' standards. If you blink, you may miss **Chinatown,** centered on 7th and H Streets NW, near the MCI Center. Missing that part of town would be a shame. Though small, Chinatown has numerous restaurants where you can dine well and inexpensively on Cantonese, Szechwan, Hunan, and Mandarin dishes (sometimes all on the same menu).

Multicultural **Adams-Morgan** has the greatest concentration of south-of-the-border, African-inspired, and what I call "hybrid" restaurants. Otherwise, ethnic restaurants are sprinkled liberally throughout the city. Or, you can head to **Baltimore,** an hour north, with its active Italian, Irish, Greek, and Jewish neighborhoods, if you are in the mood for other types of ethnic cuisine.

Dressing to Dine

To dress or not to dress, that is the question. Many people (from other places, of course) think conservative Washington natives lack fashion sense. Diners, especially on weeknights, are usually attired in their business clothes, having come straight from their offices. But you don't need to follow their leads and drag out a dark suit or black pumps. Save your fancy duds for the spots where a jacket and tie are appropriate. (I note where jackets and ties are required in the restaurant listings in Chapter 14.) Your mother or partner may carp over your unacceptable appearance, but I'm here to tell you — even if you dress like a slob, most restaurants will take your credit card with a smile.

Women seem to enjoy more leeway in the fashion department, thank heavens. Women have come a long way since I was refused entrance to a downtown restaurant for wearing a gray-flannel pantsuit. These days, you can wear jeans in dirt cheap to medium-priced places. Slacks, a skirt and blazer, or a simple dress get you into the top places, and you'll have no need to feel embarrassed. If you love dressing up, don't let me rain on your parade. Go for it.

Tips for Saving Money

Here are some suggestions for reducing your dining budget as well as your waistline. Stick to these tips, and your scale won't worry about presenting you with bad news when you return. And with the leftover coins, you can purchase an extra souvenir.

✔ Patronize small, neighborhood eateries and bypass the "in"— and often overpriced — restaurants. Set your own trends and mingle with the locals. You'll have a richer experience that won't leave you poorer.

✔ Eat a hot meal midday and graze at night. That divine lunch entrée can cost double after 5 p.m. (FYI: The Bill of Rights includes your right to stray from egg salad and BLTs at lunch.)

✔ Picnic on a pizza and watch an in-room movie for a relaxing, inexpensive evening.

✔ Save time and money by skipping sit-down lunches. Munch street food or carryout between museums. Eat outdoors or discreetly dip into your brown bag in a museum cafeteria. (Thus far, I've gotten away with it. Please don't blow my cover.)

✔ Take advantage of fixed-price, early bird, and pre-theater menus. Check your watch as well as the hours restaurants offer specials. If you arrive 5 minutes late, you'll pay full price. You snooze, you lose.

Making Reservations

In the restaurant listings in Chapter 14, when I say that a reservation is recommended for a restaurant, that means you'll need one for dinner and at the top restaurants, one for lunch as well. On Fridays and Saturdays, make dinner reservations at any place that accepts them, preferably several days in advance. On a weeknight, you'll probably be seated promptly if you arrive by 6:30 p.m. Notice I said *"probably."* On weekdays in downtown's heavy business districts and on weekends in tourist districts such as Georgetown and Adams-Morgan, arrive for lunch by 11:45 a.m. or after 1:30 to 2:00 p.m. Otherwise, you'll probably find a line.

Some restaurants serving a business clientele are open for lunch Monday through Friday only. Others cater to weekend visitors and serve lunch only on Saturday and Sunday. When in doubt, call first.

OpenTable, a rapidly expanding Web site filled with numerous D.C. restaurant descriptions, maps, and other helpful information, allows you to make reservations at numerous restaurants several days in advance (or just *30 minutes ahead*). You can find the site online at www.opentable.com.

Chapter 14

Washington, D.C.'s Best Restaurants

· ·

In This Chapter

▶ Restaurant indexes by price, location, and cuisine

▶ Full reviews of all the best restaurants in town

· ·

Time to feed your faces, friends. While you loosen your belt buckles, I'll translate the menus. As an appetizer, this chapter begins with indexes you can use for figuring out the best grazing places for your particular needs. The restaurants are indexed by location so that you can find a place near the attractions you visit, by price so that you can budget accordingly, and by cuisine so that you can satisfy your individual tastes. (The various maps I include in this chapter can also help guide you to the restaurants listed.)

From there, I move on to the main course — my picks for the best restaurants, listed alphabetically for easy referral. The price range, location, and the type of cuisine follow each restaurant's name. The price includes an appetizer, entree, dessert, one drink, taxes, and tip. If you usually skip an appetizer and/or dessert when you dine out or have kids who are unlikely to eat a full meal, adjust the price accordingly.

All the listings are for good (often better-than-good, or excellent) restaurants where you can enjoy a satisfying meal and pleasant dining experience. I'm not steering you to any dumps just because they're a bargain. And I purposely left out overpriced places that charge by the artistry of the vegetables on the plate. Selections are based on good quality food for a fair price. In other words, value. The difference between categories has more to do with extras, such as location, ambiance, decor, service, trendiness, and servers' cuteness. Yadda, yadda, yadda.

Restaurants designated as kid-friendly in this chapter have a kids' menu and/or cuisine that appeals to a younger palate.

Dining in Washington, D.C.

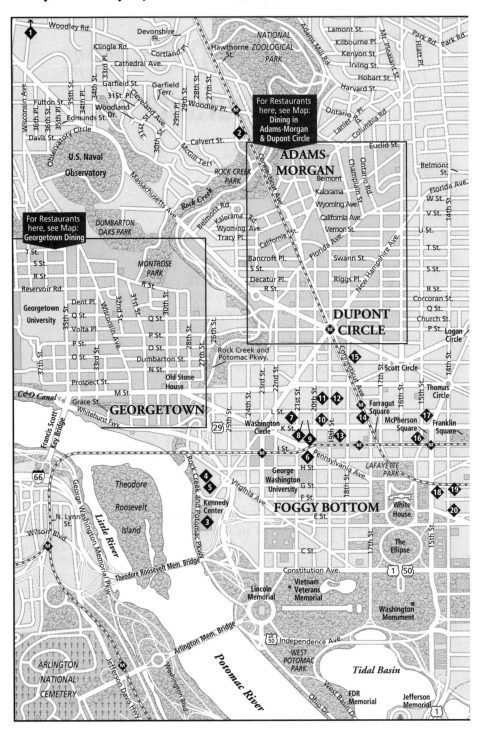

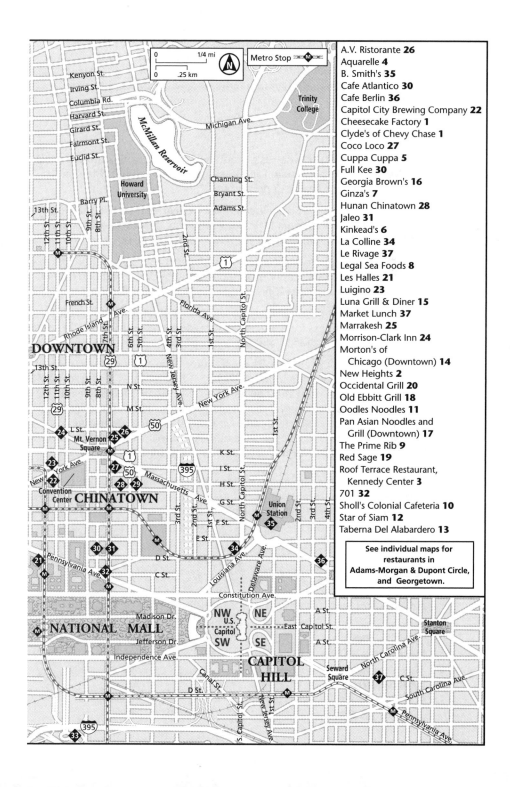

A.V. Ristorante **26**
Aquarelle **4**
B. Smith's **35**
Cafe Atlantico **30**
Cafe Berlin **36**
Capitol City Brewing Company **22**
Cheesecake Factory **1**
Clyde's of Chevy Chase **1**
Coco Loco **27**
Cuppa Cuppa **5**
Full Kee **30**
Georgia Brown's **16**
Ginza's **7**
Hunan Chinatown **28**
Jaleo **31**
Kinkead's **6**
La Colline **34**
Le Rivage **37**
Legal Sea Foods **8**
Les Halles **21**
Luigino **23**
Luna Grill & Diner **15**
Market Lunch **37**
Marrakesh **25**
Morrison-Clark Inn **24**
Morton's of
  Chicago (Downtown) **14**
New Heights **2**
Occidental Grill **20**
Old Ebbitt Grill **18**
Oodles Noodles **11**
Pan Asian Noodles and
  Grill (Downtown) **17**
The Prime Rib **9**
Red Sage **19**
Roof Terrace Restaurant,
  Kennedy Center **3**
701 **32**
Sholl's Colonial Cafeteria **10**
Star of Siam **12**
Taberna Del Alabardero **13**

See individual maps for restaurants in Adams-Morgan & Dupont Circle, and Georgetown.

I don't mean to insult your intelligence by reiterating that the price of a meal depends on what you order, but it bears repeating. If you're on an expense account or want to woo someone, don't be surprised if your bill equals the national debt. Frugal types who stick to a main course and appetizer or salad may have dessert money left over. I include two price indicators: a dollar symbol indicating what a complete meal costs and the price range of the entrees on the menu.

Here's what the symbols mean.

- ✔ **$ (Dirt Cheap):** These restaurants are popular long-standing establishments. Expect plain food in simple surroundings. Plan on spending less than $15 per person.

- ✔ **$$ (Inexpensive):** These locations are cheaper than you may expect; they may be located a little out of the way and/or may lack linen napkins or fresh flowers in the restrooms. A meal goes for $15 to $25.

- ✔ **$$$ (Medium):** You won't blow your budget by eating at one of these fine dining spots. Enjoy nice decor, good service, and better-than-good food for $25 to $35.

- ✔ **$$$$ (Expensive):** These restaurants are among the best in D.C. Expect the finest food, chefs, service, décor, and ambiance. Prepare to spend about $35 to $50 per person.

- ✔ **$$$$$ (Very Expensive):** These top-tier restaurants deserve respect. You'll find the city's influential elite at these tables. See the couple at the next table? Could be an elder statesman, media executive, lobbyist, or CIA operative and his (or her) current flavor of the month. Then again, it could be a suburban duo celebrating an anniversary. One thing's certain, they come because the restaurant is renowned for its chef, atmosphere, and high-rolling clientele.

These symbols give you a general idea how much a meal at a restaurant costs. Keep in mind that some restaurants offer prix fixe meals or other deals that may affect the dollar sign rankings. I alert you to these special prices as well.

Restaurant Index by Location

Adams-Morgan
Felix — $$$
I Matti — $$$
Meskerem — $$

Capitol Hill
B. Smith's — $$$$
Cafe Berlin — $$

Capitol City Brewing Company — $$
La Colline — $$$$
Market Lunch — $

Downtown
A.V. — $$–$$$
Austin Grill — $$

Cafe Atlantico — $$$
Capitol City Brewing Company
    — $$
Coco Loco — $$$
Dean & Deluca Cafe— $
Full Kee — $$
Georgia Brown's — $$$
Ginza's — $$$
Hunan Chinatown — $$
Il Radicchio — $$
Jaleo — $$–$$$
Le Rivage — $$$–$$$$
Legal Sea Foods — $$$$
Les Halles — $$$
Luigino — $$$
Luna Grill & Diner — $
Marrakesh — $$$
Morrison-Clark — $$$
Morton's — $$$$
Occidental Grill — $$$$
Old Ebbitt Grill — $$
Oodles Noodles — $
Pan Asian Noodles and Grill — $$
Prime Rib — $$$$
Red Sage — $$–$$$$
701 — $$$$
Sholl's Colonial Cafeteria — $
Taberna Del Alabardero — $$$$

Dupont Circle
BeDuCi — $$$
Brickskeller — $
Galileo — $$$

Il Radicchio — $$
Obelisk — $$$$
Pan Asian Noodles and Grill — $$
Pesce — $$$
Pizzeria Paradiso — $$

Foggy Bottom
Aquarelle — $$$$–$$$$$
Cuppa Cuppa — $
Kinkead's — $$$$
Roof Terrace Restaurant
    (Kennedy Center) — $$$$

Georgetown
Austin Grill (Glover Park) — $$
Bistro Français — $$$
Cafe Milano — $$$
Chadwick's — $$
Clyde's — $$
Dean and Deluca Cafe — $
Enriqueta's — $$
Houston's — $$
Morton's — $$$$
Music City Roadhouse — $$
Rockland's (Glover Park) — $
Senses — $–$$$

Uptown
Chadwick's — $$
Cheesecake Factory — $$
Clyde's — $$
New Heights — $$$$

Restaurant Index by Price

$$$
BeDuCi — Dupont Circle
Bistro Français — Georgetown
Cafe Atlantico — Downtown
Coco Loco — Downtown
Felix — Adams-Morgan
Georgia Brown's — Downtown
I Matti — Adams-Morgan
Le Rivage — Downtown
Les Halles — Downtown
Luigino — Downtown
Marrakesh — Downtown
Morrison-Clark — Downtown
Pesce — Dupont Circle

$$
A.V. — Downtown
Austin Grill — Downtown and
    Glover Park, above Georgetown
Cafe Berlin — Capitol Hill
Capitol City Brewing Company —
    Downtown and Capitol Hill
Chadwick's — Georgetown, Upper
    Northwest, Old Town,
    Alexandria
Cheesecake Factory — Upper
    Northwest
Clyde's — Georgetown, Upper
    Northwest

Enriqueta's — Georgetown
Full Kee — Downtown
Ginza's — Downtown
Houston's — Georgetown
Hunan Chinatown — Downtown
Il Radicchio — Downtown,
    Dupont Circle
Jaleo — Downtown
Meskerem — Adams Morgan
Music City Roadhouse —
    Georgetown
Old Ebbitt Grill — Downtown
Pan Asian Noodles and Grill —
    Downtown and Dupont Circle
Pizzeria Paradiso — Dupont Circle
Red Sage/Chili Bar — Downtown
Senses — Georgetown

$
Brickskeller — Dupont Circle
Cuppa Cuppa — Foggy Bottom
Dean and Deluca Cafe —
    Downtown, Georgetown
Luna Grill & Diner — Downtown
Market Lunch — Capitol Hill
Oodles Noodles — Dupont Circle
Rockland's — above Georgetown
Sholl's Colonial Cafeteria —
    Downtown

Restaurant Index by Cuisine

American
Aquarelle — Foggy Bottom
    — $$$$$
Austin Grill — Glover Park, north
    of Georgetown — $$
B. Smith's — Capitol Hill — $$$$
Brickskeller — Dupont Circle — $
Capitol City Brewing Company —
    Downtown — $$
Chadwick's — Georgetown, Upper
    Northwest — $$
Cheesecake Factory — Upper
    Northwest — $$

Clyde's — Georgetown, Upper
    Northwest — $$
Dean and Deluca Cafe —
    Downtown, Georgetown — $
Felix — Adams-Morgan — $$$
Georgia Brown's — Downtown
    — $$$
Houston's — Georgetown — $$
Kinkead's — Foggy Bottom
    — $$$$
Legal Sea Foods — Downtown
    — $$$$
Luna Grill & Diner — Downtown
    — $

Market Lunch — Capitol Hill — $
Morrison-Clark Inn — Downtown
— $$$
Morton's — Downtown,
Georgetown — $$$$
Music City Roadhouse —
Georgetown — $$
New Heights — Upper Northwest
— $$$$
Occidental Grill — Downtown
— $$$$
Old Ebbitt Grill — Downtown
— $$
Pesce — Dupont Circle — $$$
Prime Rib — Downtown — $$$$
Red Sage — Downtown —
$$–$$$$
Rocklands — Glover Park, north
of Georgetown — $
Roof Terrace Restaurant — Foggy
Bottom — $$$$
701 — Downtown — $$$$
Sholl's — Downtown — $

Asian

Oodles Noodles — Downtown
— $
Pan Asian Noodles and Grill —
Downtown, Dupont Circle — $$

Barbecue

Market Lunch — Capitol Hill — $
Rocklands — Glover Park, north
of Georgetown — $

Brazilian

Coco Loco — Downtown — $$$

Caribbean

Cafe Atlantico — Downtown
— $$$

Chinese

Full Kee — Downtown — $$
Hunan Chinatown — Downtown
— $$

Ethiopian

Meskerem — Adams-Morgan — $$

French

Bistro Français — Georgetown
— $$$
La Colline — Capitol Hill — $$$$
Le Rivage — Downtown — $$$
Les Halles — Downtown — $$$
Senses — Georgetown — $$$

German

Cafe Berlin — Capitol Hill — $$

Greek

Mykonos — Downtown — $$

Hamburgers

Chadwick's — Georgetown, Upper
Northwest — $$
Clyde's — Georgetown, Upper
Northwest — $$
Houston's — Georgetown — $$
Old Ebbitt Grill — Downtown
— $$

International

New Heights — Upper Northwest
— $$$$
701 — Downtown — $$$$

Italian

A.V. Ristorante — Downtown —
$$
Café Milano — Georgetown —
$$$–$$$$
Galileo — Dupont Circle — $$$$
I Matti — Adams-Morgan — $$$
Il Radicchio — Downtown,
Dupont Circle — $$
Luigino — Downtown — $$$
Obelisk — Dupont Circle — $$$$
Pizzeria Paradiso — Dupont Circle
— $

Japanese

Ginza's — Downtown — $$

Latin American
Cafe Atlantico — Downtown
— $$$

Mediterranean
BeDuCi — Dupont Circle — $$$

Mexican
Coco Loco — Downtown — $$$
Enriqueta's — Georgetown — $$

Moroccan
Marrakesh — Downtown — $$$

Pizza (Note: $ symbol reflects price of meal with pizza entree)
A.V. Ristorante — Downtown — $
I Matti — Adams-Morgan — $$
Luigino — Downtown — $$
Pizzeria Paradiso — Dupont Circle
— $$

Seafood
Kinkead's — Foggy Bottom
— $$$$
Legal Sea Foods — Downtown
— $$$$
Market Lunch — Capitol Hill — $
Pesce — Dupont Circle — $$$

Southern
B. Smith's — Capitol Hill — $$$$

Georgia Brown's — Downtown
— $$$
Morrison-Clark Inn — Downtown
— $$$
Music City Roadhouse —
Georgetown — $$

Southwestern
Austin Grill — Downtown and
Glover Park, north of
Georgetown — $$
Houston's — Georgetown —
$$–$$$
Red Sage — Downtown, chili bar
$$–dining room $$$$

Spanish
Jaleo — Downtown — $$
Taberna del Alabardero —
Downtown — $$$$

Steakhouse
Les Halles — Downtown — $$$
Morton's — Downtown,
Georgetown — $$$$
Prime Rib — Downtown — $$$$

Thai
Pan Asian Noodles and Grill —
Downtown, Dupont Circle — $$
Star of Siam — Adams-Morgan,
Downtown — $$

Washington, D.C. Restaurants from A to Z

Aquarelle

$$$$ Foggy Bottom   AMERICAN

Aquarelle features New American cuisine with a French twist in a sophisticated supper-club setting. Have it your way — foie gras or pheasant, that is — or try the grilled meats and fish. A window table at this romantic restaurant offers a scenic view of the Potomac. This restaurant is popular with diners attending performances at the Kennedy Center across the street; Aquarelle offers a $40 pre-theater menu nightly from 5:00 to 7:30 p.m.

Watergate Hotel, 2650 Virginia Ave. NW, at New Hampshire Ave. ☎ *202-298-4455. Reservations recommended. Metro: Foggy Bottom. Walk west 1½ blocks on I St. to left at New Hampshire Ave. Go 2 blocks, cross Virginia Ave. to Watergate. Main courses: $16.95–$20. AE, DISC, MC, V. Open: Daily 11:30 a.m.–2:30 p.m.; 5–10 p.m.*

Austin Grill

$$ Downtown   AMERICAN/SOUTHWESTERN

Come here for a shot of Tex-Mex when you're in the neighborhood. The FBI, National Archives, and Ford's Theatre are close by; the Museum of Natural History and Convention Center are each less than a 10-minute walk away. Steering clear of the crispy corn chips and flavorful salsas takes willpower, but leave room for the crabmeat quesadillas or carne asada, or the more mainstream tacos, burritos, and enchiladas. The margaritas are large and mouth-puckering, the ambiance, country roadhouse. Austin appeals to all generations, so the place is usually crowded. Seating is more prompt if you eat at off times. The music is, um, loud, but after a margarita or a longneck, it dissolves to a hum. You can dine outside in season. **Note:** A second branch of Austin Grill is situated just north of Georgetown.

750 E St. NW, between 7th and 8th Sts. ☎ *202-393-3776. Reservations not accepted. Metro: Gallery Place or Archives. Main courses: $8.95–$13.95. AE, DISC, DC, MC, V. Open: Mon–Thurs 11:30 a.m.–11:00 p.m.; Fri 11:30 a.m.–midnight; Sat 11 a.m.–midnight; Sun 11 a.m.–11 p.m. (Sat–Sun 11 a.m–3 p.m. brunch) The original Austin Grill is at 2404 Wisconsin Ave. NW.* ☎ *202-337-8080. Reservations not accepted. Metro: Tenleytown. Take No. 32, 34, or 36 bus south on Wisconsin Ave. or 15-minute walk north from Georgetown.*

A.V. Ristorante

$$ Downtown   ITALIAN

Don't be misled by the statuary outside. It would take more — a whole lot more — to prettify the Early Tenement décor of this old-timer near the Convention Center. Still, there's something charming about the grunge. The white pizza (without cheese for calorie watchers) is a must and the New York–style pizza tastes like pizza, not cardboard. Pastas with bold-flavored sauces are best shared, perhaps with simple fish or veal dishes. Drop some coins in the jukebox and sing along with your favorite aria. Snuggle in the back room with your sweetie between bites of Linguine Puttanesca and sound bites of Andrea Bocelli.

607 New York Ave. NW, between 6th and 7th Sts. ☎ *202-737-0550. Reservations for 12 or more. Metro: Mt. Vernon Sq.-UDC. Walk south on 7th St. 2 blocks to left at New York Ave. Main Courses: $7–$15. AE, CB, DC, DISC, MC, V. Open: Mon–Fri 11 a.m.–11 p.m.; Sat 5 p.m.–midnight. Closed Sun.*

B. Smith's

$$$$ Capitol Hill   SOUTHERN

Diet is a four-letter word at B. Smith's. In this vast restaurant in Union Station (once the president's waiting room), Southern cooking reigns supreme. I suggest sharing the red beans and rice appetizer before diving into a fish, seafood, or chicken dish. The fried catfish could restore even Blanche du Bois' sanity. Dessert is a toss-up between the bread pudding and the pecan praline cheesecake. Box the leftovers for late-night snacking. A jazz combo plays most evenings after 8 p.m. Because B. Smith's hosts many events, call first.

Union Station 50 Massachusetts Ave. NE. ☎ *202-289-6188. Reservations recommended. Metro: Union Station. Take escalator to main floor. Main courses: $13.95–$23.95. AE, CB, DISC, DC, MC, V. Open: Mon–Sun 11:30 a.m.–2:30 p.m. (lunch); Mon–Thurs 5:30 p.m.–10:00 p.m. (dinner); Fri–Sat 5:30 p.m.–11:00 p.m. (dinner); Sun 11:30 a.m.–3 p.m. (brunch) and 5:30–10 p.m. (dinner).*

BeDuCi

$$$ Dupont Circle   MEDITERRANEAN

BeDuCi ("Below Dupont Circle") is not just another pretty face, but it *is* a looker. With its sunny porch, sidewalk tables, and art-enhanced interior rooms, the restaurant's ambiance is evocative of Provence. The kitchen turns out Mediterranean-inspired dishes — pastas, paellas, rack of lamb, and vegetarian dishes (sometimes encased in phyllo) — that taste as good as they look. Sinful fudge-frosted brownies are the perfect ending to a meal at BeDuCi. Who cares if their Mediterranean origins are suspect?

2100 P St. NW, at 21st St. ☎ *202-223-3824. Reservations recommended. Metro: Dupont Circle. Walk west on P St. 2 blocks. Main courses: $12.95–$27.95 AE, DC, DISC, MC, V. Open: Mon–Sat lunch 11:30 a.m.–2:15 p.m.; Mon–Thurs dinner 5:30– 10 p.m.; Sat dinner 5:30–10:30 p.m.; Sun dinner (no lunch) 5:30–9:30 p.m. (Note: July–Aug, no Sat lunch)*

Bistro Français

$$$ Georgetown   FRENCH

Charming Bistro Français offers a hint of Paris on the *rive gauche* of M Street. After hanging up their toques, local French chefs gather under the hanging ferns until the wee small hours to talk shop and eat onion soup au gratin, pâtés, and pastry. The menu features well-prepared bistro fare such as coq au vin and minute steak, along with daily specials. Head straight for the succulent tarragon-flavored rotisserie chicken. The bistro celebrated its 25th birthday in October 2000. Twice a year it closes — Christmas Eve and Christmas Day.

Dining in Adams-Morgan & Dupont Circle

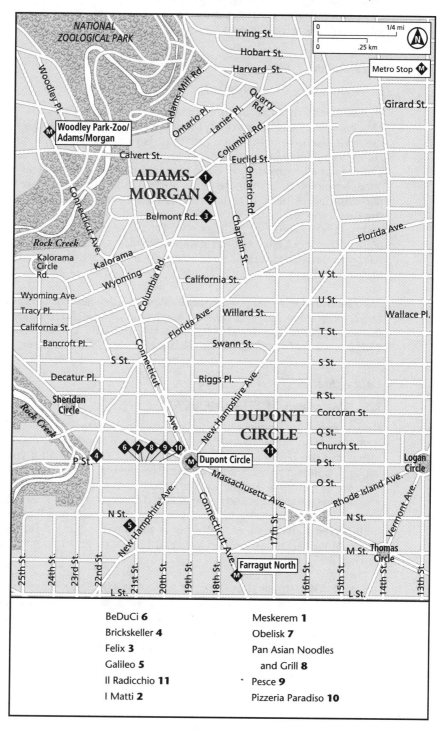

BeDuCi **6**	Meskerem **1**
Brickskeller **4**	Obelisk **7**
Felix **3**	Pan Asian Noodles
Galileo **5**	and Grill **8**
Il Radicchio **11**	Pesce **9**
I Matti **2**	Pizzeria Paradiso **10**

3128 M St. NW, between 31st and 32nd Sts. ☎ *202-338-3830. Reservations recommended. Metro: Foggy Bottom. Take any No. 30 bus on Pennsylvania Ave. or take a taxi. Main courses: $13.95–$24.95 (Average meal is $17.95). AE, MC, V. Open: daily 11 a.m.–5 p.m.; Sun–Thurs 5 p.m.–3 a.m.; Fri–Sat 5 p.m.–4 a.m.*

Brickskeller

$ Dupont Circle   AMERICAN

I remember the Brickskeller from my college days a *few* years ago. (If you believe that, I have a Van Gogh I want to sell you). Washington's quintessential pub, 44 years young in 2001, is pure frat house, minus the sticky floors. Juicy burgers, Buffalo wings, and French fries are mainstays. The menu has expanded recently to include a delish turkey and gouda cheese sandwich, crabmeat-stuffed shrimp, and other light fare. Compared to the 200 or so brands it featured back when I was swilling suds, the Brick now offers more than 850 types of beers. (The staff can help you demystify the beer choices.) Ah, for those long-gone days — and nights. The decor runs toward stale smoke, darts, and stacked empties. (Did you expect watered silk barstools?) Don't even think of driving; Metro is 3 blocks away.

1523 22nd St. NW, between P and Q Sts. ☎ *202-293-1885. Reservations accepted for 6 or more. Metro: Dupont Circle. Walk west on P St. 3 blocks. Main courses: $5.50 (bacon-cheddar burger)–$16.95 (buffalo steak). AE, DISC, MC, V. Open: Mon–Thurs 11:30 a.m.–2 a.m.; Fri 11:30 a.m.–3 a.m.; Sat 6 p.m.–3 a.m.; Sun 6 p.m.–2 a.m.*

Cafe Atlantico

$$$ Downtown   LATIN AMERICAN

Cafe Atlantico is located within walking distance of the 7th Street art galleries, the Navy Memorial, the Archives, the Ford's and Shakespeare theatres, and the FBI (also within hoofing distance of the Mall if you're a walker). Colorful panels and tiles decorate the restaurant, and the food can be as rainbow bright as the interior. Come here for seviche, empanadas, mixed grill, and jerk chicken. *Asopao,* a creamy Puerto Rican seafood stew, wins kudos, as does the chocolate bread pudding topped with glazed banana slices. Saturday is the day for "Latino Dim Sum," (Latin American tapas) served between 11:30 a.m. and 1:30 p.m. (fixed price $19.95). Deliciosa!

405 8th St. NW, between D and E Sts. ☎ *202-393-0812. Reservations accepted until 7:30 p.m. Metro: Archives/Navy Memorial. Walk north on 7th St. 2 blocks to left at D St., right at 8th St. Main courses: $9–$24. AE, DC, MC, V. Open: Mon–Fri 11:30 a.m.–2:30 p.m.; Mon–Thurs 5:30–11 p.m., Fri 5–11:30 p.m.; Sat 11:30 a.m.–1:30 p.m. (Latino Dim Sum) and 5–11:30 p.m.; Sun 5–10 p.m.*

Cafe Berlin

$$–$$$ Capitol Hill   GERMAN

This intimate town house restaurant sits in the shadow of the Capitol. If the weather is fair, you'll find congressional staffers and locals filling the outdoor tables. Desserts (strudel, black forest cake, and the like) are so scrumptious, you may want to eat that course first before moving on to sauerbraten, paprikash, or Wiener schnitzel (veal). Lunch bargains include the soup-and-sandwich specials, as well as the entrees, which cost two to three times as much at dinner. You could do a lot *wurst* than breaking pumpernickel bread at Cafe Berlin.

322 Massachusetts Ave. NE, between 3rd and 4th Sts. ☎ 202-543-7656. Reservations recommended. Metro: Union Station. Walk east 3 blocks on Massachusetts Ave. Main courses: $13.95–$16.95. AE, CB, DC, MC, V. Open: Mon–Thurs 11:30 a.m.–10 p.m.; Fri–Sat 11:30 a.m.–11 p.m.; Sun 4–10 p.m.

Cafe Milano

$$$–$$$$ Georgetown   ITALIAN

Placido Domingo and Madeline Albright are among the celebs spotted at Cafe Milano in recent months. Mr. and Ms. Average can join the fashionable folks at this trendy Georgetown restaurant. Suits and miniskirts patrol downstairs, where things heat up between 11 p.m. and 1 a.m.. For quiet and privacy, the big names sit in the back room. At lunch, enjoy a glass of Pinot Grigio with your antipasto or salad (the insalata giardino has chunks of tomatoes, potatoes, red onion, cucumber and celery in a balsamic vinegar dressing) at the sidewalk cafe. A friend recommends the ravioli in a light vegetable sauce and says the pasta outperforms other dishes. Take your autograph album.

3251 Prospect St., off Wisconsin Ave. between M and N Sts. ☎ 202-333-6183. Reservations recommended. Metro: Foggy Bottom. Take a long walk or a taxi. Main courses: $19–$35. AE, MC, V. Open: Mon–Sat 11:30 a.m.–2:30 p.m., Mon–Sat 5:30–11p.m.; Sun noon–11 p.m.

Capitol City Brewing Company

$$ Downtown   AMERICAN

Capitol City has been fruitful and multiplied, expanding to a second location. Both branches are big and boisterous. The hamburgers, chili, seasoned fries, and onion rings are better than all right. I've heard good things about the ribs from my spies, in town for business at the nearby Convention Center. Cap City is also convenient to the Ford's, National, Shakespeare, and Warner theatres. The Capitol Hill branch is across the street from Union Station. While you wait for your food, dunk the complimentary soft pretzels in the horseradish-mustard dip and try one of the in-house microwbrews. I prefer the amber. You can order food at the bar, if you are in a hurry.

1100 New York Ave, NW, corner of H and 11th Sts. ☎ *202-628-2222. No reservations. Metro: Metro Center, 11th Street exit; then walk north 1 block to H St. Main courses: $6.50 (hamburger)–$23 (steak with all the trimmings). AE, DC, DISC, MC, V. Open: Sun–Thurs 11 a.m.–11 p.m.; Fri–Sat 11a.m.–midnight. The Capitol Hill branch is in the U.S. Post Office (site of the U.S. Postal Museum) at 2 Massachusetts Ave. NE.* ☎ *202-842-BEER. Hours are the same at both locations.*

Chadwick's

$–$$ Uptown   AMERICAN

Nothing distinguished about the food here, but, like an old friend, Chadwick's is welcoming, warm, and dependable. Popular with families and folks looking for pub fare and good service at reasonable prices, Chadwick's delivers the goods to shoppers from Mazza Gallerie or Chevy Chase Pavilion. The paper tablecloths and crayons keep everyone happy until the vittles arrive. Stick with the burgers, sandwiches, and salads. Brunch here is not gourmet fare, but it's satisfying and reasonable. Additional locations: Georgetown at 3205 K St. NW; ☎ **202-333-2565** and Old Town Alexandria at 203 S. Strand St.; ☎ **703-836-4442.**

5247 Wisconsin Ave. NW. ☎ *202-362-8040. Reservations accepted. Metro: Friendship Heights. Walk south on Wisconsin Ave. 2 blocks. Main courses: $9–$17. AE, DC, DISC, MC, V. Open: Mon–Thurs 11:30 a.m.–midnight; Fri–Sat 11:30 a.m.–midnight; Sun brunch 10 a.m.–4 p.m.; Sunday dinner 4 p.m.–midnight. Bar stays open an hour after kitchen closes.*

Cheesecake Factory

$$ Uptown   AMERICAN

If you don't mind waiting in line for an hour or more to eat, you have more patience than I do. Judging by the crowds at this restaurant, most folks don't mind the long wait for the fare. My daughter once arrived here for dinner at 6 p.m., and I didn't see her for a year. The message: Get here by 11:30 a.m. for lunch; by 5:30 p.m. for dinner. The salads and pasta dishes could feed Godzilla — twice. If you're not up to the task, box the leftovers so you save room for the cheesecake. I'm a purist (no chips, nuts, fruit, or overpowering flavorings), but the selections (and calories) are all yours!

5345 Wisconsin Ave. NW, in the Chevy Chase Pavilion. ☎ *202-364-0500. No reservations (but very long lines). Metro: Friendship Heights. Walk south on Wisconsin Ave. 1 block to Chevy Chase Pavilion. Main courses: $5.95–21.95. AE, DC, DISC, MC, V. Open: Mon–Thurs 11:30 a.m.–11:30 p.m.; Fri–Sat 11:30 a.m.–12:30 a.m.; Sun 10 a.m–11 p.m.*

Clyde's of Chevy Chase

$$ Uptown   AMERICAN

At Clyde's, there's plenty that's eye-catching besides what's on the menu. A model train circles overhead, delighting kids of all ages. With all the raceway and flight-related memorabilia, you may think you're in Indianapolis or the Air and Space Museum. I prefer Clyde's for lunch; the portions are generous and fairly priced. Dinner prices run high, and though the food is above average, it's nothing to write home about. Stick with the sandwiches (the grilled Reuben gets my vote), salads, omelets, or hamburgers. Downstairs, in a cantina reminiscent of one in *Star Wars,* you can order pizza and other light fare. Also visit the original Clyde's in Georgetown (the prototypical D.C. saloon), at 3236 M St. NW; ☎ 202- 333-9180.

76 Wisconsin Circle, just across the D.C. border in Chevy Chase, MD. ☎ 301-951-9600. Reservations recommended. Metro: Friendship Heights. Walk north 1 block on Wisconsin Ave. Main courses: $10–$17. AE, DC, DISC, MC, V. Open: Mon–Sat 11 a.m.–4:30 p.m.; Sun–Thurs 4:30–11:30 p.m.; Fri–Sat 4:30 p.m.–12:30 a.m.

Coco Loco

$$$ Downtown   BRAZILIAN/MEXICAN

Whet your whistle with a potent caipirinha cocktail (lime-flavored and deadly) at this lively restaurant near the Shakespeare Theatre and 7th Street galleries. Then, if your eyes can focus, check out the Mexican tapas menu, with a wide-ranging selection of tempting vegetable, seafood, and meat dishes in mini-portions. You can create a satisfying and affordable meal for two from three or more of the choices. Larger appetites can enjoy the *churrascaria,* a Brazilian all-you-can-eat feast that begins with a self-serve cold buffet of salads and vegetables, followed by skewered meats (chicken, chorizo sausage, pork ribs, and beef), bowls of coconut rice, and roasted potatoes. Look for Brazilian dancers to stir things up on some evenings.

810 7th St. NW, between H and I Sts. ☎ 202-289-2626. Main courses: $11.95–$24.95; tapas $5.95–$10 (dinnertime only). AE, CB, DC, MC, V. Reservations recommended. Metro: Gallery Place. Walk north on H St. 2 blocks. Open: Lunch Mon–Fri 11:30 a.m.–2:30 p.m.; dinner Mon–Sat 5:30–11 p.m.

Cuppa Cuppa

$ Foggy Bottom   AMERICAN

Perfect for a quick bite before a Kennedy Center performance, Cuppa Cuppa is a no-frills self-serve cafe in the Watergate, across the street from the performing arts center. The salads, sandwiches, soups, wraps, personal pizzas, and pastry fill the bill, although they're hardly gourmet fare. From a patio table or window seat you can see the performers waltz by on their way to the stage door. Order wine by the glass or domestic and imported beers. A lengthy selection of espresso and capuccino variations is also available at the coffee bar.

600 New Hampshire Ave. at Rock Creek Parkway. ☎ *202-466-3677. No reservations. Metro: Foggy Bottom. Take free shuttle bus to Kennedy Center, walk down hill and cross New Hampshire Ave. Main courses: $3.75–$7.95 AE, MC, V. Open: breakfast, lunch, and dinner. Sun 10 a.m.–6 p.m.; Mon–Thurs 7:30 a.m.–8 p.m.; Fri–Sat. 7:30 a.m.–9 p.m.*

Dean & Deluca Café

$ **Georgetown   AMERICAN**

Shoppers, tourists, and students make for good people watching. Enjoy one of the many salads and sandwiches (like grilled veggies on a baguette or focaccia) at this branch of the legendary New York food emporium. Grab a snack, some yuppie coffee, designer water, or fresh squeezed orange juice when shopping in Georgetown. Lines can be slow at peak times, but after you're settled at an outdoor table on a sunny day, you forget the wait.

3276 M St. NW, between 32nd and 33rd Sts. ☎ *202-342-2500. No reservations. Metro: Foggy Bottom. Walk north on 23rd St. and left at Pennsylvania Ave., which merges with M St.; continue west on M St. 8 blocks. Or take any No. 30 bus headed for Georgetown from Pennsylvania Ave. Main courses: $6–$8. AE, MC, V. Open: Sun–Thurs 9 a.m.–8 p.m.; Fri–Sat 9 a.m.–9 p.m.*

Enriqueta's

$$ **Georgetown   MEXICAN**

A Georgetown landmark for as long as I can remember, Enriqueta's serves authentic fare to customers in a *barrio* apartment with too-close-for-comfort tables. The space doesn't matter — most people come here to chow, not to hang out. (And I believe the chairs are designed to promote prompt departures.) You can order tacos and enchiladas, but to truly test the kitchen, try a regional fish specialty or the flavorful chicken *mole* (a tomato and beef-based sauce flavored with onions, chiles, and Mexican chocolate). Muy deliciosa! Fans gather at lunch for a good deal that leaves them with extra pesos for dinner.

2811 M St. NW, between 28th and 29th Sts. ☎ *202-338-7772. Reservations accepted for 5 or more. Metro: Foggy Botttom. Walk north on 23rd St. to left at Pennsylvania Ave.; continue west on M St. for 5 blocks. Main courses: $11.95–$13.95. AE, MC, V. Open: Mon–Sat lunch 11:30 a.m.–2:30 p.m.; dinner 5–11 p.m. Closed Sun.*

Dining in Georgetown

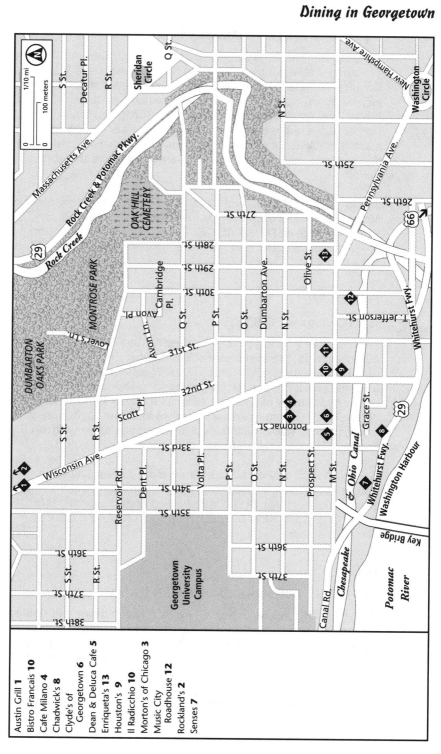

Austin Grill **1**
Bistro Francais **10**
Cafe Milano **4**
Chadwick's **8**
Clyde's of
  Georgetown **6**
Dean & Deluca Cafe **5**
Enriqueta's **13**
Houston's **9**
Il Radicchio **10**
Morton's of Chicago **3**
Music City
  Roadhouse **12**
Rockland's **2**
Senses **7**

Felix

$$$ Adams-Morgan   AMERICAN

Sip a martini, the beverage of choice, at this restaurant's first-floor bar. The atmosphere is a blend of South Beach, Soho, and a Big 10 pep rally. Couples snuggle in dimly lit corners and locals schmooze in a fantasy cityscape setting. The cuisine is predominantly American, with Italian, French, and Asian accents. The fusion (see Chapter 13) produces seafood ravioli, peppered foie gras, and charred tuna sashimi. Me? I like a vodka martini (shaken not stirred — 007 would be pleased), a double order of the smoked salmon/potato pancake appetizer, and a strawberry mousse parfait.

2406 18th St. NW, at Belmont Rd. ☎ *202-48-FELIX. Reservations recommended. Metro: Woodley Park-Zoo/Adams-Morgan. Take the shuttle bus to 18th St., or take a cab. Main courses: $16–$24. AE, CB, DC, DISC, MC, V. Sun–Thurs 6 p.m.–midnight; Fri–Sat 6 p.m.–1a.m.(bar open 6 p.m.–3 a.m.); Tues–Sat 5:30 p.m.–1:30 a.m.; Sun 5:30 p.m.–1 a.m.*

Full Kee

$$ Downtown   CHINESE

Full Kee diners smile a lot. Maybe their fortune cookies prophesy a large inheritance in the near future. Or maybe they smile because this Chinatown bastion rarely disappoints. Consistency is the hallmark of its food and service. If you have a yen for moo shoo pork in the middle of a Friday or Saturday night, Full Kee is open until 3 a.m. Join the chefs who chow down here after closing their own kitchens. Cantonese fare is featured, but Full Kee is also known for its dumpling soup, fresh fish, and seafood. The decor is basic, and the liquor policy is BYOB.

509 H St. NW. ☎ *202-371-2233. Reservations accepted for 6 or more. Metro: Gallery Place/Chinatown. Walk north 1 block on 7th St., right at H St. and continue 2 blocks. Main courses: $9.95–$14.95. No credit cards; cash only. Open: Mon–Sat lunch 11 a.m.–3 p.m.; Mon–Thurs dinner 3 p.m.–1 a.m.; Fri–Sat dinner 3 p.m.–3 a.m.; Sun 11 a.m.–1 a.m.*

Galileo

$$$$–$$$$$ Downtown   NORTHERN ITALIAN

You're equally welcome dressed up or dressed down, but Galileo is no all-you-can-eat spaghetti garden. For years, diners have groused over the prices. (Dinner for two with a bottle of good wine can run you $200.) Some complain that the food and service are inconsistent, but most concur that the quality is excellent. Galileo sets the bar by which all other D.C. Italian restaurants are measured. Award-winning Chef Roberto Donna specializes in dishes reflecting the best of Italy's Piedmont region, his birthplace. In a back room known as *Il Laboratorio,* an 11-course tasting menu is served three times a week ($90). Foodies are advised to reserve well ahead for one of the 30 coveted seats. Risotto, grilled portobello mushrooms, roasted fish and meat are highlights. And except for the bread and dessert — the meals are light. The delicious food makes you forget (almost) about the cost.

1110 21st St. NW, between L and M Sts. ☎ 202-293-7191. Reservations recommended. Metro: Farragut North. Walk west on L St. 4 blocks to right at 21st St. and north 1 block. Main courses: $20–$35. AE, CB, DC, DISC, MC, V. Open: Mon–Fri 11:30 a.m.–2 p.m.; Mon–Thurs 5:30–10 p.m.; Fri–Sat 5:30–10:30 p.m.; Sun 5–10 p.m.

Georgia Brown's

$$$ Downtown   SOUTHERN

This southern-style restaurant overlooks McPherson Square, just a short walk from the White House. You'll find the waitstaff, kitchen staff, and customers are a diverse bunch. Take your time enjoying the fare. That advice is easier said than done after the biscuits and corn bread arrive with whipped butter laced with honey and peach morsels. The menu celebrates the country cooking of the Carolinas and coastal Georgia. I'm talkin' shrimp, black-eyed peas, grits, and greens. The Sunday Jazz Brunch features your choice of one of five entrees along with a buffet table with salad, omelets, and desserts for $21.95. Vocalist and jazz quartet included.

950 15th St. NW, between I and K Sts. ☎ 202-393-4499. Reservations recommended. Metro: McPherson Square. Walk west on I St. 1 block and right at 15th St. 1 block. Or Metro: Farragut North, Conn. Ave. and K St. exit). Walk east on K St. 3 blocks to 15th St. and right half a block. Main courses: $8.95–$22.95. AE, CB, DC, DISC, MC, V. Open: Mon–Thurs 11:30 a.m.–10:30 p.m.; Fri 11:30 a.m.–midnight; Sat 5:30 p.m.–midnight; Sun 11:30 a.m.–3 p.m. (jazz brunch) and 5:30–10:30 p.m.

Ginza's

$$$ Downtown   JAPANESE

If I were going to eat something colorful that left me hungry, I'd choose flowers. But my sushi-loving friends tell me Ginza's has the best raw fish in the city. I prefer the tempura, beef or chicken teriyaki, and the other hot entrees on the extensive menu. Hey, whatever floats your sampan. The setting and service may lack energy, but you can eat well for less than $30. A fixed-price Sushi Special dinner is a deal at $19.95. If you're not sure what to order, ask the Japanese businessmen at the next table.

1009 21st St. NW, between K and L Sts. ☎ 202-833-1244. Reservations recommended. Metro: Farragut North. Walk west on L St. 3½ blocks, left at 21st St. a half block. Main courses: $9.95–$21.95. AE, MC, V. Open: Mon–Fri lunch (11:45 a.m.–2:30 p.m.) and dinner (5–10 p.m.); Sat 5–10p.m.; Sun closed.

Houston's

$$–$$$ Georgetown AMERICAN

Houston's is still the spot with the best hamburger in D.C. — big, juicy, and delicious. When I'm off beef, I tear into one of Houston's monster salads, such as the Club, with its chunks of fried chicken, real bacon bits, eggs, and avocado atop a huge bowl of mixed greens. (This is diet food?) The ribs and USDA prime strip steaks and filet mignon are big sellers, but I can't get past the hamburgers. Arrive when the restaurant opens or at off times, or you'll probably find a line. If you do, put your name on the list and take a hike. To Katmandu.

1065 Wisconsin Ave. NW, between K and M Sts. ☎ 202-338-7760. No reservations. Metro: Foggy Bottom. Take No. 30 bus to Wisconsin and M Sts. or 20-minute walk, or take a taxi. Main courses: $8 (hamburger)–$30. AE, MC, V. Open: Mon–Thurs 11:30 a.m.–11 p.m.; Fri 11:30 a.m.–midnight; Sat noon–midnight; Sun noon–10 p.m.

Hunan Chinatown

$$ Downtown HUNAN/SZECHUAN

Hunan Chinatown is something of an oxymoron: a handsome Chinese restaurant. Speak softly and carry a small chopstick. Your dining companion will hear your every word because no interference from clanging pots or cursing from the kitchen will interrupt your meal. Enjoy an order of General Tsao's chicken or Szechuan beef in a mirrored dining room with cushy chairs and soft lighting. Ask the kitchen to go easy on the chiles and hot oil if you're heat sensitive. The dumplings and tea-smoked duck are standouts. Although the menu may not be trend-setting, the fare is more than adequate when you're visiting the FBI, doing the 7th Street galleries, or attending the Shakespeare Theatre.

624 H St. NW, between 6th and 7th Sts. ☎ 202-783-5858. Reservations recommended for 6 or more. Metro: Gallery Place/Chinatown. Walk north on 7th St. 1 block to right at H St. Main courses: $7–$25 (most under $13). AE, DISC, MC, V. Open: Sun–Thurs 11 a.m.–10 p.m.; Fri–Sat 11 a.m.–11 p.m.

I Matti

$$$ Adams-Morgan ITALIAN

Fall into I Matti when you're in Adams-Morgan and yearn for moderately priced Italian fare. Pizza, pasta, polenta (a meal in itself, but available as a side order), chicken, veal, and even rabbit sausage stew are served in a no-nonsense setting. The cooking is unpretentious, the mood pleasant and upbeat. I recommend the fish or handmade pasta. (I dare you not to empty the breadbasket.)

2436 18th St. NW, between Belmont and Columbia Rds. ☎ 202-462-8844. Reservations recommended. Metro: Woodley Park-Zoo/Adams-Morgan. Take *shuttle (6 p.m.–midnight) to 18th St or take a taxi. Main courses: $12–$20. AE, DC, MC, V. Open: Tues–Sat lunch 11:30 a.m.–2 p.m.; Sun–Thurs dinner 5:30–10 p.m.; Fri–Sat dinner 5:30–11 p.m. (No lunch Sun or Mon).*

Il Radicchio

$$ Dupont Circle   ITALIAN

Indulge in a basic pizza pie with toppings from the long list of possibilities or a bottomless bowl of pasta with a variety of sauces. The prices are fair, service is efficient, and the murals are colorful (your kids should enjoy them). Another of chef Roberto Donna's successful restaurants (along with Galileo and I Matti), this is Italian fast food that's authentic and good. Sometimes very good. Another branch is on Capitol Hill at 223 Pennsylvania Ave. SE (☎ **202-547-5114**).

*1509 17th St. NW, between P and Q Sts. ☎ **202-986-2627.** No reservations. Metro: Dupont Circle. Walk east on P St. 2 blocks, turn left at 17th St. 1 block. Main courses: $7–$15. AE, CB, DC, MC, V. Open: Mon–Thurs 11:30 a.m.–10 p.m.; Fri–Sat 11:30 a.m.–11 p.m.; Sun 5–10 p.m.*

Jaleo

$$ Downtown   SPANISH

Loosely translated, *jaleo* means revelry or racket. Neither is in short supply at this lively tapas bar and restaurant. Enjoy flamenco music while perusing a menu of 50 or so possibilities. Because sharing is an unspoken rule, Jaleo is fun with a group. The restaurant is convenient to the FBI, 7th Street galleries, Shakespeare Theatre (next door), and MCI Center. The Sunday brunch attracts locals en route to a museum or an afternoon siesta. Eat your eggs with *chorizo* (sausage) or atop plantains and rice instead of sunny-side up for a change. One could graze here nightly for a week and not sample everything. I recommend the tapas with chorizo or shrimp, potatoes any way, and the grilled chicken with capers and olives. After you try these recommendations, you're on your own.

*420 7th St. NW, between D and E Sts. ☎ **202-628-7949.** Reservations recommended. Metro: Gallery Place/Chinatown; then walk south on 7th St. 3 blocks. Tapas $3–$7. Main courses: $15–$25. AE, DC, DISC, MC, V. Open: Sun–Mon 11:30 a.m.–10 p.m.; Sunday brunch 11:30 a.m.–2:30 p.m.; Tues–Thurs 11:30 a.m.–11:30 p.m.; Fri–Sat 11:30 a.m.–midnight.*

Kinkead's

$$$$ Foggy Bottom   AMERICAN/SEAFOOD

Award-winning chef Bob Kinkead wields his Midas touch on delicious seafood offerings. This is not to say his meat entrees are less than golden, but seafood is unquestionably the star attraction. Grilled squid, the creamy clam chowder, and fried clams (served with fried lemons) are fantastic. The bread and desserts are also noteworthy, with a crème brûlée as good as those in the French Quarter. I recommend sitting in the bar area, where your meal is accompanied by piano music, or in the courtyard — in both locations, you can make a terrific meal from the appetizers. The upstairs dining room is more formal and a bit stodgy for my taste.

2000 Pennsylvania Ave. NW, at I and 21st Sts. ☎ 202-296-7700. Reservations recommended. Metro: Foggy Bottom. Walk east on I St. 2 blocks. Main courses: $18–$25. AE, CB, DC, DISC, MC, V. Open: Mon–Sat 11:30 a.m–-2:30 p.m.; Sun–Thurs 5:30–10 p.m.; Fri–Sat 5:30–10:30 p.m.; Sun brunch 11:30 a.m.–2:30 p.m.

La Colline

$$$$ Capitol Hill FRENCH

The atmosphere and the clientele (mostly Hill staffers) are dignified, but the dining is comfortable and leisurely. Sit back in a leather booth and feast on classic French cuisine. Besides offering classics such as *cassoulet* (baked casserole) and *charcouterie* (pates and sausages accompanied by breads and cheeses), the kitchen also offers trendier fare, such as poached fish on red pepper coulis and wild mushroom-stuffed ravioli on its lengthy list of daily specials. Frankly, I prefer the delicious simplicity of sauteed soft-shell crabs anointed with fresh lemon juice and chopped nuts. Fridays feature bouillabaisse, in a saffron-flavored broth. You'll want to leave room for a slice of flaky-crusted apple pie or another confection from the rolling dessert cart.

400 N. Capitol St. NW, at D St. ☎ 202-737-0400. Reservations recommended. Metro: Union Station. Walk west 1 block on Massachusetts Ave., left at N. Capitol St. for 3 blocks. Main courses: $12.75–$23.75. AE, CB, DC, MC, V. Open: Mon–Fri 7–9 a.m.; 11:30 a.m.–3 p.m.; Mon–Sat 6–10 p.m. Closed Sun.

Le Rivage

$$$ Downtown FRENCH/SEAFOOD

Gracious and underappreciated, this restaurant is convenient to Arena Stage and is only a few Metro stops from the Mall. But best of all, Le Rivage enjoys a beautiful waterfront setting. And this restaurant definitely lives up to its reputation for serving fish so fresh they were flapping their fins while you drank your morning coffee. The crab bisque, mussels in white wine, and seafood au gratin are worth noting. Exotic spices and seasonings infuse the daily specials. Those who prefer turf to surf fare are directed to dishes with duck or beef. All desserts — from sorbet to fruit tarts — are homemade.

1000 Water St. SW, between Maine Ave. and 9th St. ☎ 202-488-8111. Reservations recommended. Metro: L'Enfant Plaza, 9th Street exit. Walk south 4 blocks to waterfront. Main courses: $14.50–$21.95. AE, CB, DC, DISC, MC, V. Open: Mon–Fri 11:30 a.m.–2:30 p.m.; Mon–Sat 5:30–10:30 p.m.; Sun 5–9 p.m.

Legal Sea Foods

$$$$ Downtown   SEAFOOD

Choose your favorite in-season fish and have it broiled, grilled, baked, stuffed with crabmeat, or served Cajun style (rubbed with hot spices and grilled). K Street traffic and belching buses aside (the interior is wood-paneled and softly lit), bibbed lobster lovers tear into this seafood joint's 4-pounders as if they're in Maine. Legal Sea Foods is a branch of the Boston-area chain and claims the fish is bought, still squirming, at the dock. I recommend you try the fried onion strings, fried clams, and clam chowder with your entree.

2020 K St. NW, between 20th and 21st Sts. ☎ 202-496-1111. Reservations recommended. Metro: Farragut West. Walk north on 18th St. 2 blocks, turn left at K St. and continue 3 blocks. Main courses: $14–$26. AE, DC, DISC, MC, V. Open: Mon–Thurs 11 a.m.–10 p.m.; Fri 11 a.m.–10:30 p.m.; Sat 4 p.m.–10:30p.m. Closed Sun.

Les Halles

$$$ Downtown   FRENCH/STEAKHOUSE

Located near the Warner and National theatres on revitalized Pennsylvania Avenue, this unpretentious steakhouse invites diners to relax. In good weather, customers take to the sidewalk patio. Diehards don't waver from the restaurant's signature offering — steak, pommes frites, and salade. Atypicals order the cassoulet, blood sausage, and rotisseried lamb. Les Halles fills the bill when you're downtown and dying for a good steak and puffy twice-fried potatoes.

1201 Pennsylvania Ave. NW, at 12th St. ☎ 202-347-6848. Reservations recommended. Metro: Metro Center. Walk south 3 blocks on 12th St. and hang a right at Pennsylvania Ave. Main courses: $14.75–$24. AE, DC, DISC, MC, V. Open: Daily 11:30 a.m.–midnight.

Luigino

$$$ Downtown   ITALIAN

Have you ever eaten ravioli in a bus station? Stop off for the dish at Luigino in the former Greyhound terminal and you will. My finicky New York cousin endorses the pizza. Try Luigino's take on dim sum Italian-style (raviolis). (I'm told the fish is air-freighted from Italy. Maybe they swim in garlicked waters?) Aside from the pizza, pasta, fish, veal, and chicken one expects, you can find goat stew, chicken sausage, and other more adventurous fare on the lengthy menu. Lunchtime is hoppin' when the crowds from the Convention Center cluster, but by dinnertime, the hordes somewhat diminish.

1100 New York Ave. NW, at 11th St. ☎ 202-371-0595. Reservations recommended. Metro: Metro Center. Walk north on 12th St., right at New York Ave. Main courses: $12.50–$25.50. AE, DC, MC, V. Open: Mon–Fri 11:30 a.m.–2:30 p.m.; Mon–Thurs 5:30–10:30 p.m.; Fri–Sat 5:30–11:30 p.m.; Sun 5–10 p.m.

Luna Grill & Diner

$ Downtown   AMERICAN

Convenient to the Connecticut and K business district and Dupont Circle, at Luna, you can get bacon and eggs all day. Foie gras and balsamic vinegar may be in short supply at this diner, but you can find plenty of comfort food: turkey, meatloaf, grilled cheese, cheesesteak with fried onions and mushrooms, and outstanding French fries. I recommend you try the fried sweet potatoes or gravied mashed potatoes.

1301 Connecticut Ave. NW, at N St. ☎ 202-835-2280. Reservations not accepted. Metro: Dupont Circle. Walk south on Connecticut Avenue 2 blocks. Main courses: $5.95–$15.95. AE, CB, DC, DISC, MC, V. Open: Mon–Thurs 8 a.m.–11 p.m.; Fri 8 a.m.–midnight; Sat 10 a.m.–midnight; Sun 10 a.m.–10 p.m.

Market Lunch

$ Capitol Hill   AMERICAN/SEAFOOD

Even though the crowds are thinner Tuesday through Friday, I love this place on a Saturday morning. You can find chefs shopping for dinner ingredients, neighbors chatting at produce stands, families lining up for pancakes, and bargain hunters prowling the crafts and knickknacks. Get here early for the blueberry pancakes or ham and eggs with grits on the side. The crab-cake sandwich (made with shredded or lumpmeat crab), smoky Carolina-style barbecue, fried fish, and shrimp are lunchtime favorites. Seating (for about 20) is first-come, first to grab a stool.

225 7th St. SE, between C and D Sts. ☎ 202-547-8444. Reservations not accepted. Metro: Eastern Market. Walk north 1 block on 8th St. Main courses: $4–$11. No credit cards; cash only. Open: Tues–Sat 7:30 a.m.–3 p.m. (breakfast and lunch only). Closed Sun–Mon.

Marrakesh

$$$ Downtown   MOROCCAN

Marrakesh is touristy and kitschy, but also lots of fun. Where else can you eat a seven-course meal with your hands and get away with it? Diners curled up against pillows scoop salad with bread "spoons" and then wind their way though filled phyllo pillows, chicken, lamb, couscous, fruit, nut-filled turnovers, and tea. An exotic dancer undulates and, before you know it, you're part of the entertainment. Take note: Wine is in good supply, and you can easily run up a hefty bill in excess of $$$.

617 New York Ave. NW, between 6th and 7th Sts. ☎ 202-393-9393. Reservations recommended. Metro: Mt. Vernon Sq.-UDC. Walk south on 7th St. 2 blocks and left at New York Ave. Main courses: $25 per person, fixed price. Cash and personal checks only; no plastic. Open: Daily 6–11 p.m.

Meskerem

$$ Adams-Morgan ETHIOPIAN

Injera (spongy bread) takes the place of forks and spoons at one of the city's first Ethiopian restaurants. Enjoy honey wine or a full-bodied Ethiopian beer (both from northern Virginia) to put out the fiery stews — chicken, beef, lamb, shrimp, or vegetable — flavored with red pepper paste. *Watt* items are hot and spicy. You may want to order the stews mild *(alitchas),* if you aren't used to hot foods. You dine communal-style at basketweave tables. An Ethiopian band plays late on Friday and Saturday evenings.

2434 18th St. NW, at Columbia Rd. ☎ *202-462-4100. Reservations recommended. Metro: Woodley Park-Zoo/Adams-Morgan. Take the shuttle (Sun–Thurs 6 p.m.–midnight, Fri–Sat 6 p.m.–1 a.m.) or a taxi. Main courses: $8–$12. AE, DC, MC, V. Open: Sun–Thurs noon–midnight; Fri–Sat noon–1 a.m.*

Morrison-Clark Inn

$$$–$$$$ Downtown AMERICAN/REGIONAL

The dining room of this Victorian-style inn whispers gentility, but the kitchen is far from prudish. The menu changes seasonally and features American cuisine with regional influences, such as tamarind-roasted, free-range chicken with saffron rice and sugar snap peas. The pan-seared chilean sea bass with black-bean cakes and spicy shrimp once had me swooning. In season, dine in the bricked New Orleans–style courtyard, with its hanging baskets and potted trees. Inside or out, sample the chocolate caramel tart with Praline whipped cream or the lemon chess pie with blackberry sauce and you'll wonder why the South lost the war.

1015 L St. NW, between 11th St. and Massachusetts Ave. ☎ *202-898-1200. Reservations recommended. Metro: Metro Center. Walk north 4 blocks on 12th St. and right at L St. (Take a cab after dark.) Main courses: $19–$26. AE, DISC, MC, V. Open: Mon–Fri 11:30 a.m.–2 p.m.; Sunday brunch (a la carte) 11 a.m.–2 p.m.; dinner daily 6–9 p.m.*

Morton's of Chicago

$$$$ Downtown STEAKHOUSE

Break out a jacket and tie when you visit this beef-lovers' heaven. While other similar establishments have closed up shop, Morton's has endured, and consistently serves great steak. Have your favorite prime cut black-and-blue (seared outside; purple inside), rare, or medium. Order it well done and you may end up in the meat locker. If you're not into steak, check out the giant lobsters and delicious veal chops and chicken. Keep things simple and order the crispy hashed browns; they're large enough for two or three people to share. The desserts aren't anything to write home about. And, you won't have room for sweets anyway.

1050 Connecticut Ave. NW, at L St. ☎ *202-955-5997. (Also in Georgetown at 3251 Prospect St. NW;* ☎ *202-342-6258 and Vienna, VA;* ☎ *703-883-0800.) Reservations recommended. Metro: Farragut North. Take the up escalator. Main courses: $19.95–$32.95. AE, MC, V. Open: Lunch Mon–Fri 11:30 a.m.–2:30 p.m.; Dinner Mon–Sat 5:30–11 p.m.; Sun 5–10 p.m.*

Music City Roadhouse

$$ Georgetown   AMERICAN/SOUTHERN

Enjoy your meal family-style at this down-home establishment. You can eat hearty portions from a fixed-price menu while enjoying country music. In good weather, request a table along the C&O Canal. On the menu you find fried or barbecued chicken, pot roast, ribs, fried catfish, and broiled trout. Side dishes include cole slaw, black-eyed peas, mashed potatoes, sweet potatoes, collard greens, corn bread, and biscuits. (Refills on side dishes are on the house.) Celebrate the Lord's day at the rousing Sunday gospel brunch.

1050 30th St. NW, between M and K Sts. ☎ *202-337-4444. Reservations recommended. Metro: Foggy Bottom. Walk north on 23rd Street to Pennsylvania Ave., turn left and continue 4 blocks, go left at M St. for 2 blocks, turn left at 30th St., or take a taxi. Main courses: $14.95 (family-style meal). AE, DC, DISC, MC, V. Open: Tues–Sat 5–10 p.m.; Sun (brunch)10:30 a.m.–2 p.m.; dinner 3:30–9 p.m. Closed Mon.*

New Heights

$$$$ Uptown   NEW AMERICAN

Art-filled, casually elegant New Heights overlooks Rock Creek Park. New Heights is near the National Zoo and convenient to the uptown hotels and Metro. Many Washington chefs have sharpened their knives in New Heights' kitchen. Some have pushed the culinary envelope into the next galaxy before moving on. If it's in season, try the herb-crusted Alaskan halibut (flown in fresh daily) with mild mushrooms, salsify (a delicate root) ragout, and truffle vinaigrette. This restaurant continues to transport discriminating diners to new heights. (Tell Bill, the general manager, that I sent you. Maybe he'll get the chef to put an extra truffle in your vinaigrette.)

2317 Calvert Street NW, at Connecticut Ave. ☎ *202-234-4110. Reservations recommended. Metro: Woodley-Park/Zoo. Walk south 1 block on Connecticut Ave., right at Calvert St. Complimentary valet parking. Main courses: $17.50–$24. AE, DC, DISC, MC, V. Open: Sun–Thurs 5:30–10 p.m.; Fri–Sat 5:30–11 p.m.; Sun brunch 11 a.m.–2:30 p.m.*

Obelisk

$$$$$ **Dupont Circle**   **NORTHERN ITALIAN**

Before Obelisk opened, you had to hop an Alitalia flight for food this authentic. Pure northern Italian cooking shines at this tiny Dupont Circle trattoria, where less always counts for more. The décor is spartan, with a basket of fresh vegetables and crusty house-made bread forming the centerpiece. The fixed-price menu features three, not 30, choices. The pasta is handmade, the wines carefully selected, and the waitstaff is knowledgeable and attentive. The fixed-price menu ($49) includes an hors d'oeuvre; antipasto; pasta, fish or chicken; cheese; and dessert. Make your reservations early if you want to experience Obelisk anytime soon.

2029 P St. NW, between 20th and 21st Sts. ☎ *202-872-1180. Reservations recommended (1 month ahead for Fri–Sat). Metro: Dupont Circle. Walk west 1 block on P St. Main courses: $49 fixed-price dinner. D, MC, V. Open: Tues.–Sat 6–10 p.m.*

The Occidental Grill

$$$$ **Downtown**   **AMERICAN**

Hungry for power food after a White House tour? Want a convenient place to dine before a performance at the National or Warner theatres? Celebrity photos, spacious booths, and polished dark wood color this good-old-boys restaurant that's a 5-minute walk from the Oval Office. Pols, tourists, and briefcases meet at this historic site. The menu runs from sandwiches to heartier fare. Grilled meats and fish take top honors. The business crowd goes for the grilled swordfish sandwich, a variation on a club sandwich. Service is warm, friendly, and efficient.

1475 Pennsylvania Ave. NW, in the Willard complex between 14th and 15th Sts. ☎ *202-783-1475. Reservations recommended. Metro: Federal Triangle. Walk north on 12th St. 2 blocks, left at Pennsylvania Ave. 2 blocks. Main courses: $19–$34. AE, DC, MC, V. Open: Mon–Sat 11:30 a.m.–10:30 p.m.; Sun 11 a.m.–9:30 p.m.*

Old Ebbitt Grill

$$ **Downtown**   **AMERICAN**

The Old Ebbitt, as adaptable as a chameleon, serves a diverse clientele. Suits, tourists, and theatergoers graze on upscale pub fare, main courses, and desserts before going about their business. The Ebbitt also offers seasonal specialties, such as local crabmeat, corn, vegetables, and berries in summer. And I wish I had a nickel for every hamburger the kitchen turns out in a single week. Oysters are freshly shucked at the raw bar. The Sunday brunch is extremely popular; reservations are a must.

675 15th St. NW, between F and G Sts. ☎ *202-347-4800. Reservations recommended. Metro: Metro Center. Walk west on G St. 3 blocks, left at 15th St. Main courses: $12–$19. AE, DC, DISC, MC, V. Open: Mon–Fri 7:30 a.m.–1 a.m.; Sat 8 a.m.– 1 a.m.; Sun 9:30 a.m.–1 a.m.*

Oodles Noodles

$ Downtown   ASIAN

You can fill up on dumplings, satays, and delicious and satisfying bowls of soup (seafood, chicken, or vegetable) for little more than the price of a fast-food fix. And, naturally, oodles of noodles. Noodles of many varieties, including ramen and soft udon noodles — spicy or mild, dry or wet, sauced or souped. Choose Chinese, Japanese, Indonesian, Malaysian, or Thai. In a quandary? Try the Singapore-style rice noodles. You often face a wait, but at these prices you can't have it all.

1120 19th St. NW, between L and M Sts. ☎ 202-293-3138. Reservations for 6 or more. Metro: Farragut North. Walk west on L St. 2 blocks, right on 19th St. Main courses: $6.95–$9.95. AE, DC, MC, V. Open: Mon–Sat 11:30 a.m.–3 p.m.; Mon–Thurs 5–10 p.m.; Fri–Sat 5–10:30 p.m.

Pan Asian Noodles and Grill

$$ Dupont Circle   ASIAN

On a chilly day, this cheery restaurant's drunken noodles with spicy ground chicken sauce warm faster than an extra sweater. The spring rolls, crisp nuggets, and grilled goodies on a skewer whet one's appetite for a main course of noodles with a variety of Asian toppings and flavors. You can eat here for under $12. A second location is near the McPherson Square Metro (and the White House) at 1018 Vermont Ave. NW; ☎ 202- 783-8899.

2020 P St. NW, between 20th and 21st Sts. ☎ 202-872-8889. Reservations recommended. Metro: Dupont Circle. Walk west on P St. 1½ blocks. Main courses: $8–$13. AE, DC, DISC, MC, V. Open: Mon–Sat 11:30 a.m.–2:30 p.m.; Sun–Thurs 5–10 p.m.; Fri–Sat 5–11 p.m.

Pesce

$$$ Dupont Circle   AMERICAN/SEAFOOD

Pesce is a casual, noisy, and friendly neighborhood bistro. Read the menu, chalked on a blackboard. The food is beyond good and decently priced. This simple restaurant is known for its grilled, baked, or sautéed *pesce* (fish), served with sauce, a squirt of lemon, or a plate of pasta. Lobsters and soft-shell crabs are offered in season. Many folks tell me that Pesce is their favorite seafood restaurant.

2016 P St. NW, between 20th and 21st Sts. ☎ 202-466-3474. Reservations recommended. Metro: Dupont Circle. Walk west 1½ blocks on P St. Main courses: $19.25–20.95. AE, DC, DISC, MC, V. Open: Mon–Thurs lunch 11:30 a.m.–2:30 p.m., dinner 5:30–10 p.m.; Fri–Sat lunch 11:30 a.m.–2:30 p.m., dinner 5:30–10:30 p.m.; Sun 5–9:30 p.m.

Pizzeria Paradiso

$ Dupont Circle ITALIAN

Now this is pizza! Baked in a wood-burning oven, the pies are fussed over with the same attention as the food at Obelisk, also owned by Peter Pastan. Not everyone likes shelled mussels on their dough, but few can resist the fresh vegetables or Parma ham. The thin crust is so good, piling on extra ingredients seems a shame. That's why I like the Margherita, topped only with tomato, mozzarella, and basil. The Italian cold cut and cheese sandwich on house-baked bread is superb. The menu is limited, but features other sandwiches and salads. Because the place is not much larger than a pizza box, order your pie to go. You can enjoy it on the front stoop or in nearby Dupont Circle park.

2029 P St. NW. ☎ 202-223-1245. Reservations not accepted. Metro: Dupont Circle. Walk west on P St. 2 blocks. Main courses: $7–$16. D, MC, V. Open: Mon–Thurs 11 a.m.–11 p.m.; Fri–Sat 11 a.m.–midnight.

The Prime Rib

$$$$ Downtown BEEF

Where's the beef? You find it cookin' in this black and gilt K Street supper club. A tinkling piano softens the bar scene — and it is a scene — where high rollers wearing Patek Philippes and wannabes cruise for Mr. or Ms. Right. This is the place for fantasy. The thick cut of prime rib au jus with horseradish shavings satisfies a beef lover's constant craving like little else. Many enjoy the crab imperial, but most diners order the beef. This is button-down central. Prepare to drop $50 to $60 a head for dinner, or come for lunch when prices are lower.

2020 K St. NW, between 20th and 21st Sts. ☎ 202-466-8811. Reservations recommended. Metro: Farragut West. Walk north to K St. and west 3 blocks. Main courses: $18–$40. AE, DC, MC, V. Open: Mon–Fri 1130 a.m.–3 p.m.; Mon–Thurs 5–11 p.m.; Fri–Sat 5–11:30 p.m. Closed Sun.

Red Sage

$$–$$$$ (Chili Bar–Dining Room) SOUTHWESTERN

Enjoy a margarita, a delicious burrito, a quesadilla, or a bowl of chili, but do so upstairs — the downstairs section is too formal and overpriced. You can have a terrific time in the ground-level Chili Bar and not lose your shirt. The menu offers foods that are great to share. Red Sage is a good choice when you're near the White House and downtown theaters. The walk is about 10 minutes up 14th Street from the National Museum of American History on the Mall.

605 14th St. NW, between F and G Sts. ☎ 202-638-4444. Reservations recommended for dining room; none accepted for Chili Bar. Metro: Metro Center. Walk west on G St. 2 blocks, left at 14th St. Main courses: Dining Room $20–$37 (Boo!

Hiss!); *Chili Bar $8–$13 (Yippee!) Open: Chili Bar Mon–Sat 11:30 a.m.–11:30 p.m.; Sun 4:30–11 p.m. Dining Room Mon–Fri 11:30 a.m.–2 p.m.; 5:30–10 p.m.; Sat 5– 10:30 p.m.; Sun dinner 5–10 p.m.*

Rocklands

$ Glover Park, north of Georgetown   AMERICAN/BARBECUE

Go ahead, drop your peanut shells on the floor. You may think you've entered heaven when you bite into a barbecue sandwich or Rocklands' smoky ribs. Same goes for the grilled fish on a bun, the homemade apple sauce, the tasty side salads (the Caesar is on a par with high-end restaurants), the corn pudding, and the tart lemonade. The seating is limited — stools and counters — and the decor ain't much. But Rocklands is well worth the mile trip north of Georgetown, a bit off the beaten path for most tourists. Get your order to go and watch *Steel Magnolias* or *Primary Colors*.

2418 Wisconsin Ave. NW, at Calvert St. ☎ 202-333-2558. Reservations? Surely you jest. Metro: Tenleytown. Take No. 32, 34, or 36 bus south on Wisconsin Ave. or walk (uphill) about a mile from Georgetown. Or take a cab. Main courses: $4–$19 (rack of ribs). AE. Open: Mon–Fri 11:30 a.m.–10 p.m.; Sat 11 a.m.–10 p.m.; Sun 11 a.m.–9 p.m.

Roof Terrace Restaurant, Kennedy Center

$$$$ Foggy Bottom   AMERICAN

Take in the view of the riverfront and beyond through this restaurant's glass walls. The setting is gracious and grand, with high ceilings and crystal chandeliers. Dining here is not cheap, but for Kennedy Center theatergoers the convenience can't be beat. Servers are particularly attentive to ticket holders. The restaurant offers a traditional menu (beef, fish, chicken, pasta) that changes seasonally. Appetizers and desserts are pricey ($7 to $14). Stick with a basic entree, such as grilled salmon or the special of the day. Because many people come here pre-performance, make a reservation or arrive by 5:30 p.m. or after 8 p.m. Tuesday through Saturday. For $29.95, you can enjoy an elaborate Sunday buffet brunch, complete with a glass of champagne, from 11:30 a.m. to 3 p.m.

If you snag a table by the window, you can enjoy the same fabulous view at the **Hors d'Oeuverie** without spending $50 a dinner. Order drinks and light fare. In addition, the self-service **Encore Cafe** is just down the hall from the Roof Terrace, also with a rooftop view. A mediocre dinner will set you back about $15.

New Hampshire Avenue NW and Rock Creek Parkway. ☎ 202-416-8555. Reservations recommended. Metro: Foggy Bottom. Take the free Kennedy Center shuttle bus. Main courses: $23–$30. All major credit cards. Open: Tues–Sat 5–8 p.m. (Thurs, Fri, and Sat open until a half hour after last performance, usually 11– 11:30 p.m.); Sun 11:30 a.m.–3 p.m. Encore Café is open daily, 11:30 a.m.–8 p.m. Hors d'Oeuverie's hours are the same as Roof Terrace.

Senses

$–$$$ Georgetown   BISTRO FRENCH

At breakfast, let chef/owner Bruno prepare a hearty omelette and country-style potatoes for you, perhaps with a warm croissant or brioche on the side. Soups, salads, sandwiches and hot entrees are available at lunch. Sparkling stemware and fresh flowers brighten the clothed tables. Dinner could be pan-seared salmon with truffled mashed potatoes, seafood risotto, or another seasonal specialty. Senses serves tea from 3 to 5 p.m. The tea tastes better after you dip your fork into chocolate mousse cake, an éclair, or any of Bruno's other exceptional pastries and cookies.

3206 Grace St., off Wisconsin Ave. between M and K Sts. ☎ *202-342-9083. Reservations accepted. Metro: Foggy Bottom. Main courses: Breakfast $1.50–$10; lunch $5–$12; fixed-price brunch $21; dinner $18–$28. AE, DC, DISC, MC, V. Open: Tues–Sat 8 a.m.–10 p.m.; Sun 9 a.m.–5 p.m. Closed Mon.*

701

$$$$ Downtown   AMERICAN

This elegant dining room is close to the FBI, National Gallery of Art, Archives, 7th Street galleries, and downtown theatres. Piano music plays in the background, service comes first, and the kitchen succeeds in pleasing a diverse clientele. Regulars can't see past the vodka and caviar menu when dining before enjoying a performance at the Shakespeare Theatre around the corner. Those who can handle garlic call the large Caesar salad dinner. The menu appeals to differing tastes — fish, seafood, fowl, beef, veal, and pasta. Portions are generous. 701 gets my vote in all categories. You don't need to purchase a theatre ticket to enjoy the $24.50 pre-theater menu, served from 5:30 to 7 p.m.

701 Pennsylvania Ave. NW at 7th St. ☎ *202-393-0701. Reservations recommended. Metro: Archives-Navy Memorial. Walk east 1 block on Pennsylvania Ave. Main courses: $15–$23. AE, DC, MC, V. Open: Lunch Mon–Fri 11:30 a.m.–3 p.m.; dinner Mon–Sat 5:30–11 p.m.; Sun 5–9:30 p.m.*

Sholl's Colonial Cafeteria

$ Downtown   AMERICAN

Sholl's has been a Washington institution since 1928 — a year before the big stock market crash! Sholl's continues to serve locals and busloads of visitors homestyle food at cut-rate prices. The crowds enjoy plain, dependable, comfort food. Customers come back for full breakfasts for under $6, chopped steak platters, turkey and stuffing, fresh fruit pies, and rice pudding. The decor may be uninspired, but the customers offer plenty of visual interest.

1990 K St. NW, in the Esplanade Mall between 19th and 20th Sts. ☎ *202-296-3065. Reservations not accepted. Metro: Farragut West. Walk west on K St.*

2 blocks. Main courses: $2–$6. No credit cards; cash only. Open: Mon–Sat 7 a.m.–10:30 a.m.; 11 a.m.–2:30 p.m.; 4–8 p.m.; Sun 8 a.m.–2:30 p.m.

Star of Siam

$$ Downtown THAI

Pad Thai and stir-fried rice noodles star on a menu that includes more adventurous dishes, such as curries (beef, chicken, and shrimp — alone or in combination) and crispy, fried whole fish. The popular eatery is in the heart of the central business district. The Star of Siam at 2446 18th St. NW, in Adams-Morgan ☎ **202-986-4133** is open Monday through Friday for dinner only, Saturday for lunch and dinner, Sunday for dinner only.

1136 19th St. NW, between L and M Sts. ☎ 202-785-2839. Reservations recommended. Metro: Farragut West. Main courses: $8.25–$24.95. AE, CB, DC, DISC, MC, V. Open: Mon–Sat 11:30 a.m.–11 p.m.; Sun 5 p.m.–10 p.m.

Taberna Del Alabardero

$$$$ Downtown SPANISH

This restaurant is more formal than most — men need a jacket and tie; bring your castanets if you like. (You never know when you may dine across the room from a king; Spain's King Juan Carlos and his family have dined here, for example.) The old-world style reminds me of my grandmother's house — brocade drapes, velvet upholstery, and lace. But enough about decor. Begin your meal with a glass of Spanish sherry. The lobster and seafood paella (for two) or Basque-style crabmeat dish are the signature dishes. Tapas, most of which are priced between $6 and $10, are served throughout the day, a convenience when traveling and eating at odd times. One week every March, Taberna features a week of flamenco dancing by accomplished artists. Enjoy. (If you run into King Juan Carlos, please say Hola!)

1776 I St. NW, entrance on 18th St. ☎ 202-429-2200. Reservations recommended. Metro: Farragut West. Walk west on I St. half a block, right at 18th St. Main courses: $20–$31. Open: Mon–Fri 11:30 a.m.–2 p.m.; Mon–Sat 5:30–10 p.m.; closed Sun.

Chapter 15

On the Lighter Side: Top Picks for Snacks and Meals on the Go

● ●

In This Chapter

▶ Chugging coffee and taking tea

▶ Stocking up for a picnic

▶ Searching out sweets

▶ Drinking with a view

● ●

*W*hen they're not snacking on the latest government scandal, Washingtonians love their between-meal picker-uppers. It's hard to ignore the number of people on the city's streets — from toddlers to oldsters — smacking their lips on something other than cell phones. (Of course, in D.C. many people do both at the same time.)

If you're watching your budget, keep in mind that snacking is more economical than doing the three-square-a-day bit. Snacking is also more healthful, if you can believe the nutritionists. Sightseeing burns calories and requires tremendous stamina, so you need to snack to keep body and soul together. I'm sure the founding fathers meant to include snacking among our inalienable rights. That idea in mind, read on (and check out the handy map in this chapter) for the scoop on where to get a little something to tide you over until the next big meal. Believe me, a snack by any other name — nosh, indulgence, nibble, yum-yum, munchy — tastes just as good.

Where to Grab a Snack in Washington, D.C.

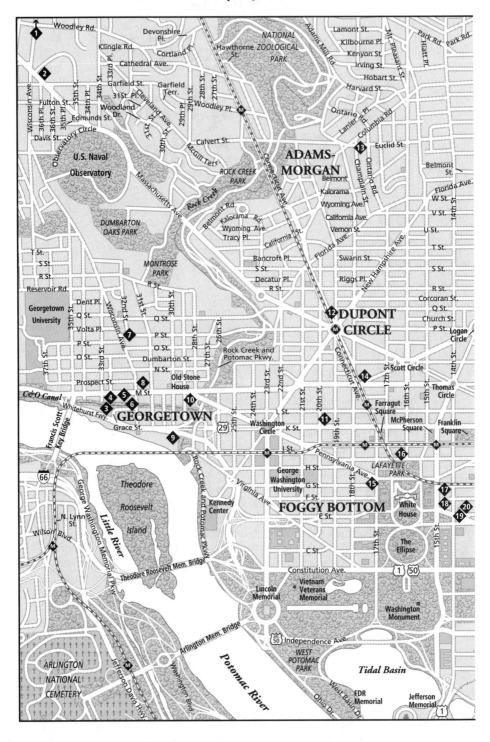

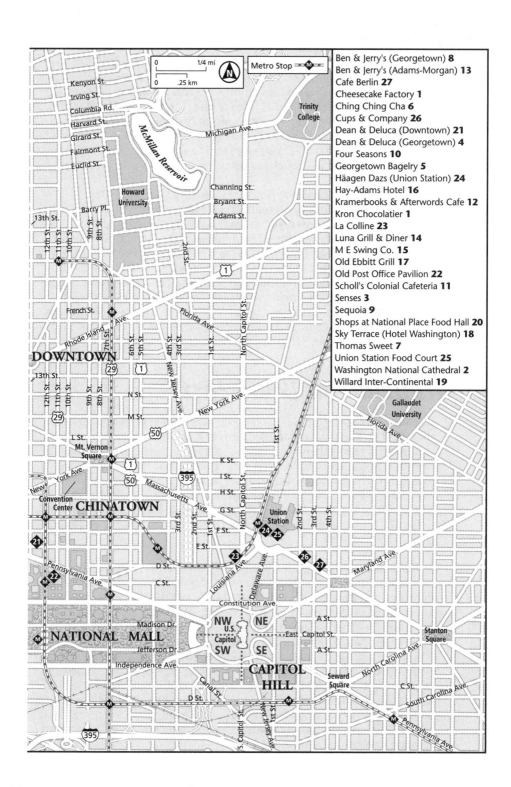

Ben & Jerry's (Georgetown) **8**
Ben & Jerry's (Adams-Morgan) **13**
Cafe Berlin **27**
Cheesecake Factory **1**
Ching Ching Cha **6**
Cups & Company **26**
Dean & Deluca (Downtown) **21**
Dean & Deluca (Georgetown) **4**
Four Seasons **10**
Georgetown Bagelry **5**
Häagen Dazs (Union Station) **24**
Hay-Adams Hotel **16**
Kramerbooks & Afterwords Cafe **12**
Kron Chocolatier **1**
La Colline **23**
Luna Grill & Diner **14**
M E Swing Co. **15**
Old Ebbitt Grill **17**
Old Post Office Pavilion **22**
Scholl's Colonial Cafeteria **11**
Senses **3**
Sequoia **9**
Shops at National Place Food Hall **20**
Sky Terrace (Hotel Washington) **18**
Thomas Sweet **7**
Union Station Food Court **25**
Washington National Cathedral **2**
Willard Inter-Continental **19**

(Coffee) Break Time

Besides a zillion branches of a certain West Coast coffee manufacturer that shall remain nameless, Washingtonians look to other sources for their caffeine fixes. One popular spot is **Cups & Company** on Capitol Hill, 201 Massachusetts Ave NE, across from Union Station, (☎ 202-546-4943). This coffeehouse is open Monday through Saturday, 7 a.m. to 6 p.m. Seating is limited; there are only eight seats inside, and only three outdoor patio tables. You can keep an eye on the Senate from here and also enjoy a sandwich, pastry, or ice cream with your java.

A few blocks from the White House, **M E Swing Co, Inc.,** 1702 G St. NW (☎ 202-628-7601), has been selling coffee and tea in the District since 1916. The coffee is roasted and ground daily, and I recommend it highly. The espresso bar seats 15 for coffee and pastry. M E Swing is open Monday through Friday, 7 a.m. to 6 p.m. Bookish coffee swillers gather at **Afterwords Café** (inside Kramerbooks), 1517 Connecticut Ave. NW, near the Dupont Circle Metro station, (☎ 202-387-1462). The help leaves you alone to read your trashy novel and nurse a cup of coffee until Bill Clinton returns to the White House as First Gentleman. Hours are Monday through Thursday from 7:30 a.m. to 1:00 a.m., and 'round the clock from 8 a.m. Friday to 1 a.m. Monday.

Capitalizing on Breakfast

Washington's power brokers start their days in a scramble — of eggs, that is. They like them scrambled with cell phones, bulging briefcases, and laptops rather than ham, cheese, or mushrooms. To check out the breakfast scene, head for a hotel dining room near the White House or Capitol. The attractive **Hay-Adams,** at 800 16th St. NW, at H Street, (☎ 202-638-6600); **Willard Inter-Continental,** 1475 Pennsylvania Ave. NW, between 14th and 15th Streets, (☎ 202-783-1475); and **Old Ebbitt Grill,** 675 15th St. NW, between F and G Streets, (☎ 202-347-4800) are good places to start.

At **La Colline**, 400 N. Capitol Street. NW (☎ 202-737-0400), a few blocks from the Capitol, lobbyists meet congressional reps to peddle influence and raise funds with their glasses of OJ. If power is not your aphrodisiac of choice — you want to jump-start *your* engine, not the economy's — try the **Luna Grill and Diner,** 1301 Connecticut Ave. NW, at N Street, (☎ 202-835-2280); or **Sholl's Colonial Cafeteria,** 1990 K St. NW, in the Esplanade Mall, (☎ 202-296-3065). At **Kramerbooks & Afterwords Cafe,** 1517 Connecticut Ave. NW, between Q Street and Dupont Circle, (☎ 202-387-1462), you can crack a book with your soft-boiled egg. When in Georgetown, get off on the right foot with breakfast at **Senses,** 3206 Grace St. NW, off Wisconsin Avenue, between M St. and the C&O Canal, (☎ 202-342-9083). The bistro has wonderful omelets, brioche, croissants, and pastries.

Tea for Two (Or One)

The Americans may have beaten the English in the American Revolution, but if the war had been a battle of tea parties, the Brits would have massacred the Yanks. Nevertheless, the United States has come a long way since the Boston Tea Party. In fact, several Washington hotels are doing their parts to perpetuate the very civilized tradition of high tea. In this context, high tea is a light meal with small, trimmed sandwiches (no crusts!), fresh-baked desserts, and potfuls of fresh-brewed tea.

If you take high tea, you can pass on dinner and opt for a snack later in the evening.

Get fancy and refined at the **Four Seasons,** 2800 Pennsylvania Ave. NW, (☎ **202-342-0444**). Soak in the view of Rock Creek Park from the Garden Terrace and nibble on finger sandwiches, breads, tartlets, scones with double Devonshire cream, fresh-brewed tea, and a nip of sherry (for medicinal purposes). Teatime is Monday through Friday, 3 to 5 p.m.; Saturday, 3:30 to 5:00 p.m.; and Sunday, from 4 to 5 p.m. (Beginning at 4 p.m. Tuesday through Sunday, a pianist tickles the ivories.) You pay $18.50 per adult and $9 per child (12 and under). As reservations are required, be sure to call ahead.

The ancient Chinese tea ritual is practiced at **Ching Ching Cha,** 1063 Wisconsin Ave. NW, near the C&O Canal in Georgetown, (☎ **202-338-8288**). The owner, Ching Ching, is a former hairstylist; the setting is serene and enhanced by classical Chinese music. The parlor lists more than two dozen teas from China and Taiwan, at $4 to $20 a serving (no charge for refills). You can also purchase loose tea here to take home.

The Gothic, Episcopal **Washington National Cathedral,** Massachusetts and Wisconsin Avenues NW (entrance on Wisconsin Ave.; ☎ **202-537-8993**), serves a grand tea at 3 p.m. in the Observation Gallery following the Tuesday and Wednesday 1:30 p.m. tours of the world's sixth largest cathedral. The tour finishes in the West Tower, where you can gaze through arched windows at the city and beyond. If you do not take the tour, meet the group inside the west entrance of the cathedral (off Massachusetts Avenue). The cost for tea is $18 per person, and reservations are required. The tour itself is free, although a donation is requested.

Picking Up Picnic Supplies

Visitors intent on cramming in a lot of sights often prefer quick bites to spending an hour or two in restaurants. Life is, after all, about choices. Most delis, coffee shops, and assorted holes-in-the-wall (as well as many restaurants) gladly pack your order to go. Enjoy your meal outdoors in one of the city's parks or squares. I'll pray for the pigeons to leave you alone. You can do your part by not feeding them.

Create a gourmet picnic at **Dean & Deluca,** situated within walking distance of the White House and Mall. The downtown store/café (with limited seating) is located in the Warner Theater Building at 1299 Pennsylvania Ave. NW (☎ **202-628-8155**). Open Monday through Friday only, 7:30 a.m. to 4:30 p.m. Take your food out and head for **Pershing Park** (Pennsylvania Avenue and 15th Street) or **Lafayette Square,** across from the White House; or continue on to the Mall. A Georgetown branch of Dean & Deluca is at 3276 M St. NW (☎ **202-342-2500**), and is open daily. The Georgetown D & D has a wider selection of yummy sandwiches, salads, desserts, and non-alcoholic beverages; it also has tables both indoors and outside.

Another option in Georgetown is the **Georgetown Bagelry,** 3245 M St. NW, just west of Wisconsin Avenue., (☎ **202-965-1011**). Their bagels are the closest thing I have found to a New York bagel (they actually have a crust!). Try them cream-cheesed or sandwiched around a choice of fillings. Counter seating is available for about 20 patrons on busy M Street. When in Georgetown, I like to brown bag it behind the **Old Stone House,** 3051 M St. MW, along the C&O Canal, or in the riverfront park at the west end of **Washington Harbour,** at 30th and K Streets NW.

Satisfying Your Sweet Tooth

Sweet tooth crave a fix? When in Georgetown, stop by **Senses,** 3206 Grace St. NW, off Wisconsin Avenue between M St. and the C&O Canal (☎ **202-342-9083**), for a Parisian brioche, napoleon, or any of its other tempting goodies. The breads, croissants, pastries, and tarts taste like grandmere's (maybe not yours or mine, but *someone's* grandmere). On Capitol Hill, skip the House of Representatives if you must, to sample the strudels, tortes, and pies at **Cafe Berlin,** 322 Massachusetts Ave. NE, (☎ **202-543-7656**).

If you are uptown, visit the **Cheesecake Factory** in Friendship Heights, near the Maryland border (no passport needed) at 5345 Wisconsin Ave. NW (☎ **202-364-0500**). Feast on 35 varieties of calorie-laden, artery-clogging desserts. (You may find a slice too rich to consume in one sitting. I can't imagine why.) **Kron Chocolatier** (☎ **202-966-4946**) is across the street in the Mazza Gallerie. This shop sells all manner of world-class chocolate. (I can empty a pound box of champagne truffles before I exit the shop.) I suggest you try the chocolate-dipped strawberries. Mention this book and they may toss you a bittersweet crumb, or not.

1 Scream, You Scream . . .

Thank heaven the ice-cream craze still drips on. If there's a quicker way to get a sugar rush and rejoin the human race when spirits lag, I don't know it. I doubt you can walk a block in D.C. without passing a push-cart or walk-in store selling ice cream or frozen yogurt. Nearly every restaurant (including those in museums and galleries), deli, and take-out sells the cool stuff. Branches of the Vermont-based **Ben & Jerry's** are located in Georgetown at 3135 M St. NW, between 31st and 32nd Streets, (☎ 202-965-2222) and in Adams-Morgan at 2503 Champlain St. NW, near 18th St. and Columbia Road (☎ 202-667-6677).

Häagen-Dazs in the Union Station Food Court, 50 Massachusetts Ave. NE, (☎ 202-789-0953) needs no introduction. **Thomas Sweet** (☎ 202-337-0616), in Georgetown at 3214 P St. NW, at Wisconsin Avenue, dishes out its own brand to locals and many area restaurants. This ice-cream parlor is old-fashioned and reminiscent of the malt shoppe in the *Archie* comic books.

Fast and Cheap Eats

Keeping up a fast pace in order to visit all the museums and attractions means you may want to eat on the run. Grab a hot dog from a street vendor before flying off to Air and Space. I'm partial to Sabrett's with mustard, kraut, and relish, when I'm downtown. You find vendors in profusion on the Mall (and adjacent to Constitution and Independence Avenues), along Connecticut Avenue and K Street and many other downtown streets, and near all Metro stations. Kids don't seem to notice, but the egg rolls and pizza are almost indistinguishable.

At the **Old Post Office Pavilion,** at 11th Street and Pennsylvania Avenue NW, or the Food Hall in the **Shops at National Place,** 1331 Pennsylvania Ave. NW (enter on Pennsylvania Avenue or F St.), you'll find plenty of food stands. Both locations are about a 10-minute walk from the Mall. On Capitol Hill, take the escalator down to the immense **Food Court** in Union Station where you can feast on hamburgers, sand-wiches, or sushi (just to name a few items) and gulp down some fresh-squeezed lemonade. End (or begin) with a cannoli from **Vacarro's** bakery stand.

Drinking In the View

Enjoy a cocktail while drinking in a primo view at the **Sky Terrace** of the **Hotel Washington,** 15th Street and Pennsylvania Avenue NW (☎ 202-638-5900). Between May and October, this spot is my favorite for catching a sundowner. Sometimes I imagine I can feel the breeze created by planes descending into Reagan National Airport. Keep it simple and stick to a cheese platter or a sandwich here. The food's nothing special and the prices are a bit high, but you can't beat the romantic setting. While you ogle the landscape, see how many buildings you can identify. One can almost peer into the East Wing of the White House. (If you could see into the West Wing, you might glimpse Martin Sheen.)

For a soothing experience, sip your poison of choice with an appetizer or some light fare by the Potomac River in Georgetown. The **Sequoia,** 3000 K St. NW (☎ **202-944-4200**), in the Washington Harbour complex hosts an interesting mix of people — from students to international businessmen — in a scenic setting. It's a great place to people-watch, so sit on the terrace and enjoy the view. If the weather is nasty, head indoors and nestle in a cozy bar-level alcove.

In Foggy Bottom, try to snag a window table in the bar area — before 5:30 or after 8:00 p.m., or you'll be competing with ticket holders — of the **Roof Terrace Restaurant** of the **Kennedy Center,** 2700 F St. NW, at New Hampshire Avenue and Rock Creek Parkway (☎ **202-416-8555**). Although the restaurant's changed chefs over the years, it consistently delivers a celestial view of downtown Washington, the Potomac River, and suburban Virginia. You can make out the eternal flame marking JFK's grave on clear evenings. Down the hall, slip into the cafeteria-style **Encore Café** and enjoy the same vista with a mini-bottle of rinky-dink wine and a sandwich or salad. No appetite? Leave your wallet in your pocket and, without spending a cent, stroll the promenade that completely encircles the performing arts center.

Part V
Exploring
Washington, D.C.

The 5th Wave   By Rich Tennant

In this part . . .

In this part, I focus on the important stuff: exploring Washington's magnificent cultural and architectural offerings, visiting the nation's most famous monuments, and touring the government's hallowed halls.

I cover all Washington's top attractions, tell you which city tours are worth your while, and give you some itineraries to make sightseeing a little easier. If you feel no trip is complete without maxing out your credit card, I also clue you in on the best shopping opportunities. Perhaps you like an occasional change of scenery; in that case, you'll like the day-trip suggestions I throw in, too.

Chapter 16

Washington, D.C.'s Top Sights

●●●

In This Chapter

▶ Indexes of the city's top attractions by location and type

▶ The best attractions in Washington, D.C.

●●●

*T*his chapter begins with indexes listing Washington's premier attractions by location and type (memorials, galleries, topless bars — just wanted to see if you were paying attention — and so on). The indexes can help you plan your sightseeing trips so that you get the most out of the time you spend here. For example, if you leave the Museum of Natural History, scratch your head, and wonder what other attractions are close by, you can check out the Mall listing to find out what's within a stone's throw . . . well, almost. When you do, you'll find that the Museum of American History is about 3 blocks west, the National Gallery of Art the same distance in the other direction (toward the U.S. Capitol). You can also consult the maps in this chapter to help you find an attraction you want to visit.

A kid-friendly icon denotes an attraction that appeals to most children. Of course, depending on the child's age, interests, and attention span, you (the parent, guardian, maiden aunt, or private valet) ultimately know what's best.

Index of Attractions by Location

Arlington, Virginia
Arlington National Cemetery

Capitol Hill
U.S. Capitol
National Postal Museum
U.S. Supreme Court

Downtown
FBI

Ford's Theatre & Lincoln
   Museum/Petersen House

Foggy Bottom
John F. Kennedy Center for the
   Performing Arts (See the
   "Presidential Tributes" listing
   later in this index.)

Georgetown

C&O Canal
Dumbarton Oaks Garden &
    Museum

National Mall (on the Mall unless otherwise indicated)

National Air and Space Museum
National Museum of American
    History
National Archives (1 block north
    of Mall, Constitution Ave. at 8th
    St. NW)
National Gallery of Art
Lincoln Memorial (west end of
    Mall at 23rd Street between
    Constitution and Independence
    Avenues)
National Gallery of Art

National Museum of Natural
    History
Washington Monument
Vietnam Veterans Memorial

Tidal Basin

Bureau of Engraving and Printing
Franklin Delano Roosevelt
    Memorial
Jefferson Memorial
Potomac Park (East and West)
U.S. Holocaust Memorial Museum

White House area

White House
White House Visitors Center

Uptown/Woodley Park

National Zoological Park

Index of Attractions by Type

Museums

Bureau of Engraving and Printing
Ford's Theatre & Lincoln
    Museum/Petersen House
U.S. Holocaust Memorial Museum
National Archives
National Gallery of Art
National Museum of Air and Space
National Museum of American
    History
National Museum of Natural
    History
National Postal Museum
White House

Parks

C&O Canal
Dumbarton Oaks Gardens

Enid A. Haupt Victorian Garden
Lafayette Square
Potomac Park (East and West)
Rock Creek Park
Theodore Roosevelt Island

Presidential Tributes

Franklin Delano Roosevelt
    Memorial
Jefferson Memorial
John F. Kennedy Center for the
    Performing Arts
Lincoln Memorial
Washington Monument
White House

The Top Attractions from A to Z

Arlington National Cemetery

Arlington, Virginia

More than 240,000 war dead and veterans (and their dependents) are buried at Arlington National Cemetery. The cemetery commands a view of the capital city from the Virginia side of Memorial Bridge. The sprawling site is hilly. Unless you're in great shape and have oodles of time, I don't advise covering it entirely on foot. I'd opt for Tourmobile (see Chapter 18), which stops at the highlights.

Just inside the entrance to the cemetery, you can see a memorial to the nearly 2 million women who have served in the military since the American Revolution. Make sure to grab a map at the Visitors Center, which is a Tourmobile stop and a good place for a pit stop because you won't find any bathrooms between here and Arlington House (the former Custis-Lee Mansion). The mansion, a gracious hybrid of Greek Revival and plantation styles, was the home of Robert E. Lee and Martha Washington's great-granddaughter. No hanky-panky there; they were married. You can take a free self-guided tour of Arlington House from 9:30 a.m. to 4:30 p.m., except when the mansion is closed on January 1 and December 25. Pierre L'Enfant's grave is nearby. He was moved here from a pauper's grave and now enjoys a front row seat for his masterwork. Below L'Enfant's gravesite, and also with a commanding view of the capital city, are the gravesites of John F. Kennedy, Jacqueline Kennedy Onassis, and Robert F. Kennedy.

The second most moving scene, after the rows of simple markers dotting the sweeping lawns, is the changing of the guard at the **Tomb of the Unknowns** (between Memorial and Roosevelt Drives). The guards change every hour on the hour (around the clock) from October through March and every half-hour April through September. About a mile north of the Visitors Center (near the Ord and Weitzel Gate) is the famous Marine Corps Memorial of the marines raising the flag on Iwo Jima, and the Netherlands Carillon, where you can catch weekend concerts April through September. Plan on spending an hour or more to take in all these attractions.

Arlington, Virginia, west side of Memorial Bridge (the Lincoln Memorial anchors the east side of the bridge). ☎ *703-607-8052. Internet:* www.arlingtoncemetery. org. *Metro: Arlington National Cemetery. Also accessible by Tourmobile. Open: Daily Apr–Sept, 8 a.m.–7 p.m.; Oct–Mar 8 a.m.–5 p.m. Admission: Free.*

The Top Attractions in Washington, D.C.

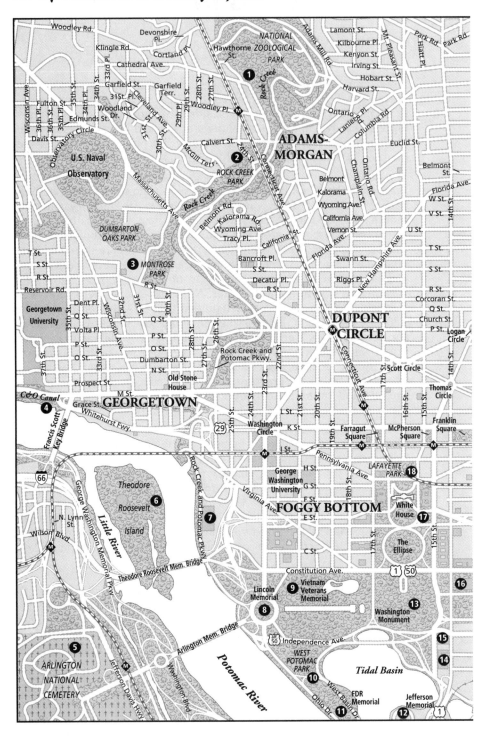

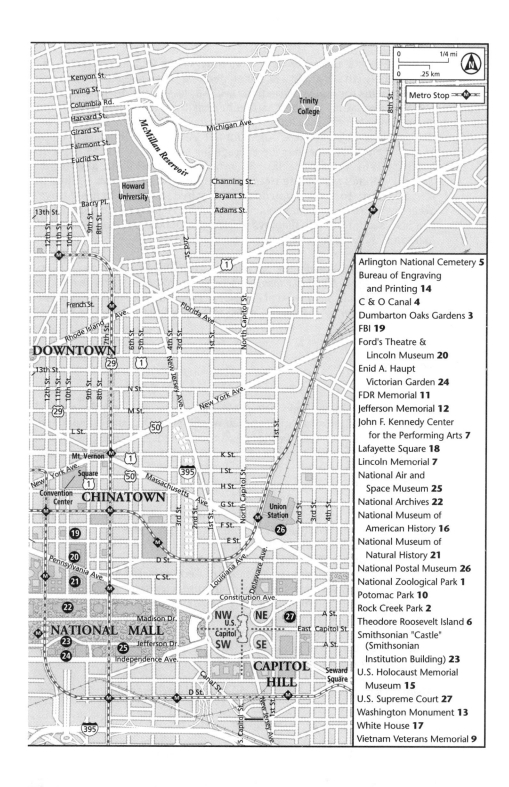

0   1/4 mi
0   .25 km

Metro Stop

Kenyon St.
Irving St.
Columbia Rd.
Harvard St.
Girard St.
Fairmont St.
Euclid St.

Trinity
College

McMillan Reservoir

Michigan Ave.

Howard
University

Channing St.
Bryant St.
Adams St.

13th St.
Barry Pl.
12th St.
11th St.
10th St.
9th St.
8th St.
2nd St.

French St.
Rhode Island Ave.
Florida Ave.
North Capitol St.

DOWNTOWN
13th St.
12th St.
11th St.
10th St.
9th St.
8th St.
7th St.
6th St.
5th St.
4th St.
3rd St.
New Jersey Ave.
New York Ave.

N St.
M St.
L St.

Mt. Vernon
Square
New York Ave.
Massachusetts Ave.
Convention
Center

CHINATOWN

K St.
I St.
H St.
G St.
F St.
E St.

1st St.
2nd St.
3rd St.
4th St.

Union
Station

Pennsylvania Ave.
D St.
C St.

Louisiana Ave.
Delaware Ave.

Constitution Ave.

Madison Dr.

NATIONAL MALL
Jefferson Dr.
Independence Ave.

NW   NE
U.S.
Capitol
SW   SE

East Capitol St.

A St.
A St.

CAPITOL
HILL

Seward
Square

Canal St.
S. Capitol St.
New Jersey Ave.

Arlington National Cemetery **5**
Bureau of Engraving
   and Printing **14**
C & O Canal **4**
Dumbarton Oaks Gardens **3**
FBI **19**
Ford's Theatre &
   Lincoln Museum **20**
Enid A. Haupt
   Victorian Garden **24**
FDR Memorial **11**
Jefferson Memorial **12**
John F. Kennedy Center
   for the Performing Arts **7**
Lafayette Square **18**
Lincoln Memorial **7**
National Air and
   Space Museum **25**
National Archives **22**
National Museum of
   American History **16**
National Museum of
   Natural History **21**
National Postal Museum **26**
National Zoological Park **1**
Potomac Park **10**
Rock Creek Park **2**
Theodore Roosevelt Island **6**
Smithsonian "Castle"
   (Smithsonian
   Institution Building) **23**
U.S. Holocaust Memorial
   Museum **15**
U.S. Supreme Court **27**
Washington Monument **13**
White House **17**
Vietnam Veterans Memorial **9**

Bureau of Engraving and Printing

Tidal Basin area

The buck starts and stops in this building, where 22.5 million notes are printed daily (that's about $77 billion per year). You need to get up early and make this top-dollar attraction the first place you stop. Between 7:30 and 8:00 a.m., April through September, visitors line up at the kiosk on Raoul Wallenberg Place (15th St. SW) for free same-day timed tickets for the guided tour. Tickets are doled out at 8:30 a.m. and often are gone by 11 a.m. (Did you know that the average life expectancy of a $1 bill is 18 months? Why does mine last 30 seconds?) The Bureau also prints Treasury bonds and White House invitations, which always get lost in the mail. Sorry to say, but you don't get any free samples when you leave. You may, however, purchase a souvenir in the Visitors Center where you can also see interactive displays. Figure on spending an hour here (not including the wait to get in).

14th and C St. SW, entrance on 14th St. ☎ 202-622-2000. Internet: www. bep.treas.gov. *Metro: Smithsonian. Walk west on Independence Ave. 1 long block to left at 14th St. (entrance) or 2 blocks to 15th St. (kiosk). Open: Mon–Fri 9 a.m.–2 p.m. Extended summer hours. Closed: Federal holidays, Jan 1, and Dec 25. Admission: Free.*

C&O Canal

Georgetown

Built in the 1800s, the old Chesapeake and Ohio Canal was the original (185 mile) transportation link between Washington, D.C. and Cumberland, Maryland. Wear your tennis shoes and rub shoulders with joggers, walkers, and bikers on the tree-lined towpaths that run alongside the canal. Recreational opportunities abound along the way. Figure on spending a half-hour or more here.

You can rent a canoe or rowboat at **Thompson's Boat Center** (☎ 202-333-4861), on the Potomac River in Foggy Bottom; Thompson's is across Rock Creek Parkway from the Watergate. Feeling less energetic? Board the *Georgetown* (☎ 202-653-5844; Internet: www.nps.gov), a 19th-century canal boat tied up in the heart of Georgetown between 30th and Thomas Jefferson Streets, NW. The 60-minute narrated canal cruise runs from mid-April through October, Wednesday through Sunday. Sit back and let the Park Service rangers steer as they regale you with local history and lore. On summer Sunday afternoons, concerts play near the boat's berth, behind the Foundry (C&O Canal between 30th and Thomas Jefferson Streets; ☎ 202-653-5190).

Metro: Foggy Bottom. Board any No. 30 bus bound for Georgetown or take a taxi.

The Mall

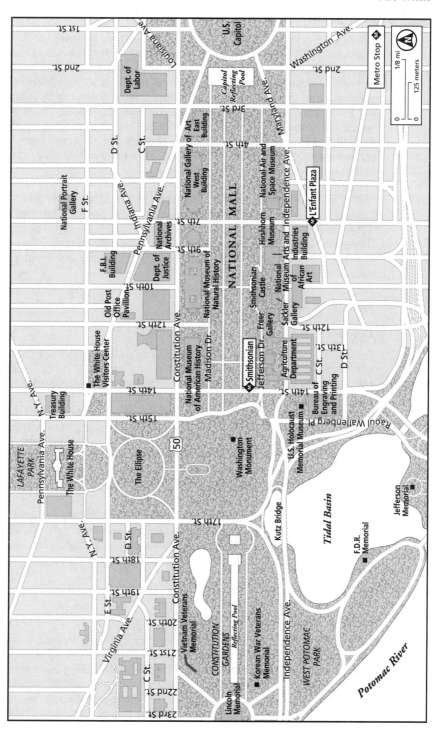

Dumbarton Oaks Gardens

Georgetown

If you plan to spend some time in Georgetown, be sure to check out Dumbarton Oaks. The former Robert Woods Bliss mansion houses a notable collection of Byzantine and pre-Columbian art. The "backyard," a 16-acre formal garden with wisteria-covered arbors, flowerbeds, and magnolia and cherry trees is, to my mind, more inspiring than anything in a museum. (Just my opinion!) Spring is especially beautiful as you can watch the roses and peonies come to life. The land is terraced, so you'd do well to wear sturdy walking shoes. Kids can let off steam here, but the terraces and steps make pushing a stroller near impossible. Plan on a half-hour at least.

1703 32nd St. NW, entrance on R St. between 31st and 32nd Sts. ☎ 202-339-6400. Internet: www.doaks.org. *Metro: Foggy Bottom and Dupont Circle (each about a mile away). Street parking is a bear. Walk if you're already in Georgetown. Otherwise, I'd take a taxi. Open: (Gardens) Daily 2–5 p.m.; (Mansion) Tues–Sun 2– 5 p.m. Closed: National holidays and sometimes during inclement weather. Admission: Free.*

Enid. A. Haupt Victorian Garden

The Mall

Seasonal flower beds make up this 4-acre park that covers the underground Sackler Gallery and Museum of African Art. In addition, flowers cascade from iron lampposts. Look for the central flower garden; it replicates the colorful rose window of the Castle. Catch your breath, reflect, or rest your feet before moving on to the next museum. A gate leads to a small island garden with benches framed by weeping cherry trees. The tea roses and magnolias are a sight for sore eyes in summer. Two Museum of American History employees constructed the brass sundial, which marks Washington's 40-degree latitude. You need 15 minutes or more to cover the highlights.

10th St. & Independence Ave. SW, between the Freer Gallery and the Arts and Industries Building; also accessible from the Sackler Gallery. ☎ 202-357-2700. Internet: www.si.edu. *Metro: Smithsonian. Open: Memorial Day–Labor Day 7 a.m.–8 p.m.; rest of the year 7:00 a.m.–5:45 p.m. Admission: Free.*

FBI

Federal Triangle

Except for the memories of J. Edgar Hoover strutting around in women's clothing, the FBI is a stellar organization. Touring its headquarters is one of the most popular activities in all of D.C., especially for youngsters. Write ahead or call your senator or representative for VIP tickets, which (if the ticket allotment has not been spoken for) ensure that you'll be admitted on the day you request and with a smaller group. Otherwise, line up no later than 8:30 a.m., especially mid-March through August. The hour-long guided tour begins with pictures and descriptions of the Ten Most Wanted criminals and a short film about how the FBI works. From there, you pass by windowed laboratories where a car's make and model can be determined from a paint chip. Don't be surprised to see technicians analyzing hair, fibers, and blood for crime-solving clues. The bang-up finish in the firing range may leave your ears ringing. Most kids over 7 go bananas for the FBI tour. Be advised that the gunfire (contained and safe but *very* loud) may scare younger children. The hour-long tour begins every 15 minutes, Monday through Friday from 8:45 a.m. to 4:15 p.m.

Pennsylvania Ave & 10th St. NW with tour entrance at E. St between 9th and 10th Sts. ☎ *202-324-3447. Internet:* www.fbi.gov. *Metro: Metro Center. Walk south on 12th St. 2 blocks to left on E St. 2 blocks; Gallery Place, National Archives, Federal Triangle stations are about equidistant. Open: Mon–Fri 8:45 a.m.–4:15 p.m. Closed: Weekends and federal holidays. Admission: Free.*

Ford's Theatre & Lincoln Museum

Downtown

As you no doubt learned in the 4th grade, on April 14, 1865, the 16th president of the United States, Abraham Lincoln, was shot by John Wilkes Booth as he watched *Our American Cousin* at this very theatre. Closed for more than 100 years after the assassination, Ford's reopened in 1968 as a venue for plays and concerts. When the theater is dark, visitors can view the presidential box, furnished as it was the night Wilkes Booth shot Lincoln. In the small basement Lincoln Museum, you can see Lincoln's death mask and Booth's derringer, along with other presidential memorabilia.

After he was shot, President Lincoln was taken to **The Petersen House** across the street from the theatre at 516 10th St. NW. At 7:22 a.m. on April 15, Lincoln died in the House's small bedroom. The exact hour is still frozen on the room's bedside clock. The Peterson House is open free to the public every day (except December 25) from 9 a.m. to 5 p.m. You can spend around 45 minutes or more touring both the house and theatre.

517 10th St. NW, between E and F Sts. ☎ *202-426-6925. Internet:* www.nps.gov. *Metro: Metro Center. Walk east on G St. 2 blocks to right at 10th St. Open: Daily 9 a.m.–5 p.m. Closed: Dec 25. Admission: Free.*

Franklin Delano Roosevelt Memorial

Tidal Basin

The latest monument honoring a U.S. president opened in 1997 and continues to garner raves for its grandeur and design. Marked by granite, fountains, and meditative areas, the site, near the Jefferson Memorial, celebrates the contributions of America's 32nd president. Exhibits cover the Great Depression, World War II, and other aspects of Roosevelt's

12-year presidency. As if to make amends for his philandering ways, the memorial features larger-than-life-size statues of Eleanor and Roosevelt's beloved dog, Fala. You can see FDR's wheelchair and other memorabilia in the Information Center. (The length of the memorial is equal to three football fields — you can find restrooms at the north and south ends.)

South end of 15th St. SW, in West Potomac Park. ☎ *202-426-6821. Internet:* www. nps.gov/frde. *Metro: Smithsonian. Walk west along Independence Ave. until you're ready to plotz (about 15 minutes), or take a taxi. Also a Tourmobile stop. Open: Daily 8 a.m.–midnight. Closed: Dec 25. Admission: Free. (Fala reproductions are extra.)*

Jefferson Memorial

Tidal Basin

Thomas Jefferson, third U.S. President and Renaissance man (author of the Declaration of Independence, founder of the University of Virginia, architect, horticulturist, and inventor are among the feathers he wore in his cap) is memorialized in a marble monument resembling the Pantheon. Jefferson liked the columned rotunda design so much, he used it at the University of Virginia and his beloved Monticello in Charlottesville. The Jefferson Memorial sits at the southern end of the Tidal Basin overseeing the Capitol, the Washington Monument, and the Lincoln Memorial. In my opinion, it's the most impressive monument in D.C., especially in the springtime when you can see the cherry blossoms blooming or at night when it's illuminated. Count on spending about 15 minutes here.

Tidal Basin, south end of 15th St. SW, in West Potomac Park. ☎ *202-426-6821. Internet:* www.nps.gov/jefm. *Metro: Smithsonian. Walk west on Independence Ave. to the Tidal Basin (watch the traffic!) and south along the Tidal Basin path. The walk takes 15 minutes from Metro, 10 minutes from the Holocaust Museum or Bureau of Engraving and Printing. You may want to take a taxi or Tourmobile.*

Lafayette Square

White House area

Once part of the White House gardens, Lafayette Square has long been a refuge for the homeless, protestors, pigeons, squirrels, and brown-bagging bookish office workers. The pretty public park across from the White House is a perfect spot for a snack; in fact, you may want to stretch out on the grass for a few minutes while you're there. Although the area is named for the Marquis de Lafayette who visited the site in 1824, the equestrian statue of General Andrew Jackson dominates the park (the Marquis is stashed in the southeast corner — go figure). This attraction sets you back 15 minutes or more.

The park's borders are H Street NW to the north, Pennsylvania Ave. to the south, between 15th and 17th Sts. (east and west). Metro: McPherson Square. Walk south on Vermont Ave. to the back of the park.

Monuments & Memorials

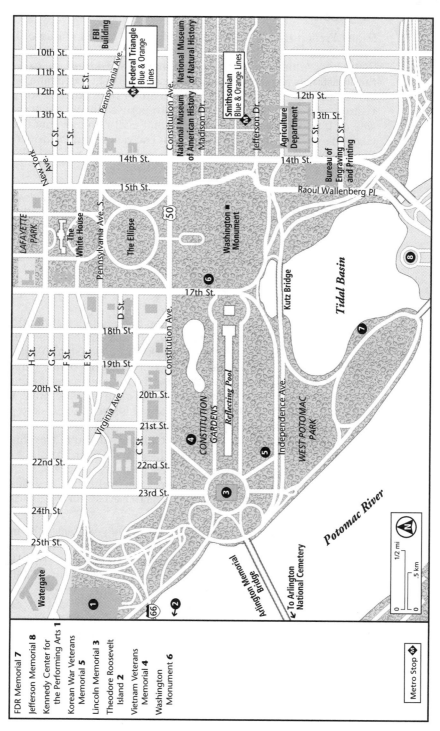

FDR Memorial **7**
Jefferson Memorial **8**
Kennedy Center for the Performing Arts **1**
Korean War Veterans Memorial **5**
Lincoln Memorial **3**
Theodore Roosevelt Island **2**
Vietnam Veterans Memorial **4**
Washington Monument **6**

Lincoln Memorial

Foggy Bottom

Daniel French took 4 years to complete the seated statue of Lincoln gazing across the Reflecting Pool and Mall to the Capitol. Lines from the Gettysburg Address and the Second Inaugural Address are carved into the limestone walls. The 36 Doric columns represent the number of states in the Union at the time of Lincoln's death in 1865. You can stop by the visitors center beneath the memorial to peruse Lincoln memorabilia as well as photographs of the protests and civil rights events that have taken place on the monument grounds. The views from the front (toward the Capitol) and back (toward Virginia), always special in daylight, are awesome after dark. Figure on spending a half-hour.

West end of Mall at 23rd St. NW, between Constitution and Independence Aves. ☎ *202-426-6895. Internet:* www.nps.gov/linc. *Metro: Foggy Bottom. Walk south 7 blocks on 23rd St. Open: Around the clock. Park staff on duty 8 a.m.–midnight. Admission: Free. (What a great city, eh?)*

National Air & Space Museum

The Mall

If it has flown, chances are it's hangared here. Aviation's milestones — the Wright brothers' 1903 *Wright Flyer,* Charles Lindbergh's *Spirit of St. Louis,* John Glenn's *Friendship 7,* Chuck *(The Right Stuff)* Yeager's *Bell X-1,* to name a few — are housed in a pink marble mausoleum that's longer than two football fields. Because the Air and Space Museum is on every visitor's list, arriving when the doors open or going late in the day to miss the crowds is wise. Stop first at the information desk to pick up a floor plan and decide if you want to take the twice-a-day free guided tour or rent an audio tour (both are bad ideas if you're travelling with kids under 8). Next, buy tickets at the Langley Theater box office for one of the movies on the multistory IMAX screen. If you haven't seen *To Fly* at least once, make it a priority for everyone over 6 in your group. Sit at least halfway back from the screen or you risk eyestrain and hearing loss.

After all the preliminaries are out of the way, you can tackle the museum itself. Introduce toddlers and preschoolers to the planes suspended over the main floor. The trick for all other age groups is to be selective. Don't try to see everything or you'll burn out. Interactive displays and exhibits cover a broad spectrum, from the earliest flying machines to rockets and flight in the computer age. In the **Albert Einstein Planetarium,** two programs are available for viewing, one of which is geared to children ages 4 to 8. An hour can slip by in seconds when you're browsing through the books and souvenirs in the **Museum Gift Shop** where the freeze-dried ice cream sandwiches frequently sell out. Fuel tank on empty? Refuel in the bright and spacious **Flight Line Cafeteria,** with a great view out the cockpit windows. Don't bother to touch down at the **Wright Place** restaurant — nice setting and aviation photos but airline-quality food.

Because of renovations lasting until sometime in 2002, some exhibits may be under wraps. You can spend at least an hour here.

South side of the Mall at Independence Ave. SW and 7th St. (enter at Independence Ave. for the full effect). ☎ *202-357-2700. Internet:* www.nasm.edu. *Metro: L'Enfant Plaza (Smithsonian Museums exit). Walk north 2 blocks on 7th St. SW to humongous marble box. You can't miss it. Open: Daily 10 a.m.–5:30 p.m. Closed: Dec 25. Admission: Free. IMAX movie tickets: $5.50 adults, $4.25 ages 2–17 and 55 and older. Planetarium show: $3.75 all ages (2 and under free, but I strongly advise against taking a 1- or 2- year old here).*

National Archives

The Mall

The Declaration of Independence, the Constitution of the United States and Bill of Rights, and a 1297 version of the Magna Carta reside in the Archives. My favorite time to visit the National Archives is right before closing when the documents are lowered into an underground vault said to be impervious to an atom bomb. It's an awesome experience. (Don't mess with the uniforms guarding our "Charters of Freedom." They're for real, and so are the firearms.) The "nation's memory," consists of *billions* of papers, documenting more than 200 years of America's history. I'm talking federal documents, passport applications, census figures, photographs, and more. The mystery, to me, is how they organize and keep track of it all. I could use some help organizing the mess on my desk. I wonder if the archivists make house calls.

Behind the 72 Corinthian columns and bronze doors, many people trace their genealogy. In fact, author Alex Haley began his research on what would become his best-selling novel, *Roots,* here at the National Archives. Researchers over 14 can do the same, by prior arrangement. Kids under 8 or 9 may find the Archives boring. Figure on spending 20 minutes or more.

Constitution Ave. & 8th St. NW. ☎ *202-501-5000. Internet:* www.nara.gov. *Metro: Archives. Open: 10:00 a.m.–5:30 p.m., usually with extended hours Apr–Labor Day. Admission: Free.*

National Museum of American History

The Mall

Vintage Americana crams three floors of the National Museum of American History (or what I like to think of as the nation's attic). You'd best arrive early or late to view some of the significant cultural, technological, and scientific advances that helped shape our country's character. By noon on weekends (and most weekdays too, actually) this place is a zoo. I advise getting up and getting out early, or you'll be staring at the backs of people's heads. I've found it to be least crowded weekdays after 3:30 p.m. when local kids are busy with activities such as soccer practice or flute lessons. Self-guided tour brochures are available to enhance your child's visit. The big exhibits here: First Ladies' contributions, the original Star-Spangled Banner (peer into the lab where weavers are preserving the original, due to be rehung sometime in 2001 or 2002), Dorothy's ruby slippers and other movie and TV memorabilia, a 280-ton steam locomotive, and the Hands-On History and Science Rooms for youngsters 5 and older.

If you have only a half-hour, head for the meat-and-potatoes exhibits on the first floor (machinery and transportation, such as a Conestoga wagon, stagecoach, and 1913 Model T). I prefer these attractions to the sweeping sociological statements attempted on the upper floors. In the Palm Court, an authentic Victorian ice cream parlor, a side dish of nostalgia comes with every malt and hot fudge sundae. If you're dying for real food, such as a sandwich or dried-out hamburger, head for the cafeteria on the lower level. Sometimes convenience is all. Plan on spending an hour or more.

14th St. and Constitution Ave. NW, with entrances on Constitution Ave. and Madison Dr. ☎ 202-357-2700. Internet: www.si.edu/namh. Metro: Smithsonian (Mall exit). Walk north across the Mall to the museum on your left (or Metro: Federal Triangle. Walk south on 12th St. NW 1 block, right at Constitution Ave.). Open: Daily 10:00 a.m.–5:30 p.m. Closed: Dec 25. Admission: Free.

National Museum of Natural History

The Mall

I still enjoy this museum. My kids loved it when they were growing up and now my grandkids are discovering its wonders. I guess we're in good company, because in 1999, Natural History overtook Air and Space as the most oft-visited museum in the *world.* (I'd like to think my big mouth had something to do with it.) Over the past decade, the museum has become increasingly user-friendly with interactive displays and multimedia exhibits. Little remains of the antiquated "Look, don't touch" attitude (except in the Harry Winston Gallery).

In the first floor, four-story rotunda, pick up a floor plan and introduce yourself to the 8-ton African Bush Elephant. Buy tickets (up to 2 weeks ahead) for a large-scale movie in the Samuel C. Johnson Theater. *Ocean Oasis* (2D) about the Baja California ecosystem, opened in Fall 2000. If it's not showing, I'm sure an equally exciting film has replaced it. Phone reservations are accepted, with a $3 per-ticket surcharge; call ☎ 202-633-7400.

Due to space constraints, I'll stifle my enthusiasm and share a few of the museum's highlights, such as the **Hooker Hall of Geology, Gems and Minerals.** The 45.5 carat Hope Diamond (see the sidebar "A girl's best friend? Nyet!" for more on this unique gem) is nothing to sneeze at, but I find the mineral collection even more impressive. Then there's the **O. Orkin Insect Zoo,** home to many creepy-crawlers and hands-on displays. Not surprisingly this exhibit is a favorite of youngsters, as are the skeletal remains of humans' prehistoric relatives in **Dinosaur Hall,** and the 92-foot replica of a blue whale and the giant squids in **Sea Life Hall.** The **Discovery Room** on the first floor invites families to inspect treasures of the natural world, Tuesday through Sunday. A newly expanded Discovery Room will open on the top floor sometime in 2002.

Meet at the Yap stone on the ground floor if you're interested in a tour of the museum's highlights, Monday through Friday. Hours vary, so inquire when you enter. One of my favorite haunts, the museum shops, are also on the ground floor and carry a wide selection of books, posters, as well

---

A girl's best friend? Nyet!

Currently on display at the National Museum of Natural History, the Hope Diamond first gained notoriety when it was stolen in the 17th century from a Hindu idol in India. The gods, it is said, had a major hissy fit and put a curse on all future wearers. Don't believe me? As you view the blue-colored stone, stop drooling long enough to consider the horrors that befell some of its owners and their nearest and dearest.

- The grandson of Englishman Henry Philip Hope — from whom the diamond takes its name — was forced to sell the gem when he went bankrupt and lost the family fortune.

- At one time, Marie Antoinette romanced the stone. We all know what happened to her. Maybe that girl lost her head because of the curse, rather than an ill-timed "Let them eat cake."

- According to the song (from *Gentlemen Prefer Blondes*), "Diamonds are a Girl's Best Friend." Maybe *some* girls, but not Evalyn Walsh McLean, who owned and proudly wore the 45.5-carat rock. McLean, a wealthy socialite, may have escaped the guillotine, but not by much. Her husband had a longstanding affair with the sauce and went insane; he ended up confined to a mental institution and their marriage dissolved — on the *rocks,* so to speak.

- Coincidence you say? Try this on for size. In short order, McLean's son died in a bizarre accident, and her family's financial empire withered. McLean failed to connect the dots and continued to wear the diamond. Then her only daughter died of a drug overdose. When McLean departed this world in 1947, her family had trouble unloading the hot rock. After 2 years of "Mister, have I got a stone for you," the family finally sold it to jeweler Harry Winston and used the proceeds to pay McLean's estate taxes.

- Winston — no fool — donated the stone to the Smithsonian in 1958. The postal carrier who delivered it supposedly had his leg crushed in a freak accident. Soon after, his wife and dog died, and his house burned to the ground.

Now you know the rest of the story. And while you're up, make mine a rhinestone.

as crafts, jewelry, and wearable art from around the world. Also on the ground floor is the **Atrium Café,** a glorified cafeteria with several food stations. It may not be worthy of *Michelin* but it's more than adequate when you're on the go. With children in tow, this museum is a must. Budget at least 2 hours and enjoy!

Constitution Ave. and 10th St. NW, 2nd entrance on Madison Dr. ☎ *202-357-2700. Internet:* www.nmnh.si.edu. *Metro: Federal Triangle. Walk south on 12th St. 2 blocks to left at Constitution (or Metro: Smithsonian. Cut across Mall to museum on your right). Open: Daily 10:00 a.m.–5:30 p.m. Admission: Free.*

National Postal Museum

Capitol Hill

A museum dedicated to the history of stamps and the postal service delivers, by extension, a large slice of American history. If only the Postal Service could deliver the mail as efficiently.

Tour a Southern Railway mail car, see floating laser images and holograms in the Customers and Consumers Gallery, and find out about the big business of junk, excuse me, direct mail that takes up so much room in your mailboxes. Children of all ages will enjoy the museum's interactive areas and video games. Plan on spending an hour or more.

2 Massachusetts Ave. NE, next to Union Station in the City Post Office Building. ☎ *202-357-2700. Internet:* www.si.edu/postal. *Metro: Union Station. Open: 10:00 a.m.–5:30 p.m. Admission: Free.*

National Zoological Park

Woodley Park

Several thousand animals representing more than 500 species call the National Zoo home. I suggest you arrive here early spring through fall because busloads of school children and families can quickly overrun the 163 acres of forested hills. The park houses animals in spacious enclosures similar to their natural habitats. You can crisscross the park on 3 miles of trails, so be sure to wear your walking shoes.

Be sure to grab a map and schedule of special programs at the Education Building near the main Connecticut Avenue entrance. Twice on most mornings, you can catch the elephants demonstrating a trunkload of tricks, and around 11:30 a.m., you can see the sea lions frolic (in exchange for fish). In late 2000, the zoo acquired two giant pandas to replace Ling-Ling and Hsing-Hsing, the dearly departed pandas given by the People's Republic of China to the children of America during Tricky Dick's regime. Be sure to visit Mei Xiang and Tian Tian — on loan to the zoo for the next 10 years — at their bamboo home off Connecticut Avenue

National Zoological Park

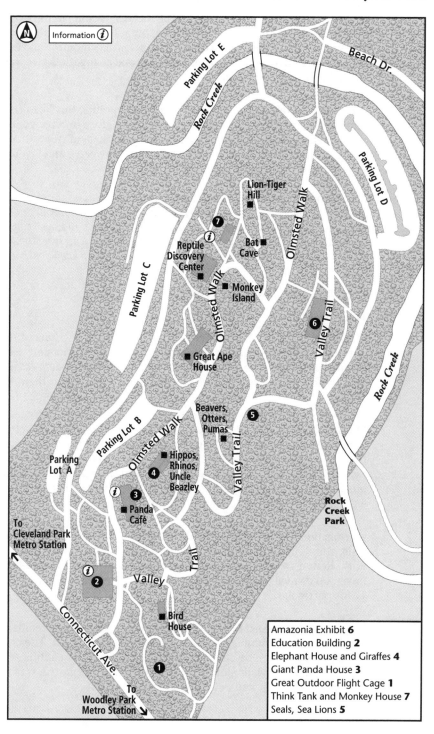

Information (i)

Parking Lot E

Beach Dr.

Rock Creek

Parking Lot D

Lion-Tiger
Hill

Olmsted Walk

Reptile
Discovery
Center

Bat
Cave

Monkey
Island

Parking Lot C

Olmsted Walk

Valley Trail

6

Great Ape
House

Beavers,
Otters,
Pumas

5

Parking Lot B

Olmsted Walk

Hippos,
Rhinos,
Uncle
Beazley

4

Valley Trail

Parking
Lot A

Rock
Creek
Park

3

Panda
Café

To
Cleveland Park
Metro Station

Trail

2

Valley

Connecticut Ave.

Bird
House

1

To
Woodley Park
Metro Station

Amazonia Exhibit **6**
Education Building **2**
Elephant House and Giraffes **4**
Giant Panda House **3**
Great Outdoor Flight Cage **1**
Think Tank and Monkey House **7**
Seals, Sea Lions **5**

Watch your head as you enter the **Great Outdoor Flight Cage,** home to many of our feathered friends. (If it's true that good luck comes to those nailed by bird droppings, I must be the luckiest woman in the world.) To see a remarkable re-creation, visit **Amazonia,** the zoo's rainforest. Come in winter to warm up. In the **Think Tank,** scientists monitor and examine animals' cognitive behavior. The macaques and orangutans give their pin-striped counterparts a run for their money.

A zoo visit to talk to the animals never disappoints, but I can't say the same for the food. Unless you plan on eating before or after your visit, I recommend toting sandwiches and buying drinks and dessert. You can rent a stroller for a few bucks. You can spend between 2 and 5 hours here depending on your pace and interest level.

3001 Connecticut Ave. NW. ☎ *202-673-4800. Internet:* www.si.edu.natzoo. *Metro: Woodley Park-Zoo. Take the northbound L-2 or L-4 bus, or walk three-tenths of a mile (Note: It's uphill). Open: Buildings, May–mid-Sept, 10 a.m.–6 p.m.; rest of year 10:00 a.m.–4:30 p.m. Grounds, May–mid-Sept, 6 a.m.–8 p.m.; rest of year 6 a.m.–6 p.m. Admission: Free. Parking: $5 for first 3 hours, $2 each additional hour.*

Potomac Park (East and West)

Tidal Basin area

You won't find chain-link fences delineating the two sections of 700-acre Potomac Park. The area surrounding the Tidal Basin and Jefferson Memorial is West Potomac Park; East Potomac Park is *south* of the Tidal Basin. (Hey, I don't decide these things, I only write about them.)

The park's main claims to fame are the more than 3,000 cherry trees that bloom every spring. Because of D.C.'s fickle weather, the blossoms appear anywhere from late March to mid-April. April 5 is the average date to catch peak blossoms, but in 2000, the trees bloomed around St. Patrick's Day. In other words, winning the lottery may be easier than pinning down the exact date of the blooms. Regardless, this park provides a great spot to stroll or picnic any time of the year.

You can find the Lincoln, Roosevelt, Korean and Vietnam Veterans memorials, the Reflecting Pool, and Constitution Gardens, in West Potomac Park. Rent a two-seater or four-seater paddleboat and cruise the Tidal Basin; boats available from 10 a.m. to an hour before sunset (see Chapter 17 for particulars).

Larger than West, East Potomac Park features golf courses, tennis courts, picnic areas, a swimming pool, and hiking and biking paths. The only easy ways to get here are by car or taxi. The peninsula is a beautiful place for a scenic drive or walk along Ohio Drive, which fronts the Washington Channel to the east and Potomac River to the west.

Rooting around for cherry blossoms

When most people hear Washington, D.C., the first thought that pops into their minds is cherry blossoms. The scene enchants even the most jaded visitor. Every spring more than 3,700 trees flower, embracing the Tidal Basin, East Potomac Park, and the Washington Monument grounds with their pale, lacy arms. A gift from Japan, the original 3,000 Yoshino trees (white and soft pink flowers) were planted by First Lady Helen Taft and the Viscountess Chinda of Japan in 1912.

Of the original 3,000 trees, fewer than 200 survive. More Yoshinos have been added over the years, however, along with Akebonos (single pale pink flowers) and Kwansans (deeper pink pompom blossoms). The Yoshinos bloom first, usually in early April, followed by the Kwansans a week or two later. The timetable depends on Mother Nature. The trees have blossomed as early as mid-March, and as late as mid-April. Suffice it to say, if you're planning a visit during the 2-week National Cherry Blossom Festival (beginning in late March), you have a 50-50 chance of seeing the trees at their peak. If you strike it right, you'll never forget it. Bring plenty of film.

For more information, call the Park Service (☎ 202-619-7222) or check the cherry trees' Web site at www.nps.gov/nacc/cherry/index.htm. (As yet, you can't e-mail the trees directly.) Also, local newspapers and television newscasts maintain a daily blossom watch in the weeks preceding the festival. Around here, the trees are monitored more scrupulously than moms-to-be in their ninth month.

West Potomac Park: Boundaries are Constitution Ave. to the north, 14th St. to the east, Jefferson Memorial to the south, and Potomac River to the west. ☎ 202-619-7222. Internet: www.nps.gov. *Metro: Smithsonian. Walk west on Independence Ave. (It's about a 10-minute walk, but don't try it after dark). Open: Dawn to dusk. Admission: Free.*

East Potomac Park: Ohio Dr. SW, south of the Tidal Basin and Independence Ave. ☎ 202-426-6765. Internet: www.nps.gov. *Metro: Uh-uh. If you're on foot, I advise leaving the park by dark. Open: Dawn to dusk. Admission: Free. Charge for golf, tennis, and so forth.*

Rock Creek National Park

Foggy Bottom into Chevy Chase, Maryland

Rock Creek cuts through the District and measures nearly 12 miles top (suburban Maryland) to bottom (Potomac River). Besides hiking, biking, and fitness trails, the park has an 18-hole golf course, horseback riding, 25 tennis courts, a nature center and planetarium, playgrounds, picnic areas, and the remnants of several forts built to protect Washington during the Civil War.

Rock Creek Park Area

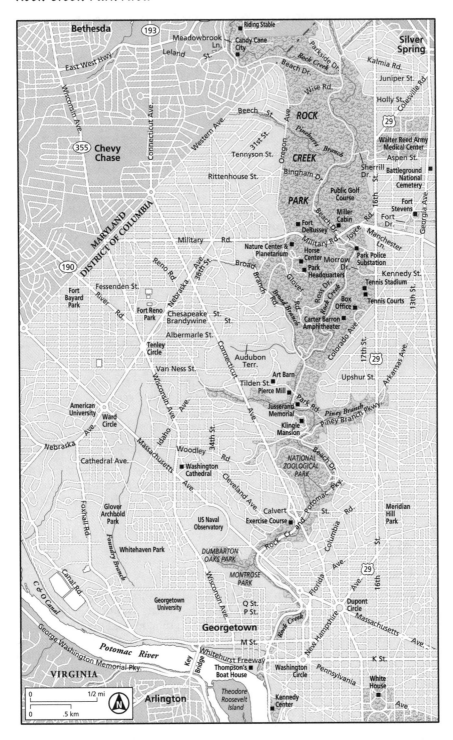

In summer, audiences at the Carter Barron Amphitheatre enjoy the National Symphony and Shakespeare in the Park (both free) as well as various musical groups. The men's Legg Mason Tennis Classic is played at the park's H. G. FitzGerald Tennis Center (16th & Kennedy Streets NW; ☎ 202-291-9888) the third week in July. Dress lightly because this is invariably the hottest week of the summer.

Because the sprawling park takes a 2,000-acre bite out of D.C., I suggest focusing on one area at a time if you are traveling by Metro. If you're familiar with the roads, drive (free parking is available throughout the park). Otherwise, take a taxi. You could spend weeks here trying to find your way out. Use the buddy system and hike in pairs.

5000 Glover Rd. NW (Visitors Information Center). ☎ *202-282-1063. Internet:* www.nps.gov/rocr. *Metro: Friendship Heights. Transfer to bus No. E1 or E3 to Military Rd. and Oregon Ave./Glover Rd. Open: To vehicular traffic around the clock; on foot, dawn to dusk. Admission: Free.*

Theodore Roosevelt Island

The 88-acre preserve, an island once inhabited by Native Americans, sits smack in the middle of the Potomac River, between D.C. and Virginia. The place is a fitting tribute to the old Rough Rider and his numerous conservation efforts. Rabbits, chipmunks, fox, and owls now call this diverse ecosystem their home. Enjoy more than 2 miles of trails that snake through the pristine setting; try to ignore the roar of airplanes descending into Reagan National Airport. A bronze statue of Roosevelt oversees a moat-enclosed terrace. You are permitted to picnic on the grounds near the island, but no food is allowed after you enter. From June through September, be sure to bring insect repellant — you'll thank me. Budget an hour or more.

Off the Virginia side of G.W. Memorial Parkway, between Key and Roosevelt bridges. ☎ *703-285-2598. Internet:* www.nps.gov. *Directions: Roosevelt Bridge to G.W. Memorial Parkway north. (Note: You cannot get to the island if you're traveling southbound on the parkway. Trust me. I tried and spent an unscheduled week in Virginia.). Occasional visitors: Don't even try to drive here; take a taxi. Or paddle over from Thompson's Boat Center* ☎ *202-333-4861.*

U.S. Capitol

Capitol Hill

All visitors, regardless of citizenry, should put this attraction on their must-see lists. The architecture and history, which symbolize the United States government, and the many art treasures kept within its hallowed halls make the U.S. Capitol a necessary stop for all travelers. I'll lay odds that a visit here will accelerate your pacemaker. If not, you need to recharge your battery.

The building served as a hospital and barracks for Union troops during the Civil War. Believe it or not, bread was baked in ovens beneath the West Wing to feed soldiers stationed at nearby forts. The 180-foot-high dome resembles a chocolate-covered cherry and the cherry stem is the statue of Freedom. You'll find that the Capitol dominates the Washington landscape.

Nine presidents have lain in state in the Rotunda. Above it, lining the dome, you can see the allegorical fresco, *The Apotheosis of Washington.* Constantino Brumidi spent close to a year on his back to complete it. Statues of prominent Americans — political and otherwise — fill Statuary Hall, once the House of Representatives. Start your visit with the half-hour guided tour (offered Monday through Saturday from 9:30 a.m. to 4:30 p.m., sometimes with extended summer hours), and then strike out on your own. During your visit, if you trip over the Capitol cornerstone, misplaced during a 1950s restoration and still missing, please report it to the authorities. For a real "moment," watch the sunset from the West Lawn or attend a concert here on Memorial Day or Labor Day weekends, or the 4th of July. You'll spend an hour or more, less time with very young children.

East end of the Mall, entrance on E. Capitol St. and 1st St. NE. ☎ *202-225-6827. Internet:* www.senate.gov. *Metro: Capitol South. Walk north 3 blocks on 3rd St., left at E. Capitol St. (watch those steps!). Open: Daily 9:00 a.m.–4:30 p.m. (often with extended hours Mar–Sept as determined annually by Congress). Tours: Mon–Sat Closed: Jan 1, Thanksgiving, Dec 25. Admission: Free (Ain't Washington grand?).*

U.S. Holocaust Memorial Museum

Tidal Basin area

I have yet to meet a soul who was unmoved by a visit to this museum. You can easily spend 5 or 6 hours here, but most visitors max out after 2 or 3. Don't be surprised if you're emotionally exhausted by the time you leave. The museum recommends that children under 11 stay behind, *except* to visit the two exhibits described in the next few paragraphs. Parents of older children should prepare their kids for what they will see and hear.

The national memorial honors the 6 million Jews and millions of others exterminated during the Holocaust. Multimedia exhibitions, with interactive videos and films, document this obscene chapter of history. When they enter, visitors pick up an identity card of a Holocaust victim, which adds to the immediacy of the experience.

The self-guided tour begins on the fourth floor with the rise of Nazism. On the third floor, the Nazis' "Final Solution" is depicted. Aboard a freight car that was used to transport Jews to Treblinka, visitors listen to recordings by survivors. Take tissues. The second floor is dedicated to the liberation of the camps and the many non-Jews who, at great risk, hid Jews during the war. Time-specific tickets are required to view the exhibits I've described. They're available at the museum beginning daily at 10 a.m. or by calling Tickets.com at ☎ **703-218-6500,** or by visiting the company's Web site at www.tickets.com. All visitors may view the exhibit areas on the first floor and concourse *without* tickets. Among them is **Daniel's Story,** a watered-down version of the Holocaust appropriate for children 10 and under. Awe-inspiring and eloquent in its simplicity, the **Children's Wall** consists of colorful tiles painted by American schoolchildren to commemorate the 1.5 million children who perished in the Holocaust. You'll need at least an hour, although two or more is better.

100 Raoul Wallenberg Place, at 15th St. SW near Independence Ave. and the south-west corner of the Mall. ☎ *202-488-0400. Internet:* www.ushmm.org. *Metro: Smithsonian. Walk west 2 blocks on Independence Ave. and left at Raoul Wallenberg Place. Open: Daily 10:00 a.m.–5:30 p.m. Closed: Yom Kippur (usually in September) and Dec 25. Admission: Free, but Tickets.com charges a small surcharge.*

U.S. Supreme Court

Capitol Hill

Most visitors may not consider the nation's highest court worthy of a stop, but I say the heart of our judicial branch deserves at least a few minutes. About 150 cases are heard annually, Monday through Wednesday from the first Monday in October through April (but not all weeks). Arrive by 9 a.m., if you're interested in sitting in on the proceedings. Seating is limited to 100.

The judges release orders and opinions from mid-May to early July. Call the information office (☎ **202-479-3211**) for a courtroom calendar. Year-round you can check out free lectures (every hour on the half-hour between 9:30 a.m. and 3:30 p.m.) and a three-star film on the workings of the Court. Court-related exhibits and a gift shop are on the ground floor. The cafeteria is open weekdays for breakfast and lunch. The carryout snack bar is open weekdays *only* when the court is in session.

Be sure to enjoy the view of the Capitol from the steps on your way in or out.

1st St. & Maryland Ave. NE, opposite the Capitol. ☎ *202-479-3000. Internet:* www.supremecourtus.gov. *Metro: Capitol South. Walk north 3 blocks on 1st Street NE. Open: Mon–Fri 9:00 a.m.–4:30 p.m. Closed: All holidays. Admission: Free.*

Vietnam Veterans Memorial

The Mall

The Wall, as it is known, is a low-slung V-shaped monument in Constitution Gardens, near the Lincoln Memorial. Remember when the Vietnam War was called "a conflict"? Well, etched on 140 black granite panels are the 60,000 names of the men and women who lost their lives or remain missing as a result of the Conflict.

Loved ones come from all over the world to leave mementos near the names of the deceased and missing. The casualties are listed chronologically from the first skirmish in 1959 to the last in 1975. The scene is a moving one, even for those with no personal connection to the Conflict. Since its dedication in 1982, the Wall has continually been one of Washington's most visited sites.

Don't get so caught up in the emotion of the moment that you're careless with your wallet or purse. A friend of mine had her purse snatched right from her shoulder some years ago.

Constitution Ave. and 21st St. NW, in Constitution Gardens near the Lincoln Memorial. ☎ *202-634-1568. Internet:* www.nps.gov/vive. *Metro: Foggy Bottom. Walk south on 23rd St. 7 blocks, left at Constitution Ave. 2 blocks. Open: Daily, around the clock. Park rangers on duty 8 a.m.–midnight. Admission: Free.*

Washington Monument

The Mall

Surely, this towering marble obelisk is one of the most recognizable sights in all of America. In mid-winter, I've seen the lines coil around the base, so make sure to arrive early or late for the shortest wait. For $1.50, you can order a ticket in advance through Ticketmaster ☎ 800-505-5040. The same timed-admission tickets are also available for free at the monument. On summer evenings, you can hear military bands playing on the grounds, and the monument provides a spectacular background each year for the impressive 4th of July fireworks. The gridlike scaffolding that had covered the monument during a 3-year-restoration came down when the monument reopened in July 2000. Y'all come!

15th St. and Constitution Ave. NW. ☎ *202-426-6839. Internet:* www.nps. gov/wamo. *Metro: Smithsonian. Walk north 2 blocks on 12th St., left at Madison Dr. (on the Mall) 2 blocks. Open: Apr–Labor Day 8 a.m.–midnight; rest of year 9 a.m.– 5 p.m. Closed: July 4 and Dec 25. Admission: Free.*

White House

White House area

Here's the bad news up front: On a *regular* tour, you won't be allowed inside the Oval Office (where more than affairs of state have been consummated). The good news: The public areas are available for viewing. I hope you arranged for VIP tickets (see Chapter 9 for details on arranging VIP tickets). If not, from March to September, stop first at the White House Visitors Center (1450 Pennsylvania Ave. NW; ☎ 202-208-1631), for same-day tickets. Showing up at 8 a.m. is not too early; the doors open at 7:30 a.m. The half-hour video, "Inside These Walls," may give you a closer look at the presidential mansion than the actual tour when visitors are herded through, cattle-call style. I may sound like a broken record, but I urge visitors to at least try to secure passes for a VIP tour.

The White House Area

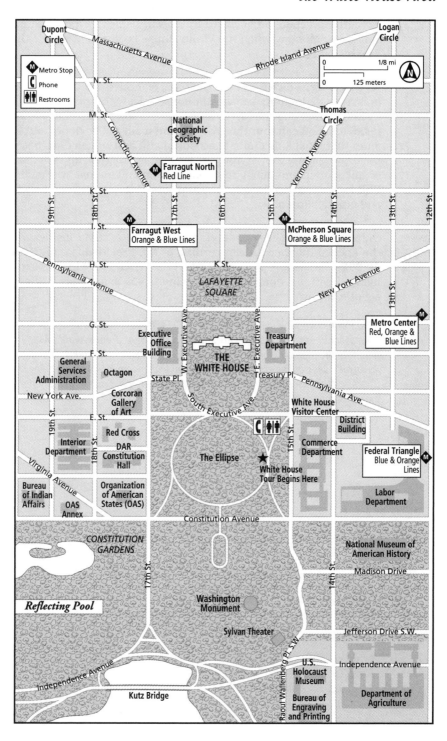

Dupont Circle

Massachusetts Avenue

Logan Circle

Rhode Island Avenue

M Metro Stop
C Phone
♥ Restrooms

N. St.

0   1/8 mi
0   125 meters

M. St.

Thomas Circle

National Geographic Society

L. St.

Connecticut Avenue

Vermont Avenue

M Farragut North
Red Line

K. St.

19th St.
18th St.
17th St.
16th St.
15th St.
14th St.
13th St.
12th St.

I. St.

M Farragut West
Orange & Blue Lines

M McPherson Square
Orange & Blue Lines

Pennsylvania Avenue

H. St.

K St.

LAFAYETTE SQUARE

New York Avenue

13th St.

G. St.

W. Executive Ave.
E. Executive Ave.

Metro Center
Red, Orange & Blue Lines **M**

Executive Office Building

Treasury Department

F. St.

THE WHITE HOUSE

General Services Administration

Octagon

State Pl.

Treasury Pl.

Pennsylvania Ave.

New York Ave.

Corcoran Gallery of Art

South Executive Ave.

White House Visitor Center

District Building

19th St.

E. St.

C **♥**

15th St.

Interior Department

Red Cross

DAR Constitution Hall

18th St.

Commerce Department

Federal Triangle
Blue & Orange Lines **M**

The Ellipse

★
White House Tour Begins Here

Virginia Avenue

Bureau of Indian Affairs

OAS Annex

Organization of American States (OAS)

Labor Department

Constitution Avenue

CONSTITUTION GARDENS

National Museum of American History

17th St.

Madison Drive

14th St.

Reflecting Pool

Washington Monument

Jefferson Drive S.W.

Sylvan Theater

Raoul Wallenberg Pl. S.W.

U.S. Holocaust Museum

Independence Avenue

Independence Avenue

Kutz Bridge

Bureau of Engraving and Printing

Department of Agriculture

October through February, when things are less busy, you can bypass the Visitors Center and queue up at the East Visitors Gate on East Executive Avenue, adjacent to *la maison blanche*. Don't line up on a Sunday or Monday when the White House is closed to all but the First Family and staff.

All U.S. citizens own a piece of the rock, er, house, but don't try claiming it as a tax deduction. And what a house it is, with priceless art and furnishings reflecting the tastes and contributions of its current and past residents. You can tour the grounds and main public floors, but keep in mind that most kids under 8 are bored stiff and/or can't see because of the crowd. If you visit in April or October, try to hook up with the spring or fall, garden and house tour, offered annually on *one* weekend. In the **Children's Garden,** look for the imprints of former presidents' children and grandchildren.

During your visit to Washington, pretend you're an insider and dial the special number for a recording of the President's daily schedule, ☎ 202-456-2343. A parting bit of trivia: When the White House flag is flying, the Prez is home. Maybe he'll invite you in for some barbecue and a guitar pickin'.

1600 Pennsylvania Ave. NW. ☎ *800-717-1450. Internet:* www.nps.gov/whho. *Metro: McPherson Square. Walk south on 15th St. to Pennsylvania Ave. and hang a right to the biggest house on the block. For the Visitors Center, 1450 Pennsylvania Ave., take Metro: Federal Triangle Station. Walk west 2½ blocks on Pennsylvania (toward White House). Open: Tues–Sat 10 a.m.–noon. Closed: Some days for official functions (call first!). Admission: Free.*

Chapter 17

More Cool Things to See and Do

*W*ashington has much more to offer you than bureaucratic red tape and marble memorials. If you've seen and done everything recommended in Chapter 16, keep reading. You can find plenty more to do and see while you're here. To locate the attractions you are interested in, see the map in this chapter.

Especially for Kids

Capital Children's Museum

Union Station

Learning is fun at this museum a few blocks from Union Station. The Capital Children's Museum's hands-on activities and interactive displays are a big hit with kids under 12. Most exhibits focus on world cultures, communication, and technology. Preschoolers can drive a bus and explore the underside of city streets while older siblings do the Mexican hat dance and make tortillas in the International Hall. Cartoon lovers create their own animations in the exhibition devoted to Bugs Bunny's creator, Chuck Jones. Pint-sized news-anchor wannabes can try out the latest bells and whistles of a working TV studio. The museum hosts special weekend activities, workshops, and performances. The opportunities for learning at this struggling private museum far outweigh the peeling paint. Plan on spending an hour or more here.

More Cool Things to See and Do

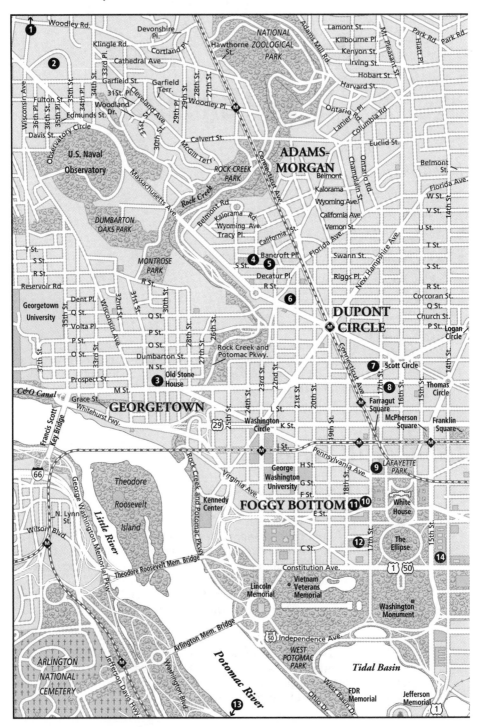

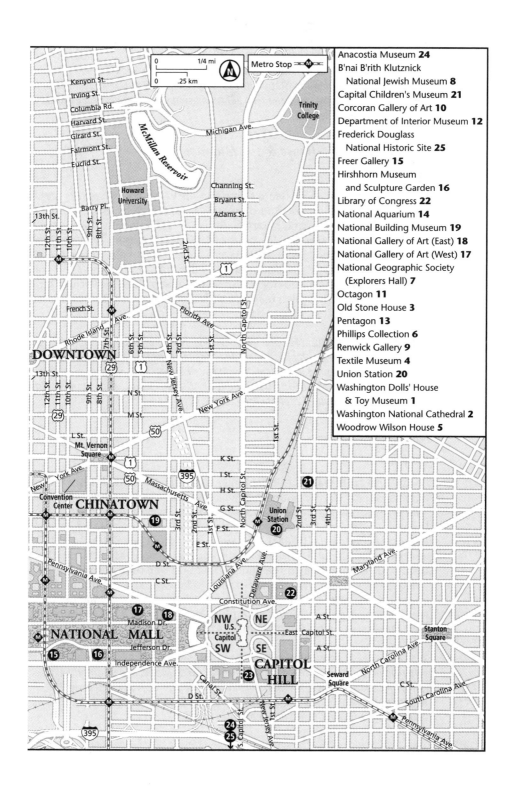

Anacostia Museum **24**
B'nai B'rith Klutznick
   National Jewish Museum **8**
Capital Children's Museum **21**
Corcoran Gallery of Art **10**
Department of Interior Museum **12**
Frederick Douglass
   National Historic Site **25**
Freer Gallery **15**
Hirshhorn Museum
   and Sculpture Garden **16**
Library of Congress **22**
National Aquarium **14**
National Building Museum **19**
National Gallery of Art (East) **18**
National Gallery of Art (West) **17**
National Geographic Society
   (Explorers Hall) **7**
Octagon **11**
Old Stone House **3**
Pentagon **13**
Phillips Collection **6**
Renwick Gallery **9**
Textile Museum **4**
Union Station **20**
Washington Dolls' House
   & Toy Museum **1**
Washington National Cathedral **2**
Woodrow Wilson House **5**

800 3rd St. NE, at H St. ☎ 202-675-4125. Internet: www.ccm.org. *Metro: Union Station. Hearty souls can hoof it the rest of the way. Take the escalator to the 3rd floor of the parking garage, walk through it and out the back. Right onto H St. and over the bridge (a bit of a climb); cross the street to the red brick museum. Or take a short taxi ride from Union Station (Mass. Ave. exit). Hours: Daily 10 a.m.–5 p.m. Closed: Jan 1, Thanksgiving, and Dec 25. Admission: $6 for adults and children 2 and older, free for kids under 2.*

Washington Dolls' House & Toy Museum

Uptown

Kids may forget all about Santa Claus and his workshop when they get a load of this museum. Located on a side street close to the Friendship Heights Metro station and Mazza Gallerie, the Washington Dolls' House and Toy Museum houses collections of dollhouses and antique toys that enthrall kids and those who are kids at heart. Serious collectors can find doll-related periodicals, dollhouses, and miniature accessories (new and consigned) in the second-floor shops. Youngsters can celebrate their birthdays in the Edwardian tearoom with advance reservations. Plan on spending 45 minutes or more here.

5236 44th St. NW. ☎ 202-244-0024. Metro: Friendship Heights (Jenifer St. exit). Left on Wisconsin ½ block to Jenifer, left on Jenifer 1 block to 44th, left at 44th and walk a ½ block. It may sound like a trek, but the walk takes no more than 5 minutes. (Remember: left, left, left.) Hours: Tues–Sat 10 a.m.–5 p.m., Sun noon–5 p.m. Admission: $4 for adults, $2 for children under 12.

National Aquarium

Downtown

Locals bring their tadpoles here long before they're ready for the heavy-duty museums. At the nation's oldest aquarium, youngsters can watch sharks, eels, and koi (Japanese carp) get along swimmingly. (It's lucky for the rest of the fish that a separate tank holds the piranhas.) Although this aquarium doesn't boast the latest in technological advances, 270 species of fish, amphibians and reptiles do reside here. Kids can dip their little starfish hands into the touch tank and get the rare pleasure of petting a horseshoe crab. (And it's nice to know that *some* piranhas are contained in tanks and not feeding on the federal payroll.) Incidentally, feeding time is 2 p.m. Don't let your kids get too close to the piranhas. A visit here sets you back a half-hour or more.

14th Street NW, between Constitution and Pennsylvania Aves., lower level of Department of Commerce building. ☎ 202-482-2825. Metro: Federal Triangle. Walk north on 12th St. 1 block. Left at Pennsylvania Ave., go 2 blocks and left at 14th St. to entrance. Open: Daily 9 a.m.–5 p.m. Closed: Dec 25. Admission: $3 adults, 75 cents children 2–10, free for kids 1 or under.

National Geographic Society's Explorers Hall

Downtown

At the National Geographic Society's headquarters, human evolution, global and space expeditions, and ancient civilizations take center stage. Kids 6 and older can get up close and personal with the hall's many interactive displays and videos. You can feel what orbital flight 23,000 miles above Earth is like in the Earth Station One amphitheater. Visitors can experience a tornado and other geophysical phenomena in Geographica. Visit the National Geographic Store to pick up nature books, photography collections, globes, maps, and back issues of *National Geographic* magazine. Plan on spending at least an hour.

17th and M Sts. NW. ☎ *202-857-7588. Internet:* www.nationalgeographic. com. *Metro: Farragut North (Connecticut Ave. & L St. exit). Walk east on L St. 1 block, left at 17th St. and continue 2 blocks. Hours: Mon–Sat and holidays 9 a.m.– 5 p.m., Sun 10 a.m.–5 p.m. Closed: Dec 25. Admission: Free.*

Especially for Teens

If you can drag them out of bed, steer your teens to the American History, Natural History, and Air and Space museums; the White House; the FBI tour; and the Bureau of Engraving and Printing. Your teenagers will, no doubt, visit other attractions that appeal to them (see Chapter 16) after they satisfy their familial obligations. Places with food, shopping, and other nose rings.

Mom and Dad: If your kids blaze new trails at home, unleashing them in Washington is okay. I do advocate the buddy system though, especially at night.

Georgetown

Teens have been making Georgetown their own since the days of pegged pants and poodle skirts. Shops, restaurants, and clubs (entry with valid ID) populate this historic neighborhood, whose main intersection is Wisconsin Avenue and M Street NW.

On summer weekends, free concerts take place behind the Foundry Mall (30th Street below M). **Washington Harbour,** with a park and more places where teenagers can stuff their faces and shopping bags, fronts the Potomac at 30th and K Streets. In the Georgetown Park Mall (Wisconsin Avenue and M Street), teens can browse for souvenirs — Fit to a Tee, Sunglass Hut, Record Town, and Waldenbooks — grab a snack at the Canal Walk Food Court, and commiserate with their peers. Teens can lick an ice cream cone from Ben & Jerry's (3135 M St.), Häagen-Dazs (3120 M St.), or Thomas Sweet (Wisconsin and P Streets); pick up a souvenir T-shirt (Fit to a Tee in Georgetown Park); have their palms read by Mrs. Natalie (1500 Wisconsin Ave. at Volta Place); or just hang out.

Georgetown is always hopping. Pick up a Visitors Guide and map at the Georgetown Partnership Information Center, 3242 M St. NW (next to Clyde's restaurant), at the concierge desk on the first level of George-town Park, or at the White House Visitors Center (1450 Pennsylvania Ave. NW) when you first arrive. (For more information on shopping, see Chapter 19; for restaurant information, check out Chapters 14 and 15; see Chapter 23 for the lowdown on Washington's clubs.)

Wisconsin Ave., from Potomac River north to R St., and M St., from 28th to 35th Sts. Metro: Foggy Bottom. Walk north on 23rd St. and cross Pennsylvania Ave.; board any bus traveling west over M St. to Georgetown. Get off at Wisconsin Ave.

Union Station

Young people are drawn to Union Station like iron filings to a magnet. Come here any afternoon or weekend if you don't believe me. Who'd have thought that a train station would become a glorified mall? But that's exactly what's happened since its restoration in the 1980s. Union Station has all the right stuff that young people crave: a nine-screen movie theater complex, more than 100 retail and food shops on three levels, and a lower-level food court with more than 20 vendors.

50 Massachusetts Ave. NE. ☎ 202-371-9441. Metro: Union Station. Ride the esca-lator up and you've arrived. Shops open: Mon–Sat 10 a.m.–9 p.m., Sun 10 a.m.–6 p.m. Restaurants open: varying hours. Admission: Free, but you'll be hard-pressed not to spend money during your visit.

Especially for History Buffs

Deciding what attractions fall into this category is a tough call, because history perfumes Washington's air. When you're done with the monu-ments, memorials, and federal buildings, I suggest investigating the following sites.

Old Stone House

Georgetown

In the heart of Georgetown and easy to pass given its diminutive size, the only pre-Revolutionary house still stands in the District. The Old Stone House dates back to 1765 and is furnished as it was when Georgetown was a thriving tobacco port. No formal tours here, but a charming and knowledgeable park ranger is available to answer questions. Most visitors are struck by the interior space, or lack thereof. (How did folks back then manage without three bathrooms and a computer room?) When you exit the small fieldstone house be sure to look out back at the lovely English-style garden, abloom from April to November. You're invited to bring lunch and join picnickers who brown-bag it on the lawn.

3051 M St., between 30th and 31st Sts. ☎ 202-426-6851. Internet: www.nps.gov. *Metro: Foggy Bottom. Walk north on 23rd St. to Washington Circle and west on*

Pennsylvania Ave. (Ask anyone you see if you're headed toward Georgetown). At 28th St., Pennsylvania merges with M St. Continue 2½ blocks to the house between 30th and 31st Sts. (Figure a 20-minute walk). Or walk north on 23rd St. to Pennsylvania Ave. and cross, and then board any bus traveling west over M St. to Georgetown. Open: noon–5 p.m. Wed–Sun. Closed: Mon–Tues and major holidays.

Woodrow Wilson House

North of Dupont Circle

After his term ended in 1921, Woodrow Wilson, America's 28th president and leader of the League of Nations, lived the last 3 years of his life in a Georgian Revival home. When Wilson was president, he didn't have to hand over the gifts he received while in office. Now many of those gifts, as well as Wilson's inaugural Bible, specs, and a shell casing from World War I are displayed throughout the house. According to the s-m-a-r-t docents, the residence/museum looks very much as it did when Wilson lived in it. Touring the house properly takes about an hour.

(And, because I'm in a historical kind of mood, for $1: What was Mrs. Woodrow Wilson's first name? . . . Huh? . . . Sure? . . . Is that your final answer? Answer: Edith.)

2340 S St. NW. ☎ 202-387-4062. Internet: www.woodrowwilsonhouse.org. *Metro: Dupont Circle (Q St. exit). Walk north about 5 blocks on Massachusetts Ave. NW (also known as Embassy Row), right at 24th St., go half a block to S St. and turn right. (Note: It's an uphill climb.) Open: Tues–Sun 10 a.m.–4 p.m. Guided tours last about 1 hour. Admission: $5 adults, $4 seniors, $2.50 students, free kids under 7.*

Especially for Art Lovers

Private art galleries paint many D.C. neighborhoods, but the majority are situated in Georgetown and along 7th Street NW. For the **Georgetown galleries,** take Metro to Foggy Bottom, walk north to Pennsylvania Avenue and left. Continue onto M Street. Most are on M Street, along Wisconsin Avenue (between M and R Streets) and on the side streets. To reach the **7th Street galleries** (between D and G Streets), take Metro to the Archives-Navy Memorial station and walk north on 7th Street.

Corcoran Gallery

Downtown

You can find Washington's first private art museum just a block away from the White House. The art, in rotating exhibits, spans the 18th through 20th centuries and features the works of Flemish and Dutch masters, several Impressionists, and the Hudson River School (Cassatt, Homer, and Whistler, to drop a few names). The museum is small in size, but grand in stature. The Corcoran has a first-floor café, an auditorium with top-flight entertainment many evenings (admission), and a noteworthy museum shop. Seeing the collection takes about an hour.

500 17th St. NW, between D and E Sts. ☎ *202-639-1700. Internet:* www.corcoran. org. *Metro: Farragut West. Walk east on I St. one block, right at 17th and continue 5 blocks. Hours: 10 a.m.–5 p.m. Fri–Mon and Wed; 10 a.m.–9 p.m. Thursday. Closed: Tuesday, Dec 25, and Jan 1. Free tours are conducted at noon daily and 7:30 p.m. on Thursday.*

Freer Gallery of Art

The Mall

Behind the Freer's beautiful Renaissance-style façade, you'll find the world's largest collection of Whistlers (that's James McNeill Whistler). If you've never seen *Harmony in Blue and Gold: The Peacock Room,* I encourage you to do so. In fact, try to get in on one of the docent-led tours. On the tour, you can discover the fascinating history behind Whistler's stunning dining room, created for industrialist Charles Lang Freer, who was Whistler's chief patron. The Freer's collection of Asian art spans 6,000 years. At any given time, less than 10 percent of the museum's collection is on view. Budget at least a half-hour for the museum.

Jefferson Dr. and 12th St. SW, south side of the Mall. ☎ *202-357-2104. Internet:* www.asia.si.edu. *Metro: Smithsonian. Walk north on 12th St. 1 block (toward the Mall), right at Jefferson Dr. Hours: Daily 10:00 a.m.–5:30 p.m. Closed: Dec 25. Admission: Free.*

Hirshhorn Museum and Sculpture Garden

The Mall

Lovers of 20th-century paintings, drawings, and sculptures fall in love all over again whenever they visit the Hirshhorn. All the top guns are here, from Auguste Rodin and Matisse to Larry Rivers and Ellsworth Kelly. Decompress in the Sculpture Garden next to works by Calder, Moore, and other mallet-and-chisel masters. You can easily spend an hour or more here.

Independence Ave. at 7th St. SW, south side of the Mall. ☎ *202-357-2700. Internet:* www.si.edu/hirshhorn. *Metro: L'Enfant Plaza (Smithsonian exit). Walk north on 7th St. 3 blocks to Independence Ave. Hours: Daily 10:00 a.m.–5:30 p.m. The Sculpture Garden is open from dawn to dusk.*

National Gallery of Art and Sculpture Garden

The Mall

Topping the list of Washington's world-renowned art museums is this masterpiece. The National Gallery is actually composed of two separate buildings (East Building and West Building) connected by an underground moving walkway.

The **West Building** is a treasure chest of 12th- to 20th-century paintings and sculpture. Special exhibitions augment the sizable permanent collection, only a portion of which is on view at any one time. In the Micro Gallery, visitors (aided by computer touch screens) can zoom in on details of their favorite works. The gift shop sells unframed prints, a wide selection of gorgeous art books, stationery, and gifts. John Russell Pope's architecture is glorious.

I. M. Pei designed the trapezoid-shaped **East Building.** Even if you're not an art lover, you have to admit the museum design is ingenious and awesome. An immense Calder mobile dominates the soaring ground-level central court. The museum brims with a wealth of 20th-century master-works. Come here when your soul seeks nourishment — the gallery can elevate your mood faster than Prozac. Passes are usually required for special exhibitions. Pick up a floor plan and inquire about tours and special events at the information desk.

Families take note: Most kids prefer the East Building and Sculpture Garden, which opened to great and well-deserved fanfare in 1999.

Do stop at the Sculpture Garden before or after your visit to the National Gallery. You'll need at least an hour, and probably more, to see the museum's highlights.

North side of the Mall, between 3rd and 7th Sts., NW (Entrances at 6th St. & Constitution Ave. or Madison Dr.). ☎ 202-737-4215. Internet: www.nga.gov. _Metro: Archives-Navy Memorial. Walk south 1 block on 7th St., cross Constitution Ave., and left 1 block. Open: Mon–Sat 10 a.m.–5 p.m.; Sun 11 a.m.–6 p.m. Closed: Jan 1 and Dec 25. Admission: Free._

Phillips Collection

Dupont Circle

In the former home of collector and benefactor Duncan Phillips, you'll find French Impressionist, Postimpressionist, and contemporary master-pieces. Art connoisseurs rank the Phillips among the world's top private collections for its breadth and depth. (Perhaps the Renoirs, Matisses, Klees, and Picassos have something to do with it.) Concerts and educa-tional activities are ongoing and involve all ages.

1600 21st St. NW, at Q St. ☎ 202-387-0961. Internet: www.phillipscollection. org. _Metro: Dupont Circle (Q St. exit). Walk west on Q St. 1 block. Hours: Tues–Wed and Fri–Sat 10 a.m.–5 p.m.; Thurs 10:00 a.m.–8:30 p.m.; Sun noon–5 p.m. Closed: Mon. Admission: $7.50 adults (weekends), contributions sought Tues–Fri; always free 18 and under._

The Renwick Gallery

Downtown

Across from the White House, this striking 19th-century landmark building is filled with contemporary crafts and decorative arts. The Renwick

Gallery is done in the French Second Empire style. Chief among the gallery's holdings are the Ghost Clock, carved from a solid piece of mahogany, and Larry Fuente's colorful *Game Fish,* with its glittering scales of game pieces and toys.

Northeast corner of 17th St. and Pennsylvania Ave. NW. ☎ *202-357-2700. Internet:* www.nmaa.si.edu. *Metro: Farragut West. Walk east 1 block on I St, right at 17th St.; continue 2 blocks to Pennsylvania Ave. Hours: Daily 10:00 a.m.–5:30 p.m. Admission: Free.*

The Textile Museum

Dupont Circle

The textile arts are magnificently represented at this museum. The collection began with George Hewitt Myers's Chinese silks, tapestries, and hand-woven Oriental rugs. Some of the pieces are 3,000 years old. The gift shop is noteworthy too, featuring silk scarves and ties, Kilim pillows, and Tibetan rug squares.

2320 S St. NW, off Embassy Row. ☎ *202-667-0441. Internet:* www.textilemuseum.org. *Metro: Dupont Circle. Walk north about 5 blocks on Massachusetts Ave. to right at S St. Open: Mon–Sat 10 a.m.–5 p.m., Sun 1 p.m.–5 p.m. A suggested donation of $5 is requested. (It's worth it.)*

Seeing the City's Architectural Highlights

Washington's striking and diverse architecture always leaves me awestruck — the Capitol, the White House, the Smithsonian "Castle," the Freer Gallery, and the National Gallery's East and West buildings are just a few of the city's architectural masterpieces. (Of course, Washington has its share of losers, such as the Rayburn Office Building and the Air and Space Museum, but I don't want to dwell on negatives.) Here are some more of Washington's architectural winners

Library of Congress

Capitol Hill

Borrowing books isn't allowed at this library (the nation's and *world's* largest), but if you're over high-school age, you can do research here in the **Jefferson Building.** And you can admire the soaring arches, the mosaic ceiling, and the marble staircase in the Great Hall. Check out the Gutenberg Bible and Giant (I'm talking really huge) Bible of Mainz on the main floor, along with exhibits of posters, music, and photographs. You can take a free hour-long guided tour (given three times a day) that starts inside the Library of Congress Visitors Center on the Jefferson's sidewalk level; the tour is well worth the time.

Next door in the **Madison Building** is the **Copyright Office.** Outside the Copyright Office on the fourth floor, Star Wars masks and pop icons (Bert and Ernie, Barbie and What's His Name, and more) are on display. The building is open to the public Monday through Friday from 8:30 a.m. to 9:00 p.m. and Saturday 8:30 a.m. to 6:00 p.m. However, if you wish to copyright your latest invention, you need to show up during business hours, Monday through Friday, 8:30 a.m. to 5:00 p.m.

1st St. SE, at Independence Ave. ☎ *202-707-8000. Internet:* www.lcweb.loc. gov. *Metro: Capitol South. Walk north on 1st St. 2 blocks, cross Independence Ave. to Jefferson Building. Open: Mon–Sat 10 a.m–5 p.m. (exhibits). Closed: Sunday and federal holidays. Admission: Free.*

National Building Museum

Downtown

Formerly the Pension Building, The National Building Museum is now dedicated to architecture and building history. Stop by to take in the museum's Renaissance-style palazzo design and its majestic Great Hall, which sports awesome 75-foot-high columns. *Washington: Symbol and City,* is a permanent exhibition that focuses on the construction of Washington, D.C. Temporary exhibits change two or three times a year.

Trivia buffs: The TV special, *Christmas in Washington,* is filmed at the Building Museum, which has also been the site of numerous inaugural balls and the prestigious Smithsonian's Craft Show. All in all, plan to spend at least a half-hour here.

North side of Judiciary Square at 401 F. St., NW, between 4th and 5th Sts. ☎ *202-272-2448. Internet:* www.nbm.org. *Metro: Judiciary Square. Ride the escalator up and you've arrived. Hours: Mon–Sat 10 a.m.–4 p.m.; Sun 1–4 p.m. Admission: Free.*

The Octagon

Downtown

The oldest museum of architecture in the United States is maintained by the American Architecture Foundation and serves as the American Institute of Architects (AIA) headquarters. This Federal-style town house was designed for wealthy Virginia planter John Tayloe and his 15 children by architect William Thornton; Thornton also designed the U.S. Capitol. If you take the half-hour guided tour you'll discover the roles that several U.S. presidents played in the home's history. After you visit the Octagon Museum, stop at the gallery behind the house, maintained by the AIA. The changing exhibits are open 8:30 a.m. to 5:00 p.m. daily; admission is free.

1799 New York Ave. NW, between 17th and 18th Sts., just west of the White House. ☎ *202-638-3105. Internet:* www.aafpages.org. *Metro: Farragut West (Street exit). Walk west 1 block on I to 18th St., south 5 blocks to the corner of New York Ave. Open: Tues–Sun 10 a.m.–4 p.m. Admission: $3.*

The Pentagon

Arlington, Virginia

One of the most recognizable structures in the world, the Pentagon is not only five-sided, but is also the planet's largest office building (3.7 million square feet). More than 22,000 employees navigate the 17.5 miles of corridors at the headquarters for the Department of Defense — that's the army, navy, air force and Joint Chiefs of Staff. If you're a military buff, this is an obvious stop, but if you aren't or if you're traveling with young children, the Pentagon doesn't rate as a must-see. Nevertheless, it is extremely popular and the tours of the building are usually full by 10 a.m., so get here by 8:45 a.m. in the summer. The 90-minute guided tours showcase the service branches' art collections and Medal of Honor recipients, but you can forget about seeing the War Room or anything else of strategic importance. The current décor is military drab and somewhat depressing. The good news, however, is that thanks to a deep-pocketed Uncle Sam, the building is getting a 14-year, $1.1 *billion* face-lift (and you thought Hollywood spent a lot of money on cosmetic surgery!). So, by 2007, the Pentagon will be in shipshape condition, and if they spruce up the tour, it will definitely be worth a look.

Arlington, Virginia, across the 14th St. Bridge. ☎ *703-695-1776. Internet:* www.defenselink.mil./pubs/pentagon. *Metro: Pentagon. Enter at the tour window, next to the entrance to the station. Open: Mon–Fri 9 a.m.–3 p.m. Guided tours leave every hour on the hour. Closed: Federal holidays. Visitors 16 and older must show a photo ID. Groups of 10 or more must reserve 2 weeks ahead. Admission: Free.*

Union Station

Capitol Hill

Amtrak passengers are welcomed by Daniel Burnham's exceptionally attractive beaux-arts neoclassical design known as Union Station. Modeled after the Diocletian Baths and the Arch of Constantine in Rome, the station is marked by 50-foot columns, stenciled skylights, and coffered ceilings brushed with 22-karat gold leaf. I can still remember when the plaster fell in chunks and boards crisscrossed the wet marble flooring before a huge restoration project in the 1980s. Since the grand reopening and Union Station's rise to major attraction status, I can't help wondering what Burnham would think about the hordes who come here to eat, shop, and see a movie.

50 Massachusetts Ave. NE. ☎ *202-371-9441. Internet:* www.unionstationdc.com. *Metro: Union Station. Take the escalator up and you've arrived. Shops open:*

Mon–Sat 10 a.m.–9 p.m.; Sun 10 a.m.– 6 p.m. Restaurants open: varying hours. Admission: Free, but you'll be hard-pressed not to spend money during your visit.

Washington National Cathedral

Uptown

Officially the Cathedral Church of St. Peter and St. Paul, this imposing structure is the sixth largest in the world and, along with the Capitol and the Washington Monument, it dominates the city's skyline. The nave measures 518 feet, and the vaulted ceiling is 102 feet high. Begun in 1907, the cathedral wasn't completed until 1990 thanks to bureaucratic red tape and blown budgets. Located a mile north of Georgetown, this Episcopal English-Gothic cathedral serves as the national house of worship. Especially noteworthy here are the **Children's Chapel,** furnished with a pint-sized pipe organ, and the medieval inspired **Bishop's Garden.** The free 45-minute tour runs every 15 minutes Monday through Saturday, 10:00 a.m. to 3:15 p.m. and Sunday 12:30 p.m. to 2:45 p.m. You can spend anywhere from a half-hour to 2 hours here.

Massachusetts and Wisconsin Aves. (You can't miss it!) ☎ 202-537-6207. Metro: Dupont Circle. Take N bus up Massachusetts Ave. NW. Open: Mon–Sat 10:00 a.m.– 4:30 p.m.; times vary on Sunday according to the schedule of services, call ahead. Admission: Free.

Exploring Museums of Many Cultures

When you consider how many cultures influenced, shaped, and spiced the nation's character, you won't be surprised to find out that Washington has many ethnic attractions. A visit to one or more of these round out any capital experience.

Anacostia Museum

Anacostia

With a special focus on the Washington, D.C. area, the Anacostia Museum, promotes public understanding and knowledge of the African American experience. The Smithsonian manages a large permanent collection of historic documents, art, and sheet music at this museum named after Washington's lesser-known river. Special exhibitions, talks, workshops, and educational programs are available. Visitors can take a short guided walk along the George Washington Carver nature trail on the museum grounds with advance reservations. (I don't recommend strolling this neighborhood alone.) Allow plenty of travel time as this museum is a bit off the beaten path. Budget a half-hour to an hour for this attraction.

1901 Fort Place SE, off Martin Luther King Jr. Ave. ☎ 202-287-3382. Internet: www.si.edu/anacostia. Metro: Anacostia. Take a W1 or W2 bus to the museum's door. Hours: Daily: 10 a.m.–5 p.m. Admission: Free.

B'nai B'rith Klutznick National Jewish Museum

Downtown

More than 20 centuries of Jewish history and culture are housed here. The permanent collection is composed of religious books, Torahs, Judaic art, and ceremonial objects. Artifacts and memorabilia reflect aspects of immigration, the Holocaust, and other facets of the Jewish experience. The museum shop sells books, ceremonial items, and imported crafts. Educational events are ongoing.

1640 Rhode Island Ave. NW ☎ *202-857-6583. Internet:* http://bnaibrith. org/museum/ . *Metro: Farragut North. Walk north 1.5 blocks on Connecticut Ave., right at Rhode Island Ave. 2 blocks. Hours: Sun–Fri 10 a.m.–5 p.m. Closed: All federal and Jewish holidays. Admission: Free.*

Department of Interior Museum

Downtown

Get one thing straight, this museum doesn't represent a government decorating firm. You can see many examples of Interior's business (the National Park Service, Geological Survey, and Bureau of Indian Affairs) here. My personal recommendation is for the exhibits relating to Native American life, featuring pottery, artifacts, crafts, and beadwork. A Native American docent is usually on hand. Don't be shy with your questions. Check out the Indian Craft Shop, in Room 1023, if you're in the mood for a little gift or souvenir shopping.

Adult visitors need to show a photo ID, such as a driver's license to enter.

1849 C St. NW, near DAR Constitution Hall. ☎ *202-208-4743. Internet:* www.doi. gov. *Metro: Farragut West. Walk south 5 blocks on 18th St., right at C St. and continue 1 short block. Hours: Mon–Fri 8 a.m.–4 p.m. Admission: Free.*

Frederick Douglass National Historic Site

Anacostia

This 20-room Victorian house on the Anacostia River was home to the abolitionist and orator Frederick Douglass. The site features original furnishings and Douglass memorabilia in commemoration of his contributions. I recommend seeing the short film in the visitors center for an overview of Douglass' life. The Anacostia River, Washington Navy Yard, U.S. Capitol, and Washington Monument are visible from the hill in front of the house. Watch for special programs in February, which is Black History Month. Plan to spend an hour here.

1411 W St. SE. ☎ *800-365-2267. Internet:* www.nps.gov. *Metro: Anacostia. Take B-2/Mt. Rainier bus (8 blocks), which stops at the door. Or take the Tourmobile tour here. Open: Mid-Oct–mid-April 9 a.m.–4 p.m.; mid-April–mid-Oct 9 a.m.–5 p.m. Admission: $3 ages 7–61, $1.50 62 and over, free kids 6 and under.*

Chapter 18

And on Your Left, the White House: Seeing Washington, D.C. by Guided Tour

* *

In This Chapter

▶ Seeing the city by guided tour

▶ Taking a special-interest tour

* *

*T*ravelers with limited time and/or limited mobility can benefit from taking a general orientation tour. So can visitors who like to check out the forest before inspecting the trees. Guided tours make sense, as well, for those with kids in tow, the elderly, and travelers with special interests. In Washington, you can tour historic, cultural, and even scandal-ridden sites. And you can do it by bus, bike, or boat and on foot — for an hour, after dark, or a day or more. The Guild of Professional Tour Guides (☎ 202-298-1474), keeps the city's tour companies and guides in line, so you can count on interesting, informative, and accurate information along the way.

Seeing the City on General Orientation Tours

Tourmobile (☎ 202-554-5100; Internet: www.tourmobile.com), takes the prize as the best general tour operator in the city. The area's largest sightseeing organization is run by the National Park Service and operates year-round. Tourmobile is the only touring company licensed to stop at several sites on the Mall.

Tourmobile Route

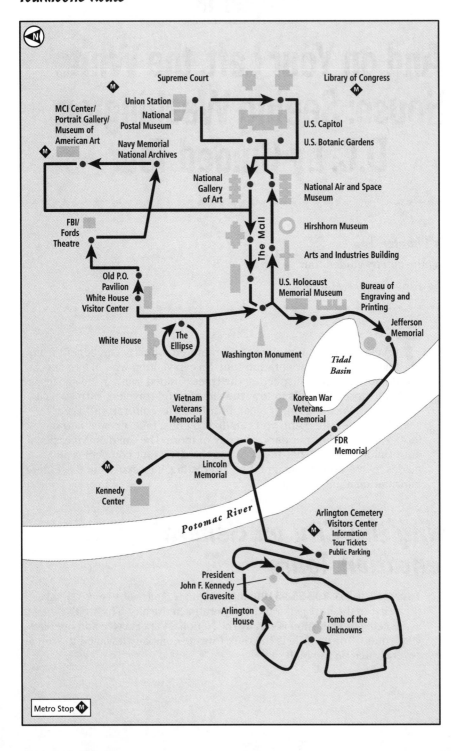

The company's **Heritage Tour** makes about two dozen tram stops on or near the Mall and Pennsylvania Avenue, and then heads off to Arlington Cemetery, for another three stops. You can get off and on the trams as often as you like. Some visitors remain on board for an entire figure-eight loop, and then get off on the second go-round. Using Tourmobile is an excellent way to familiarize yourself with the major tourist areas. The tour costs $16 for adults, $7 for kids 3 to 11, and is free for kids 2 and under. You can purchase tickets from the driver or at ticket booths at select boarding points along the tram route. (See the "Tourmobile" map in this chapter to locate stops that have ticket booths, or surf over to www.tourmobile.com.) You can order tickets in advance from Ticketmaster (☎ 800-551-SEAT); a small surcharge applies. Be sure to ask about other tours, some of which require advance reservations.

If you find the prospect of tackling both D.C. and Arlington in the space of a day too taxing, Tourmobile offers a separate **Arlington Cemetery Tour.** The cost is $4.75 for adults, $2.25 kids 3 to 11, and free for children 2 and under. You can purchase tickets at the Arlington Cemetery Visitors Center and via Ticketmaster. The company also offers a few site-specific tours, so check its Web site or call to find out what's being offered when you're in town.

Old Town Trolley Tour (☎ 301-985-3021 or 202-832-9800; Internet: www.historictours.com) has an advantage over Tourmobile in that it offers pick-up and drop-off service at several hotels. This tour company also makes stops at places farther away, such as Georgetown and near the National Zoo. For a full list of boarding stops, see the company's Web site or call. Like Tourmobile, you can get on and off the trolley tour whenever the spirit moves you. However, the Trolley does not stop on the Mall (no matter what its Web site says) and operates March through December only. It takes about 2¼ hours for a Trolley to complete one loop. Departures are from Union Station, 50 Massachusetts Ave. NE (Metro: Union Station), beginning at 9 a.m. Prices are $24 adults, $12 ages 4 to 12, free kids 3 and under.

The company also offers a 2½-hour **Monuments by Moonlight** tour that offers you a chance to see D.C.'s memorials and monuments illuminated in all their nighttime glory. And you can discover neat things, such as which president's ghost haunts Congress (Which ones don't?). The tour departs nightly from Union Station, 50 Massachusetts Ave. NE (Metro: Union Station), and costs $25 per adult, $13 per child. The times vary according to season, so call ahead.

Gray Line Sightseeing Tours (☎ 202-289-1995; Internet: www.graylinedc.com) offers an extensive array of city tours and trips to the Maryland and Virginia boonies by motor coach, usually from the Gray Line terminal in Union Station (Metro: Union Station). Always call ahead to confirm departure times and points because they are subject to change. Here's a sampling of the company's touring options:

✓ **L'il Red Trolley Tours** are similar to Tourmobile and Old Town Trolley and make a 2-hour continuous loop around Washington, D.C. Some stops include several hotels, the National Zoo, Arlington Cemetery, and Georgetown. Riders can hop on and off as they choose. The tour costs $25 for adults and kids 12 and older, $12 for kids ages 3 to 11.

✓ **The Public Buildings Tour** is a 9-hour trek through some of the city's most famous buildings, including the White House (when open), the Capitol, the Supreme Court, the American History Museum and the National Archives. The tour operates Monday through Saturday and costs $36 for adults and kids 12 and older, $18 for kids ages 3 to 11.

✓ **The Washington After Dark Tour** offers proof that the city only looks better when the sun sets. You'll be taken past a number of illuminated Washington landmarks and will actually visit the Jefferson, Lincoln, Vietnam, Korean, and FDR Memorials and the Kennedy Center. The tour costs $25 for adults and kids 12 and older, $12 for kids ages 3 to 11.

✓ A 9-hour **Combination Tour** combines a sightseeing tour of Washington, D.C. and Arlington National Cemetery with a visit to George Washington's home at Mount Vernon and nearby Old Town Alexandria. The tour runs daily and costs $44 for adults and kids 12 and older, $22 for kids ages 3 to 11. Lunch, alas, isn't included although the tour does allot some time for you to chow down at a food court.

Gray Line also offers multilingual and black heritage tours; tours to Monticello; and overnight packages to Williamsburg, Virginia.

DC Ducks (☎ **202-966-DUCK;** Internet: www.historictours.com) can best be described as a hybrid tour. Utilizing amphibious vehicles that transported troops and supplies during World War II, the Duck ferries up to 28 visitors to several downtown sights before plunging into the Virginia side of the Potomac for a half-hour swim. Then the Duck waddles ashore near Reagan National Airport for the return trip on asphalt. The 90-minute keels-on-wheels tour departs April through October from Union Station, 50 Massachusetts Ave. NE (Metro: Union Station), weekdays on the hour, 10 a.m. to 4 p.m. (every half-hour on weekends and as demand warrants). The narrated 90-minute ride is $24 for adults, $12 for children 4 to 12, free kids 3 and under. You may not hear as much history as on some of the other tours, but the experience will quack you up.

Pounding the Pavement with Walking Tours

If your feet aren't too tired, consider a walking tour to discover historic sights and architectural gems. When you shop around for a walking tour, ask about group size. Here's a case where smaller is better.

Architectural and historical tours

Anthony S. Pitch serves as your tour guide in Adams-Morgan and Georgetown on alternate Sundays. Pitch, a former Brit with abundant charm and an encyclopedic memory, doles out an impressive amount of historical and architectural information. He charges $10 per person for his 2-hour walking tours. If it's raining, no tour. C-SPAN filmed one of his tours, which takes in the homes of U.S. presidents before and after they occupied the White House. Pitch's "Capitol Hill to the White House" tour is based on his book, *The Burning of Washington* (referring to the British invasion of 1814). He'll craft a tour for your group (of 3 to 30) for a flat rate of $200. For information call, ☎ **301-294-9514** or visit www.dcsightseeing.com. Reservations are suggested.

Scandal tours

Gross National Product (GNP), a local comedy troupe, leaves tourists rolling in the aisles on its narrated **Scandal Tours.** These bus tours are guaranteed to tickle your funny bone. Tours depart Saturdays (usually April to September, when GNP is not performing elsewhere) at 1 p.m. from the Old Post Office Pavilion at 11th St. and Pennsylvania Ave. NW. You'll visit more than 100 scandalous sites, including the White House, Tidal Basin, U.S. Capitol, and some infamous hotels. You pay $30 for the tour, but the laughs are priceless. Call ☎ **202-783-7212** for more information.

Riding the Waves on River Tours

Hit the deck and see the capital city's prettiest face from the Potomac. For a 50-minute narrated river cruise, take **Capitol River Cruises'** *Nightingale II,* a 150-year-old steel riverboat from Georgetown's Washington Harbour dock (end of 31st Street). The cruise runs hourly from noon to 8 p.m. (or sometimes later), April through October. The cost is $10 for adults, $5 for kids 3 to 12. Bring your own lunch or dinner; the boat has a snack bar. Call ☎ **800-405-5511** or check out the Web site www.capitolrivercruises.com for details.

Cruising on the C&O Canal

Board a mule-drawn canal boat for a trip along the historic C&O Canal. The *Georgetown* (☎ 202-653-5844) is berthed in (where else?) Georgetown, at the foot of Thomas Jefferson Street (below M Street). From April through October, the mules depart several times on Wednesday through Sunday; more frequent departures are available from mid-June to mid-September. Call to find out exact schedules. The boat plies the canal for a delightful hour while Park Service rangers narrate. Tickets are $7.50 for adults, $6 seniors 62 and older, $4 kids 2 to 12, and free 2 years and under.

Wheeling around D.C.

Several guided tours on 21-speed hybrid Trek bicycles are available through **Bike the Sites** (☎ 202-966-8662; Internet: www.bikethesites. com). The 10-mile Capital Sites Ride begins and ends at the Freer Gallery of Art on the Mall (Metro: Smithsonian). The tour passes about two dozen sights, and the guide stops frequently so that bikers can consume some history and humor with their granola bars. Most of the terrain is flat on paved and gravel trails. The tour costs $35 and includes a bike, helmet, snack, and water bottle. These bicycle tours are popular with families; kids must be at least 9 years old to participate, adults must accompany those under 14. The company will create a customized tour for you, so give them a call if that's something you would be interested in.

Chapter 19

A Shopper's Guide to Washington, D.C.

- -

In This Chapter

▶ Getting a feel for the shopping scene

▶ Browsing the big names in D.C. shopping

▶ Visiting the outdoor markets

▶ Exploring the great shopping neighborhoods and their stores

▶ Finding shops for specific needs

- -

1 know you came to Washington to visit monuments and memorials, to gaze at the *Spirit of St. Louis,* and to scrutinize government in action. But that doesn't mean shopping should be relegated to the bottom of your list. D.C. may not be a shopping mecca like New York or Paris, but the city has plenty of places to palm your plastic and find good deals (see the map in this chapter). Washington doesn't feature many department stores, with the exception of Lord & Taylor, Neiman-Marcus (also known as Needless Mark-Up), and Hecht's, but that doesn't stop the locals from contributing their two cents worth (or more) to the latest consumer spending figures or traveling to big-name department stores in the 'burbs. Collect your coins and shopping bag as I take you on a Mall-to-mall shopping tour of the nation's capital.

Surveying the Shopping Scene

You won't find clothing, furniture, or fashion made here. Washington focuses more on making laws, headlines, red tape, scandals, and plenty of bureaucracy. The D.C. stores are more than adequate for tourists in search of a souvenir or everyday stuff (ties, pantyhose, ho-hum clothing), but you don't see much that's distinctive, except for items in the museum and specialty shops noted later in this chapter.

Shopping in Washington, D.C.

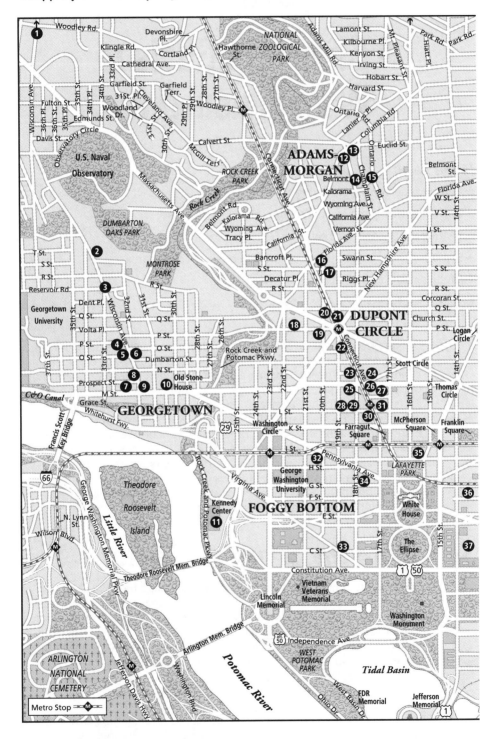

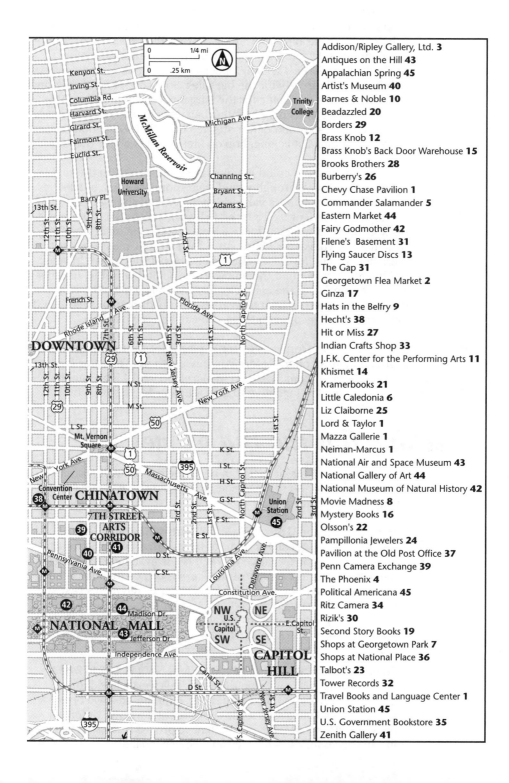

Addison/Ripley Gallery, Ltd. **3**
Antiques on the Hill **43**
Appalachian Spring **45**
Artist's Museum **40**
Barnes & Noble **10**
Beadazzled **20**
Borders **29**
Brass Knob **12**
Brass Knob's Back Door Warehouse **15**
Brooks Brothers **28**
Burberry's **26**
Chevy Chase Pavilion **1**
Commander Salamander **5**
Eastern Market **44**
Fairy Godmother **42**
Filene's Basement **31**
Flying Saucer Discs **13**
The Gap **31**
Georgetown Flea Market **2**
Ginza **17**
Hats in the Belfry **9**
Hecht's **38**
Hit or Miss **27**
Indian Crafts Shop **33**
J.F.K. Center for the Performing Arts **11**
Khismet **14**
Kramerbooks **21**
Little Caledonia **6**
Liz Claiborne **25**
Lord & Taylor **1**
Mazza Gallerie **1**
Neiman-Marcus **1**
National Air and Space Museum **43**
National Gallery of Art **44**
National Museum of Natural History **42**
Movie Madness **8**
Mystery Books **16**
Olsson's **22**
Pampillonia Jewelers **24**
Pavilion at the Old Post Office **37**
Penn Camera Exchange **39**
The Phoenix **4**
Political Americana **45**
Ritz Camera **34**
Rizik's **30**
Second Story Books **19**
Shops at Georgetown Park **7**
Shops at National Place **36**
Talbot's **23**
Tower Records **32**
Travel Books and Language Center **1**
Union Station **45**
U.S. Government Bookstore **35**
Zenith Gallery **41**

Washington being a government town, the stores have 3- and 4-day (extended weekend) sales around all federal holidays. If it's not a holiday, the stores invent one. I'm waiting for the "Kids are Back in School, Let's Celebrate" sale, and the "Bored with Winter and Waiting for Spring" sale. For what it's worth, "special" merchandise (read: junk) is often brought in expressly for the big sales. Still, shoppers jam parking lots to spend hours searching for the bargain of the millennium. (Me, I'd rather go to the movies.) The suburban department stores are more plentiful, larger in size, and better stocked than their D.C. counterparts. So, if your shopping list is long, hop on Metro and head for the hills.

If only the store owners could get together and operate on the same schedule — this breakthrough would save shoppers some headaches. As it stands, business hours vary widely by type of shop and location. Most shops open at 9 or 9:30 a.m. and close at 5:30 or 6 p.m. (Some stores stay open later one or more evenings.) Keep in mind that D.C. is not a 24-hour town like New York. After the sun sets, most Washington workers flee the city for their suburban homes; if they're not burning the midnight oil, you'll find them unwinding behind picket fences miles away. The exception to the early-closing rule can be found in heavily trafficked areas, such as Georgetown, especially during the spring and summer seasons. I recommend that you call before you shop.

And, of course, don't forget to factor in your contribution to the local government's coffers before you buy anything. The sales tax is 6 percent in Washington, 5 percent in Maryland, and 4.5 percent in Virginia — not a lot of incentive to cross the border to save a buck.

Checking Out the Big Names

Washington sports a major deficit in big-name department stores — most of them fled to the suburbs ages ago — but you can still find the following famous names in town:

- ✔ **Hecht's,** 12th and G Sts. NW. (☎ **202-628-6661;** Metro: Metro Center; ride the escalator up into the store). A mix of clothing styles — from conservative to trendy — is available at this department store. Hecht's strongest retail areas can be found in their cosmetics, housewares, furnishings, lingerie, and men's casual wear departments. For pantyhose, ties, or a quick tube of lipstick, Hecht's is a good place to shop. Actually, it's the *only* downtown place to shop if you seek the breadth offered by a department store.

- ✔ **Filene's Basement,** 1133 Connecticut Ave. NW. (☎ **202-872-8430;** Metro: Farragut North at the L St. exit; walk west a few doors to Connecticut Ave., and then turn right). I purchased a $49 blazer at a Boston-based Filene's a decade ago, and I still wear it. Unfortunately, my visits to the D.C. location have proved fruitless. The clothing and accessories — for men and women, no kidswear — run the gamut from quality to schlock. Prepare to dig through piles of merchandise to find big savings (sort of like kissing a lot of toads to find a prince). A second location of Filene's is in the Mazza Gallerie at 5300 Wisconsin Ave. NW (☎ **202-966-0208;** Metro: Friendship Heights).

✔ **Lord & Taylor,** 5225 Western Ave. NW. (☎ **202-362-9600;** Metro: Friendship Heights; walk west 1 block on Western Ave. to the big white building at the corner of Jenifer St.). This branch of the New York chain offers substantial women's wear, children's clothing, and accessories departments. Many people come here to shop for their kids and grandkids. I always seem to find at least one department of Lord & Taylor that is having a sale. During these sales, you can find plenty of quality merchandise with terrific markdowns.

✔ **Neiman-Marcus,** Mazza Gallerie, 5300 Wisconsin Ave. NW. (☎ **202-966-9700;** Metro: Friendship Heights; walk south on Wisconsin Ave. a block or so). Weekdays you can shoot a cannon off in Neiman's with no casualties. I don't get it. How does this place stay in business? The merchandise is well-made; well-displayed; and, well, expensive. I left quickly after I selected a tie for my Dad and found out it cost $75. (I love my father, but one spaghetti stain and. . . .) Fortunately, it's free to window-shop. And the sales clerks keep an ample supply of smelling salts handy for the shoppers who swoon from the high prices. Shopping for birthday gifts is fun here (as long as it's someone else's birthday). Browse the china and crystal departments; the selections are remarkable. You could lose your fingers reaching for a discounted item during the store's semi-annual sales. Don't come here for recliners, polyester housedresses, or $2 gadgets. (Neiman's and Filene's in the same mall? From the sublime to the ridiculous, as they say.)

To Market, to Market: Flea Markets and Crafts Shopping

Washington, D.C. may be America's First City, but it's not a capital spot for flea and crafts markets. If open-air markets and early morning haggling are your idea of fun, you need to head to Maryland or Virginia. That said, a few places in town do merit a visit.

✔ At **Eastern Market,** 7th and C Sts. SE, south of N. Carolina Ave. (☎ **202-546-2698;** Metro: Eastern Market). This redbrick market was built in 1873 and offers a variety of common to outlandish merchandise. On weekends, you can rummage through the outdoor stalls and stands for antiques, knickknacks, and various junk (or treasure to some). Chefs join the locals and party-givers who shop here on Saturday, when the produce and flowers are especially fresh. You'll find the atmosphere charged with eccentricity. In addition, the shops on 7th Street sell clothing, antiques, and food. (Try to find the bread lady across from the market. I "loave" her dough.)

✔ The **Georgetown Flea Market** is flooded every Sunday from March through December with frenzied shoppers hoping for that once-in-a-lifetime bargain. Nearly 100 vendors sell furniture, clothing, antiques, and the odd knickknack. Although you'll have fun rooting through the loot, you won't have any laughs getting here. The flea market takes place in a parking lot at Wisconsin Avenue NW, between S and T Streets on Georgetown's north end. If you take Metro to Foggy Bottom or Dupont Circle, the flea market is at least a 30-minute walk. Unless you're an avid walker, take a taxi. Skip the bus, because service on Sunday doesn't run regularly.

✔ If you prefer to do your crafts shopping indoors, visit **Appalachian Spring,** 50 Massachusetts Ave. NE (☎ 202-682-0505; Metro: Union Station). This shop sells quality crafts such as rag rugs, pottery, kaleidoscopes, new quilts, weavings, and more. All merchandise is made in the U. S. of A. And another branch is located in Georgetown at 1415 Wisconsin Ave. NW, but the Union Station store is easier to reach because a Metro station is located downstairs.

✔ The **Indian Crafts Shop,** 1849 C St. NW, Room 1023 in the Department of the Interior (☎ 202-208-4056; Metro: Farragut West), is an excellent place to find Native American crafts and hand-crafted jewelry. The pieces are priced for every budget — from a few to a few thousand dollars.

Hunting Down Bargains in D.C.'s Prime Shopping Zones

During your time in D.C., perhaps as a break from all that sightseeing, you may want to check out the following shopping areas. Each area has its own unique characteristics.

Adams-Morgan

In Adams-Morgan, you'll find more restaurants and clubs than shops, but the shops are unique. You'll enjoy a number of secondhand and one-of-a-kind stores here. Maybe while you're walking off dinner or people-watching, you can pick up a trinket or two. This ethnically diverse neighborhood's center can be found at the intersection of 18th Street and Columbia Road NW. Take Metro to Woodley Park-Zoo/Adams-Morgan, and then walk south 1 long block on Connecticut Avenue, east on Calvert Street about 5 blocks, bear right ½ block to 18th Street and Columbia Road.

Getting to Adams-Morgan during the evenings has been made easier with the addition of Metrobus shuttle service from the Woodley Park-Zoo/Adams-Morgan station. Here's how it works: When you enter Metro, get a transfer ticket from the machine on the mezzanine level. Ride Metro to the Woodley Park-Zoo/Adams-Morgan station, and then transfer to Metrobus No. 98 (first pickup at 6:28 p.m., last at 10:50 p.m.). Hand the driver the transfer and 25 cents. If you forgot the transfer, the fare is $1. Carry exact fare; the drivers do not make change. The 5-minute ride lands you at 18th Street and Columbia Road NW, the heart of Adams-Morgan. The return shuttle departs 18th and Columbia weeknights from about 6:00 to 11:45 p.m. Saturday and Sunday until 12:45 a.m. The fare is $1 (exact fare only; transfers not accepted on return to Metro). After dark, I advise taking the shuttle to Metro or catching a taxi.

Flying Saucer Discs, 2318 18th St. NW (☎ 202-265-DISC), sells used jazz, pop, rock and classical CDs from its basement store. Decorators and do-it-yourselfers mine **The Brass Knob,** 2311 18th St. NW (☎ 202-332-3370), and **Brass Knob's Back Door Warehouse,** 2329 Champlain St. NW (☎ 202-332-3370), for architectural acquisitions recovered from demolished houses and office buildings. African-inspired fabrics make up the colorful clothing by designer Millee Spears of Ghana; you can purchase these garments at **Khismet Wearable Art,** 1800 Belmont Rd. NW (☎ 202-234-7778), open to walk-ins weekends or by appointment.

Connecticut Avenue/Dupont Circle

On the lower end of Connecticut Avenue (between K and M Streets NW) is a collection of stores that reflects the Wall Street–like nature of the area. You can browse such conservative shops as **Brooks Brothers,** 1840 L St. NW (☎ 202-659-4650); **Talbot's,** 1227 Connecticut Ave. (☎ 202-887-6973); **Burberry's,** 1155 Connecticut Ave. (☎ 202-463-3000); and **Liz Claiborne,** 1144 Connecticut Ave. (☎ 202-785-8625). For casual wear, stroll into the **Gap,** 1120 Connecticut Ave. (☎ 202-429-0691), my preferred house of couture. Women who need a little something to wear to a black-tie affair at the White House shop at **Rizik's,** 1100 Connecticut Ave. NW (☎ 202-223-4050), for designer garments and excellent service. For affordable office and casual wear, locals browse **Hit or Miss,** 1140 Connecticut Ave. (☎ 202-223-8231).

You can sense a definite change in the mood as you get closer to **Dupont Circle.** Suddenly you see fewer three-piece suits and briefcases, and more jeans and multi-pierced body parts. Check out the galleries, bookstores, secondhand shops, and gay boutiques in this unconventional neighborhood reminiscent of New York's Greenwich Village. Try **Kramerbooks & Afterwords** for books and a cappuccino (1517 Connecticut Ave. NW; ☎ 202-387-1400), or **Backstage,** 2101 P St. NW (☎ 202-775-1488), for scripts, sheet music, and theatrical make-up (helpful in hiding imperfections on non-theatrical faces too). The staff at **Beadazzled,** 1507 Connecticut Ave. NW (☎ 202-265-BEAD), can help you make a necklace from a large selection of beads. In search of a kimono and fan? Look no further than **Ginza,** 1721 Connecticut Ave. NW (☎ 202-331-7991).

Downtown/Federal Triangle

Between 11th and 14th Streets NW on Pennsylvania Avenue, you'll find a mass of federal and district office buildings. At the corner of 14th Street is the historic Willard Inter-Continental Hotel. The National Press Club, National Theater, and J.W. Marriott, as well as **The Shops at National Place** (entrance on F St. NW between 13th and 14th Streets; ☎ 202-783-9090) are close by. The multilevel mall in the National Press Building has **Electronique** (electronic gizmos), **Capitol Image** (souvenirs), and **B. Dalton** (books), as well as numerous places to purchase shoes, clothing, and accessories. For a vast selection of fast foods and desserts, visit the Food Hall on the top level. Metro Center is only 1 block away.

If you're an architecture buff, you will want to visit the **Pavilion at the Old Post Office,** Pennsylvania Ave. and 11th St. NW (☎ 202-289-4224). The elevator ride to the clock tower also provides a stunning view of the city. Touristy shops sell souvenirs and glorified junk for the most part; maybe that's why kids enjoy coming here. Food stands feature more than adequate grub (spicy chicken wings and bleu cheese dip, sushi, sandwiches and burgers, and Indian and Oriental fare).

Georgetown

I liked Georgetown better when there were fewer shops selling CDs and elevator shoes, and more boutiques, parking spaces, and tastefully attired blue-haired ladies. Georgetown still has a certain cache, however, and shoppers of all ages enjoy spending money here.

Shops line both sides of M Street NW, from 28th to 36th Streets, and Wisconsin Avenue, from the C&O Canal (below M Street) north to about R Street. In addition, many of the side streets are dotted with stores as well. Unfortunately, the nearest Metro station is Foggy Bottom, a mile away. I enjoy the walk, but many complain about it. They take a taxi the rest of the way or walk to Pennsylvania Avenue and hop on a Metrobus bound for Georgetown. Street parking is scarce, and the few lots fill quickly, especially on weekends.

If you park in the garage beneath Shops at Georgetown Park (enter on Wisconsin Avenue, just below M Street) you get a break on parking with proof of a $10 purchase. Otherwise, I suggest taking a taxi from wherever you stay.

You find a bounty of record stores and branches of national chains such as **Gap, Banana Republic, Benetton,** and the **Original Levi's Store** in Georgetown. In addition, I want to mention some treasured old-timers:

- ✔ **Movie Madness,** 1083 Thomas Jefferson St. (☎ 202- 337-7064), sells movie posters.

- ✔ **Commander Salamander,** 1420 Wisconsin Ave. (☎ 202-337-2265), offers the latest in black leather, or you can have your hair streaked with DayGlo orange.

- ✔ The original **Hats in the Belfry,** 1237 Wisconsin Ave. (☎ 202-342-2006), sells a large selection of stylish and bizarre chapeaus from its tiny, but highly successful shop.

- ✔ **The Phoenix,** 1514 Wisconsin Ave. NW (☎ 202-338-4404), has been selling Mexican folk art and bric-a-brac, handcrafted silver jewelry, and those gauzy peasant blouses once favored by Joan Baez since 1955.

- ✔ **Little Caledonia,** 1419 Wisconsin Ave. (☎ 202-333-4700), is my all-time favorite Georgetown shop. For 60 years, the Lilliputian rooms have been crammed with china, home and kitchen furnishings, and toys. I have spent hours browsing this shopping wonderland. If Little Caledonia closes, I'm renouncing my citizenship.

If you're still looking for some more locations to spend your greenbacks, the **Shops at Georgetown Park,** 3222 M St. NW (☎ 202-342-8180) can help you drain your checking account in a hurry. These stores are housed in a handsome mall done in brick, brass, and potted plants. Well-heeled travelers, diplomats, and mature women from the city and the 'burbs shop the galleries and expensive boutiques for art, leather goods, imported children's clothing (**Benetton 0-12**), outrageously priced toys (**FAO Schwarz**), and new apparel (**Polo, J. Crew, bebe**). The rest of us head for **Mrs. Fields** for a bag of double-chocolate chip cookies and munch a few among the stacks at **Waldenbooks.** The Shops offer great browsing, but you won't be buying unless your wallet is padded — heavily padded — with cash.

Union Station

This magnificent railway station was restored in the 1980s at great expense (and worth every dollar, I'd say). Look around before bolting for the shops. Many are branches of national chains, such as **Brookstone** (gadgets), **B. Dalton** (books), and the **Discovery Channel Store** (environmentally themed books and trinkets). The rest of the station holds stores offering everything from women's wear to political memorabilia and handcrafted jewelry. You'd be way off track if you bypassed the **Great Train Store** on the main floor, especially with little cabooses. **B. Smith's** and other very good restaurants are located throughout the station. Washington's quintessential Food Court is on the lower level with about three dozen choices. Whatever else you eat, try the chocolate cannoli at **Vaccaro's. Union Station,** 50 Massachusetts Ave. NE (☎ 202-371-9441) is near the U.S. Capitol with a Metro station available downstairs.

Upper Wisconsin Avenue NW

An exclusive shopping zone begins at Mazza Gallerie and Chevy Chase Pavilion in Friendship Heights (D.C.) and continues on into Chevy Chase, Maryland. The largely residential area features a bunch of upscale and designer shops on Wisconsin Avenue (**Tiffany's, Gianni Versace, Cartier, Saks-Jandel,** to name just a few). To the north is **Saks Fifth Avenue.** Within Washington's boundaries are **Lord & Taylor** and two malls: the **Mazza Gallerie** (5300 Wisconsin Ave. NW, ☎ 202-966-6114), with **Neiman-Marcus, Filene's,** and numerous specialty shops; and **Chevy Chase Pavilion** (5345 Wisconsin Ave. NW, ☎ 202-686-5335), with a wide range of offerings, from the classic, tailored clothing at **Country Road Australia** to the consummate container store, **Hold Everything.** One of the area's most popular restaurants, **The Cheesecake Factory,** is located here, as are many other dining spots.

Take Metro to Friendship Heights. Come up the escalator and look around for the stores listed in this section. What you don't see immediately is within a few blocks.

D.C. Shopping from A to Z

Whatever you're looking for, you'll find it in Washington. In this section, I tell you where to get the merchandise you desire.

Antiques

Throughout the city, you can find lovely old furniture, art, jewelry, and the like at antique shops, but don't expect any bargains. The greatest concentration of antiques stores is on **Capitol Hill** and in **Georgetown.**

Begin your search at **Antiques-on-the-Hill,** 701 North Carolina Ave. SE (☎ 202-543-1819; Metro: Eastern Market). You'll enjoy a little of this and a little of that, good prices, and a personable staff. Or shop **The Brass Knob,** 2311 18th St. NW (☎ 202-332-3370; Metro: Woodley Park-Zoo/Adams-Morgan), if you are in pursuit of architectural treasures salvaged from demolished homes and buildings.

Head for **Antique Row** in Kensington, Maryland, where close to 50 antiques and collectible shops line Howard Avenue off upper Connecticut Avenue. The half-hour drive from D.C. is worthwhile when you consider the good deals you can get on everything from accessories to furniture. Drive north on Connecticut Avenue (S.R. 185) into Maryland. About 5½ miles past the D.C. line, go right at Howard Avenue; look for the Safeway on the corner. Or take a northbound L8 (Aspen Hill) bus from the Friendship Heights Metro station at Wisconsin and Western Avenues NW.

Art galleries

Most of D.C.'s galleries are concentrated in Dupont Circle, Georgetown, and on 7th Street NW (known in official circles as the 7th Street Arts Corridor) between D and H Streets.

Among the well-known are the **Addison/Ripley Gallery, Ltd.,** 1670 Wisconsin Ave. NW in Georgetown (☎ **202-338-5180;** take a taxi), for works by contemporary artists; some of the artists are locals. Along the **7th Street Arts Corridor,** you can find a slew of contemporary paintings, prints, and drawings, by national and international artists. The **Artists Museum,** 406 7th St. NW (☎ **202-638-7001**), is a coopera- tive with the **Touchstone Gallery** (☎ **202-347-2787**), **Adamson Gallery** (☎ **202-628-0257**), and others. Across the street is the **Zenith Gallery,** 413 7th St. NW (☎ **202-783-2963**), with contemporary mixed media works and much-publicized annual neon and humor shows.

Bookstores

Washington is a literary town with a number of chain bookstores and a wealth of independent booksellers. Here's a sampling of places to pick up the latest page-turners:

 ✔ You can spend an entire afternoon browsing at a Barnes & Noble (or Borders) superstore. More than 150,000 titles fill the three- level **Barnes & Noble** in Georgetown, 3040 M St. NW (☎ **202- 965-9880**). B & N features couches and chairs for you to relax in, a coffee bar, and an extensive selection of newspapers and maga- zines. The closest Metro is Foggy Bottom, and then walk north on 23rd to Pennsylvania and catch any bus traveling westbound, or you can walk the 7 blocks from 23rd and Pennsylvania.

 ✔ **Borders,** 1800 L St. NW, at 18th Street (☎ **202-466-4999**), stocks about 200,000 titles, as well as videos, tapes, and CDs in its down- town megastore. Kids can attend Saturday morning story hours while their parents catch up on the latest best-seller or drink cap- puccinos from the café/coffee bar. Take Metro to Farragut North, and then walk south half a block on Connecticut Avenue, right at L Street one block to Borders.

 ✔ Of the independent booksellers, I like the personal service at **Olsson's.** Various locations: 1307 19th St. NW, off Dupont Circle (☎ **202-785-1133;** Metro: Dupont Circle); 1200 F St. NW (☎ **202- 347-3686;** Metro: Metro Center); 1239 Wisconsin Ave., in

Georgetown (☎ 202-338-9544; Metro: Foggy Bottom); and 418 7th St. NW, in the Lansburgh Building between D and E Streets NW (☎ 202-638-7610; Metro: Archives-Navy Memorial). In September and April, Olsson's has storewide sales with pretty substantial discounts. At other times of the year, some hardcovers and paperbacks are marked down, and you can usually trust the sales staff's recommendations to be pretty good selections.

✔ **Fairy Godmother,** 319 7th St. SE, on Capitol Hill (☎ 202-547-5474; Metro: Eastern Market), carries a wide selection of children's books and has story times for pre-schoolers. Toys are also available from the Godmother. Stop on your way to or from Eastern Market.

✔ **Second Story Books,** 2000 P St. NW (☎ 202-659-8884; Metro: Dupont Circle), is the place for old and out-of-print books, used CDs, and advertising posters.

✔ **Travel Books and Language Center,** 4437 Wisconsin Ave. NW (☎ 202-237-1322; Metro: Tenleytown), is one of the foremost suppliers of travel books, guides, memoirs, diaries, fiction, photography, maps, language dictionaries, and tapes *in the country.*

✔ The **U.S. Government Printing Office Bookstore,** 1510 H St. NW, between 15th and 16th Sts. (☎ 202-653-5075; Metro: McPherson Square). Pick up or order any Government Printing Office document and publication here. Don't laugh. The Printing Office Bookstore publishes a lot of valuable consumer information. It's not all long-winded drivel and statistics. (If you didn't have your fill of Monica and Bill in the '90s, you may find a dusty copy of their grand jury testimonies lying around.) The store is open Monday through Friday, 8 a.m. to 4 p.m.

✔ **Mystery Books,** 1715 Connecticut Ave. NW (☎ 202-483-1600; Metro: Dupont Circle). The game's afoot at this bookstore. Sherlock Holmes, Ellery Queen, and Hercule Poirot wannabes can find plenty of reading matter that will exercise their little grey cells. You won't leave clueless.

Bibliophiles and collectors shouldn't overlook the museum stores (described later in this section), which carry a wide selection of special interest books.

Cameras

Penn Camera Exchange, 915 E St. NW (☎ 202-347-5777; Metro: Metro Center or Gallery Place), is the place for discounts on brand names and quality processing for amateur and professional shutterbugs alike. Penn also buys, trades, rents, and repairs used equipment.

Ritz Camera, 1740 Pennsylvania Ave. NW (☎ 202-466-3470; Metro: Farragut West), is a one-stop photo shop, with 1-hour photo-finishing and an on-site enlarger for your favorite D.C. photos. Ritz has several other locations scattered throughout D.C.

CDs and tapes

Tower Records, 2000 Pennsylvania Ave. NW (☎ 202-331-2400; Metro: Foggy Bottom), has the area's largest selection of music, as well as videos and laser discs on two floors.

Olsson's Books & Records, with locations in Georgetown (☎ 202-338-9544); Dupont Circle (☎ 202-785-1133); near Metro Center (☎ 202-347-3686); and 7th St. NW, on the 7th Street Arts Corridor (☎ 202-638-7610) is strong in all categories of music and books, especially classical and folk. Shopping here is easy because the sales-people are always eager to assist you. (For street addresses and Metro information, look for Olsson's listing under "Bookstores," earlier in this section.)

Jewelry

Notice to all significant others who can't decide what to get their partners: Consider baubles or beads from **Pampillonia Jewelers,** at 1213 Connecticut Ave. NW (☎ 202-628-6305; Metro: Farragut North); or Mazza Gallerie, 5300 Wisconsin Ave. NW(☎ 202-363-6305; Metro: Friendship Heights). This family-owned business is the quintessential Washington jeweler, with traditional and custom-designed pieces for women and men.

Museum shopping

This may be the best-kept secret in Washington. Some of the best shopping — for quality crafts, books, clothing, jewelry, and souvenirs — is in museum and gallery shops. Because the museums themselves are already on your sightseeing list, you won't waste any travel time. Here are some of my favorites:

✔ **John F. Kennedy Center for the Performing Arts,** 2700 F St. NW and Rock Creek Parkway (☎ 202-416-8350), for posters, performing arts memorabilia, videos and CDs.

✔ **National Air and Space Museum,** Independence Ave. and 7th St. SW (☎ 202-357-1387), for flight-related books, posters, souvenirs.

✔ **National Gallery of Art,** Constitution Ave. between 4th and 6th Sts. NW (☎ 202-737-4215), for posters, books, stationery, and gifts.

✔ **National Museum of Natural History,** 10th St. and Constitution Ave. NW (☎ 202-357-1537), for crafts, books, clothing, and jewelry.

Political memorabilia

It's fun, especially at the start of a new administration, to pick through the campaign buttons, books, bumper stickers, and other politically inspired novelties at **Political Americana,** 50 Massachusetts Ave. NW, in Union Station (☎ **202-547-1685;** Metro: Union Station). A second branch is at 685 15th St. NW, between F and G Sts. NW (☎ **202-547-1817;** Metro: McPherson Square).

Chapter 20

Itineraries for Cutting Washington, D.C. Down to Size

. . . .

In This Chapter

▶Getting a fix on Washington's top sightseeing priorities

▶Understanding some tips for a hassle-free visit

. . . .

*T*o help you focus your sightseeing plans, this travel spin doctor has spun itineraries that include Washington's top attractions. Follow my prescriptions to alleviate motion sickness and anxiety over the myriad choices facing D.C. visitors. For more information on each attraction, please see Chapters 16 and 17.

Exploring Washington in Three Days

Direct from the oval office, mine, not the prez's, the following is a 3-day agenda for visiting many of the top sights and getting a taste of the city. The choices are not written in stone, so you can exercise your right to choose or substitute without penalty. It's your America!

Day one

Go first to the **Smithsonian Institution Building,** also known as the "Castle" (open at 9 a.m., an hour before the museums) for visitor information. When your pockets are stuffed, cross the Mall to the **National Museum of Natural History.** Buy tickets for the large-screen movie (see Chapter 16 for more on the movie offerings there) before glimpsing the gems and minerals, dinosaurs, and creepy crawlers. Get a breath of fresh air on your way to the **National Museum of American History.** When you've had your fill of Old Glory and First Ladies, grab a quick lunch in the museum's Victorian-style **Palm Court** café, the cafeteria, or from a street vendor.

Stroll over to the **Washington Monument.** If the line is horrendous, come back after 4 p.m. or during the evenings in the summer. Continue to **Constitution Gardens** (with the **Reflecting Pool, Vietnam** and **Korean Veterans' memorials**). Take plenty of pictures of the **Lincoln Memorial** and the **U.S. Capitol.**

Still rarin' to go? Walk to the **Tidal Basin** and pay your respects to FDR and Mr. Jefferson. Rent a paddleboat, near Raoul Wallenberg Place SW and East Basin Drive. Grab a soda, ice cream, or snack here. From the Tidal Basin, you can take about a 15-minute walk back to the Smithsonian Metro station.

Otherwise, return to your hotel. If you bought tickets to an evening performance and didn't made dinner reservations, do so immediately. Numerous restaurants offer pre-theater *prix fixe* menus (see Chapters 13, 14, and 15 for my top restaurant suggestions). Loll by the pool or watch an in-room movie. Siesta time! If you're hanging loose, dine in **Georgetown.** Take an after-dinner stroll on M Street and/or Wisconsin Avenue or along the Potomac riverfront. Enjoy a drink at **Sequoia** (see Chapter 15 for more on Sequoia's charm) or duck into a restaurant with live music or an ice cream parlor for something sinful.

Day two

Up and at 'em! Unless you've secured so-called VIP passes (see Chapter 9 for instructions on that), go to the **White House Visitors Center** first thing for timed tickets to the presidential mansion. Be prepared to spend the better part of the morning waiting in line to tour 1600 Pennsylvania Avenue. If your patience wears thin, buy souvenir post-cards of the presidential mansion and visit instead the **Corcoran** or **Renwick galleries,** the **Octagon,** or **National Geographic Society's Explorers Hall** (all an easy walk from the *Maison Blanche*). See Chapter 17 for more details on those attractions. Take a break in **Lafayette Square** where protestors demonstrate inches away from preppy hair-cuts and business suits. Feed the squirrels; then feed yourself.

Eat lunch at the **Sky Terrace** of the **Hotel Washington** (more for the view than the food). Or head to the **Old Ebbitt Grill, Red Sage,** or the Food Court at the **Shops at National Place.** You can find plenty of fast-food joints near the White House on Pennsylvania and Connecticut Avenues, and on 17th Street.

Glimpse the **Ellipse** and the **White House** posterior on your way to the **Washington Monument.** (If you have trouble finding this one, you'd better schedule an eye exam.) Ride the elevator to the observation level or come back another time if the line is too long.

Depending on your energy level, you can visit some more presidential memorials. Too pooped to peep, much less walk? Take **Tourmobile** (see Chapter 11 for details) and give your feet a rest. If you've had it up to here with history, refresh yourself with some real *soul* food at the **National Gallery of Art** (East or West Building; your call) or the **Hirshhorn.** Be sure to check out the **sculpture gardens** at each.

Go back to your hotel and have a quiet dinner in your neighborhood. Crash early.

Day three

Head first to the **Bureau of Engraving and Printing,** where the buck *starts.* If greenbacks don't turn you on, substitute the **U.S. Holocaust Memorial Museum** for a sobering and thought-provoking experience. Take a coffee break in the museum's self-serve café. Go for a brisk walk on the **Tidal Basin** or **Mall.** You'll need it.

Take Metro to **Capitol Hill.** Have lunch with your senator or congressional representative or try one of the Hill's many fine dining restaurants or casual, drop-in pubs and cafes. Visit the **U.S. Capitol** (see Chapter 16 for more on the Capitol).

Be sure to take in the view from the **West Front** before going to the **U.S. Supreme Court** and/or the **Library of Congress.**

Relax, swim laps, or hit the health club at your hotel. Dine early at **Union Station.** Browse the shops and have a cannoli at **Vacarro's;** then catch the Gray Line after-dark tour that departs from the station. Drink a pint of stout at **Irish Times** or the **Dubliner** before turning in.

Washington for Government Groupies

I prefer oysters and chocolate, but for many, big government (and those who drive it) are powerful aphrodisiacs. If the possibility of glimpsing the commander in chief raises goosebumps on your flesh, or the desire to pump your congressional rep's hand sends shivers up your spine, join the government groupie patrol at the following sights.

Stop at pretty **Bartholdi Park** on your way to the **U.S. Capitol.** Take the guided tour or sprint up the stairs like Rocky Balboa and do it yourself. If you want, look up your senator or congressional representative. If he or she is on the floor (of the Senate or House chamber, not passed out) or on the road, leave a message with an aide. Pass-holders may sit in the Senate or House Gallery (see Chapter 9 for information on getting gallery passes).

Ride the $18 million subway (your tax dollars at work) connecting the Capitol to the **Dirksen** and **Hart Senate office buildings.** Walk to the **West Front** of the Capitol for an unobstructed view of the Mall, all the way to the **Lincoln Memorial.**

In trivial pursuit of the White House

Headlines usually focus on the occupants of 1600 Pennsylvania Avenue, but on November 1, 2000, the White House made page one as it celebrated its 200th birthday.

Everyone past the goo-goo stage knows the White House is the official residence of the First Family, First Dog and, sometimes, First Cat and First Intern. Pierre Charles L'Enfant's original design for the "President's Palace" was actually four times the size of the present structure. You can credit James Hoban with cutting it down to size. (Little did he know he'd set a precedent for attempts at downsizing government.)

Construction took 8 years and cost $232,372. The White House measures 85 feet, 6 inches wide without the porticoes, 152 feet wide with them tacked on. Before Pennsylvania Avenue was carved out in 1822 (establishing Lafayette Square north of the mansion), the area had been a public common for fairs and parades. Since that time the space has been the site of countless protests. What goes around, comes around.

The White House has most certainly come a long way from its humble origins in a D.C. swamp. Here are some of the changes the house has been through:

- **Restrooms:** Of the structure's 132 rooms, 31 are bathrooms — a lot of toilet bowl cleaner, friends. Speaking of bathrooms, the first bathtubs were portable and made of tin. In 1833 (during Andrew Jackson's term), piped water flowed into the house for the first time to clean all those bathrooms. William Howard Taft (president from 1909 to 1913) had to install a special bathtub — big enough to hold four men — after he got stuck in the White House's tub the first time he used it (Taft weighed in at 322 pounds).

- **Outside walls:** Despite two major fires — in 1814 and 1929 — and a major gutting during "Give 'em Hell" Harry's presidency (1945 to 1953), the exterior stone walls are the originals. During George Bush's term, a 1990 restoration of the exterior uncovered battle scars from the 1814 fire (during the War of 1812, when James Madison was president).

- **Stoves:** In 1801, Thomas Jefferson moved in and replaced the open-hearth fireplaces with stoves. (Note: He didn't do the work himself. He called Home Depot. And country gentleman Jefferson reportedly answered the door in a robe.)

- **Telephones:** In 1879, Rutherford B. Hayes used the first White House phone, whose number was 1.

- **Electricity:** The first electric lamps blinked on and off in 1891 during Benjamin Harrison's presidency.

- **Presidential broadcasts:** "Silent" Calvin Coolidge delivered the first White House radio broadcast in 1925. While Ike gave the first televised presidential news conference in 1955, JFK was the first to do a live television broadcast.

- **Pool table:** President Ulysses S. Grant added a billiard room to the house in the 1870s. (This is the same witty guy who said, "I know only two tunes — one is "Yankee Doodle" and the other isn't.")

✔ **Pools:** Other presidential sportsmen include Franklin Delano Roosevelt (FDR's term spanned 1933 to 1945), who installed an indoor pool. The indoor pool became a press pool — er, briefing room — in the early 1970s during Nixon's presidency. During Gerald Ford's administration (1974 to 1977), an outdoor pool was installed.

✔ **Golf green:** Dwight Eisenhower built a putting green outside the Oval Office during his term from 1953 to 1961.

✔ **Bowling alley:** The Nixons — big-time bowlers — constructed a one-lane alley under the driveway leading to the North Portico (Nixon's stay ran from 1969 to 1974).

✔ **Jogging track:** William Jefferson Clinton (1993 to 2001) added a jogging track around the South Grounds driveway and practice green. (I'll leave a discussion of presidential indoor sports for another time.)

Despite its revolving door of residents, the White House is and will undoubtedly remain an enduring and beloved symbol of the United States and the presidency. John Adams may have penned the quintessential birthday toast (now inscribed on a mantel in the mansion) in a note to his wife on their second day in the White House: "I pray Heaven to bestow the best of blessings on this House . . . and all that shall hereafter inhabit it. May none but honest and wise Men ever rule beneath this roof."

Well put, John. I'll drink to that.

Have lunch in the Dirksen Building South Buffet Room, the **Montpelier Dining Room** (Madison Building of the Library of Congress), or in a Hill café. Keep your eyes peeled for prominent legislators.

If the **U.S. Botanic Garden** has reopened (it's scheduled to reopen in fall 2001, but it may not open until winter 2002), after extensive renovation, run, don't walk, to the conservatory. If not, walk off lunch and browse on **Pennsylvania Avenue SE.** Make a quick stop at the **Thomas Jefferson Building** of the **Library of Congress.** Count the more than 17 million volumes if you wish and/or visit Bert and Ernie and other pop culture icons in the **Madison Building.**

Afterward, take your case to the **Supreme Court.** Oyez! Oyez! (Hear ye! Hear ye!). The decision on the view from the steps is unanimous: Guilty of providing a spectacular vista. Upon leaving the hallowed halls of justice, take a walk to check out the architecture and homes on the Hill. Or shop, snack, and see a late afternoon movie (cheaper before 6 p.m.!) at **Union Station.** Catch Metro back to your hotel. Put your feet up or check your e-mail. Have dinner in **Dupont Circle** or **Adams-Morgan;** then people-watch, listen to live music, or dance the night away.

Georgetown for Shoppers

On her way to a state dinner, consummate shopper Imelda Marcos may have detoured to **Georgetown** for an extra dozen pairs of gentian violet pumps. And Jackie O is said to have dropped a bundle in the Wisconsin Avenue boutiques when JFK was president. Closet shoppers, casual browsers, shopaholics, and Jackie wannabes, unite! In Georgetown you have nothing to lose but the contents of your designer wallets.

Before the stores open, fortify yourself with breakfast at **Senses.** Walk off the omelet and croissants with a stroll along the **Washington Harbour** promenade. Shops line both sides of **M Street,** from 28th Street west to Key Bridge. (If you make it to 36th Street, you see the nasty steps immortalized in the recently re-released *Exorcist* movie.) Overspending is a local as well as a government pastime. If you doubt this statement, step into the **Shops at Georgetown Park,** which attracts a high-rolling clientele. Cool your plastic and take a break at **Dean & Deluca,** or have a **Mrs. Fields** sugar fix.

Among the familiar (Original Levi's Store, Gap, Bennetton, HMV) you can find more distinctive boutiques, such as **Hats in the Belfry, Betsey Johnson, Commander Salamander** (for leather, feather boas, and nose rings), and **Little Caledonia** (kitchenware and home furnishings).

I never ate a bad meal in Georgetown. Consult Chapters 14 and 15 for a list of great dining spots in the area. For lunch, two of my favorites are **Clyde's** and **Houston's.**

After you refuel, walk by **3307 N St. NW.** John F. Kennedy called it home from shortly after Caroline's birth in 1957 until he moved into larger quarters at 1600 Pennsylvania Avenue on January 20, 1961. Temper any further shopping urges with a visit to **Dumbarton Oaks.** See Chapter 16 for more on the magnificent art and spectacular gardens housed here.

Take a break and scarf down an ice cream soda or sundae at **Thomas Sweet.** Let palmist, psychic, and tarot-reader extraordinaire **Mrs. Natalie** (just a few doors down at 1500 Wisconsin Ave.; ☎ **202-333-1245**), read your palm. She'll probably tell you that you're tired and need a nap. Follow Mrs. Natalie's advice. Revitalized, enjoy dinner downtown and see a play or in summer, enjoy a free outdoor concert.

Washington, D.C. for Family Planners

Don't despair if your in-laws change their minds about staying with the kids (so that you can enjoy a nice, relaxing vacation). Bring the rugrats! Kids take to Washington like reporters to a bad story. You may want to modify the itineraries below to suit your kids' ages and interests. And, puh-leeze, take several time-outs and snack often.

With kids under 8 years old . . .

Your first stop is the **National Aquarium,** where children can pet a horseshoe crab in the touch tanks. Cross Constitution Avenue to the **Museum of American History.** Browse the **Museum Shop.** Let them buy a souvenir *first,* and they may not bug you the rest of the day. See the first-floor exhibits devoted to farm and power machinery and transportation. Pick up a snack in the museum's **Main Street Cafe** or from a street vendor on the Mall.

Next, ride the **Carousel on the Mall,** near the Smithsonian "Castle." A short walk away is the **Museum of Natural History.** Spend an hour seeing the Insect Zoo, giant squids, Dinosaur Hall, and maybe one other exhibition and the Museum Shop. Eat lunch in the museum cafeteria or break into the brown bag you picked up on the way. If the kids are antsy after their visit to the Insect Zoo, let them run around the Mall. (Depending on your kids' interests, you may wish to substitute the **Air and Space Museum** for the American History or Natural History museums.)

Or, forget the Mall and take them directly to the **National Zoo.** (With any luck, Metro's motion will lull your little ones to sleep.) Spend 2 to 4 hours, depending on your youngsters' ages. Refuel at one of the zoo restaurants or snack stands. I'd call it quits after the zoo; return to your hotel for quiet time.

If they've napped and are still raring to go, head to the **Capital Children's Museum** and eat a snack in the **Food Hall (Union Station).** Then crawl back to your hotel, take a dip in the pool, watch an in-room movie, or take another nap. Eat dinner in or near the hotel or order a pizza and watch a G-rated movie. Lights out early.

With kids over 8 years old . . .

Tour the **FBI** or **Bureau of Engraving and Printing** (see Chapter 16 for more on both attractions) first thing and then head for the Mall. Buy tickets to see a movie in the IMAX Theater at the **Air and Space Museum.** Munch an early lunch in the **Flight Line** cafeteria (before it gets too crowded) or step outside for a hot dog or slice of pizza. See the movie and single out a few exhibits, or vice-versa. Nobody in his or her right mind does this entire museum in one visit. Don't even try. Buy a kite in the **Museum Shop** and fly it on the Mall.

Weather permitting, rent a pedal boat on the **Tidal Basin,** row or canoe on the river or the **C&O Canal,** or return to your hotel for a swim. If the weather is nasty, go to **Union Station** to shop, see a movie, and eat some more. If there's still steam in your kettle, return to the Mall late afternoon when the crowds have thinned (theoretically, at least), and visit the **Natural History** or **American History** museum.

For dinner, take your brood to a casual, kid-friendly place such as **Capital City Brewing Co., Austin Grill, Houston's, Planet Hollywood, Red Sage** (cantina), or the **Food Court at Union Station.** Catch a movie and chill.

With teens . . .

Give them money, a map, money, Metro fare, money, a curfew, more money, and point them toward Georgetown or Old Town, Alexandria. Chapter 17 has more on attractions geared toward teenagers.

Avoiding Common Sightseeing Hassles

To make sure you get the most out of your sightseeing excursions, I offer the following advice:

- ✔ Most important, budget your time wisely. Bear in mind every traveler's first commandment: Thou shalt spend more time and money than anticipated.

- ✔ Get a feel for the city on a guided tour. Then play bureaucrat and do what's politically expedient — develop a strategy.

- ✔ Ricocheting like a stray bullet gets old fast. If you zigzag from the White House to the Capitol to Georgetown to the Mall, you waste time and wear yourself out. Concentrate your sightseeing in one or two adjacent neighborhoods, such as the Mall and Downtown, or Foggy Bottom and Georgetown.

- ✔ Visit no more than three or four museums in a day (and that's pushing it!), fewer if your kids are under 10 or if you tire easily.

- ✔ Earmark an average 1½ to 2 hours for each site (that means *each* Smithsonian Museum). Some attractions — the presidential monuments and memorials, for example — can take a half-hour or less. Make sure that you factor commuting time into your sightseeing schedule.

- ✔ If possible, show up at the busiest museums and attractions (the Air and Space, American History, and Natural History museums; the White House, FBI, and Bureau of Engraving and Printing) when the doors open or after 3 p.m. (except at the White House, which is not open in the afternoon). Take advantage of extended summer and holiday hours. Pick up tickets for special exhibitions and IMAX movies *before* touring.

✔ Allow some downtime for meals, shopping, phoning home, and yes, even quiet reflection. Prevent brain drain by alternating museums with outdoor activities (a stroll around the Tidal Basin, kite flying on the Mall, or a Potomac River cruise, perhaps).

✔ Wear comfortable shoes and layer clothing, except in summer when you should wear the minimum allowed by law.

Chapter 21

Exploring beyond Washington, D.C.: Three Great Day Trips

● ●

In This Chapter

▶ Visiting Old Town, Virginia

▶ Touring Mt. Vernon

▶ Exploring Annapolis, Maryland

● ●

*I*f time permits, you may want to get out of Dodge for a day or longer. Excursion opportunities abound in the capital region. You can reach historic sites, shopping outlets, state parks, and theme parks faster than Congress can answer a roll call. I offer a few destinations within 1 to 2 hours travel time from the White House, in case you stay there. Using your hotel as a base, you can spend a day at one of the following locations and still return in time for a nightcap and the 10 o'clock news. In the spots where you're better off spending the night, I also suggest places to stay.

Day Trip #1: Discovering Old Town, Alexandria, Virginia

With its scenic riverfront setting, historic sites, and myriad dining and shopping choices, **Old Town** charms all who visit. George Washington was a teenage surveyor's assistant when Alexandria became a city in 1749. The once-thriving colonial port on the western shore of the Potomac River is about 6 miles south of D.C. (see the map in this chapter). Picturesque and steeped in history, Old Town boasts fine restorations of 18th- and 19th-century buildings on cobblestone streets, an active waterfront, an artisans cooperative, boutiques, and fine and casual dining. In February, visitors pack their powdered wigs and celebrate Washington's birthday at the largest G.W. Day parade in the nation.

Getting there

If you drive, take the Arlington Memorial or 14th Street Bridge to the picturesque George Washington Memorial Parkway southbound, which becomes Washington Street. Make a left at King Street, Alexandria's main thoroughfare that continues 6 blocks to Union Street and the waterfront. Thumbs down on driving here in rush hour, when the 6 miles from D.C. may feel more like 60. Short-term parking permits, good for 2 hours at a meter, are available at the Ramsay House Visitors Center. Traffic creeps on the narrow streets, and parking can be a hassle, especially on weekends.

To travel by Metro, hop on a Yellow line train bound for Reagan National Airport. Get off at the King Street Metro station and transfer to a DASH (Alexandria's public transportation system) bus to King and Fairfax (at the door of the Ramsay House). Or walk the 15 blocks.

Seeing the sights

Write, call, or stop at the **Ramsay House Visitors Center,** 221 King St. (☎ 703-838-4200; Internet: www.funside.com), a faithful reconstruction of Alexandria's first house. The center provides brochures, self-guided walking-tour maps, and a special events calendar. You can also purchase admission tickets for many historic homes and sights. The Ramsay House is open every day but Thanksgiving, Christmas, and New Year's Day from 9 a.m. to 5 p.m.

A self-guided walking tour is outlined in a brochure at the Visitors Center. Otherwise, it's first-come, first-served every day for **Doorways to Old Virginia** (☎ 703-548-0100) a 90-minute docent-led walking tour (Monday through Saturday 10:30 a.m.; Sunday 2 p.m.). The cost is $10 per person. Doorways also runs an hour-long docent-led **Ghost and Graveyard Tour** (Friday and Saturday 7:30 and 9:00 p.m.; Sunday 7:30 p.m.; $6 adults, $4 kids 7 to 12, free ages 6 and under). You may want to consider an early dinner before taking this informative walk through Old Town.

Because Alexandria enjoys a waterfront setting, beginning your visit with a cruise makes sense. Take a 40-minute narrated cruise on the **Admiral Tilp** (☎ 703-548-9000), or a 90-minute ride on the **Matthew Hayes** past several monuments and memorials. Tickets for the longer cruise are $14 for adults, $12 for seniors, $6 for kiddies 6 to 12. Cruises depart from the Alexandria City Marina, at Union and Cameron Streets behind the Torpedo Factory. Metro: King Street. Then a DASH bus to King and Fairfax, walk down King toward the river, or take a taxi.

Gadsby's Tavern, 134 N. Royal St. (☎ 703-838-4242), is said to have been visited by Washington, Madison, and Jefferson (but not on the same evening). The tavern is now a museum of colonial furnishings and artifacts. Strolling minstrels play period music during dinner and Sunday brunch in the first-floor restaurant.

Old Town Alexandria

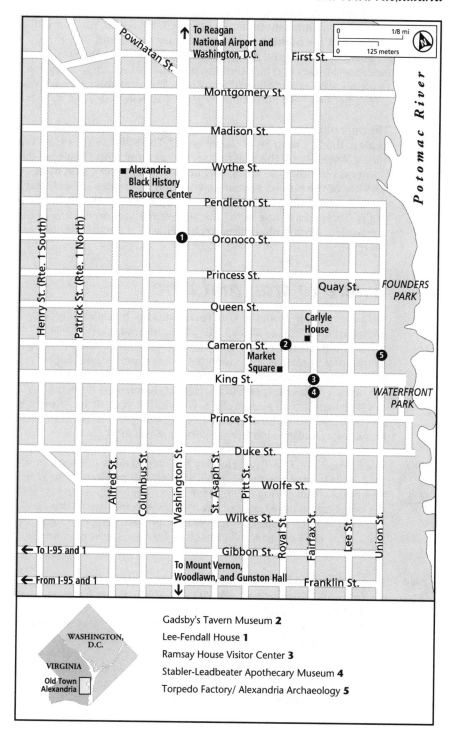

Gadsby's Tavern Museum **2**

Lee-Fendall House **1**

Ramsay House Visitor Center **3**

Stabler-Leadbeater Apothecary Museum **4**

Torpedo Factory/ Alexandria Archaeology **5**

The **Lee-Fendall House,** 614 Oronoco St. (☎ **703-548-1789**), is the city's only Victorian house-museum. Docents are on hand to answer visitors' questions about family life way back when. You can't fill a prescription at the **Stabler-Leadbeter Apothecary Shop,** 105-107 S. Fairfax St. between Prince and King (☎**703-836-3713**), with its hand-blown medicine bottles and bloodletting paraphernalia, but you can read a request for cod liver oil written by Mrs. Bushrod Washington (wife of G. W.'s nephew). To find out more, take the self-guided audio tour.

The only thing to be fired in recent years at the **Torpedo Factory Art Center,** 105 N. Union St. at Cameron (☎ **703-838-4565**), is clay. But during World War I, the building served as a torpedo shell-case factory. Painters, sculptors, weavers, and other artisans work side by side in full view of the public. Voyeurs are invited inside the artists' studios to observe and make purchases (great shopping opportunity!). While you're here, take a look at the unearthed artifacts on display in the **Alexandria Archaeology Research Lab,** which occupies space in the Center.

Where to stay and dine

Walk everywhere from the **Old Town Holiday Inn,** 480 King St., Alexandria, VA 22314 (☎ **703-549-6080;** Internet: www.holiday-inn. com), which offers 227 rooms in the thick of things. Amenities include continental breakfast, afternoon tea, a large indoor pool (open year-round), and an exercise room with treadmills and bikes. **101 Royal** is the hotel's restaurant, serving breakfast, lunch, and dinner. Stop for a drink or light fare in **Annabelle's.** Or ask that your drink or meal be served in the quiet, flowered courtyard. Complimentary continental breakfast and afternoon tea are served in the lobby.

Woof! Woof! The Old Town Holiday Inn invites dogs under 40 pounds (and their human caretakers) to its Doggy Happy Hour, held Thursday afternoons from spring through fall. The weekly happening is held in the courtyard where Gatorade and doggy biscuits are enthusiastically received. A hotel staff person says the dogs are very well behaved. Rack rates are $149 to $189. Fido stays for free, but remember, he must weigh in under 40 pounds.

It may be touristy, but the waterside setting of the **Chart House Restaurant,** 1 Cameron St. (☎ **703-684-5080**), floats my boat. Steer clear of the beef and fish and cruise straight toward the coconut shrimp ($21.95). A slab (this is no slice) of the famous ice cream mud pie is big enough for two consenting adults. You can easily create a meal from the 50-or-so items on the salad bar ($12.95). Reservations are recommended. Open for dinner only Monday through Saturday, brunch and dinner Sunday. The menu for kids 11 and younger features chicken strips, spaghetti, and other mini-portions.

Head for the **Warehouse Bar & Grill,** 214 King St. (☎ **703-683-6868**), for a sandwich, full dinner, or Sunday brunch in a casual setting that in former lives served as a trolley warehouse, boat repair business, and pool hall.

I suggest sticking to things you can pronounce, like grilled fish or steak. The fried clams enjoy a rep for being crunchy and greaseless. (Let me know if they still measure up.) Dinner entrees run from $12.95 to $23.95. On Sundays, the popular a la carte brunch (10 a.m. to 4 p.m.) fills faster than church. Kids are always welcome.

I've been trying for years to lure the **Hard Times Café,** 1404 King St. (☎ **703-683-5340**), to my neighborhood. For a quick-and-dirty meal on your way to or from Old Town, this place can't be beat. Though 12 blocks from Old Town, it's worth the walk on a nice day. (Think of it as working off the French fries.) Or take the DASH bus from the King Street Metro station or Visitors Center. Chili comes three ways: Texas-style (spiciest of the three with chunks of beef rather than ground meat), Vegetarian, and Cincinnati-style (plenty of ground beef in a tomato-based sauce spiced with cinnamon). I like the burger topped with Cincinnati chili, accompanied by a side of onion rings, a Dixie longneck, and an antacid chaser. You can pig out here for less than $15. Leave your lasso at the door.

The **Union Street Public House,** 121 S. Union St. between King and Prince (☎ **703-548-1785**), has long been a favorite for its casual, neighborhood saloon ambiance, bar food, New Orleans–inspired fare (gumbo, jambalaya, and Creole chicken with Remoulade sauce), and local beer. Old brickwork, gas lamps, and polished wood enhance the pubby-clubby atmosphere. Open for lunch and dinner daily with an extensive menu. The average dinner entrée is in the $11 to $12 range; some entrées are in the low $20s. This restaurant has racked up dining awards for several years running. A kids' menu is available too.

Day Trip #2: Exploring Mt. Vernon

Mount Vernon lies on the Potomac River, 16 miles and more than 200 years in ambiance away from modern-day D.C. A stop at George Washington's riverfront estate, restored to the original paint colors on the walls, is the perfect complement to a visit of the federal district bearing his name. The land was granted to Washington's great-grandfather in 1674. G.W. spent 2 years in retirement here before he died and was buried here in 1799. What a setting! (He certainly had an eye for prime real estate!) Some of the furnishings are original, others are authentic reproductions, and all are positioned as they were when George and Martha squabbled at the breakfast table.

Getting there

Drive across the Potomac River to the George Washington Memorial Parkway and head south. The parkway ends at Mount Vernon. Easy, no? **Tourmobile** buses (☎ 202-554-5100) depart daily (April through October) for 4-hour tours from the ticket booths at Arlington National Cemetery and the Washington Monument. Reserve a seat 30 minutes before departure at either location. The fare ($22 adults, $11 kids 3 to 11) includes admission to Mount Vernon. Payment is in cash or traveler's checks *only.* From January through October, the **Spirit of Mount Vernon** cruises twice daily to Mount Vernon from Pier 4 (6th and Water Streets SW; ☎ 202-554-8000). Tickets ($28 adults, $18 kids 6 to 11, free 5 and under) include admission to Mount Vernon.

Seeing the sights

For information before you arrive, contact the **Mount Vernon Ladies' Association,** at Mount Vernon, VA 22121 (☎ 703-780-2000), or visit its Web site at www.mountvernon.org. Mount Vernon is open daily with varying hours. Call ahead!

Aside from the addition of air conditioning in 1998, Mount Vernon is a typical 18th century aristocratic estate. (Sort of like Mel Gibson's place in the movie *The Patriot.*) About 30 of Mount Vernon's original 8,000 acres are yours to explore. Tour on your own and ask the docents your questions, even the silliest ones. Take a minute, especially with youngsters, to inspect the family kitchen and outbuildings where baking, weaving, and washing took place. George and other family members are interred in a tomb a short walk from the mansion. On the third Monday of February, a memorial service commemorates Washington's birthday.

On weekends from Memorial Day through Labor Day, volunteers re-create 18th-century plantation life. From May through September, children can card and spin wool, roll hoops, and try on colonial clothing in the **Hands-On-History** tent next to the mansion.

April through October the **Potomac Spirit** (☎ 703-780-2000) departs the Mount Vernon dock for a 45-minute river cruise ($7 adults, $6 kids 4 to 11), a pleasant interlude before heading back to the city.

Where to dine

Outside the main gate are a snack bar (breakfast, lunch, and light fare), and the **Mount Vernon Inn** (☎ 703-780-0011). The inn is open daily for lunch, and if you make reservations, you can eat dinner here Monday through Saturday. Picnicking is allowed 1 mile north at Riverside Park. Or stop on the way back to D.C. and dine in Old Town, Alexandria. (See "Day Trip #1: Discovering Old Town, Alexandria, Virginia", earlier in this chapter.)

I cannot tell a lie

George Washington was a truthful dude (as politicians go), and is generally regarded as a decent human being. He's the only one of the Founding Fathers to have freed his slaves. Thomas Jefferson, on the other hand, was all declaration and no action. G.W. liked fighting fires when not otherwise engaged. He also tried to ban swearing in the army (wouldn't Patton have loved him?). Nevertheless, although America's first president was revered as a symbol of integrity and honesty, many beloved stories regarding his life are down-and-out lies. Sorry to shake the powder from your wig . . .

Some of the more popular legends about the father of our country are:

✔ **He chopped down his father's cherry tree.** Perhaps the most famous story about George Washington — Is there an American child who hasn't learned this one in school? — is, in fact, one giant lie. An early biographer of Washington, Parson Mason Weems, made the story up to illustrate the president's integrity. Obviously, Weems didn't heed the lesson he was imparting.

✔ **He had wooden teeth.** This enduring myth about Washington's false teeth is, um, false! Which is not to say that George had a grandiose set of gums either. His dentures were made out of material that, in all likelihood, was even more uncomfortable than wood. Made of cow's teeth, human teeth, and elephant ivory, his teeth were set in a lead base with springs that allowed him to open and close his mouth (ouch!). Not surprisingly, his choppers fit poorly and distorted the shape of his mouth.

✔ **He threw a silver dollar across the Potomac River.** Although a pretty good athlete, George Washington didn't have the major-league throwing arm attributed to him. He did reportedly throw a piece of slate across the Rappahannock River near Fredericksburg, but that body of water is far narrower than the Potomac. And, in any case, he couldn't have tossed a silver dollar across the river because silver dollars didn't exist back then!

Day Trip #3: Visiting Annapolis, Maryland

Cruise up to **Annapolis,** located about 35 miles as the gull flies, from downtown D.C. (betcha your heart rate slows). The once prosperous 18th-century seaport supports hundreds of maritime-related businesses and is a magnet for boaters from all over the world. The home of the U.S. Naval Academy, Maryland's state capital, St. John's College, and exemplary 18th- and 19th-century architecture has a small-town feel. With more than 30,000 registered pleasure craft, Annapolis has earned the title, "sailing capital of the United States." A vocal and active preservation group oversees the historic district, some think with an iron fist. But the efforts have paid off handsomely: No high-rises, billboards, fast-food restaurants, or tacky buildings interfere with the architectural integrity of downtown. I've included a handy map of Annapolis in this chapter to help you understand the layout of the city.

Getting there

Annapolis has retained its resort-town flavor, in part, because the city is not linked to D.C. by a public transportation system. This excursion is one time when a car comes in handy. The ride is 45 minutes from downtown D.C., longer during rush hour. Exit Washington, D.C. via New York Avenue/U.S. 50 eastbound; from U.S. 50 take Exit 24, Rowe (rhymes with cow) Boulevard. Continue about 1 mile, hang a right at the governor's mansion (or crash the iron fence), and go halfway around Church Circle. Take a right at the Maryland Inn (Duke of Gloucester Street) and follow signs to Main Street, City Dock, and the Historic District. On-street parking is 50 cents an hour, with a 2-hour max.

The local meter maids are as vigilant as vultures awaiting fresh road-kill. Parking is also available in the Hillman Garage (entrances on Duke of Gloucester Street and Main Street) or Gott's Court Garage (enter on Calvert Street between Rowe and West Streets). Fringe parking is at the Navy-Marine Corps Stadium (Rowe Boulevard and Taylor Avenue), where all-day parking is $4 and includes a shuttle to downtown, 10 a.m. to 9 p.m. (extended hours during special events). *Note:* The shuttle often runs on its own mysterious internal clock.

Commuter bus transport is available Monday through Friday only during rush hour(s) between the District and Annapolis, via **Dillon's Bus Service** (☎ 410-647-2321). The one-way el cheapo fare is $3.35. Dillon's also runs commuter service from the New Carrollton Metro station (last stop on the Orange line) to several points in Annapolis, a distance of about 20 miles. This service is helpful to Annapolitans who commute to Washington, but not to visitors.

Seeing the sights

Write to the **Annapolis and Anne Arundel County Conference and Visitors Center,** 26 West St., Annapolis, MD 21401 (☎ 410-280-0445), open from 9 a.m. to 5 p.m. daily, or surf over to www.visit-annapolis. org. You can get comprehensive information from the walk-in Visitors Center, off Church Circle. Access the "Whiz Bang Machine," a touch-screen video guide, for more information about sights and special events. If you land downtown, pick up a brochure or calendar of events and ask questions at the **Visitor Information booth** (next to the public restrooms at the City Dock) in the heart of town, daily from 9 a.m. to 5 p.m. For information on B&Bs, try Bed-and-Breakfasts of Maryland (☎ 410-269-6232).

Annapolis

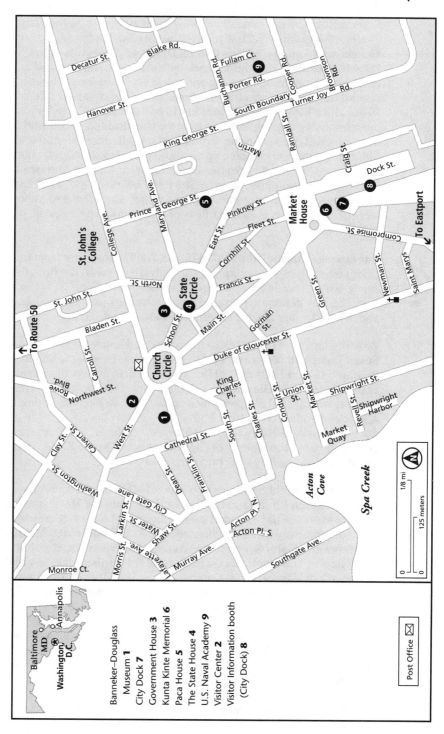

Banneker–Douglass
Museum **1**
City Dock **7**
Government House **3**
Kunta Kinte Memorial **6**
Paca House **5**
The State House **4**
U.S. Naval Academy **9**
Visitor Center **2**
Visitor Information booth
(City Dock) **8**

Post Office ⊠

Three Centuries Tours (☎ **410-263-5401**) leads 2-hour walking tours of the historic district, State House, Naval Academy, and St. John's College. Reservations are not taken, just show up at 10:30 a.m. at the Visitors Center, 26 West St. or at 1:30 p.m. at the City Dock information booth. Tickets are $9 adults, $3 kids 6 to 18. **Discover Annapolis Tours** (☎ **410-626-6000**) shuttles visitors by 350 years of history and architecture aboard minibuses with big windows. The hour-long tours depart several times a day from the Visitors Center. The cost is $12 for adults, $6 for 11- to 18-year-olds, $3 for kids 10 and under, and free for preschoolers. I recommend this tour for the disabled, those who can't walk long distances, and the terminally lazy. All others should get out there and walk! You can pick up an audio tour (lasting about 1 hour and 15 minutes), narrated by Walter Cronkite, or an **African American Heritage tour,** from the **Museum Store** at 77 Main St. (☎ **410-268-5576**). Although these tours are informative, I prefer a real live person to a recording. The cost is $5 regardless of sex, political persuasion, or sailing experience.

Chesapeake Marine Tours (☎ **410-268-7600**) runs tours from City Dock several times a day, spring through fall. Go with the flow. Because every visitor should view Annapolis at least once from the water, I recommend the 40-minute narrated tour of the harbor and Naval Academy aboard the *Harbor Queen,* $7 adults, $4 kids 11 and under.

Walk the length of City Dock to the water and enjoy the panorama from **Susan Campbell Memorial Park.** Get a double-scooper from **Storm Bros. Ice Cream Factory,** 130 Dock St., and drip across the street to the seawall along **Ego Alley,** appropriately named for the informal parade of boats and flesh that takes place on summer weekends. Where Ego Alley dead-ends, across from Market House, is a life-size bronze of *Roots* author Alex Haley reading to several children. The sculpture commemorates the landing of Haley's ancestor, Kunta Kinte, aboard the slave ship *Lord Ligonier* on September 29, 1767.

Check out the architecture as you ascend **Main Street** from City Dock to Church Circle, and the harbor view from the Maryland Inn. Downtown's face has changed dramatically in the past decade. Among the independently owned businesses are **A. L. Goodie,** 100 Main St., for souvenirs, T-shirts, and fudge; **Avoca Handweavers,** at 141 Main, woolens and household accessories from the British Isles; **Snyder's Bootery,** 170 Main Street at Conduit Street, with the area's largest selection of boat shoes; and **Chick and Ruth's Delly,** an Annapolis institution since the 1960s (see "Where to Dine" later in this section).

History buffs may wish to detour to the **Banneker-Douglass Museum,** 84 Franklin Street (☎ **410-974-2893**), dedicated to African American history, especially in Maryland. From the top of Main Street, go left at Church Circle, left at Franklin. The museum is housed in a Victorian Gothic church that was built in 1874 by former slaves. The museum's exhibits change periodically; call ahead to find out about current shows.

If you go right onto Church Circle from Main Street, and right again at School Street to **State Circle,** you discover an Annapolis that many overlook. The **State House** (☎ **410-974-3400**), the oldest state capitol in continuous use, still watches over the town below. Site of the ratification of The Treaty of Paris, it served as the U.S. Capitol for 8 months in the 1780s. View the grounds and public areas on your own or take the free tour, daily at 11 a.m. and 3 p.m. Private tours are by appointment. When you exit the rear of the building, cross **Lawyers Mall,** with its statue of Thurgood Marshall, to **Government House,** the official residence of Maryland's governor. (I had the pleasure of attending a function there a few years ago. Nice spread! Wonderful art!) Unfortunately, walk-ins are not admitted. On State Circle are some of the town's premier shops and galleries. **Annapolis Pottery** (No. 40) is a workshop/gallery with a wide selection of attractive and functional pieces. At **Nancy Hammond Editions** (No. 64-A), the award-winning local artist sells her limited-edition silk-screen prints, watercolors, note cards, clothing, and gifts. The **Maryland Federation of Art Gallery** (No. 18 State Circle), in a restored 1840 building with exposed brick and modern lighting, mounts solo and small group exhibits of multimedia works and three national shows per year.

From State Circle, turn down **Maryland Avenue,** with its many home design and antiques shops, boutiques, and galleries. Reminiscent of a gentler era, and a lot less touristy than Main Street, Maryland Avenue merits exploration. Shops line the cobblestone street from State Circle to Prince George Street. A personal favorite is the **Aurora Gallery** (No. 67), a few doors from the State House, with American-made crafts, pottery, jewelry, paintings and sculpture (some created by the artist-owners). Across the street is the **Briarwood Book Shop** (No. 88) for used and out-of-print books. The **Ship and Soldier Shop** (No. 58) draws miniaturists and model train collectors from near and far. The **Dawson Gallery** (No. 44) sells 18th-, 19th-, and early 20th-century American and European paintings. Among the gallery's better-known customers is Harrison Ford who purchased paintings here while filming *Patriot Games* in Annapolis several years ago.

Anyone who's been in Annapolis 5 minutes knows it's a sailing mecca. Many people come here from all over the country to learn to sail. If you're one of them, try the **Annapolis Sailing School,** 601 6th St. (☎ **800-638-9192** or 410-267-7205), where you can learn the basics in a weekend. The school has classes for kids as young as 4 and no upper-age limit. In the meantime, feel the wind on your face aboard the ***Woodwind*** or its twin, ***Woodwind II,*** with several departures most days, April through October, from Pusser's Landing (behind Marriott Waterfront Hotel, 80 Compromise St.; ☎ **410-263-7837**). Owner/Captain Ken Kaye knows how to put crew members at ease and encourages them to raise the sails or take the wheel of the classic 74-foot wood schooner during the 2-hour cruise ($24 adults, $22 seniors, and $15 kids 2 to 11). When the Bay breezes beckon, I head for the *Woodwind.* (Doing so is much cheaper than owning a boat.)

Annapolis lays claim to numerous fine examples of 18th- and 19th-century architecture. As you tour, notice the colored plaques on many buildings designating their historic status and the period in which they were built. (An explanation is provided in the Annapolis Visitors Guide, available at the Visitors Center.) If forced to choose, I would go see the **William Paca House and Gardens,** 186 Prince George St. (☎ **410-263-5533,** Internet: www.annapolis.org), open daily. Admission is adults $7 (house and gardens), $5 (house only), $4 (gardens only); half price for ages 6 to 18. Who was this Paca (pronounced Pay-ca, not Pack-a) character? Well, he signed the Declaration of Independence and served as governor of Maryland during the Revolution. Not a bad resume. The five-part Georgian mansion, built between 1763 and 1765, nearly succumbed to the wrecker's ball in 1965. The Historic Annapolis Foundation stepped in, restoring the house and gardens to their former grandeur. If you're short on time, or period furnishings fail to set your heart aflutter, skip the house and enjoy the gardens, with its terraces, parterres, and flowers in bloom from March to November. A self-guided audio tour is only $1.

Many people use the words Annapolis and the **U.S. Naval Academy** interchangeably. Whatever you call it, it's a must-see. At the very least, drive through and stop occasionally to snap a picture. If you park downtown, it's a 5-minute walk from City Dock via Randall Street to King George Street and Gate 1, the visitors' entrance. If you drive, limited parking is available next to the Halsey Field House, just inside Gate 1. A U.S. Marine greets you, perhaps, even salutes you. (No jokes, please, about whether the gun is loaded. It is.) To get information before you arrive, call ☎ **410-263-6933,** or visit the academy's Web site at www.usna.edu.

You are free to roam on your own, but I strongly recommend stopping first in the **Armel-Leftwich Visitors Center,** just inside Gate 1 and next to the Field House, for a map and to see the short film, *To Lead and to Serve.* Check out the interactive exhibits, gift shop, and stroll the waterfront promenade behind the building. Upstairs, you can ogle David Robinson's basketball and other significant memorabilia. I've taken the hour-long guided tour at least six times. Each guide gives it a different spin, and I always learn something new ($6 adults, $5 seniors, $4 kids 1st to 12th grades, and free for preschoolers). Tours are offered several times daily throughout the year. During the academic year (September through May) try to hook up with a morning tour which allows you to see noon meal formation (about 12:10 p.m. weekdays, 12:20 p.m. weekends, weather permitting) in front of **Bancroft Hall.** If you tour on your own, arrive a little before noon at **Tecumseh Court,** in front of Bancroft. The procession into **King Hall** (the world's largest dining room, it can accommodate all 4,000 midshipmen at one time) is preceded by bayonet drills and music, and it is incredibly moving. The food inside, alas, is hardly fit for royal consumption.

In **Lejeune Hall,** across from the Visitors Center, you find athletic trophies and photographs and maybe can catch swim practice in the Olympic-size pool. Close by is **Dahlgren Hall,** where a chrome yellow biplane "flies" from the ceiling. The Navy's ice hockey team plays here, and the Hall has also been the site of figure skating competitions and ice shows. Cross the Yard — as in Navy Yard because this is a military base — to the awesome **Navy Chapel** and **John Paul Jones's crypt.** Nearby is the Naval Academy Museum, **Preble Hall** (☎ 410-293-2108), filled with 200 years of naval art and artifacts. See the ground-floor **Gallery of Ships,** many of which are original builder's models. From the **Robert Crown Sailing Center,** the *plebes* (freshmen) learn to sail, and the academy's team races aboard *Knockabouts* (a type of schooner). *Mids* (short for Midshipmen) are required to learn sailing basics in preparation for *YP* (Yard Patrol) duty, even though most never board a sailboat again after graduation. **Bancroft Hall** (a huge H from the air) is the dormitory for all 4,000 midshipmen. Visitors are welcome to tour the public areas on their own, but must be with an escorted group to enter a *bunk* (room). Y'all come and take part in some of the activities during **Commissioning Week** — graduation, to the uninitiated — in late May. Locals leave work early for the spectacular air show by the **Blue Angels,** always a waker-upper. Most academy athletic events are free and open to the public. For information and tickets call the Naval Academy Athletic Association (☎ 800-US-4-NAVY).

Where to stay and dine

The **Annapolis Marriott Waterfront,** 80 Compromise St., Annapolis, MD 21401 (☎ 800-336-0072 or 410-268-7555), has 150 rooms (some overlooking the harbor and Spa Creek) and many amenities, but no pool. The location is in the heart of downtown and a 5-minute walk to the Naval Academy. Staying here does not come cheaply. Rack rates in season are $239 to $379 (waterfront suite). Off-season (November to mid-February) the price drops to $134 to $309. Occasionally, the Marriott runs a special, so be sure to inquire. On-site parking is an additional $12 per day. **Pusser's Landing** restaurant and dockside bar/lounge are out back with so-so food but a commanding view of Ego Alley's preening muscle boats and tattooed blondes (male and female). During special events, like the in-water boat shows in October, this place is booked a year or more ahead.

On a quiet side street in the Historic District and convenient to the sights is the warm and welcoming **Chez Amis B&B,** 85 East St., Annapolis, MD 21401 (☎ 410-263-6631; Internet: www.chezamis.com). Rooms are $115 to $140 per night, sometimes with special rates off-season. Carved from a corner store, the original tin ceilings, pine floors, and oak counters were retained in the store-to-inn renovation. Furnishings acquired during the owner's European travels fill the rooms. The colorful quilts that blanket the walls were pieced by the proprietor's grandmother. Air-conditioning, TVs, terry robes, and fresh flowers are standard in all rooms. Each room has a private bathroom, one with a claw-foot tub. A full breakfast is served. Kids 10 and older are welcome. Garage parking is $4 per day a few blocks away.

For the ultimate Annapolis experience, bed down on the water. Well, sort of. **Private Pleasure,** Annapolis City Marina, Severn Ave., Annapolis, MD 21403 (behind Carrolls Creek Café; ☎ **800-877-9390** or 410-267-7802; Internet: www.harborviewbnb.com) is a classic 1947 Trumpy yacht accommodating six. (I'd stay here if I didn't live down the road.) Guests enjoy an hour-long sunset cruise and the marina's pool and cafe in season. Continental breakfast is served in the paneled main salon or aft deck. The Giardinis are congenial hosts who love what they do. An overnight stay starts at $230 for a standard cabin and includes the amenities described above.

Stay smack on Main Street at the **Scotlaur Inn,** 165 Main St., Annapolis, MD 21401 (☎ **410-268-5665;** Internet: www.scotlaurinn.com). The 10 rooms, though smallish, are comfortable and surprisingly quiet. They don't build fortress-thick walls like that anymore. All rooms were redecorated in 1999 and come with air-conditioning, cable TVs, hair dryers, and irons and ironing boards (so you can press your wrinkled T-shirts). Some bathrooms are equipped with showers only. Rack rates run $80 to $110, and an extra person over the age of 2 costs an additional $10. Go downstairs to **Chick and Ruth's Delly** for a full complimentary breakfast and to kibbitz with owner Ted Levitt. Patrons salute the flag at 8:30 a.m. weekdays, 9:30 a.m. Saturday and Sunday. Garaged parking a block away is $4 night.

Café Normandie, 185 Main St. (☎ **410-280-6470**), a cozy, plant-filled French bistro tries to be all things to its customers. Most of the time, the kitchen succeeds, but the service can be inconsistent. Come for a hearty breakfast (eggs, omelets, and French toast), lunch (tomato-crab or onion soup, grilled chicken Caesar salad, and crepes), or dinner (veal, fish, beef many ways, seafood-filled crepes, and pasta). Except for the obscene ice cream-filled or fruit-filled crepes, the desserts are ho-hum. Main courses run from $7 to $23. Good value here, especially for the $18.50, 3-course Early Bird Special, served 5:00 to 6:30 p.m. The restaurant is open Sunday to Thursday 8 a.m. to 10 p.m., Friday to Saturday 8 a.m. to 11 p.m.

From May to October, visit **Cantler's Riverside Inn on Mill Creek,** 458 Forest Beach Rd. (☎ **410-757-1311**), and dig into a pile of steamed Maryland blue crabs. This place is packed in summer, especially on weekends (when the restaurant won't take a reservation). I urge you to arrive at off times. Have an early or late lunch or a *very* early dinner. Otherwise, you may find the crabs AWOL. Also try the steamed shrimp, crab-vegetable soup, soft-shell crab sandwich, fried or broiled fish, and the fried chicken for landlubbers. In shedding boxes beneath the restaurant, the crabs striptease to become *soft shells,* which are then sautéed or fried. Cantler's is open Sunday to Thursday 11 a.m. to 11 p.m., Friday to Saturday 11 a.m. to midnight. The inn is about a 15-minute ride from City Dock.

A bit of advice from this old crab picker: At Cantler's, order large or jumbo males (jimmys) or fuggedaboutit. A dozen of these jimmys set you back about $40 in summer. The mediums are too much work for too little meat. The roe in the female crabs (sooks) puts most people off.

With its long wooden bar, chatty bartender, high-decibel noise level, and garage-sale accessories, **Riordan's,** 26 Market Space (☎ **410-263-5449**), is a quintessential neighborhood saloon. The servers are pleasant and efficient, the food is consistent and reasonably priced (nothing on the menu is more than $19), and the beer is cold. Start with potato skins with the works, or a seafood appetizer and then move on to a burger, roast beef sandwich, or Reuben. The soups are, um, soup-er, especially the New England clam chowder and crab vegetable. The a la carte Sunday brunch (mimosa or glass of champagne included) is an Annapolis tradition and also a bargain, with most entrees under $10. At lunch and dinner, a kids' menu for the 10-and-under set lists burgers, chicken, and spaghetti. The restaurant is open daily 11 a.m. to 2 a.m.; Brunch is Sun 10 a.m. to 1 p.m.

Chick and Ruth's Delly, 165 Main St. (☎ **410-269-6737**), has anchored the corner of Main and Conduit streets since the '60s, before Annapolis became a yuppie outpost. Come for the breakfast platters (served all day), the tasty sandwiches (named for Maryland pols and local characters), milkshakes, malteds, or banana splits. Try the *delly fries* (home fries with plenty of pepper and onions), my favorite diet treat. The kitschy décor — orange Formica and bagel light pulls are décor? — is pure 1950s. So are the cheeky waitresses and prices (most items are $2 to $9) at this friendly eatery, which has served four generations of Annapolitans. One booth is stocked with newspapers and reserved for the governor. Join the locals in the Pledge of Allegiance weekdays at 8:30 a.m., weekends at 9:30 a.m.. The restaurant is open Sunday, Wednesday, and Thursday from 6:30 a.m. to 10 p.m.; Monday and Tuesday from 6:30 a.m. to 4 p.m.; and Friday and Saturday 6:30 a.m. to 11:30 p.m. Closed Thanksgiving and Christmas. Credit cards aren't accepted.

Part VI

Living It Up after the Sun Goes Down: D.C. Nightlife

The 5th Wave   By Rich Tennant

"Yes, we are going to hear Pachelbel's Canon next, but maybe I should explain..."

In this part . . .

*R*ead my lips: D.C. ain't no Vegas! For many,
Washington, D.C. is a place to work. Period. Some
federal workers rise at 4:30 a.m. to boot up their computers by 6:30 a.m. After working 8 to 9½ hours, they may face
a 1- to 2-hour commute. A Washington worker's idea of
nightlife may be a peanut butter and jelly sandwich and
crawling into bed.

But that doesn't mean you should do the same! Nightlife in
Washington can mean cocktails in a discreet lounge or a
warm pint in a noisy pub. You can indulge in a leisurely
dinner, perhaps a movie, show, concert, or an after-dark
tour. Neighborhood watering holes and music/dance clubs
abound, drawing the young and awake. Whatever your
pleasure (within the law), this part helps you plan your
evenings in D.C.

Chapter 22

Washington, D.C.'s Cultural Scene

. . . .

In This Chapter

▶ Getting information and tickets

▶ Dining before the curtain goes up

▶ Knowing what's hot on the cultural scene

▶ Taking in a play, concert, or dance performance

. . . .

*U*nlike the famous cherry trees, Washington's cultural scene knows no particular season and blooms year-round. When I immigrated in the '60s, the National Theatre and Arena Stage were the only games in town. Today, a dazzling array of theatrical and cultural offerings confronts residents and visitors. Except for New York's performing arts scene, Washington takes a back seat to no one. Like the old car commercial, D.C.'s number two, so we try harder.

What to Know before Taking in a Show

I recommend doing a little homework before you touch down in the capital city. Check out www.washington.org or call ☎ 202-789-7000 to gather info from the **Washington, D.C. Convention and Visitors Association.** You can also peruse the *Guide to the Lively Arts* (daily) or the *Weekend* magazine (Friday) in the *Washington Post,* or visit its Web site at www.washingtonpost.com.

Tickets, please!

Due to the sterling caliber of performances, competition for tickets is keen. To get the best seats (or any seats) for a popular performance, buying tickets in advance is a necessity. It's your call, but I prefer to pass on a performance if the seats are in the upper deck or behind a post. When I splurge, I want to see what's going on. All of it.

If you order tickets over the phone, ask about the location; at the box office, ask to see a diagram of the theater.

To order tickets to most city events, call **Ticketmaster** (☎ 202-432-SEAT), or visit Hecht's, at 12th and G streets NW at Metro Center. **Tickets.com** (☎ **703-218-6500;** Internet: www.tickets.com), formerly known as Protix, pretty much covers what Ticketmaster doesn't, and sells tickets for productions at the Arena Stage and Ford's Theatre. Expect to pay a surcharge ($2 to $3.50 per ticket and $1 per order) for this service.

Located just one block from the Federal Triangle Metro station, **TicketPlace** (in the mezzanine of the Old Post Office Pavilion, 11th Street and Pennsylvania Ave. NW; ☎ **202-TICKETS**) allows you to purchase half-price tickets (with a 10 percent surcharge) for same-day performances. Call first and listen to the recording of what's available and then decide whether you want to make the trip to the pavilion. TicketPlace is open Tuesday through Friday, 11 a.m. to 6 p.m.; Saturday, 11 a.m. to 5 p.m. Tickets for Sunday and Monday shows are sold on Saturday. TicketPlace is closed Thanksgiving, Christmas, and New Year's Day. No credit cards are accepted for half-price tickets, but you can also purchase full-price tickets here and, for these, your plastic is good.

The concierge at your hotel should be able to get you tickets to any event, within reason. This is Washington, however, and greasing a palm or two goes with the territory. Nobody does the concierge a favor for free, however, so you can expect to pay a surcharge. This charge can vary from a few dollars per ticket to $10 or more. Whatever the case, tip the concierge $5 for his service.

Many theaters set aside tickets for seniors and full-time students that go on sale the day of the performance. If you don't ask, you don't get! Gamblers are advised to arrive at the box office a half-hour before curtain time. Sometimes unclaimed reserved tickets are available. If you're determined to attend a performance that's sold out, ask about SRO (Standing Room Only) tickets. These tickets usually go for $20 or less. If someone leaves at intermission, you may get lucky and snag a seat.

Pre-theater dining

If you're catching a theater performance, be seated for dinner no later than 6 p.m., as most curtains go up at 7:30 or 8:00 p.m. Choose some-place near the theater, in case the service is slow. (Wouldn't you rather sprint a couple of blocks than hail a cab and maybe miss Act I?) When you sit down tell the host or waiter (or both) that you're going to an event and need to be out by X time. Order soon after you're seated and save the soufflé and other dishes requiring lots of preparation for a non-theater evening.

Many restaurants within walking distance of the theaters offer a pre-theater, fixed-price menu. This menu usually includes an appetizer or salad, entree, dessert, and a beverage (non-alcoholic). Pre-theater specials are usually in effect from 4:30 or 5:00 p.m. to 6:00 or 6:30 p.m. You can make out like a bandit and spend considerably less than you would ordering a la carte later in the evening.

If you have tickets for a show, consider the following restaurants (the price is in parentheses):

- ✔ The **Roof Terrace Restaurant** ($39), at the Kennedy Center; ☎ 202-416-8555.

- ✔ **Aquarelle** ($40), across from the Kennedy Center in the Watergate, 2650 Virginia Ave. NW at New Hampshire Ave.; ☎ 202-298-4455.

- ✔ **Le Rivage** ($18.95), near Arena Stage, at 1000 Water St. SW, between Maine Ave. and 9th St. SW; ☎ 202-488-8111.

- ✔ **701** ($24.50), near the Shakespeare Theatre and Ford's Theatre, 6 blocks from the National and Warner Theaters, 701 Pennsylvania Ave.; ☎ 202-393-0701.

For more information on these restaurants or for a larger selection of restaurant choices, see Chapter 14.

Curtain calls

Blame it on all those bureaucratic ions in the water, but Washingtonians are a punctual lot. So you can count on the curtain rising on time. A good rule of thumb is to arrive at least 15 minutes early so you can visit the restroom and buy a $2 bag of candy — ouch! (I've seen the line to the ladies room snake all the way to Kentucky 5 minutes before a performance.) Latecomers may not be seated until intermission.

Because every rule has an exception, naturally, the curtain one does too. If the President is in attendance, and it's happened to me a few times, the performance will start late. You can bank on it. Smile as you pass through the metal detector and hand over your purse when asked. No jokes about explosives, please. If you're carrying a pocket-knife you'll lose it, temporarily. The security guards won't confiscate your chocolate-covered mints.

The Performing Arts Scene in Washington, D.C.

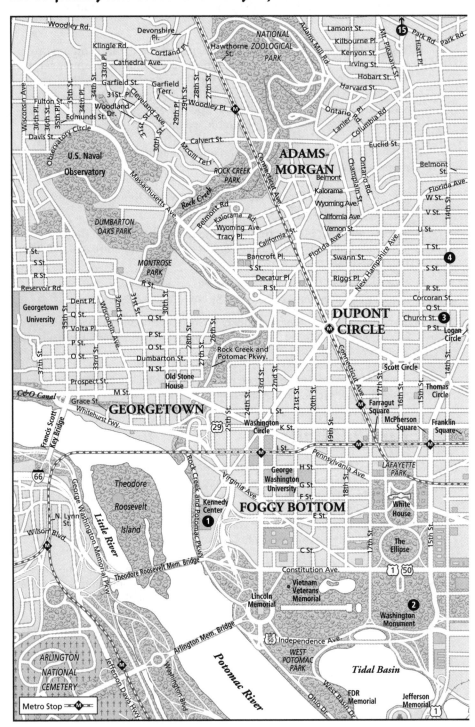

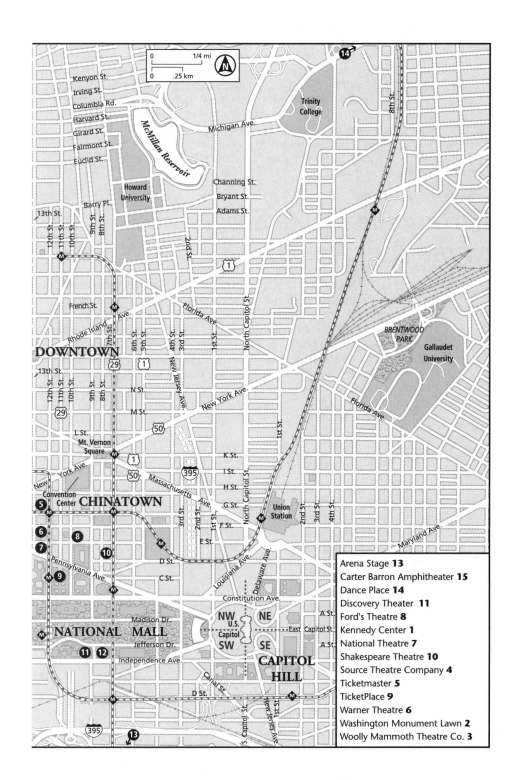

Arena Stage **13**
Carter Barron Amphitheater **15**
Dance Place **14**
Discovery Theater **11**
Ford's Theatre **8**
Kennedy Center **1**
National Theatre **7**
Shakespeare Theatre **10**
Source Theatre Company **4**
Ticketmaster **5**
TicketPlace **9**
Warner Theatre **6**
Washington Monument Lawn **2**
Woolly Mammoth Theatre Co. **3**

Dressing the part

A night at the theater no longer means a suit and tie or dress and high heels. (Choose sides!) Oh, you may see the occasional bouffant 'do and décolletage, but most Washington theatergoers are a shade or two less formal and flamboyant. Knock yourself out and preen your feathers if that's your style, but the usher will show you to your seat no matter what your attire. When in doubt, follow your mother's advice and "wash behind your ears, comb your hair, and look presentable." Try slacks or a skirt, a clean shirt or blouse, a jacket or sweater. Now, go make your entrance.

Getting the Inside Scoop on the D.C. Arts Scene

The **Kennedy Center,** with 6 stages, is the most visited and best-attended arts center in the nation. Home of the National Symphony and the Washington Opera, it plays host to the Washington Ballet as well as internationally acclaimed artists and such star-studded companies as the American Ballet Theatre and Alvin Ailey. D.C. also sports no less than six acclaimed theaters, which showcase a variety of performances, from Broadway standards to Shakespeare to experimental theater. Year-round, on any given day, D.C.'s cultural treats provide opportunities for locals and visitors alike. (See the map in this chapter for more on the locations of the performing arts venues.)

The play's the thing

In a city that generates more than its share of political drama, the *legitimate* theater also thrives. (I guess audiences don't get enough sturm und drang from their leaders.) Broadway-bound shows and resurrected classics account for most of the theatrical activity at the **Kennedy Center,** 2700 F Street NW (at Rock Creek Parkway; ☎ **202-467-4600;** Internet: www.kennedy-center.org). Perhaps it's a generous bow to democracy, but the Ken Cen has a history of playing it safe, pleasing audiences with first-rate productions that lack bite, while many theatergoers are hungry for more adventurous fare.

On the other hand, the **Arena Stage,** 6th Street and Maine Ave. SW, (at the Maine Avenue waterfront; ☎ **202-488-3300**) presents a theater season that always includes a mix of old and new performances that are superbly acted and rarely dull. Several productions that debuted at the Arena, such as *The Great White Hope* and *Dancing at Lughnasa,* ended up on Broadway and/or on film.

Fabulous freebies

The best news for those traveling on a tight budget is that free performances are as much a part of Washington as spin doctors and filibusters. The Kennedy Center offers free performances on the **Millennium Stage** in the Grand Foyer, daily at 6 p.m. Discounted tickets (50 percent off full price) for Kennedy Center performances are available to the following: full-time students, seniors 65 and older, those with permanent disabilities, enlisted military personnel, and those on fixed income. Proof of eligibility must be presented in person at the Friends Desk in the Hall of States (before ordering tickets by mail) or at the box office when purchasing tickets.

Every summer for 2 or more weeks, audiences applaud **Shakespeare in the Park** when the Shakespeare Theatre plays its thing (for free) in **Rock Creek Park at the Carter Barron Amphitheatre** (off 16th Street and Colorado Ave. NW), a 20-minute to half-hour drive (or taxi or bus ride) from downtown. And free outdoor concerts, given by the National Symphony and military bands, take place at several downtown sites from Memorial Day through Labor Day.

For the past couple of summers, the Washington Monument lawn has become a screening room for **"Screen on the Green."** On five Monday evenings, vintage films *(Singin' in the Rain, North by Northwest)* have been shown on huge drive-in–type screens. Ya' gotta love it! For information and schedules check the *Washington Post,* especially the Friday *Weekend* magazine or go to www.washingtonpost.com.

D.C.'s diminutive Great White Way, and I hesitate to compare ours to New York's, is downtown, east of the White House. The most active stages are as follows:

- ✔ **National Theatre,** 1321 E St. NW, between 13th and 14th Streets; ☎ 202-628-6161.

- ✔ **Shakespeare Theatre,** 450 7th St. NW, between D and E Streets; ☎ 202-547-1122.

- ✔ **Warner Theatre,** 511 10th St. NW, between E and F Streets; ☎ 202-783-4000.

- ✔ **Ford's Theatre,** 511 10th St. NW, between E and F Streets; ☎ 202-347-4833.

Don't overlook the more experimental **Source Theatre Company,** 1835 14th St NW, between S and T Streets; ☎ 202-462-1073, and the **Woolly Mammoth Theatre Co.,** 1401 Church St. NW; ☎ 202-393-3939.

Hearing the sounds of music

D.C.'s **National Symphony Orchestra** plays in the Kennedy Center Concert Hall, at F Street NW and Rock Creek Parkway. Leonard Slatkin is the conductor, with world renowned guest conductors filling in when Maestro Slatkin is on the road. For information, call ☎ **202-416-8100;** if you want to order tickets (with a 9 percent service charge), call ☎ **800-444-1324** or 202-467-4600. You can also check out the orchestra on the Web at www.kennedy-center.org.

National Symphony Orchestra (NSO) performances frequently sell out during the regular season, September to June. But don't let that stop you. Subscribers occasionally show up pre-performance with seats they can't use. Sometimes unsold tickets are available at the box office up until the conductor raises his baton. Whaddaya have to lose? If a performance is sold out, you may be able to snag SRO (Standing Room Only) tickets, which usually go for $20 or less. If you get one, keep an eye peeled for empty seats. You could luck out when someone leaves to attend an emergency White House meeting. (I've seen it happen.)

Hot time: Summer in the city

For those of you visiting Washington in the summer: If you enjoy classical music, consider taking in the Mozart festival at the Kennedy Center. This event takes place in June and sells out quickly. Order your tickets early if you are interested. (See the previous section for Ken Cen contact information.)

In addition, the NSO offers free concerts on the West Lawn of the Capitol each Sunday of the Memorial Day and Labor Day weekends, and on the 4th of July. These events are some of the top perks of summer in the city. You can also catch a free concert by the NSO several times in July at the **Carter Barron Amphitheatre** in Rock Creek Park (☎ **202-426-6837**).

The rousing 4th of July concert — a scene worthy of Norman Rockwell — features guest artists, choral groups, and an enthusiastic audience. Aye, it's a grand old flag! The evening ends with a bang when the 1812 Overture accompanies the fireworks display on the Mall. (Or vice versa, depending on your viewpoint.) Bring something to sit on. You can also catch a live broadcast of the concert on TV, which is precisely what I did in 2000 because of a heat and humidity index of about 4,000.

From early June to Labor Day, the Kennedy Center features free musical entertainment — everything from bluegrass to R & B to classical — Tuesday and Thursday at noon at the East Front of the U.S. Capitol (the same location as the visitors entrance). The world's top orchestras, soloists, and chamber ensembles also concertize at the Ken Cen.

A night at the opera (minus the Marx Brothers)

Snagging tickets for the **Washington Opera** was difficult *before* Placido Domingo became artistic director. Now it's tougher than getting elected. About 95 percent of the seats are sold to series subscribers. Still, you can have a go at it and call ☎ **800-870-OPERA** or 202-295-2400. Also, returned tickets are sold at the box office an hour before curtain time. If you want to go SRO, the tickets are sold Saturday at 10 a.m. for the upcoming week. You can't purchase single tickets off the Web site at www.dc-opera, but you can find out which diva will be singing *Turandot.*

Enjoying an evening of dance

The best in the dance world grace Washington's stages. In 2000, the Alvin Ailey Company, American Ballet Theatre, Bolshoi, Merce Cunningham, Paul Taylor and many, many other stellar companies performed here. The Kennedy Center and **Washington Performing Arts Society** (WPAS) are the leading presenters. The city is also quite proud of its own **Washington Ballet** (☎ **202-362-3606** for info; **202-432-SEAT** for tickets), a fine ensemble troupe with a varied repertory. The Washington Ballet presents a fall, winter, and spring series at the Kennedy Center, and spreads holiday cheer with a full-length *Nutcracker* at the Warner Theatre and at George Mason University in suburban Virginia.

Located near Catholic University, **Dance Place,** 3225 8th St. NE (☎ **202-269-1600,** Internet: www.danceplace.org), is the site of weekend performances by local and visiting troupes: contemporary, postmodern, tap, ethnic, performance art, and styles as yet unnamed. Tickets are a steal at $5 to $15. In addition, many high-caliber D.C.–based companies perform regularly in their own backyard. Keep an eye peeled for Bowen-McCauley Dance, Juan Rincones, and Tony Powell.

Cool for kids

Washington offers wonderful cultural opportunities for families, especially during the school year. Look to the following for entertaining productions that are geared to youngsters:

- ✔ **The Discovery Theater,** in the Smithsonian's Arts and Industries Building, 900 Jefferson Dr. SW (☎ 202-357-1500).

- ✔ **The Kennedy Center's Theater for Young People,** F Street NW and Rock Creek Parkway (☎ 202-416-8830).

- ✔ **Saturday Morning at the National,** 1321 E St. NW (☎ 202-783-3372).

The (free) **Navy Band Lollipop Concert** on the Washington Monument grounds in August (☎ 202-433-2394), and (free) summertime military band concerts at several downtown sites (☎ 202-433-4011), are always big hits with little ones. Holiday highlights include the **Washington Ballet's Nutcracker** (late November through December) at the Warner Theatre, 1299 Pennsylvania Ave. NW (☎ 202-432-SEAT); and the **Pageant of Peace** (December evenings) on the Ellipse, between the White House and Constitution Avenue NW (☎ 202-619-7222 for more information).

Chapter 23

Hitting the Clubs and Bars

- -

In This Chapter

▶ Spying the best spots to hear your favorite music

▶ Checking out clubs where you can dance the night away

▶ Taking some time out for a laugh (or two)

- -

*T*aking in Mozart or *Swan Lake* at the Kennedy Center, or *Hamlet* at the Shakespeare Theatre may quench your cultural appetite. But it may leave you thirsty for a chilled cocktail and some hot jazz. When your aesthetic sensibilities have been fed but you feel the urge to get down or wet your whistle, you won't lack for a place to go. Rest assured, after the lights go off in the White House, you can take the party elsewhere, such as Adams-Morgan or Georgetown. Washington's large international population has spawned several music clubs, bars and other nightspots that appeal to its multicultural citizenry (see the map in this chapter for details).

Before you go off to strut your stuff, however, keep in mind that Metro stops running at midnight Sunday through Thursday, and at 2 a.m. Friday and Saturday. Allow plenty of time to get to the station, or you may need to catch a taxi back to your hotel.

For a comprehensive listing of the entertainment scene, see the "Weekend" section of the Friday *Washington Post.* The free *City Paper,* available in bookstores, restaurants, bars, and cafes all around town, is another good source for information on what's goin' on.

Finding Hot Spots for Cool Jazz

D.C.'s premier jazz club, **Blues Alley,** rear of 1037 Wisconsin Ave. NW (☎ 202-337-4141), presents top blues and jazz musicians — Nancy Wilson, Wynton Marsalis, Julie Wilson, Maynard Ferguson, and so forth — twice nightly, sometimes with a third midnight show on the weekends. Book early and arrive by 7 p.m. for the 8 p.m. show as it's first-come, first-served seating. The cover runs $15 to $50 with a $7 food or drink minimum. Take a cab; the Foggy Bottom Metro station is about a mile away.

Washington, D.C. Bars & Clubs

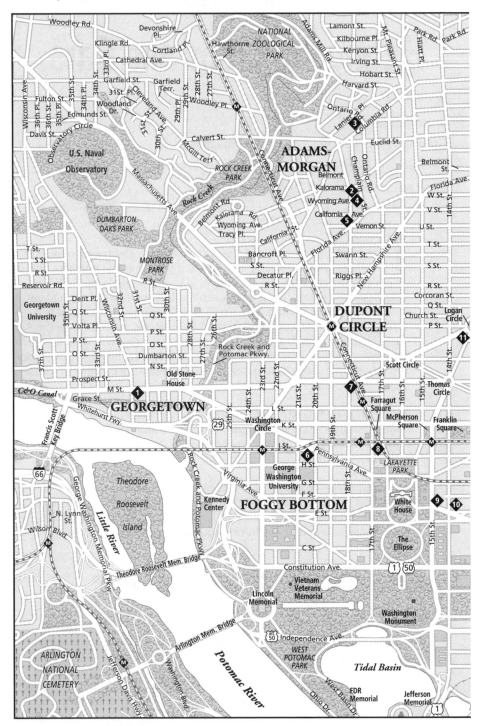

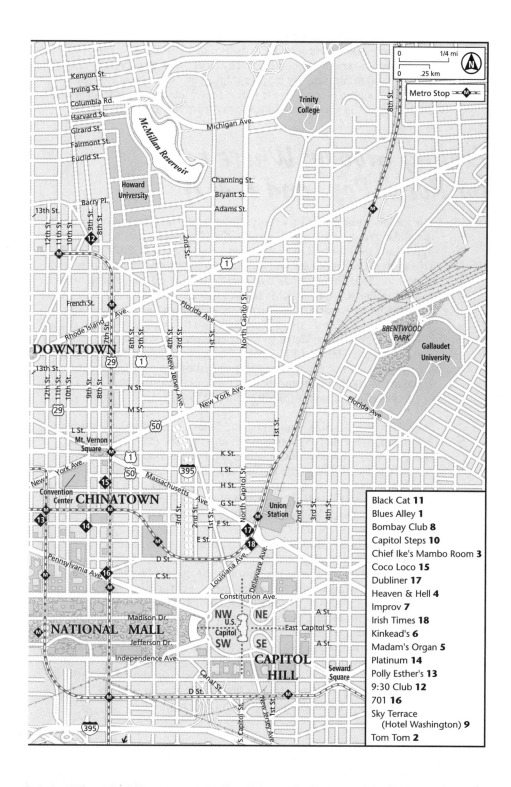

Kenyon St.
Irving St.
Columbia Rd.
Harvard St.
Girard St.
Fairmont St.
Euclid St.

McMillan Reservoir

Trinity College

Michigan Ave.

8th St.

Metro Stop Ⓜ

Channing St.
Bryant St.
Adams St.

Howard University

Barry Pl.

13th St.
12th St.
11th St.
10th St.
9th St.
8th St.

2nd St.

French St.

Rhode Island Ave.
7th St.

6th St.
5th St.
4th St.
3rd St.
2nd St.
1st St.

Florida Ave.

North Capitol St.

BRENTWOOD PARK

Gallaudet University

DOWNTOWN

13th St.
12th St.
11th St.
10th St.
9th St.
8th St.

N St.
M St.

New Jersey Ave.

New York Ave.

Florida Ave.

L St.
Mt. Vernon Square

Convention Center

CHINATOWN

New York Ave.

Massachusetts Ave.

3rd St.
2nd St.
1st St.

K St.
I St.
H St.
G St.
F St.
E St.

1st St.

Union Station

2nd St.
3rd St.
4th St.

Pennsylvania Ave.

D St.
C St.

Louisiana Ave.
Delaware Ave.

Constitution Ave.

NW   NE
U.S.
Capitol
SW   SE

A St.
East Capitol St.
A St.

Madison Dr.

NATIONAL MALL

Jefferson Dr.

Independence Ave.

CAPITOL HILL

Seward Square

Canal St.

D St.

S. Capitol St.
New Jersey Ave.

Black Cat **11**
Blues Alley **1**
Bombay Club **8**
Capitol Steps **10**
Chief Ike's Mambo Room **3**
Coco Loco **15**
Dubliner **17**
Heaven & Hell **4**
Improv **7**
Irish Times **18**
Kinkead's **6**
Madam's Organ **5**
Platinum **14**
Polly Esther's **13**
9:30 Club **12**
701 **16**
Sky Terrace
   (Hotel Washington) **9**
Tom Tom **2**

In the lounge at **701,** 701 Pennsylvania Ave., at 7th St. NW (☎ 202-393-0701), you can nurse a Cosmopolitan (or a pot of coffee) and listen to the three-piece Alex Jenkins Trio, Monday through Saturday, 7:30 to 11:30 p.m. The trio has been a fixture at 701 for several years. There's no cover, no minimum. My mother might say, "Change out of your shorts, it's a nice place." To get there, take Metro to Archives/Navy Memorial. 701 is less than a block away from the station.

Feeling Groovy: Where to Go for Rock, Pop, and R & B

The music scene heats up evenly throughout the city, but it sizzles in the clubs around 14th and U Streets NW. The coolest felines purr at the **Black Cat,** 1831 14th St. NW, between S and T Sts. (☎ 202-667-7960). This club showcases new and alternative bands and has a dance floor that holds 400. The club has two parts. You pay no cover or minimum in the smaller room that holds pinball machines and a jukebox with mostly alternative and classic rock selections. In the big room, the cover is $5 to $15, with no minimum. A mostly vegetarian menu of light fare is available. Take Metro to U Street/Cardozo, walk west 1 block on U Street, make a left at 14th, and go 2 blocks. Or take a taxi. (Maybe it's my age, but I'm not crazy about this neighborhood.) The Black Cat also sponsors workshops for musicians. Buy tickets at the club's box office or through Ticketmaster (☎ 202-432-SEAT).

Sheryl Crow, Smashing Pumpkins, and Shawn Colvin have all played the **9:30 Club,** 815 V St. NW, between 8th and 9th Sts. (☎ 202-393-0930). Lords of Acid, Cowboy Mouth, and Deep Banana Blackout have too. (How do they come up with these names?) The 9:30 has a state-of-the-art sound system, 3 dance floors, and 4 bars. Cover is $5 to $25. Take Metro to U Street/Cardozo, go east 4 blocks on U Street, make a left at 9th Street, and walk half a block. Better yet, take a taxi.

Big Daddy's Love Lounge & Pick-Up Joint, the second-floor bar at **Madam's Organ** (a play on Adams-Morgan where it's located) is worth a visit. Voted one of the 23 best bars in the country by *Playboy* in 2000, Madam's has a varied musical menu, served nightly from 9 p.m. Monday, it's funky jazz; Tuesday, delta blues; Wednesday, hillbilly bluegrass (with local TV news anchor Doug McKelway playing banjo); Thursday, salsa; Friday and Saturday, national, local, and regional blues bands. Redheads get half-price drinks every night. The bar is located at 2003 18th St. NW (☎ 202-667-5370). To get here, take Metro to Woodley Park/Adams-Morgan, and then hop on the free shuttle. If you insist on driving here, there's limited parking in a lot on 18th Street, between Belmont and Columbia Roads.

Relaxing with Cocktails for Two

After a rough day of sightseeing, kicking back with your favorite aperi-
tif can be therapeutic. The following places don't charge a minimum or
a cover.

At the south end of the 7th Street Arts Corridor and near the Shakespeare
Theatre is the dimly lit, elegant lounge area of **701,** 701 Pennsylvania
Ave. NW, at 7th Street (☎ **202-393-0701**). As I noted earlier in this chapter, 701 is a great place not only to dine (see Chapter 14) and listen to
jazz, but also to enjoy a cocktail and good conversation. Check out the
vodka and caviar menu and enjoy a jazz trio Sunday through Friday,
and classical piano on Saturday. Take Metro to Archives/Navy Memorial,
and then look around until you spot 701 on the corner.

In the downtown business district, the **Bombay Club,** 815 Connecticut
Ave. NW, between H and I Streets (☎ **202-659-3727**), is the perfect spot
for sipping a Pimm's Cup in days-of-the-raj splendor. A pianist enter-
tains from 6:45 to 10:15 p.m. in the lounge area. Take Metro to Farragut
West, and then go east for half a block, make a right at Connecticut
Ave. and go another half a block.

In the city's West End, a pianist accompanies the lively bar-and-grazing
scene at **Kinkead's,** 2000 Pennsylvania Ave. NW (☎ **202-296-7700**).
Enjoy the tickling of the ivories from around 6:00 to 10:00 or 10:30 p.m.,
later on weekends. Metro: Foggy Bottom, and then walk east on I Street
for 3 blocks. Look for the entrance on I street between 20th and 21st
Streets.

The **Sky Terrace** on the 11th floor of the Hotel Washington, 15th Street
and Pennsylvania Avenue, NW (☎ **202-638-5900**) is D.C.'s premiere bar
with a view. You'll probably have to wait anytime after 5 or 5:30 p.m.
The Sky Terrace is open April to October, weather permitting, from
11:30 a.m. to 1 a.m. To get here, take Metro to McPherson Square and
walk south on 15th Street for 2 ½ blocks. The hotel is on the northeast
corner.

Searching for International Sound Bites

After a thought-provoking play at the Shakespeare Theatre, walk up the
street, and shake your coconuts at **Coco Loco,** 801 7th St. NW, between
H and I Sts. (☎ **202-289-2626**). Join the conga line and limbo contest
held around 2 a.m. on Thursday, and 3 a.m. on Friday and Saturday.

The Brazilian dancers' gyrations have been known to stop diners dead in their tapas. Take Metro to Chinatown/Gallery Place, and then walk north 2 blocks on 7th Street.

On Thursday through Saturday evenings from 9 p.m. to 1 a.m. (or later), join the students swillin' and spillin' their stout at the folk sing-alongs at **Irish Times,** 14 F St. NW, between N. Capitol St. and New Jersey Ave., opposite Union Station (☎ **202-543-5433**). Irish music also cuts through the suds nightly at **The Dubliner,** in the Phoenix Park Hotel opposite Union Station, 520 N. Capitol St. NW (☎ **202-737-3773**) from 9 p.m. on most evenings, and from 7:30 p.m. on Sundays. Last call is at 2 or 3 a.m.

Getting Down Tonight: Where to Shake Your Booty

Take your dancin' feet to **Coco Loco** (see the previous section for details) or **Chief Ike's Mambo Room,** 1725 Columbia Rd. NW, in Adams-Morgan (☎ **202-332-2211**), where a mostly under-30-somethings crowd the small dance floor Friday and Saturday nights to DJ-spun, R & B, hip-hop, '70s tunes. Also check out the other music clubs described in this chapter, many of which have crowded dance floors.

Tom Tom, 2333 18th St. NW, at Columbia Road (☎ **202-588-1300**), attracts a mostly dining and drinking clientele of 20-somethings to 50-plusers who come for the tapas, pizza, and designer beers on tap. Weekends (and nightly in summer) the crowd swells, swings, and sticks (to the floor). If you can, snag a table on the rooftop patio where space heaters keep patrons toasty warm. Take Metro to Woodley Park-Zoo/Adams-Morgan, and then shuttle to 18th Street and Columbia Road. Late at night, cab it back to your hotel.

As you might expect, **Heaven & Hell,** 2327 18th St. NW, at Columbia Road (☎ **202-667-HELL**), welcomes both angels and devils. Leave your wings and pitchforks at the door of the Green Island Café (why don't they just call it Purgatory?) which separates the mirrored upstairs dance bar (Heaven) from the smoky subterranean bar (Hell). Even Heaven sizzles here, with music (jazz, swing, industrial, techno, house) that is sometimes live, sometimes DJ-generated. Lines form early for the Thursday night '80s dance party ($5 cover). On weekends, the pearly gates don't close until 3 a.m. Take Metro to Woodley Park-Zoo/Adams-Morgan, and then shuttle to 18th Street and Columbia Road. Take a taxi back to your hotel if the hour is late.

A well-heeled international clientele bellies up to the sushi bar at **Platinum,** 915 F St. NW (☎ **202-393-3555**; Internet: www.platinumclubdc.com) to snack, sip, and swap e-mail addresses.

The music playing on this downtown meetery's three dance floors is international, too (techno, hip-hop, Latin, house). Platinum shines Thursday through Sunday. The cover is $10 Thursday (9 p.m. to 2 a.m.) and Sunday (9:30 p.m. to 2:30 a.m.), $15 Friday and Saturday (9 p.m. to 3 a.m.). Take Metro to Metro Center, walk south on 12th Street for 1 block to F Street, and then make a left and go 2½ blocks.

Grab your platforms and flared pants and hustle (as in the dance craze) to **Polly Esther's,** 605 12th St. NW, between F and G Sts. (☎ 202-737-1970; Internet: www.pollyesters.com). Couples stay alive to '70s disco, '80s retro, and '90s music on three dance floors at the D.C. branch of this national chain. Expect many bars and much noise at this happening, fun spot. The club is open Thursday through Saturday from 8 a.m. to 3 a.m. (Do people really stay up that late?). On Thursday nights, you can get in if you're 18 or older; Friday and Saturday you better carry proof that you're 21. The cover charge is $10.

Laughing It Up: Where to Go for Comedy

Headliners on the comedy club circuit perform at Washington's enduring **The Improv,** 1140 Connecticut Ave. NW, between L and M Sts. (☎ 202-296-7008). Top bananas such as Ellen DeGeneres, Jerry Seinfeld, and Robin Williams have told a few jokes on The Improv's stage. (Maybe you can do shtick at open mike night?) Diners at the early show get priority seating. You can charge tickets ($15 to $20 plus a surcharge) over the phone. Shows are Thursday and Sunday at 8:30 p.m.; Friday and Saturday at 8:00 and 10:30 p.m.

When not on tour, the **Gross National Product** (☎ 202-783-7212) returns home to spoof D.C.'s major players at different venues. GNP also conducts **Scandal Tours** Saturday afternoons aboard motor coaches from the Old Post Office Pavilion that'll leave you rolling in the aisles (see Chapter 18 for more details regarding these tours). The ever-popular **Capitol Steps** (☎ 703-683-8330), comprised of former congressional staffers, deflate Washington institutions with their probing political satire. Catch their hilarious spoofs at their new home in the Ronald Reagan Building, 1300 Pennsylvania Avenue NW, every Saturday at 7:30 p.m. Tickets cost $31.50 and are available through Ticketmaster (☎ 202-432-SEAT).

Part VII
The Part of Tens

The 5th Wave   By Rich Tennant

"That? That's Schedule LVES-1.
We've never had to use it. But,
if anyone actually discovers how
to grow money on trees, Uncle
Sam's got a form to get his
fair share of the leaves."

In this part . . .

Ah, tradition. The Part of Tens is to ...*For Dummies* books what museum hopping is to Washington, D.C. — an integral part of the experience. In this area of the book, I feed you some useful and fun information, just to give you some interesting topics of conversation, if nothing else.

In the chapters in this part, I let you in on some of D.C.'s most scandalous affairs and tell you where to find the best views of the city.

Chapter 24

Top Ten D.C. Views

In This Chapter

▶ Finding great places to watch D.C. sunsets

▶ Checking out cool spots overlooking the capital

*S*ooner or later, even the most jaded visitor succumbs to Washington's beauty (I don't mean George; he was a fine general and commander in chief, but no looker). During your visit, I hope you can find the time to admire Washington's pretty face from one or more of the following sites. And don't forget to put film in your camera.

Washington Monument

An updated **Washington Monument,** 15th Street and Constitution Ave. NW (☎ 202-426-6841), reopened to the public on August 1, 2000 after 3 years of restoration. I can't speak for the improved infrastructure, but the new, narrower window frames have enhanced the view from the top.

For a truly magical experience, go at night. (See Chapter 16 for more information on this grand attraction.)

Old Post Office Pavilion

Ride the elevator to the clock tower in the **Old Post Office Pavilion,** Pennsylvania Ave. and 11th St. NW (☎ 202-606-8691). Here, on the equivalent of the building's 12th floor, is a view of downtown and beyond that many think is second only to the vista from the Washington Monument. On your way up or down, you may want to stop at the 10th floor to check out the 10 Congress Bells, replicas of those at Westminster Abbey. A full peal honors national holidays, state occasions, and the opening and closing of Congress. Self-guided tours of the tower are ongoing from 9 a.m. to 9 p.m. in summer, 9 a.m. to 5 p.m. from Labor Day to early April. Catch the elevator in the lower lobby near the 12th Street entrance.

Sky Terrace

The food may be forgettable at the Hotel Washington's **Sky Terrace,** 15th Street and Pennsylvania Ave. NW (☎ **202-638-5900**), but the bird's-eye view of downtown is not. Take the elevator to the 11th floor and arrive by 5:30 p.m. if you want to beat out the executives and other tourists for a seat. Face south for the best view. With any luck, you'll see the sun set over the White House. Stick martini olives in your ears to block out the roar of planes approaching Reagan National. Washington's favorite hotel bar is open from May to October.

Lincoln Memorial

Take a break from reading the Gettysburg Address and gaze at the Reflecting Pool, the Mall, and the Capitol from the steps of the **Lincoln Memorial,** 23rd Street NW, between Constitution and Independence Aves. (☎ **202-426-6895**). Then walk around to the back of the monument for a glimpse of Arlington National Cemetery. On a clear day you can make out the eternal flame marking JFK's grave. This is what's known as a "twofer."

Roof Terrace of the Kennedy Center

You don't need orchestra seats to visit the **Kennedy Center.** In fact, one of the best shows in town is center stage night and day, and it's free. Although you may wish to dine in the Roof Terrace Restaurant or Encore Café (☎ **202-416-8555** for both), you can feast on the view from the promenade *outside* the restaurants without spending a cent. Circle the promenade once for a 360-degree vista. Stop here before or after a performance or tour of the performing arts center, or just come because you feel like it. You don't need a reason.

National Cathedral

The **Cathedral Church of St. Peter and St. Paul,** Massachusetts and Wisconsin Aves. NW (☎ **202-537-6200**), center of the nation's Anglican/ Episcopalian faith, perches on Mt. St. Albans, the city's highest point. For a small donation, you can tour the cathedral on your own and gaze at the commanding view of Washington and beyond from the **Pilgrim Observation Gallery.** The cathedral also runs guided tours daily (☎ **202-537-6207**). On Tuesdays and Wednesdays, you can also enjoy a spot of tea in the Observation Gallery. (See Chapter 17 for more information on the cathedral and Chapter 15 for the tea service.)

Washington Harbour

Walk along the riverfront promenade at **Washington Harbour,** 30th and K Streets NW in Georgetown, and gaze across the Potomac to Rosslyn, Virginia. Dead ahead is Theodore Roosevelt Island. To the left, you can make out the Watergate and, beyond it, the Kennedy Center. To the right, Key Bridge connects Georgetown and Arlington, Virginia. On a summer evening, take in la dolce vita — D.C. style — at **Sequoia,** 3000 K St. (☎ **202-944-4200**). See Chapter 15 for more on Sequoia's charms.

West Front of Capitol

If your timing is right — maybe after an afternoon tour of the Capitol in winter or on your way to dinner in summer — you can watch the sun set over the Lincoln Memorial and Potomac River from the West Front of the Capitol. (Stand with your back to the Capitol and face the Mall.) I discovered this hint by accident one evening, when I was walking on the Hill. I can tell you that seeing the museums bathed in golden light, with purple and pink streaking the sky over the Potomac is an awesome sight.

Arlington National Cemetery

If you don't own one, I suggest picking up a disposable panoramic camera before touring **Arlington National Cemetery,** on the west side of Memorial Bridge (☎ **202-703-697-2131**). You can get some great shots of the capital city from the Arlington House lawn (a Tourmobile stop), or from Pierre L'Enfant's grave below the house. If you have the wherewithal, hike here from the Arlington Cemetery Metro station at dawn or dusk for a heart-stopping moment. For more on Arlington, see Chapter 16.

Marriott Key Bridge

Visitors and locals have been flocking to the 14th floor of the *first* hotel in the Marriott chain since it opened in 1959. Although the hotel's restaurant has had more lives than a cat, the primo view has endured. Diners at J.W.'s **View Steakhouse** look out over Arlington and the Potomac, and Georgetown and Foggy Bottom on the far shore. The **Marriott Key Bridge,** 1401 Lee Highway, Virginia side of F. Scott Key Bridge (☎ **703-524-6400**), is a 2-block walk from the Rosslyn Metro station, about 20 minutes from Georgetown over Key Bridge. The restaurant is open for dinner Monday through Saturday and for Sunday brunch. (Please don't quote me, but if you're in the neighborhood and wearing shoes, you can probably wander in before the restaurant opens and take a peek. Make like a local and *spin* a story about how you're looking at sites for a political fundraiser.)

Chapter 25

Top Ten Scandal Sites

∙ ∙

In This Chapter

▶Famous political dust-ups

▶Notorious "affairs" of state

∙ ∙

*Y*ou can't walk down a Washington street without recalling some scandal that has besmirched it. D.C.'s dirt has tarnished the image of the nation's capital time and time again during America's history. Although not widely publicized, Potomac River pollution has been directly traced to hazardous runoff from government leaders' after-work affairs. When you're done with the Mall and the memorials, you may want to round out your education by visiting this hit parade of top 10 scandal sites, here grouped by location.

Watergate

A security guard, arriving early on the morning of June 17, 1972, at the Watergate in Foggy Bottom (2600 Virginia Ave. NW), found tape over the lock to the bugged offices of the Democratic Party's national head-quarters. Inside he came across, not the janitor, but five rubber-gloved men clutching $100 bills and binoculars — and not a broom or mop in sight. Two years later (August 4, 1974, for the trivial pursuers among you), Tricky Dick Nixon resigned. In the fallout, Judge "Maximum John" Sirica sent 25 members of the president's staff to camp (the kind with bars on the cabin doors and windows).

During Monica Lewinsky's White House internship and, ahem, special friendship with President Clinton, she shared an apartment and confi-dences with her mother at the Watergate. (Not wishing to rekindle the embers — and the *ad nauseum* media coverage — of that liaison, I'll bid adieu to the Watergate.)

Howard Johnson Hotel

Across the street from the Watergate, at the Howard Johnson Hotel, 2601 Virginia Ave. NW (now a George Washington University dormitory), G. Gordon Liddy got his hands dirty on behalf of the Watergate caper. Liddy collected $235,000 for his efforts as the former counsel to the Committee to Re-elect the President (otherwise known as CREEP — an appropriate acronym?).

John F. Kennedy Center for the Performing Arts

Around the corner at the Kennedy Center, 2700 F St., NW and Rock Creek Parkway, a smiling JFK bust greets incoming Opera House audiences in the Grand Foyer. The Lancelot of Camelot, Kennedy mucked up the Bay of Pigs, consorted with mobsters and molls, and welcomed women through a revolving bedroom door in the White House. He definitely did a lot for his country.

Washington Monument

Now George may not have been a sex symbol during his term as president, but George did have an eye for the ladies and a hand in the country's cookie jar. Think about that when you're waiting in line to ride to the top of the Washington Monument. I cannot tell a lie — when George was a mere general, he granted himself an 8-year expense account of $449,261 — and that's in the currency of the time. (Given inflation, Bill Gates has nothing on George!) He also revealed (hush-hush) military plans to Mary Gibbons, one of his mistresses. She, in turn, blabbed to William Tryon, the royal governor of New York. (And you thought he was posing for Gilbert Stuart in his spare time.) Oops.

Tidal Basin

On October 7, 1974, Representative Wilbur Mills (one-time Arkansas congressman and chairman of the powerful House Ways and Means Committee) and a woman were stopped at 2 a.m. near the Tidal Basin for speeding in a car without headlights. (Perhaps they were paying their respects at the nearby Jefferson Memorial?) Accompanying Mills was Fanne (no "i") Foxe, a stripper better known as "the Argentine firecracker." With Jefferson looking on, the firecracker cracked and took a swan dive into the Tidal Basin, ending Mills' career. He subsequently resigned from the Ways and Means Committee and did not seek reelection in 1976. (Is it me or are there self-destructive atoms in the Arkansas H_2O?)

Old Executive Office Building

Nixon had Watergate and Ronald Reagan had his Waterloo, known as Iran Contra, in 1986. Consider the startling similarities when you pass the Old Executive Office Building, 17 Street and Pennsylvania Avenue NW, on the west side of the White House. In an attempt to down Nicaragua's socialist Sandinista government, Reagan's administration sold arms to Iran's Ayatollah Khomeini and used the payoff to subsidize a pickup army of freedom fighters known as the Contras. Perhaps the Teflon president's memory problems had already begun as Reagan, grinning ear to ear, disavowed any knowledge of his underlings' illegal machinations.

Remember Ollie North? He was the G. Gordon Liddy of the Iran Contra scandal who did his dirty work in the bowels of this building, a stone's throw from the presidential mansion. North's secretary, doe-like Fawn Hall, shredded the evidence, something Rosemary Wood wished — a thousand or so times a day — she had done to the Watergate tapes. During a congressional hearing, Hall was heard to say, "Sometimes you have to go above the written law." Way to go, Fawn.

The White House

Here's something to mull over while you wait to tour the White House, 1600 Pennsylvania Ave. NW. Ever wonder how many presidents have respected their marriage vows? That list is short. Very short. It's unsurprising that psychologists have linked politicians' voracious desire for power with their other expanded appetites.

Here are a few to consider. Warren G. Harding enjoyed Nan Britton's company in the Oval Office (sound familiar?). Britton claimed that Harding fathered her illegitimate daughter when he was a senator. Harding also carried on with Carrie Fulton Phillips, the wife of a good friend. FDR was busy with Missy Lehand and Lucy Mercer, who was with the president when he died in Warm Springs, Georgia. Eisenhower had Kay Summersby. Lyndon B. Johnson had . . . shoot, who can count that high? LBJ enjoyed a rep as a womanizer all his life, probably because he was so suave and debonair? President Clinton needs no bibliography from me. Stay tuned for his 20-volume memoir.

The Jefferson, Willard, and Vista hotels

Several D.C. hotels have made headline news — and not for their low rates. Dick Morris, one-time political consultant to President Clinton, kept company with Sherry Rowlands, a $200-an-hour prostitute at The

Jefferson Hotel, 16th and M Streets NW. The twosome was caught snuggling on the balcony of Suite 205. Smooth Sherry claimed that Morris shared insider secrets with her and also let her listen in on conversations with the Clintons.

Ulysses S. Grant met with influence peddlers over brandy and cigars in the lobby (hence the term lobbyist) of the Willard Hotel, 1455 Pennsylvania Ave. NW. Various robber barons also wheeled and dealed here, buying politicians' votes in exchange for whiskey and cash during the Civil War.

On January 18, 1990, in Room 727 of the Vista Hotel, 1400 M St. NW on Scott Circle, hizzoner Marion Barry (former D.C. mayor, drug addict, and ladies man) was caught in an FBI sting taking hits from a crack pipe. Hey, it's a pressured job. A guy has a right to relax once in a while. At the trial, where he faced 14 separate drug charges, he was convicted on *one* measly count of cocaine possession and did 6 months in Petersburg, Virginia. While incarcerated, a prostitute helped Barry de-stress in the prison's visiting room, in plain view of about 40 inmates and their families. Despite his "poor judgement," and despite the censure of 14 members of his administration for fiscal wrongdoings, Barry was reelected and was sworn in for a fourth term on January 2, 1995. Definitely a "Ripley's Believe it or Not" moment.

Capitol Hill

Let me refresh your memory about the layout of the U.S. Capitol. Facing the west facade (actually the back, which overlooks the Mall), look left to find the Senate and right to view the House of Representatives. Members of the House and Senate have found themselves in some pretty sticky situations over the years, usually outside the walls of their bureaucratic offices. Consider the following as you gaze at these imposing structures:

> ✔ Pity poor Massachusetts senator **Ted Kennedy.** Despite legislative success, wealth, and power (and at least 60 extra pounds), he doesn't have the Midas touch. To wit, two of his brothers have been assassinated; he took an unscheduled swim one summer night in Chappaquiddick, ending his presidential aspirations; his first marriage dissolved; he was at the family's Palm Beach compound the night of nephew Willy Smith's "incident" (Smith was accused and acquitted of rape). And then there's his ongoing struggle with wine, women, and calories. Oh well, what's in a name?

✔ Former South Carolina congressman **John Jenrette** also had a run of bad luck. You may recall that he was nailed for his part in Abscam. He and some buddies sold Congressional favors to "sheiks" who were really FBI agents wearing robes over their three-piece suits. During the investigation, his wife, Rita, testified to finding $25,000 in one of John's shoes. Yuppie arch supports? During a break in a late-night House session, Jenrette was caught with his pants down, having sex with a woman on the west steps of the Capitol. The woman turned out to be his wife. But not for long. The model couple separated, and soon after, John was arrested for shoplifting. The ex-Mrs. J capitalized on the publicity and penned *My Capitol Secrets,* which did not make the *Times* bestseller list. She then shed more of her inhibitions in *Playboy.*

✔ As you tour the Hill, think of **Gary Hart.** Remember *Monkey Business?* Hart and Donna Rice monkeying around on the luxury yacht? The Democratic senator from Colorado (and former divinity student) finally fessed up after a *Miami Herald* reporter spied Rice exiting Hart's town house at 517 6th St. SE, after a 24-hour visit. What's the big deal? Maybe she was waxing the floors. So much for Hart's 1988 presidential hopes. Easy come, easy go.

✔ And, a short walk from the Capitol, **Stephen Gobie,** former boyfriend and housekeeper of **Rep. Barney Frank** (Democratic congressman from Massachusetts), ran a male escort service — out of Frank's home. When the story hit the airwaves, Frank said he didn't have a clue. Right. And I'm Senator Hillary Rodham Clinton.

Longworth Office Building

When you stop in the Longworth Office Building, at Independence and New Jersey Aves. SE, to ask your congressional rep for a favor, consider this: Back in 1974, Elizabeth Ray earned $14,000 a year in Room 1506 as a secretary to Rep. Wayne Hays of Ohio. So? Bear with me. The average secretary's salary was half that in the mid-'70s. Ms. Ray, far from average, couldn't type, and she didn't answer phones. Despite a generous salary for her extracurricular performance, she had grown weary of Hays' friendships with other women. Fearful that she would lose her job after her boss married *another* of his secretaries, Ray went to the *Washington Post* with her story (hey, she was no dumb blonde). The paper spelled Hays' name right, but the publicity didn't help his career. In fact, it ended soon after. He subsequently overdosed on pills, but survived.

Appendix

Quick Concierge

●●

*T*his handy section is where I've condensed the practical and perti-
nent information — from airline phone numbers to mailbox locations — that you need to make certain you have a successful and
stress-free Washington, D.C. vacation. And, for those of you who
believe in being *really prepared,* I also give you some additional
resources to check out.

Washington, D.C. A to Z: Facts at Your Fingertips

AAA

The most centrally located AAA is at 701 15th
St. NW ☎202-331-3000. For emergency road
service, call ☎ 800-763-5500.

American Express

There is an American Express Travel Service
office downtown at 1001 G St. NW, between
10th and 11th Streets, (☎ 202-393-2368);
1150 Connecticut Ave. NW, between L and M
Streets, (☎ 202-457-1300); one uptown near
Chevy Chase, Maryland, at 5300 Wisconsin
Ave. NW, (☎ 202-362-4000); and several in
the Maryland/Virginia suburbs. Call ☎ 800-
528-4800 for exact office locations.

Area Codes

If you are calling a D.C. number from somewhere else, dial **202.** If you are in D.C. and
calling D.C., no area code is needed. For the
close-in Maryland suburbs dial **301; 410** for
Baltimore, Annapolis, and the Eastern Shore
of Maryland; and **703** for suburban Virginia.

ATMs

ATMs may soon outnumber bureaucrats in
Washington. They're located in or near

hotels, restaurants, attractions, and Metro
stations. Most, if not all, banks have them.
For specific locations, call Cirrus ☎ 800-
424-7787 or Plus ☎ 800-843-7587. (ATMs are
also discussed in Chapters 3 and 12.)

Baby-sitters

Most hotels will secure a bonded sitter for
your brood. Wee Sit (☎ 703-764-1542) provides hotel childcare by bonded sitters, as
does White House Nannies (☎ 301-652-8088;
Internet: www.whitehousenannies.com).

Camera Repair

If your shutter won't shut, head to Penn
Camera at 915 E. St. NW (☎ 202-347-5777),
or at 1015 18th St. NW (☎ 202-785-7366).

Congressional Representatives

To locate a senator or congressional representative, call the Capitol switchboard
(☎ 202-224-3121).

Convention Center

The Washington Convention Center is located
at 900 9th St. NW, at H Street (☎ 202-
789-1600). Take Metro to Metro Center

(12th and G Sts. NW), walk north 1 block on 12th Street, and then walk east 3 blocks on H St.

Credit Cards

If your card is lost or stolen, call Citicorp Visa (☎ 800-645-6556), American Express (☎ 800-221-7282), or MasterCard (☎ 800-307-7309). For all other cards, call information at ☎ 800-555-1212 to find out the number.

Customs

For information regarding U.S. Customs, call your embassy or consulate, or contact the U.S. Customs office at ☎ 202-927-1770.

Dentists

For a dental emergency, call the Dental Referral Service at ☎ 202-723-5323 or the D.C. Dental Society at ☎ 202-547-7615.

Disabled Visitors

For information on accessibility in Washington, call ☎ 202-962-1245.

Doctors

There are no walk-in clinics in Washington, D.C. If you get sick, call the hotel's front desk or concierge for the name of the physician who treats hotel guests. You can also call Prologue (☎ 800-DOCTORS), a physicians referral service.

Emergencies

For police, fire, and ambulance, call ☎ 911. The 24-hour poison control hotline is ☎ 202-625-3333.

Eyeglasses

For same-day service on single-vision prescriptions, call Atlantic Optical, 1747 Pennsylvania Ave. NW (☎ 202-466-2050), or Sterling Optical, 1900 M St. NW (☎ 202-728-1041).

Hospitals

For life-threatening emergencies, call ☎ 911. For emergency-room treatment, contact one of the following hospitals: Children's Hospital National Medical Center, 111 Michigan Ave. NW, near Catholic University (☎ 202-884-5000); George Washington University Hospital, 901 23rd St. NW (☎ 202-994-3211); Georgetown University Hospital, 3800 Reservoir Rd. NW, (☎ 202-784-2118). If you have a car, now is not the time to drive in D.C. I suggest you take a taxi.

Hotlines

The city's 24-hour crisis line is ☎ 202-561-7000; for an alcohol- or drug-related problem, call ☎ 800-234-0420; for Alcoholics Anonymous, dial ☎ 800-222-0828.

Information

For tourist information, contact the Washington, D.C. Convention and Visitors Association, 1212 New York Ave. NW (☎ 202-789-7000; Internet: www.washington.org) or the White House Visitors Center, 1450 Pennsylvania Ave. NW (☎ 202-208-1631). For D.C. telephone directory information, dial ☎ 411; for telephone numbers outside the Washington area, dial the area code plus 555-1212.

Internet Access & Cyber Cafes

Check your e-mail at Kramerbooks & Afterwords, 1517 Connecticut Ave. NW, between Dupont Circle and Q St. (☎ 202-638-5900) or cyberSTOP Café, 1513 17th St. NW, between P and Q Sts. (☎ 202-234-2470).

Laundry & Dry Cleaning

For a self-service, coin-operated laundry, try Washtub Laundromat, 1511 17th St. NW (☎ 202-332-9455). For pickup and delivery service, contact Bergmann's (☎ 202-737-5400). For same-day dry-cleaning service, go to MacDee Quality Cleaners at 1639 L St. NW, between 16th and 17th Streets (☎ 202-296-6100). Most hotels provide laundry and dry-cleaning services or have coin-operated laundry facilities.

Liquor Laws

You must be 21 years old to drink in D.C. Establishments can serve alcohol Monday through Thursday from 8 a.m. to 2 a.m.; Friday and Saturday from 8:00 a.m. to 2:30 a.m.; and Sunday from 10 a.m. to 2 a.m. Liquor stores are closed on Sunday, but grocery stores and convenience stores often sell beer and wine 7 days a week.

Lost Property

If you lose something on an Amtrak train, call ☎ 800-872-7245; on Metro (rail or bus), go to 600 5th St. NW, 5th Floor, Room 5C (☎ 202-962-1195); on a Greyhound bus, 1005 1st St. NE (☎ 800-231-2222). If you leave something in a taxi, call the individual company or the nearest police precinct. If you left something in a hotel room, check with the front desk or concierge.

Mail

The National Capital Post Office, at North Capitol St. and Massachusetts Ave. NE, across from Union Station (☎ 202-682-9595), is open Monday through Friday from 7 a.m. to midnight, and Saturday and Sunday from 7 a.m. to 8 p.m. For the nearest post office, ask at your hotel's front desk. For ZIP code information, call ☎ 202-682-9595.

Maps

Free city maps are available at most hotels and tourist sites and at the Washington, D.C. Convention and Visitors Association, 1212 New York Ave. NW, between 12th and 13th Sts. (☎ 202-789-7000).

Newspapers & Magazines

The two major dailies are the *Washington Post* and the *Washington Times. Washington City Paper* is a weekly that is distributed free every Thursday. The *Washingtonian* magazine is published monthly.

Pharmacies

CVS has more than 40 locations; its two 24-hour locations are at 1211 Vermont Ave. NW, at 14th St. on Thomas Circle (☎ 202- 628-0729) and at 67 Dupont Circle (☎ 202- 785-1466).

Police

In case of emergency, dial ☎ **911.** For the nearest district police headquarters, call ☎ 202-727-1000.

Radio Stations

Turn the dial to 88.5 FM (National Public Radio), 90.9 FM (Classical & NPR news), 94.7 FM (Classic Rock), 98.7 FM (Country), 100.3 FM (Oldies), 101.1 FM (Rock), 104.1 FM (Top 40), 105.9 FM (Smooth Jazz), 106.7 FM (Talk & Sports), 730 AM (CNN News), and 980 AM (Sports).

Safety

The safe zones include the major tourist areas, presidential monuments, and Metro. At night, use the buddy system and stick to the main commercial blocks of Adams-Morgan and Capitol Hill. If Metro's service has stopped for the day, and you are still out on the town, I suggest you take a taxi. Keep your wits about you after dark in the southwest and southeast sections of the city. Know your destination before you set out. Hold your kids' hands on city streets and on all Metro escalators. Lock your hotel room door, car doors, and trunk. Lock valuables in a safe deposit box (if not in your room, at the front desk). Keep a close eye on your pocketbook, camera, and wallet. Hold onto your purse in a restaurant. Put your money and credit cards away and secure your wallet before going on the street. Leave the family jewels at home; what you do bring, don't flash. For a copy of the useful "Take a Bite Out of Crime," by the Crime Prevention Coalition, contact the U.S. Government Printing Office (☎ 202-512-1993).

Smoking

Smoking in D.C. restaurants is virtually unregulated. No specific requirements are enforced by the city's health department. Most restaurants provide smoking and non-smoking areas.

Taxes

The sales taxes on merchandise are 6 percent in D.C., 5 percent in Maryland, and

4.5 percent in Virginia. The restaurant taxes are 10 percent in D.C., 5 percent in Maryland, and 4.5 percent in Virginia. The hotel sales taxes are 14.5 percent in D.C., 5 percent (plus another 5 to 7 percent local or city tax) in Maryland, and 10 percent in Virginia.

Taxis

D.C. cabs operate on a zone system. Between two points in the same zone, the minimum fare is $4. Drivers are allowed to pick up as many passengers as they can fit into the cab. A $1.50 charge applies to call a taxi.

Time Zone

Washington, D.C. is on Eastern Standard Time, except when Daylight Saving Time (DST) is in effect. DST is observed from the first Sunday in April, when clocks are moved ahead one hour, until the last Sunday in October. For the correct time, dial ☎ 202-844-2525.

Transit Info

For Metrorail (subway) and Metrobus information call ☎ 202-637-7000. If you left a personal item on Metro, call Lost and Found at ☎ 202-962-1326.

Weather Updates

For the D.C. weather forecast, call ☎ 202-936-1212, watch the Weather Channel, or visit www.weather.com. If you want the extended outlook for the area, call ☎ 202-899-3240.

Toll-Free Numbers & Web Sites

Major airlines

Air Canada
☎ 800-776-3000
Internet: www.aircanada.ca

Airtran Airlines
☎ 800-247-8726
Internet: www.airtran.com

Alaska Airlines
☎ 800-426-0333
Internet: www.alaskaair.com

American Airlines
☎ 800-433-7300
Internet: www.americanair.com

American Trans Air
☎ 800-225-2995
Internet: www.ata.com

America West Airlines
☎ 800-235-9292
Internet: www.americawest.com

British Airways
☎ 800-247-9297
☎ 0345-222-111 (in Britain)
Internet: www.british-airways.com

Canadian Airlines International
☎ 800-426-7000
Internet: www.cdnair.ca

Continental Airlines
☎ 800-525-0280
Internet: www.continental.com

Delta Air Lines
☎ 800-221-1212
Internet: www.delta-air.com

Midway Airlines
☎ 800-446-4392
Internet: www.midwayair.com

Northwest Airlines
☎ 800-225-2525
Internet: www.nwa.com

Southwest Airlines
☎ 800-435-9792
Internet: www.iflyswa.com

Trans World Airlines (TWA)
☎ 800-221-2000
Internet: www.twa.com

United Airlines
☎ 800-241-6522
Internet: www.ual.com

US Airways
☎ 800-428-4322
Internet: www.usairways.com

Virgin Atlantic Airways
☎ 800-862-8621 (in Continental
United States)
☎ 0293-747-747 (in Britain)
Internet: www.fly.virgin.com

Car rental agencies

Advantage
☎ 800-777-5500
Internet: www.arac.com

Alamo
☎ 800-327-9633
Internet: www.goalamo.com

Auto Europe
☎ 800-223-5555
Internet: www.autoeurope.com

Avis
☎ 800-331-1212 (in Continental
United States)
☎ 800-TRY-AVIS (in Canada)
Internet: www.avis.com

Budget
☎ 800-527-0700
Internet: www.budgetrentacar.com

Dollar
☎ 800-800-4000
Internet: www.dollarcar.com

Enterprise
☎ 800-325-8007
Internet: www.pickenterprise.com

Hertz
☎ 800-654-3131
Internet: www.hertz.com

Kemwel Holiday Auto (KHA)
☎ 800-678-0678
Internet: www.kemwel.com

National
☎ 800-CAR-RENT
Internet: www.nationalcar.com

Payless
☎ 800-PAYLESS
Internet: www.paylesscar.com

Rent-A-Wreck
☎ 800-535-1391
Internet: rent-a-wreck.com

Thrifty
☎ 800-367-2277
Internet: www.thrifty.com

Major hotel and motel chains

Best Western International
☎ 800-528-1234
Internet: www.bestwestern.com

Clarion Hotel
☎ 800-CLARION
Internet: www.hotelchoice.com

Comfort Inn
☎ 800-228-5150
Internet: www.hotelchoice.com

Courtyard by Marriott
☎ 800-321-2211
Internet: www.courtyard.com

Days Inn
☎ 800-325-2525
Internet: www.daysinn.com

Doubletree Hotel
☎ 800-222-TREE
Internet: www.doubletreehotels.com

Econo Lodge
☎ 800-55-ECONO
Internet: www.hotelchoice.com

Fairfield Inn by Marriott
☎ 800-228-2800
Internet: www.fairfieldinn.com

Hampton Inn
☎ 800-HAMPTON
Internet: www.hampton-inn.com

Hilton Hotel
☎ 800-HILTONS
Internet: www.hilton.com

Holiday Inn
☎ 800-HOLIDAY
Internet: www.basshotels.com

Howard Johnson
☎ 800-654-2000
Internet: www.hojo.com

Hyatt Hotels & Resorts
☎ 800-228-9000
Internet: www.hyatt.com

ITT Sheraton
☎ 800-325-3535
Internet: www.sheraton.com

La Quinta Motor Inn
☎ 800-531-5900
Internet: www.laquinta.com

Marriott Hotel
☎ 800-228-9290
Internet: www.marriott.com

Motel 6
☎ 800-4-MOTEL6
Internet: www.motel6.com

Quality Inn
☎ 800-228-5151
Internet: www.hotelchoice.com

Radisson Hotels International
☎ 800-333-3333
Internet: www.radisson.com

Ramada Inn
☎ 800-2-RAMADA
Internet: www.ramada.com

Red Carpet Inn
☎ 800-251-1962
Internet: www.reservahost.com

Red Lion Hotels & Inns
☎ 800-547-8010
Internet: www.redlion.com

Red Roof Inn
☎ 800-843-7663
Internet: www.redroof.com

Residence Inn by Marriott
☎ 800-331-3131
Internet: www.residenceinn.com

Rodeway Inn
☎ 800-228-2000
Internet: www.hotelchoice.com

Vagabond Inn
☎ 800-522-1555
Internet: www.vagabondinns.com

Super 8 Motel
☎ 800-800-8000
Internet: www.super8motels.com

Wyndham Hotels and Resorts
☎ 800-822-4200 in Continental U.S.
and Canada
Internet: www.wyndham.com

Travelodge
☎ 800-255-3050
Internet: www.travelodge.com

Where to Get More Information

I packed this book with information, but if you still haven't had
enough, you can consult the following resources for additional info.

Washington, D.C. Convention and Visitors Association

Call or write the Washington, D.C. Convention and Visitors Association
(1212 New York Ave. NW, Washington, D.C. 20005, ☎ **202-789-7000**)
and ask them to send you a free copy of the *Washington, D.C. Visitors
Guide,* which details hotels, restaurants, sights, shops, and more.
They'll also be happy to answer specific questions. The association's
Web site (Internet: www.washington.org) gives a broad overview of
what to see and do in D.C. The vacation planning section includes an
up-to-date calendar of events and a list of 101 Free Things to Do in D.C.

Information on the Web

National Capital Parks Central

Internet: www.nps.gov/nacc

You can find links to the approximately dozen memorials and monuments maintained by the National Park Service on this site. You find
among the links: the Washington Monument, Jefferson Memorial,
National Mall, and Vietnam Veterans Memorial. Each page has a brief
description of the memorial or monument, some images, and basic visitor information. You can also find information about special events held
in the capital city, such as the Fourth of July festivities.

Metropolitan Washington Airports Authority

Internet: www.metwashairports.com

Ground transport, terminal maps, flight status, and airport facilities for Dulles International and Reagan National airports are available at this site.

Smithsonian Institution

Internet: www.nasm.si.edu

The range of museums covered on this site is phenomenal; you can wander from the National Museum of the American Indian to the National Air and Space Museum. This Web site includes information about what's happening at each of the Smithsonian's museums, and has updates on special exhibitions and general events. If you allow sufficient time, you can get a better education at the Smithsonian than you can at many American colleges — for a lot less money too.

TimeOut.com: Washington, D.C.

Internet: www.timeout.com/washingtondc

This lively online magazine includes reviews and a calendar of events covering the latest happenings in the nation's capital. You won't find mammoth directories here, instead TimeOut selects a handful of worthy events and covers them in some detail.

Visit Washington, D.C.

Internet: www.dchomepage.net

A production of the D.C. Office of Tourism and Promotions, this site links you to many popular Web pages for D.C. attractions. You can also find links to information on lodging and the local transit system.

Washington Metropolitan Area Transit Authority

Internet: www.wmata.com

Here you can find timetables, maps, fares, and more information regarding the buses and trains that serve the Washington, D.C. metro area.

Washington Post Online

Internet: www.washingtonpost.com

The *Washington Post's* Web site provides up-to-the-minute news, weather, visitor information, restaurant reviews, and online discussions on specific subjects. The entertainment guide in the *Style* section includes an events calendar, nightlife advice, theater and dance listings. Especially useful is the "Destination D.C." section; this section's content is fantastic and includes a clickable map of the Smithsonian and the Mall, a guide to the FDR monument, restaurant reviews, a tour of scandal sights, and a guide to Washington's theater productions.

Washingtonian Online

Internet: www.washingtonian.com

The "Visitors Guide" on this magazine's Web site offers advice on where to stay and dine and what to see. You can find features such as "The 100 Best Bargain Restaurants" in the dining section, and "The Four-Hour Mall" in the Attractions and Events section. "What's Happening" is a monthly guide to what's going on at museums, theaters, and other cultural showplaces around town.

The White House

Internet: www.whitehouse.gov

Click on "White House Tours" to find out more about seeing the White House and upcoming public events. You can also find a link to "Congressional Tours" on this page. If you bring children with you on your trip, the site offers a special Web tour and newsletter designed especially for children.

Making Dollars and Sense of It

Expense	Amount
Airfare	
Car Rental	
Lodging	
Parking	
Breakfast	
Lunch	
Dinner	
Babysitting	
Attractions	
Transportation	
Souvenirs	
Tips	
Grand Total	

Notes

Fare Game: Choosing an Airline

Travel Agency:_____ Phone:_____

Agent's Name:_____ Quoted Fare:_____

Departure Schedule & Flight Information

Airline:_____ Airport:_____

Flight #:_____ Date:_____ Time:_____ a.m./p.m.

Arrives in:_____ Time:_____ a.m./p.m.

Connecting Flight (if any)

Amount of time between flights:_____ hours/mins

Airline:_____ Airport:_____

Flight #:_____ Date:_____ Time:_____ a.m./p.m.

Arrives in:_____ Time:_____ a.m./p.m.

Return Trip Schedule & Flight Information

Airline:_____ Airport:_____

Flight #:_____ Date:_____ Time:_____ a.m./p.m.

Arrives in:_____ Time:_____ a.m./p.m.

Connecting Flight (if any)

Amount of time between flights:_____ hours/mins

Airline:_____ Airport:_____

Flight #:_____ Date:_____ Time:_____ a.m./p.m.

Arrives in:_____ Time:_____ a.m./p.m.

Notes

Sweet Dreams: Choosing Your Hotel

Enter the hotels where you'd prefer to stay based on location and price. Then use the worksheet below to plan your itinerary.

Hotel	Location	Price per night

Menus & Venues

Enter the restaurants where you'd most like to dine. Then use the worksheet below to plan your itinerary.

Name	Address/Phone	Cuisine/Price

Places to Go, People to See, Things to Do

Enter the attractions you would most like to see. Then use the worksheet below to plan your itinerary.

Attractions	Amount of time you expect to spend there	Best day and time to go

Going "My" Way

Itinerary #1

☐ _____
☐ _____
☐ _____
☐ _____

Itinerary #2

☐ _____
☐ _____
☐ _____
☐ _____

Itinerary #3

☐ _____
☐ _____
☐ _____
☐ _____

Itinerary #4

☐ _____
☐ _____
☐ _____
☐ _____

Itinerary #5

☐ _____
☐ _____
☐ _____
☐ _____

Itinerary #6

☐ _____
☐ _____
☐ _____
☐ _____

Itinerary #7

☐ _____
☐ _____
☐ _____
☐ _____

Itinerary #8

☐ _____
☐ _____
☐ _____
☐ _____

Itinerary #9

☐ _____
☐ _____
☐ _____
☐ _____

Itinerary #10

☐ _____
☐ _____
☐ _____
☐ _____

Notes

Index

• *B* •

• N •

• *Accommodations* •

• Restaurant Index •

Notes

Notes

Notes

Notes

Notes

Notes

Discover Dummies Online!

The Dummies Web Site is your fun and friendly online resource for the latest information about *For Dummies*® books and your favorite topics. The Web site is the place to communicate with us, exchange ideas with other *For Dummies* readers, chat with authors, and have fun!

Ten Fun and Useful Things You Can Do at www.dummies.com

1. Win free *For Dummies* books and more!
2. Register your book and be entered in a prize drawing.
3. Meet your favorite authors through the IDG Books Worldwide Author Chat Series.
4. Exchange helpful information with other *For Dummies* readers.
5. Discover other great *For Dummies* books you must have!
6. Purchase Dummieswear® exclusively from our Web site.
7. Buy *For Dummies* books online.
8. Talk to us. Make comments, ask questions, get answers!
9. Download free software.
10. Find additional useful resources from authors.

Link directly to these ten fun and useful things at
http://www.dummies.com/10useful

For other technology titles from IDG Books Worldwide, go to
www.idgbooks.com

Not on the Web yet? It's easy to get started with *Dummies 101*®: *The Internet For Windows*® *98* or *The Internet For Dummies*® at local retailers everywhere.

Find other *For Dummies* books on these topics:
Business • Career • Databases • Food & Beverage • Games • Gardening • Graphics • Hardware
Health & Fitness • Internet and the World Wide Web • Networking • Office Suites
Operating Systems • Personal Finance • Pets • Programming • Recreation • Sports
Spreadsheets • Teacher Resources • Test Prep • Word Processing

IDG BOOKS WORLDWIDE BOOK REGISTRATION

Register This Book and Win!

We want to hear from you!

Visit **http://my2cents.dummies.com** to register this book and tell us how you liked it!

- ✔ Get entered in our monthly prize giveaway.

- ✔ Give us feedback about this book — tell us what you like best, what you like least, or maybe what you'd like to ask the author and us to change!

- ✔ Let us know any other *For Dummies*® topics that interest you.

Your feedback helps us determine what books to publish, tells us what coverage to add as we revise our books, and lets us know whether we're meeting your needs as a *For Dummies* reader. You're our most valuable resource, and what you have to say is important to us!

Not on the Web yet? It's easy to get started with *Dummies 101*®: *The Internet For Windows*® *98* or *The Internet For Dummies*® at local retailers everywhere.

Or let us know what you think by sending us a letter at the following address:

For Dummies Book Registration
Dummies Press
10475 Crosspoint Blvd.
Indianapolis, IN 46256

BESTSELLING
BOOK SERIES